D1196324

Lorette Wilmot Library
Nazareth College of Rochester

DEMCO

THE GERMAN TRADITION OF PSYCHOLOGY IN LITERATURE AND THOUGHT, 1700–1840

The beginnings of psychology are usually dated from experimental psychology and Freudian psychoanalysis in the late nineteenth century. Yet the period from 1700 to 1840 produced some highly sophisticated psychological theorising that became central to German intellectual and cultural life, well in advance of similar developments in the English-speaking world. Matthew Bell explores how this happened, by analysing the expressions of psychological theory in Goethe's *Faust*, Kant's *Critique of Pure Reason*, and in the works of Lessing, Schiller, Kleist, and E. T. A. Hoffmann. This study pays special attention to the role of the German literary renaissance of the last third of the eighteenth century in bringing psychological theory into popular consciousness and shaping its transmission to the nineteenth century. All German texts are translated into English, making this fascinating area of European thought fully accessible to English readers for the first time.

MATTHEW BELL is Senior Lecturer in German and Director of the Comparative Literature Programme at King's College London. He is Honorary Secretary and Treasurer of the English Goethe Society and author of *Goethe's Naturalistic Anthropology: Man and Other Plants* (1994).

CAMBRIDGE STUDIES IN GERMAN

General editors
H. B. NISBET, *University of Cambridge*
MARTIN SWALES, *University of London*

Advisory editor
THEODORE J. ZIOLKOWSKI, *Princeton University*

THE GERMAN TRADITION OF PSYCHOLOGY IN LITERATURE AND THOUGHT, 1700–1840

MATTHEW BELL
King's College London

CAMBRIDGE
UNIVERSITY PRESS

WITHDRAWN

LORETTE WILMOT LIBRARY
NAZARETH COLLEGE

CAMBRIDGE UNIVERSITY PRESS

Cambridge, New York, Melbourne, Madrid, Cape Town, Singapore, São Paulo

Cambridge University Press
The Edinburgh Building, Cambridge CB2 2RU, UK

Published in the United States of America by Cambridge University Press, New York

www.cambridge.org
Information on this title: www.cambridge.org/9780521846264

© Matthew Bell 2005

This book is in copyright. Subject to statutory exception
and to the provisions of relevant collective licensing agreements,
no reproduction of any part may take place without
the written permission of Cambridge University Press.

First published 2005

Printed in the United Kingdom at the University Press, Cambridge

A catalogue record for this book is available from the British Library

Library of Congress Cataloguing in Publication data

Bell, Matthew
The German tradition of psychology in literature and thought, 1700–1840 / Matthew Bell.
p.   cm. – (Cambridge studies in German)
Includes bibliographical references (p. 280) and index.
ISBN 0 521 84626 9
1. German literature – 18th century – History and criticism.   2. German
literature – 19th century – History and criticism.   3. Psychology in literature.
I. Title.   II. Series.
PT289.B37   2005
830.9′353′09033–dc22   2004058601

ISBN-13 978-0-521-84626-4   - hardback
ISBN-10 0-521-84626-9   - hardback

Cambridge University Press has no responsibility for the persistence or accuracy of URLs for external or
third-party internet websites referred to in this book, and does not guarantee that any content on such
websites is, or will remain, accurate or appropriate.

730.9353
Bel

For
Lou
my light
Neu

Genieß ich nun durch dich das weite Licht
Des Tages.

> facilis descensus Averno:
> noctes atque dies patet atri ianua Ditis;
> sed revocare gradum superasque evadere ad auras,
> hoc opus, hic labor est.
>
> Virgil, *Aeneid*, VI, 126–9

Contents

Acknowledgements

Some of the arguments advanced in Chapter 2 were first published in 'Psychological conceptions in Lessing's dramas', *Lessing Yearbook* 28 (1996), 53–81. Parts of Chapter 5 appeared in 'Sorge, Epicurean psychology, and the classical *Faust*', *Oxford German Studies* 28 (1999) 82–130, and 'The revenge of the *untere Seelenvermögen* in Schiller's plays', *German Life and Letters* 52 (1999) 197–210. I would like to thank the editors and publishers of *Lessing Yearbook*, *Oxford German Studies* and *German Life and Letters* for granting me permission to use the material.

Help comes in many shapes and sizes. The library staff at the Institute of Germanic Studies in London and the Schiller-Nationalmuseum/ Deutsches Literaturarchiv in Marbach gave generously of their time and expertise. The professionalism and patience of staff in the Humanities and Rare Books Reading Rooms at the British Library, where most of the research for this book was done, never cease to amaze. The Arts and Humanities Research Board (AHRB) provided funds for a period of research in Marbach. The project was begun, many years ago, while I was a Septcentenary Junior Research Fellow at Balliol College, Oxford. Since then I have been privileged to work with inspiring colleagues and students in the Department of German at King's College London. To the following I am grateful for providing the stimuli to ask questions and the means to answer them: Jeremy Adler, Nick Boyle, Jörg Drews, Howard Gaskill, Simon Glendinning, David Hill, Roger Paulin, Ritchie Robertson, John Whaley, and John Williams. Derek Glass sharpened my ideas on Kleist and E. T. A. Hoffmann: he is sorely missed. John White stopped the project going off the rails at an early stage. It was expertly steered through the Press by Linda Bree, Maartje Scheltens, and Joanna Breeze. Robert Whitelock has been as thorough and scholarly a copy-editor as one could hope for, dispensing order, intelligibility, and good sense. To the editors of the series, Barry Nisbet and Martin Swales, I owe profound thanks for their support and critical judgement. To friends and family I owe deep debts of a more or less tangible nature: thanks to my mother and Pete, my father and Christine, Sarah, Simon, John, and Meg. I hope that Florence and Cecily will not begrudge their mother her proper place as dedicatee of this book and are not too disappointed when they discover what sort of book I have been writing.

Abbreviations

KAA   Immanuel Kant, *Gesammelte Schriften, herausgegeben von der Königlich Preussischen Akademie der Wissenschaften*, Berlin: de Gruyter, 1900–.

KWS   Heinrich von Kleist, *Sämtliche Werke und Briefe*, ed. Helmut Sembdner, 2 vols. Munich: dtv, 1993.

KWW   Immanuel Kant, *Werke*, ed. Wilhelm Weischedel, 10 vols. Darmstadt: Wissenschaftliche Buchgesellschaft, 1983.

LPW   G. W Leibniz, *Philosophical Writings*, ed. G. H. R. Parkinson, London: Everyman, 1973.

LW   Gotthold Ephraim Lessing, *Werke*, ed. Herbert G. Göpfert *et al.*, 8 vols. Munich: Winkler, 1970–9.

MW   Karl Philipp Moritz, *Werke*, 3 vols. ed. Horst Günther, Frankfurt am Main: Insel, 1981.

NA   Friedrich Schiller, *Werke. Nationalausgabe*, ed. Julius Petersen, Hermann Schneider *et al.*, Stuttgart: Böhlau 1943–.

NS   Novalis (Friedrich von Hardenberg), *Schriften*, ed. Paul Kluckhohn and Richard Samuel, 4 vols. Stuttgart: Kohlhammer, 1960.

PEGS *Publications of the English Goethe Society.*

ROC   Jean-Jacques Rousseau, *Oeuvres complètes*, ed. Bernard Gagnebin and Marcel Raymond, Paris: Gallimard, 1959.

RR   Johann Christian Reil, *Rhapsodien über die Anwendung der psychischen Curmethode auf Geisteszerrüttungen*, Halle: Curtsche Buchhandlung, 1803.

SSW   Friedrich Wilhelm Joseph Schelling, *Sämmtliche Werke*, ed. K. F. A. Schelling, 14 vols. Stuttgart: Cotta, 1856–61.

SuD   *Sturm und Drang. Dramatische Schriften*, ed. E. Loewenthal and L. Schneider, 2 vols. Heidelberg: Schneider, 1972.

SWL   Arthur Schopenhauer, *Sämtliche Werke*, ed. Wolfgang Freiherr von Löhneysen, 5 vols. Frankfurt am Main: Suhrkamp, 1986.

SWS   Friedrich Wilhelm Joseph Schelling, *Werke*, ed. M. Schröter, 6 vols. Munich: Beck and Oldenbourg, 1927–8.

WA   Johann Wolfgang Goethe, *Werke, herausgegeben im Auftrage der Großherzogin Sophie von Sachsen*, ed. Erich Schmidt *et al.*, 146 vols. Weimar: Böhlau, 1887–1919.

WAA   Christoph Martin Wieland, *Gesammelte Schriften*, ed. E. Schmidt *et al.*, Berlin: Weidmann, 1909–.

WGW   Christian Wolff, *Gesammelte Werke*, ed. J. Ecole *et al.*, Hildesheim: Olms, 1965–.

WMS   Christoph Martin Wieland, *Werke*, ed. Fritz Martini and Hans
      Werner Seiffert, Munich: Hanser, 1964.

Introduction

During the eighteenth and early nineteenth centuries in Germany, psychology grew from a minor branch of philosophical doctrine into one of the central pillars of intellectual culture. In the process psychology's evidential basis, theoretical structure, forms of articulation, and status both as a scientific discipline and as a cultural phenomenon took on a recognisably modern form. It became a fixture in the curricula of German universities, a subject in public and academic debate, and a popular publishing phenomenon, with collections of case histories, journals, and factual and fictionalised life-histories appearing in ever increasing numbers. By the middle of the nineteenth century psychology was – if the pun can be forgiven – institutionalised.

My argument is that the rise of psychology had a significant impact on German literature and thought of the period. Indeed, it is hard to form a historically faithful picture of German intellectual and cultural life without an understanding of psychology's role in it. One of my reasons for writing this book was that students of the philosophy and literature of the period often seem not to appreciate the importance that the writers and thinkers they study attached to psychology. There is a failure, perhaps, to recognise just how aware these early moderns were of a subject that we tend to think of as belonging to our age and not theirs. My argument will be that the eighteenth and early nineteenth centuries had at their disposal some quite sophisticated means of conceptualising psychological states. Subsequent developments in psychology have made this hard to see; we have become used to talking about psychology in a language that was formed in the late nineteenth and early twentieth centuries. Consequently, when we try to read the writing and thought of an earlier period in psychological terms, the result is often anachronism. This might be the relatively harmless anachronism of using terms such as 'intuition', 'intelligence', and 'imagination' in ways that would not have been understood two hundred years ago. Or, more damagingly, earlier psychology is read as if it were merely unconceptualised psychoanalysis.[1] More cautious readers have reacted against the retrospective application of modern psychology, with results that can be damaging in a different way. In his study of Schiller, for instance, Emil Staiger argued that psychology was not a significant force in Schiller's writing.[2] Because Staiger disliked the retrospective application of psychoanalysis, he dismissed psychology *tout court*. Yet it was surely obvious in Staiger's day – and has since become even more so, thanks to the work of Wolfgang Riedel and Peter-André Alt – that the young dramatist Schiller was intensely interested in psychology.[3] Part of my aim in this study is to show just how fully conceptualised the psychology of eighteenth- and early nineteenth-century writers and thinkers was and so how unnecessary the retrospective application of psychoanalysis is.

This book presents a series of case studies in the interaction of psychology with literature and philosophy between 1700 and 1840. A complete account of the subject is well beyond the scope of a single study; instead I have chosen to show how some of the canonical writers and thinkers of the period assimilated and applied psychological ideas. It follows that part of my subject will be the emergence of psychology itself. One element of this book is a history of the evolution of psychology. I have largely confined myself to looking at the main theoretical developments in psychology. The history of how psychology became a discipline – the social and institutional history of psychology, if you like – forms the background to this study, but will remain largely invisible. The details of who practised psychology and where, how much they published and what form their publications took, what institutional status they had – these factors are of great interest, and much has been done in recent years to illuminate them. A picture has emerged of the confluence of initially isolated discourses, such as the autobiographical and devotional literature of German Pietism rediscovered by Hans-Jürgen Schings, followed by more integrated and institutionalised activity after 1750, first at the University of Göttingen, then in philosophical circles in Berlin, and then around 1800 at the University of Jena.[4]

The social and institutional context is of great importance, but it forms the background of this study, not its foreground. Our interest is in psychological *theory* – psychology's conceptual contents, not its social and institutional context. Some reference to the historical context and the detail of who drew on what sources is essential, of course, but this is not in the first place a study in 'bottom–up', contextualised history. Nor does it aim at completeness. I have chosen to look at individual works or historical moments, rather than attempt a complete account of a writer's knowledge and use of psychology. My aim is to show that psychology was important, not that it saturated every text. My evidence is a number of canonical works, which serve as test cases. My purpose in examining them has not been to provide an analysis – let alone a complete one – of a given author's handling of the psychology of his characters, but rather to consider representative instances of that author's awareness of, or contribution to, psychological theory. I am also aware of the danger of the kind of reductive reading that seeks to interpret a work through a single theme or from a single perspective. I only mean to argue that the psychological element must be built into readings of the works. Some omissions deserve explanation. All the writers and thinkers discussed in the following pages are men. I have made no attempt to redress this imbalance, not wishing to misrepresent an age in which philosophical and avant-garde literary discourse was overwhelmingly male. When gender issues arise, I have addressed these in an explicit and, I hope, conscientious way. Some important authors and texts have been omitted for reasons of space or in order to avoid unnecessary duplication. The former excluded Wezel, Tieck, and Jean Paul, the latter E. T. A. Hoffmann's novels. As this is a study of the period 1700 to 1840, I have not discussed or used Freudian or other psychoanalytical ideas. The only circumstance in which I could conceive of its being helpful to apply Freud's theories retrospectively would be if they could be shown to be true.

CHAPTER I

The 'long past': psychology before 1700

It is not uncommon for histories of psychology to begin by quoting Hermann Ebbinghaus's dictum that psychology has 'a short history but a long past'.[1] This implies that until psychology became a science and acquired a history, it was uneventful. It suggests the long persistence of a stable paradigm, and in some respects it is true. It is indeed the case that from antiquity up to the nineteenth century most European philosophy of mind derived directly or indirectly from Aristotle's *De anima*. The underlying model of mind is a group of distinct faculties with a physiological basis, each located in a separate organ and each defined by its function. One can find evidence for this model as far back as the Homeric poems.[2] Given systematic and philosophical form by Aristotle, it became the standard model of mind and lasted well into the modern period. For instance, the belief, explicitly held by Aristotle and implicit in Homer, that humans share with animals all of their psychic faculties except for reason would have been accepted by most thinkers of the eighteenth century.[3]

The aim of this chapter is to identify the key features of psychology's long past. This will involve a brief summary of Aristotle's *De anima*, followed by an account of the fate of the much less influential Platonic tradition. Finally, to gain a sense of what an educated person around 1700 might have understood by 'psychology', we will consider how some important German, British, and French reference books presented the subject.

Aristotle

De anima deals chiefly with the biological aspect of soul.[4] Later it would be used to provide answers to questions that were quite foreign to its intentions, in particular the Christian need to demonstrate the immortality of the soul. In fact, *De anima* presents the powers of the soul – motor powers, instincts, the emotions, sensation – as dependent on the body. Aristotle's key argument is that soul is the 'actuality' (*entelecheia*) of the body (412a16). It is what a body must be in order to carry out its functions. Aristotle compares this to vision: soul and body are to a person what seeing and pupil are to an eye (412b18–24). Soul is what a body is for, its purpose. In general, then, soul is the essence of body: the formal, efficient, and final causes of body converge in it (415b8 ff.). That is not to say that the soul is the person. Aristotle distinguishes between the person and his or her intellect. It is neither the person alone nor the intellect alone that thinks: rather a person thinks by means of the intellect (408b13–14).

Five different types of soul occur and each has different capacities (*dynameis*). The most basic form of soul has the powers of nutrition and growth (413a21–34). Plants have souls of this kind. The second type of soul has these powers plus sensation (413b1–10). This is the kind of soul that immobile animals have. The third type of soul has all the above plus desire. The fourth has the above plus movement: all mobile animals have this species of soul. The fifth type has the above plus 'intellect and the reflective capacity' (*nous kai hē theorētikē dynamis*, 413b24). In each case the higher soul comprises the lower. Thus, although the highest species of soul comprises a multiplicity of powers, it is also ultimately a unity, for the higher capacities contain the possibility of the lower (414b29–30).

Cognition begins when the senses receive the forms of external objects. The form of a thing imprints itself on the sense like a ring in wax; the imprint in the wax consists of the form of the ring, not the ring itself (424a18–23). The process of sensation itself is free of errors (418a31–33). When we see a white object, we cannot be wrong in sensing it is white (428b19–22). The power of the senses does vary, however, for it often happens that after a loud noise we are less able to hear (429a31–b2). Moreover, we can be wrong in imagining what the white thing is. We form an image (*phantasma*) of the thing in our imagination (431a16). We never think without these images. Imagination leads to error because it makes us susceptible to illusion (427b18–19). This is why when we sleep or when we are ill we do not perceive the world as it is; in these states we are governed by imagination (429a1–8).

Normally, the intellect (*nous*) is in control. Intellect is of two kinds. If, as seems to be the case, the mind can potentially think everything, then it must have no limitations and must therefore contain nothing but itself (429a18–21). In this sense the mind 'cannot have any nature of its own except just this, to be potential' (429a21–2). However, the intellect is also the location of forms. In this aspect – what Aristotle calls its 'actualised' state – the intellect takes on the form of what it is thinking about: 'the intellect, in its actualised state, is the facts' (431b17). The intellect's capacities are potentially the forms of the objects themselves. The same is true of the senses. The sense of touch is the power to take on the forms of all touchable things (431b24 ff.).

Chapter 5 of *De anima* introduces a new idea, the productive (*poiētikos*) intellect. This provides a metaphysical grounding for intellect. Just as the potential intellect has the capacity to become things, so the intellect must also have the power to initiate things. This productive intellect is like light. Light enables coloured things to be coloured; without light, although they possess the same qualities, they are only potentially coloured. Similarly, the active intellect renders potential qualities actual. In its essence this power is 'separated, unaffected, and unmixed, being in substance activity (*energeia*)'. Its action is constant. Unlike the potential intellect, which is affected, productive intellect is not. Though it perdures the destruction of the physical body, we have no memory of our pre-existence, because the productive intellect is unaffected. Here Aristotle appears to be thinking of Plato's theory of *anamnēsis* or recollection, according to which the process of acquiring knowledge is in fact a recollecting of things hidden within us.[5] The Platonic tradition of psychology coexisted and commingled with the dominant Aristotelian tradition from late antiquity onwards to varying degrees. Its main contributions were the notions of the duality of soul, the belief that the psyche is driven by desire, and the theory of *anamnēsis*, which can be seen as the source of the idea of the unconscious in European thought and is thus of considerable importance for our story.

The idea of the unconscious in the Platonic tradition

Although some elements of Plato's psychology resemble Aristotle's physiological faculty psychology, a quite different, dualist psychology appears in the *Meno* and *Phaedo*. Its central idea is *anamnēsis*.[6] In the *Meno* this forms part of an argument about cognition. Socrates argues that we cannot find something if we do not know what to look for. The mind must in some way be pre-equipped for knowledge. Hence it is more true to speak of remembering than knowing. Our knowing is not a becoming acquainted by seeing sensible objects, for what we know is not in fact sensible particulars but the forms of things. An ideal principle in us knows or recollects these forms: the immortal soul. In the *Phaedo* Socrates defines soul as a substance that is entirely different and separate from the body, an idea that derives perhaps from Pythagorean cult beliefs.[7] Soul can be hindered in exercising its powers of cognition by the body. Cognition involves separating thought from the sense organs. Only when the soul is apart from the body does it have intelligence (*phronēsis*).[8] The soul is driven by eros, first bodily eros, then through release and purification from the body towards spiritual eros.[9] Eros and reason (*logos*) are the constitutive forces of the soul. Both remind us of our prenatal contact with the world of ideas, before soul was imprisoned in body.

Late-Antique Neoplatonist psychology is an amalgam of Platonic and Aristotelian ideas, the former providing the structure and the latter much of the content. For Plotinus, the soul is independent of the body and immortal. As in Plato's *Timaeus*, it is divinely born (*theion gennēton*) and partakes in the universal world-soul. Individual souls are emanations from the universal soul. In this sense, there is only one soul, present everywhere in many bodies.[10] It might be objected that if all souls were one, people should not differ in their knowledge. Plotinus answers that such differences occur because bodies are different, not souls. Even within one body, the different parts of the body have different experiences. This is because the body obscures the truth.

Humans are inhabitants of two worlds. The soul is situated at the point where the universal intellect and the individual bodily sensibility meet:

The operation of the Intellectual-Principle [*nous*] enters from above us as that of the sensitive faculty [*aisthēsis*] from below; the We is the soul at its highest, the mid-point between two powers [*dynameis*], between the sensitive principle, inferior to us, and the intellectual principle superior.[11]

Plotinus agrees with Plato that the soul is divided into rational and irrational parts.[12] The two parts of the soul are the 'intellectual' (*noētikos*) and the 'psychic' (*psychikos*). The *noētikos* is immortal, the *psychikos* is not. These two parts together consist of a further five parts corresponding to the five *dynameis* of Aristotelian souls. The intellectual soul consists of 'a kind of unthinking activity', and *noēsis* itself. The psychic soul consists of three parts: *dianoia, aisthēsis,* and *physis. Physis* is the power of the unconscious, vegetative soul; *aisthēsis* that of the sensitive, animal soul; and *dianoia* the capacity for reasoning.[13]

The soul's power of *aisthēsis* apprehends sensible objects. The representations to which these give rise, however, are handled by another power, the *logizomenon*, which assesses and judges the representations coming from perception. The *logizomenon* can also judge the impressions (*typoi*, literally 'blows') that come down from *nous*. It has a middle position between sensation and intellect. Its role is liaison:

The reasoning-principle [*logizomenon*] in the Soul acts on the representations [*ta phantasmata*] standing before it as the result of sense-perception [*aisthēsis*]; these it judges, combining, distinguishing: or it may also observe the impressions [*typoi*], so to speak, rising from the Intellectual-Principle, and has the same power of handling these; and reasoning will develop to wisdom where it recognises the new and late-coming impressions (those of sense) and adapts them, so to speak, to those it holds from long before – the act which may be described as the soul's reminiscence [*anamnēsis*].[14]

In this life we seek to strip away the matter from sensible particulars so as to reach ideas. This is sometimes conceived of as an upwards striving of the soul, but more often as a remembering of ideas already in our mind of which we are not conscious. And yet inasmuch as this involves stripping away the (obstructive) knowledge of sensible particulars, to learn is to forget.[15]

This leads to what one might fairly term the first theory of the unconscious. There are two states in which we can think whilst not being conscious of what we are doing. The first is in habitual actions, when we are not attentive to the world:

Circumstances, purely accidental, need not be present to the imaging faculty [*phantasia*], and if they do so appear they need not be retained or even observed, and in fact the impression [*typos*] of any such circumstance does not entail awareness [*synaisthēsis*]. Thus in local movement, if there is no particular importance to us in the fact that we pass through first this then that portion of air, or that we proceed from some particular point, we do not take notice, or even know it as we walk.[16]

In such situations we have unconscious instincts that guide us. This is unconscious in the sense of 'not known', and whilst it might be psychologically interesting, it is not philosophically significant. We are also unaware of our mental activity when concentrating intently on something. Plotinus cites the example of acts of great bravery, in which one is conscious of one's objective but not of oneself:

And even in our conscious life we can point to many noble activities, of mind and of hand alike, which at the time in no way compel our consciousness [*praxeis . . . to parakolouthein hēmas autais ouk ekhousai*: literally 'actions that do not have us following along with ourselves']. A reader will often be quite unconscious when he is most intent: in a feat of courage there can be no sense either of the brave action or of the fact that all that is done conforms to the rules of courage . . . So that it would even seem that consciousness tends to blunt the activities upon which it is exercised, and that in the degree in which these pass unobserved they are purer and have more effect, more vitality, and that, consequently, the Proficient arrived at this state has the truer fullness of life, life not spilled out in sensation but gathered closely within itself.[17]

This inwardness is a key to Plotinus' mysticism.[18] If we can escape our consciousness of the actions we are performing, we will be better able to perform them, even if they are mental activities. The intellect may remain conscious of its object, but the person as a whole is not. This unconscious mental activity is like the movement of a mystic towards God. It embodies a tendency towards the fourth *hypostasis*, that of pure *nous*, in which the thinking subject becomes one with its object. Beyond that is the fifth *hypostasis*, the One, or the complete identity of self to itself.

The psychology of Platonism and Neoplatonism, obscured by Scholasticism in the Middle Ages, was rediscovered in the Renaissance by Marsilio Ficino and others. Broadly speaking, Ficino followed Plotinus' metaphysics of soul. There are five essences: the One, mind (the angels), soul (humans), quality (the forms of things in the world), and physical matter. Soul occupies a position between the earthly and the divine, and it partakes of both.[19] Man also has five aspects, in which he imitates and brings together the Universe. Ficino emphasises the power of the human soul over nature: 'Man imitates all the works of divine nature and perfects, corrects and changes those of the inferior world.'[20] Man is therefore a smaller earthly version of God.[21] With divine powers come divine aspirations. Humans can know sensible realities, but they quest for ultimate reasons that are beyond them. The result is disquiet ('inquietudo animi', 1.i; vol. 1 p.38). This accounts in part for Ficino's interest in the figure of the melancholy genius from the pseudo-Aristotelian *Problemata*.[22] Humans are the most perfect and the most wanting of creatures, yet their very shortcomings turn out to constitute their true worth.[23] Inclination and inadequacy combine in desire. Humans experience both the presence and the absence of the desired object. Desire fires man's progress towards God.[24] Herein lies the dignity of man: his desire to ascend to the divine. Ficino's conception of love owes much to Plato's *Phaedrus*, in which Socrates imagines that the soul resembles a chariot. The charioteer represents the rational part of the soul (*nous*), struggling to keep control of two horses of opposed natures, one divine and one not:

The soul resembles the naturally joined power of a winged team [of horses] under its charioteer. The God's horses and charioteers are all of good nature and good stock, but all others have been cross-bred. As for us the charioteer does hold the reins, but one of the horses is of fair and good nature and of like stock and the other is of the opposite nature and stock. (*Phaedrus*, 246a5–b4)

For Ficino it is love, not reason, that binds together the two aspects of the world. Through love the world of appearance strives towards the world of ideas.

The Neoplatonism of Ficino was a formative influence on the Cambridge Neoplatonist school led by Ralph Cudworth, with which we reach the threshold of the Enlightenment.[25] The immediate context of Cambridge Neoplatonism was the religious conflicts of the seventeenth century. It originated in the Latitudinarian response to Puritanical Calvinism and the restrictions on the Church of England during the Interregnum.[26] The 'latitude-men' objected to Calvinist pessimism, stressing instead the capacity of man for moral improvement and drawing their inspiration from classical ethics, especially Plato. Another philosophical difference between Florentine and Cambridge Neoplatonism was the influence of Descartes on the latter.[27] Cudworth was generally well disposed towards Descartes. He agreed with Descartes that bodies can only be known by the understanding and that all knowledge of bodies aspires to the status of physics. However, Cudworth believed that real knowledge involves the identity of knower and known. From this he drew the Cartesian conclusion that only knowledge of the self can count as certain.[28] It follows that perception and knowledge are two quite different processes with very different results.[29] However, Cudworth disliked Descartes's dualism of matter and mind, which he believed made most of the mind material. He rejected Descartes's view that animals are machines. Human mental behaviour is like that of animals in some respects: like animals humans have instincts, which are purposive and must therefore be essentially incorporeal.[30]

Cudworth replaced Descartes's dualism of mind and matter with a new dualism of activity and passivity. Sensation arises from the combination of the pressure of external objects on our senses and mind's own vital, attentive energy.[31] Because they contain a material element, sensations are not pure cognitions. Yet attentive consciousness is not the sum of the mind's activity, as it was for Descartes; the soul is active even when we are not conscious. Accordingly, unconscious states such as dreaming are of great importance to Cudworth.[32] Citing Plotinus' argument that there can be thought without the unifying central focus of *synaisthēsis*, he uses this against 'those philosophers . . . who make the essence of the soul to consist in cogitation', by which he means Descartes.[33] This leads into an extended discussion of the mind's unconscious 'plastic power' that recalls Plotinus:

It is certain that our human souls themselves are not always conscious of whatever they have in them; for even the sleeping geometrician hath, at that time, all his geometrical theorems and knowledges some way in him; as also the sleeping musician, all his musical skill and songs: and therefore, why may it not be possible for the soul to have likewise some actual energy in it, which it is not expressly conscious of? We have all experience of our doing many animal actions non-attendingly, which we reflect upon afterwards; as also that we often continue a long series of bodily motions, by a mere virtual intention of our minds, as it were by half a cogitation. That vital sympathy by which our soul is united and tied fast, as it were in a knot, to the body, is a thing that we have no direct consciousness of, but only in its effects. Nor can we tell how we come to be so differently affected in our souls, from the many different motions made upon our bodies. As likewise we are not conscious to ourselves of that energy whereby we impress a variety of motions and figurations upon the animal spirits of our brain in our fantastic thoughts. For though the geometrician perceive himself to make lines, triangles, and circles in the dust with his finger, yet he is not aware how he makes all those same figures first upon the corporeal spirits of his brain. . . . There is also another more interior kind of plastic power in the soul, . . . whereby it is formative of its own cogitations, which itself is not always conscious of; as when, in sleep or dreams, it frames interlocutory discourses betwixt itself and other persons, in a long series, with coherent sense and apt connexions, in which oftentimes it seems to be surprised with unexpected answers and repartees, though itself were all the while the poet and inventor of the whole fable.[34]

This constellation of ideas passes into the German tradition of psychology at its very font, via Shaftesbury and Leibniz, as we shall see in Chapter 2.

DEFINITIONS OF PSYCHOLOGY IN THE EIGHTEENTH CENTURY

If some of the content of the Platonic tradition passed into eighteenth-century European psychology, its form and defining features remained unmistakably Aristotelian. The word *psychologia* appears to have been invented by sixteenth-century German Aristotelian humanists. The first confirmable printed occurrences of the word date from the 1570s, in the work of the German Semiramist philosopher Johann Thomas Freigius. The discipline named psychology originates from the organising principles of Semiramism, which, by unifying philosophy into a single discipline, strove to overcome the confusion into which Scholasticism had fallen. Within this the sub-disciplines were arranged by means of dichotomised divisions, often presented in the form now used for cladistics, with the general discipline ramifying into more specific sub-disciplines. The adherents of Semiramism included Freigius, Rodolphus Goclenius (Goeckel),

Johannes Comenius (Komensky), and Otto Casmann. In 1590 Goclenius became the first to publish a work with *psychologia* in its title, an anthology of pieces on the (theological) question of how souls originate.[35] The first monograph titled *Psychologia* was Casmann's *Psychologia anthropologica; sive, animae humanae doctrina (Anthropological Psychology; or, Doctrine of the Human Soul)* of 1594.[36] For Casmann *psychologia* was one of the two branches of *anthropologia*, the other being *somatologia*. According to Casmann's scheme, anthropology was the study of the interaction of mind and body. Psychology, the study of mind, and somatology, the study of body, were its sub-disciplines. Anthropology was in turn one of the two sub-disciplines of the study of spirited beings, the other being the study of angels, *angelographia*.[37] Casmann's positioning of psychology as a subset of the more general science of anthropology held good until the late eighteenth century, when psychology fully established itself as a discipline, so eclipsing anthropology, which then allied itself with ethnology.

The first dictionary appearance of the word *psychologia* was in the German Semiramist Johannes Micraelius's *Lexicon philosophicum* of 1653. The entry for *psychologia* consists of the statement that '*Psychologia* is the doctrine of soul.'[38] Under *anima* there is an Aristotelian definition of soul, a list of the parts and powers of the soul, and attacks on false doctrines such as the Manichaean view that human souls are part of God. It ends with a cross-reference to the article for *psychologia*. The article on *philosophia* locates the science of psychology within the Semiramist classification of subjects. Metaphysics has two components, ontology and pneumatology, and the latter consists of *theologia, angelographia*, and *psychologia*. The article on *metaphysica* gives the same classification, and notes that there is some debate as to whether theology, angelography, and psychology should be counted as parts of metaphysics or as separate disciplines. By contrast, the Frenchman Pierre Godard's *Lexicon philosophicum* of 1675 gives the standard Aristotelian treatment of *anima*, but makes no reference to *psychologia*.[39] Similarly, the *Lexicon philosophicum* of the Huguenot Etienne Chauvin, published from exile in Holland, has articles on *anima* and *anima rationalis*, but not *psychologia*.[40] Whilst German Semiramism recognised psychology as a distinct subject, French Scholasticism evidently did not.

The general encyclopedias of the late seventeenth and early eighteenth centuries present a similar picture. Sponsored by the Académie Française and reflecting the interests of the French elite, Thomas Corneille's *Dictionnaire des arts et des sciences* (1694) contains no entries for psychology in its two volumes of dictionary and two of encyclopedia. The dictionary entry *Ame* gives a brief, common-sense definition: 'Soul . . . which is the principle of life in living things. It is used particularly of man, and signifies that thing in him that makes him capable of thinking, wanting, and reasoning.'[41] The British counterpart to Corneille, the *Lexicon technicum* of Royal Society Fellow John Harris, is even less forthcoming, containing no philosophical entries at all. Harris explains his anti-metaphysical stance thus:

That which I have aimed at, is to make it a Dictionary not only of bare *Words* but *Things*; and that the Reader may not only find here an Explication of the *Technical* Words, or the Terms of Art made use of in all the *Liberal Sciences*, and such as border nearly upon them, but also those *Arts themselves*; and especially *such*, and *such* Parts of them as are most Useful and Advantagious to Mankind. In this, which was the chief of my Design, I found much less help from Dictionaries already published, then one would have expected from their *Titles*: *Chauvin's Lexicon Rationale*, or *Thesaurus Philosophicus*, is a well Printed Book, and the figures are finely Graved; but 'tis too much filled with the School Terms, to be usefully instructive; and is as defective in the Modern Improvements of Mathematical and Physical Learning, as it abounds with a Cant which was once mistaken for *Science*.[42]

The result is an encyclopedia that, in useful subjects such as anatomy, is 'very large and full', but in '*Logick, Metaphysicks, Ethicks, Grammar, Rhetorick,* &c.' is 'designedly short'.[43]

The *Universal-Lexicon* produced between 1732 and 1754 in Leipzig by the Protestant publisher Johann Heinrich Zedler is altogether different. Zedler's encyclopedia was written in the shadow of the philosophical system of Christian Wolff, which gave an unusually prominent place to psychology. It is also on a much grander scale than either Corneille's or Harris's. Even so, the comparison shows how far Germany's systematisation of psychology was ahead of France's and England's. The entry *Seelen-Lehre* provides, in one-and-a-half folio columns, a detailed summary of Wolff's theories. Entries under *psychologia* and *Psychologie* refer back to *Seelen-Lehre*, as does an entry under *Seelen-Wissenschaft*. These are complemented by a further tantalising entry:

PSYCHOMETRIA, is a science not yet available in books, which constitutes the mathematical knowledge of the soul and has been proposed by Herr Christian Wolff.[44]

Zedler thus does for psychology what Harris does for the physical sciences and medicine. He gives the philosophically inclined reader the most up-to-date knowledge of the subject.

With its grand format and lavish plates, the *Encyclopédie* of Diderot and D'Alembert far surpasses Zedler in coverage and in the modernity of its content. The *Encyclopédie* is the first non-German reference work to contain an entry for psychology and gives a similar account to Zedler's. Psychology is defined in the Wolffian manner as 'part of philosophy which treats the human soul, defines its essence, and gives account of its operations.'[45] The subject is divided into two parts, rational and empirical. It is a foundational discipline that furnishes other areas with concepts, in particular theology, ethics, and logic. It is also pleasing and useful, for 'Nothing is more suitable than the study of *psychology* for giving the most lively pleasures to a mind that loves solid and practical knowledge.'[46] In summary, the article offers a description of and advertisement for Wolffian psychology. This contrasts with the article for *Ame*, which does not mention Wolff, but instead presents a critique of Leibniz, Spinoza, Lucretius, and Hobbes.[47] Similarly, the article *Ame des bêtes* consists of an extended critique of Descartes's mechanistic view of animal souls.[48] These articles are essentially ideological.

The *Encyclopædia Britannica* is oriented towards utility and, like Harris's *Lexicon*, is impatient of metaphysics. The article 'Soul', after a conventional Aristotelian definition ('a spiritual substance, which animates the bodies of living creatures: it is the principle of life and activity within them') is mainly theological, with two paragraphs weighing up proofs of the immortality of the soul and coming down in favour of a providentialist argument from the goodness of God.[49] 'Anima' has a dismissively brief entry.[50] Psychology appears under the heading 'metaphysics',[51] where a broadly Wolffian scheme is evident:

METAPHYSICS, . . . is divided according to the objects that it considers, into six principal parts, which are called, 1. Ontology: 2. Cosmology: 3. Antrophology [*sic*]: 4. Psychology: 5. Pneumatology: and, 6. Theodicy, or metaphysical theology.

The misspelling of anthropology, repeated in the body of the article, suggests unfamiliarity – whether the author's or the printer's – with the ideas being described. Discussion of the spiritual aspect of anthropology (psychology) is dismissed as airy and empty:

Concerning [psychology] the most subtle and abstract researches have been made, that the human reason is capable of producing; and concerning [it] in spite of all these efforts, it is yet extremely difficult to assert any thing that is rational, and still less any thing that is positive and well supported.

The *Encyclopædia* accepts a Wolffian framework, but rejects its contents. It also reflects the status of psychology in Britain. The concept had still not entered British philosophical discourse by the 1770s. In 1702 a controversy was sparked by William Coward's *Second Thoughts Concerning the Human Soul, demonstrating the Notion of Human Soul, as believ'd to be a spiritual, immortal substance, united to human body, to be a plain heathenish invention* (1702),[52] during which the term psychology briefly enjoyed currency.[53] This did not spill over into academic psychology, however, where the older scholastic term (pneumatology), with its archaic connotations, was still preferred.[54]

CHAPTER 2

The Enlightenment: Rationalism and Sensibility

DESCARTES AND LEIBNIZ

It is often said that modern Western philosophy begins with Descartes. The German tradition of psychology certainly does, in both the general and a particular sense. Descartes turned Western philosophy inwards from metaphysical to epistemological questions and originated the idea of consciousness in its modern form. More specifically, the modifications made by Leibniz and Wolff to Descartes's system created the need for a philosophical psychology in Germany. In the *Discourse on Method* (1637), Descartes argued that the physical qualities and essences of Scholasticism could be dispensed with. Science should be mathematical. Bodies with measurable characteristics would replace qualities. By 1700, however, Descartes's influence was increasingly subject to criticism. The Cartesians, it was felt, had thrown out the qualities of Aristotle only to replace them with innate ideas. The tone of Enlightenment philosophy, set by Bayle and Locke, became anti-Cartesian. However, German philosophy continued to operate within a Cartesian framework. In Germany Wolff's popularity was at its height when Descartes was in eclipse in Britain and France. This is one of the reasons why the rise of psychology as a distinct discipline in the eighteenth century was confined to Germany.

The German tradition of psychology originated from a problem in Descartes. In his efforts to fend off scepticism, Descartes gave a special role to consciousness. Even if we reject all knowledge that might plausibly be doubted, we must still admit the truth of the proposition 'I am', for thinking requires that there be a subject that can think. Seen in this way, consciousness – the state in which we are aware of ourselves as subjects – has a special significance: it confers certainty in a very uncertain world. We can be certain about truths that depend on consciousness, but not on anything a posteriori. This dualistic epistemology corresponds to a dualistic ontology. The world consists of *res cogitans*, thinking stuff or souls, and *res extensa*, physical bodies. The former works according to laws of reason, the latter according to mechanical laws. Human beings are composed of both. They have a rational, thinking part that can conceive of clear and distinct ideas, and they have a mechanical part, whose behaviour is irrational. The passions belong to the latter.

Leibniz accepted Descartes's theory of truth, but not his equation of soul with consciousness or his view that bodies were simply machines. The *cogito* only answers the sceptic's denial that I can be certain of my existence *now*, not whether I will still exist when I am no longer conscious. It does not prove that the personal soul is immortal. For this reason, in German rationalism consciousness does not enjoy a high status. For Leibniz mental activity was more important than consciousness. He argued, inspired perhaps by Plotinus, that the mind's activity is incessant.[1]

In Leibniz's system the ultimate substances are 'monads'.[2] These have no spatial extension, and are therefore immortal, as indivisible things cannot have any parts taken away from them. Because they have no parts, monads are also without 'windows': nothing can enter or leave them. They must have properties, or they would be indistinguishable and not separate things. They must also be subject to change, or else time, which Leibniz thinks is only a property of objects, would stand still. But the change must come from within because monads are windowless. The only possible properties monads can have, then, are representations. What constitutes a monad and makes it different from all other monads is that it has representations that are unique to it. More precisely, monads all represent the same thing, namely the Universe, but their representations differ in the degree of their clarity and distinctness. Hence, the changes monads undergo are changes in the clarity and distinctness of their representations.

The internal principle that drives change in monads is 'appetition'.[3] It is the desire of a monad to improve its representations. Appetition is directed towards perfection. Being at different stages on the route to their goal, monads fall into different classes distinguished by the degree of perfection of their representations. Monads with only perception are the lowest form; they constitute physical matter. The next highest are animal souls, which have feeling and memory and are capable of knowing contingent truths. (This is in contrast to Descartes's view that animals are machines.) Memory gives these souls consecutiveness in time and the capacity to develop cognitive habits. Cognitive habits can have the same empirical characteristics as reason; indeed they mimic reason, to which monads all aspire. Humans act on habit, like animals, most of the time.

What distinguishes humans is the capacity, whether they use it or not, to reason.

The system of monads is designed to overcome Descartes's dualism and establish the unity and immortality of the soul. For Leibniz the psyche is a single unit, powered by a single force (appetition) and grounded in a single activity, the production of representations. This corresponds to a feature of Leibniz's epistemology. In the *Meditations on Cognition, Truth and Ideas* (1684) Leibniz shows that the different forms of knowledge are arranged in a graduated scale from clear and distinct ideas down to sense perception, and not in two separate classes, as Descartes believed.[4] At the lowest level of mental activity are obscure and confused sensations of which we are not even conscious. Leibniz later termed these *petites perceptions*. He gives a beguiling argument for these *petites perceptions* in the *New Essays on Human Understanding*.[5] Our perception of a wave breaking on a shingle beach is in reality composed of minute, separately indiscernible perceptions of each bit of the wave striking each individual pebble. We cannot separate each perception of each pebble being struck by each bit of the wave, but we know that each such perception must exist, because if it did not, and were nothing, then, since a multiple of zero equals zero, the whole perception of the wave could not exist for us. Therefore unconscious perceptions must exist, and there must be a practically infinite number of them. They must be continuously present, even when we are asleep.

Leibniz secured the inalienability and continuity of thinking by enhancing the status of the unconscious mind.[6] Yet this also threatens the rationality it is designed to defend. All action in the mind is grounded in the imagination, and all ideas are dependent on the character of the primary representations. However, representations behave according to their own, not necessarily rational rationale. The *petites perceptions* are an unruly rabble that arises in complete spontaneity with regard to the world and uncontrolled by the attention. As Cudworth and many eighteenth-century writers, including Kant, believed, the imagination is 'blind'.[7] Leibniz reasoned, citing Plotinus, that whereas we know some things clearly and distinctly, we have a great chaotic mass of unconscious ideas: 'Although the mind, as Plotinus rightly says, contains a kind of intelligible world within it, very few things in us can be known distinctly, and the remainder are hidden in confusion, in the chaos of our perceptions as it were.'[8] Representations force themselves upon the consciousness, as when we remember something we would rather have forgotten. In this sense, reason is subject to things that are beyond its control.

Leibniz believes that we access our unconscious when our normal waking sensations are too weak to drown it out, such as when we sleep.[9] Our *petites perceptions* emerge in dreams, which, since all states of mind or matter are products of previous states, can contain in them experiences that they precede and can, therefore, be prophetic.[10] The argument is expanded in the *New Essays*:

These minute perceptions . . . are more effective in their results than has been recognized. They constitute that *je ne sais quoi*, those flavours, those images of sensible qualities, vivid in the aggregate but confused as to the parts; those impressions which are made on us by the bodies around us and which involve the infinite; that connection which each being has with the rest of the universe. It can even be said that by virtue of these minute perceptions the present is big with the future and burdened with the past, that all things harmonize – *sympnoia panta* [everything is in sympathy], as Hippocrates put it – and that eyes as piercing as God's could read in the lowliest substance the universe's whole sequence of events – 'What is, what was, and what will soon be brought in by the future.'[11]

The influence of renaissance Neoplatonism is plain to see.

WOLFF

Christian Wolff (1679–1754) stands at the head of the German tradition of philosophical psychology. The content of his psychology is not especially original, deriving mostly from Leibniz, Descartes, and the Aristotelian tradition, and much of his empirical psychology is not empirical at all. However, viewed as a whole, his project is highly innovative. Wolff systematised psychology and formed it into a discipline. He was the first to accord *psychologia* the same status as such venerable disciplines as *theologia, physiologia,* and *cosmologia.* His *Psychologia empirica* was the first work of psychology to be worthy of the title, to treat psychology as the systematic and thorough study of mind.[12] He divided psychology into empirical and theoretical sub-disciplines. He realised that some aspects of psychology, such as the measurement of responses and affects, could be given a quantitative basis and gave this form of psychology the label *psycheometria,* so pre-empting by more than a hundred years the development of psychometrics (*WGW* 11.v.403). For Wolff, the psychologist is no less a scientist than the astronomer, who builds a theory out of observations and subjects the theory to empirical testing (*WGW* 11. v.4).[13] Empirical psychology provides the principles with which rational psychology works, and the theories developed in rational psychology could be subjected to confirmation by empirical psychology. Wolff made serious and systematic philosophical reflection about the soul possible. His influence can be found in such disparate and important eighteenth-century thinkers as Hartley, Diderot, and Herder.[14]

The innovative character of Wolff's undertaking is reflected in the prominence it has in his philosophical system. The order in which Wolff published his Latin system corresponds broadly to his philosophical priorities. His two Latin psychologies, the *Psychologia empirica* and the *Psychologia rationalis*, published in 1732 and 1734 respectively, appeared after the volumes on logic (1728), ontology (1729), and cosmology (1731), but before those on physics, physiology, ethics, politics, and theology. In the German version of his philosophy, empirical psychology forms the long third chapter of the system's 'hub',[15] *Vernünfftige Gedancken von Gott, der Welt und der Seele des Menschen, auch allen Dingen überhaupt,* 1720 [*Rational Thoughts on God, the World and the Soul of Man and All Things in General*], where it precedes the cosmology and shares a volume with the general metaphysics. This reflects the work psychology has to do. Empirical psychology provides the principles from which rational psychology then derives the nature of soul. It also provides principles for natural law, natural theology, ethics, and logic (*WGW* 11.v.3–8). If this were not justification enough, Wolff observes that psychology is a source of pleasure in its own right and is relatively accessible: it is 'more agreeable for beginners and can be learnt separately from all the other disciplines' ('für Anfänger anmutiger und kann ohne alle übrigen Disziplinen erkannt werden', *WGW* 1.i.152). This is not to say that it is unserious. Wolff promotes psychology because it is philosophically fundamental; its accessibility is secondary.[16]

Consciousness and sense perception

Wolff's empirical psychology begins with the Cartesian argument that consciousness entails the existence of a conscious subject. Wolff, however, does not define consciousness only in terms of subjecthood. Consciousness requires both a subject and an object. Soul is not just consciousness, but 'that thing which is conscious of itself and other things outside it'. If soul were identified with subjecthood, dangerous consequences would follow for the immortality of the soul. However, these questions belong to rational, not empirical, psychology. Empirical psychology is concerned with 'what we perceive of [the soul] through our everyday experience'.[17] Here Wolff has two arguments against Descartes. One is an empirical analogue of the ontological argument for the soul's immortality. There is evidence to suggest that whereas the mind is not continuously conscious of its activity, it is continuously active. In dreams our mind is active, but not conscious. The second argument concerns the nature of sensation. For Descartes sensation is a purely physical process. Animals, which are soulless machines, have sensations just as humans do. Sensations belong to the body, not the soul. Wolff, following Leibniz, conceives of sense perception as comprising two stages. The first is physical. Impressions strike the sense organs and cause activity in them. However, this is only part of the story. If physical stimulation of the sense organs were all that was needed for me to be able to say 'I hear', then I would just as well be able to say 'I hear' when asleep as when awake, for a sleeping person's ears are physically no different from a waking person's. This obvious absurdity confirms Wolff in his belief in the duality of perception. The first stage, then, is the physical stimulation of the organs. The second, in Leibniz's terminology, is apperception, the mind's consciousness of itself as a perceiving subject. In order to hear I must receive a stimulus and apperceive my attending to the stimulus. This suggests that Descartes was wrong to distinguish so cleanly between consciousness and sensation. For Wolff they are implicated in one another. Between sensation and rationality there is a continuity: as Wolff's follower Alexander Gottlieb Baumgarten put it, 'nature leaves no gaps between obscurity and clarity'.[18]

The ideas produced by sensation are physical. Wolff calls them *phantasmata* or *ideae* in the Latin psychology (following the Latin translations of Aristotle) and *Einbildungen* in the German. He is happy to accept the doctrine of 'material ideas' (and its troublesome consequences), as long as apperception remains immaterial (*WGW* 11.vi.29). As ideas are material, they cannot be erased or altered by thought alone. Sense impressions are permanent (*WGW* 11.v.43). The mind's lack of control over impressions extends also to the degree of force they possess. If we imagine impressions competing for the mind's attention, the stronger will prevail over the weaker (*WGW* 11.v.41–2). We are most aware of the ideas that have struck us most forcefully, not those that possess, say, the most intellectual or moral appeal.

Wolff seems untroubled by this. Our faculty of imagination (*Einbildung*) organises and stores impressions, but according to protocols that we do not determine (*WGW* 1.ii.135). Impressions enter the mind and are permanently impressed on it without the mind's active participation. All the mind can do is attend to itself as a percipient subject. The principle, or 'law' (*Gesetz*), as Wolff terms it, by which impressions are organised holds that they are linked to the other impressions that first accompanied them. My idea of a person is linked to the circumstances in which I first saw him or her. When I recollect the person, I will also recollect the place associated with him or her, whether I like it or not. This law of association, Wolff says, is of great importance, because of what it says about us. We are creatures of habit. Because our impressions are stored and recalled according to how we experience them, we can build a reliable picture of the world, but we are bound to repeat the same habits of thought, no matter how profitable or unprofitable they are. When we are remembering our experiences, the uncontrolled and associative memory is in charge. The faculty of recollecting (*Gedächtnis, recordatio* or *reminiscentia*), is merely the ability to recognise that what is presented to us is indeed a recollection of an earlier impression (*WGW* 11.v.164–5). What makes us re-experience the memories is the *Einbildungskraft*, and that, as we have seen, is beyond our control.

A further consequence of the doctrine of material ideas is that the rational faculties of attention and understanding are at odds with the irrational ones. As well as clamouring for our attention, impressions dull and confuse our reasoning. This is why it is easier to think if we are not distracted by sensations. Wolff relates an anecdote about the seventeenth-century mathematician Johannes Wallis, who claimed that one night he had succeeded in deriving, without pen and paper, the square root of the 53-digit number 24 681 357 910 121 411 131 516 182 017 192 122 242 628 302 325 272 931 (*WGW* 1.ii.146–7).[19] The point is that Wallis would not have been capable of this feat during daytime, when his mental faculties would have been clouded by light and noise.

Faculty Psychology

Wolff's general theory of cognition is not as mechanical as his theory of the imagination. The largely passive imaginative faculty (*Einbildungsvermögen*) is complemented by an active fantasy (*Dichtungsvermögen*). This faculty has the power to create new ideas by dismantling and reassembling already existing ideas. Thus we might separate the idea of the wings of a bird from the idea of the whole bird and combine them with a human body to create the idea of an angel (*WGW* 1.ii.134–5). However, Wolff is sceptical about this faculty, which creates only 'empty impressions' (*leere Einbildungen, WGW* 1.ii.136). The mind's true creativity is its ability to abstract from experience by compiling the best examples of a given object and creating from them its ideal form (*WGW* i.ii.136). Unlike empty impressions, these Platonic forms can have a truth content.

One of Wolff's aims is to define mental faculties sharply and systematically. The mind is equipped with an array of tools for performing distinct tasks. The sense organs receive physical impressions. Apperception focuses the mind on the senses. The imagination stores impressions. Attention (*Aufmerksamkeit*) isolates one thought from the rest (*WGW* i.ii.149). Memory distinguishes between known and unknown ideas. The inventive faculty creates new, but empty ideas out of existing ones. The understanding (*Verstand*) is the capacity to imagine the truly possible (as distinct from what we erroneously think possible, such as human bodies with birds' wings, *WGW* i.ii.153–4). The theory of cognition is thus largely concerned with questions of definition, a feature that was criticised by philosophers in the empiricist and realist traditions. The Scottish common-sense philosopher Thomas Reid was scornful:

Among modern philosophers I know none that has abused definition so much as Carolus Wolfius [*sic*], the famous German philosopher, who, in a work on the human mind called *Psychologia empirica* consisting of many hundred propositions, fortified by demonstrations, with a proportional accompaniment of definitions, corollaries, and scholia, has given so many definitions of things that cannot be defined, and so many demonstrations of things self-evident, that the greatest part of the work consists of tautology and ringing changes upon words.[20]

Wolff needed clear distinctions between forms of cognition. The most important of these were between clear and unclear, and distinct and confused ideas. Clear ideas can be distinguished from other ideas; unclear ideas are those of which one cannot say what they represent, such as an object seen in a dim light or from a distance. Distinct ideas can be defined and their qualities fully enumerated; indistinct ideas cannot (*WGW* ii. v.20–33 and i.ii.109–20). The function of thought is to render ideas clear and distinct; that is, to progress them from sense perceptions at the bottom of the cognitive ladder to clarity and distinctness at its top. One of Wolff's aims is to show how, in real situations, the mind does this. The definitions that Wolff gives the faculties must correspond to cognitive tasks. The attentive faculty has the task of isolating a perception from other perceptions; the faculty of understanding has the task of deciding which ideas are possible, and so on.

A second criticism is that Wolff defines realia teleologically, as contributions towards the providential ordering of the Universe: so it might be argued, infamously, that rats exist in order to feed cats. If the mental design of humans is teleologically orientated and cognitive tasks have mental faculties that correspond to them, it could be objected that there is nothing to check the proliferation of faculties. Might there not be a faculty for the British sense of humour, as the Göttingen materialist Michael Hißmann ironically observed?[21] In this light, Wolff's project appears flawed. Yet, as Hißmann pointed out, properly speaking Wolff's faculties are no more than dispositions. To say that someone has a faculty of understanding, with which they can determine what things are truly possible, is to say no more than that they are *disposed* to determine what things are truly possible. Any cognitive psychology will talk in this way. Moreover, Wolff's argument that our faculties are *designed* to deal with certain tasks might reasonably be given a minimalist, naturalistic interpretation: we are equipped with mental dispositions that can cope more or less well with the cognitive tasks that confront us. (We do not normally have to derive the square roots of 53-digit numbers.) Replace Providence with evolution by natural selection, and Wolff's psychology looks perfectly plausible.

Wolff's project differs from the mainstream of Enlightenment philosophy of mind in important ways. First, Wolff is not concerned with the *limits* of our understanding, as the empiricist tradition was. For Wolff, as for Leibniz, philosophy is the science of what is conceptually possible (*WGW* 11.i.13). He accepts the main claims of rationalism about our cognitive powers. In particular, he accepts Leibniz's view that philosophy must start from the 'primitive' principles of sufficient reason and identity. His psychology describes the structure of the cognitive apparatus that enables us to think in this way. This is why Wolff's project has more in common with Kant's than with Locke's. The difference between Wolff and Kant is that for Wolff our mental apparatus is real, whereas for Kant it is subjective or ideal. Wolff believes that a psychology of cognition is a valid enterprise, whereas Kant does not.

There is, however, a streak of empiricism in Wolff's psychology. Although each faculty represents a separate compartment, into which only a particular cognitive activity fits, Wolff repeatedly says that in empirical psychology everything is a matter of degree. Mental states are not absolutes; they are positions on a graduated scale. Our attention is never simply on or off; it is always somewhere between fully active and completely dormant. This suggests, of course, that the faculties are distinguished by quantity and not quality, which is why he can envisage a physical science of 'psycheometria'. On the other hand, the gradualism of a scientific psychology runs directly counter to the rationalism of clearly delineated faculties. It is unlikely that Wolff saw any incompatibility. Leibniz himself had insisted on a principle of continuity according to which there are no gaps in the series of existent things. It is one of the unresolved problems in Wolff's system.

To return to the higher faculties, attention underpins our ability to give clarity to perceptions. It enables us to say that we are having a particular experience now. This leads on to definitions of more specific faculties. Reflection enables us to attend to experiences in a temporal sequence. Our ability to attend to things distinctly comes from apprehension. This is the grasping of an object's full concept. To think of a triangle as a two-dimensional polygon with three straight sides is to apprehend it. From this, Wolff proceeds to the recognition of singularity and commonality, and thence to symbolic knowledge, propositional judgements, and logic.

Ethical psychology

The final part of empirical psychology is ethical psychology (*WGW*. ii.247–322). Wolff combines Leibniz's cognitive ethics and the classical tradition of ethical psychology. The classical tradition treated the mind as an organic whole or 'economy'. A precondition of goodness was that the individual had a well-ordered mind, in which the emotions and the mental faculties each carried out their proper functions. For Leibniz, by contrast, the rightness of actions flows from their consequences. To act rightly, I must know what is at stake. Wolff integrates these approaches. In the normal run of things I have emotions to guide me, such as my sense of pleasure or displeasure. From pain and pleasure comes my intuitive sense of a thing's goodness. Pain and pleasure have a cognitive basis. Pleasure accompanies the experience of completeness, pain incompleteness. This has a pronouncedly Leibnizian flavour. For Leibniz the world is good insofar as it is a divine totality, in which the realm of natural laws will (finally) coincide with the realm of moral ends. Wolff sees emotions in the light of Leibnizian totality. Hence sadness has a cognitive function, as it signals ways in which the world is incomplete. Not all emotions are cognitively useful in this way. Hatred is the experience of pleasure at another person's misfortunes, whether those are deserved or not (in which case pity would be more appropriate). Envy is the feeling that another is unworthy of his or her fortune, regardless of whether it is truly deserved. Hatred and envy do not necessarily have any cognitive content. Moreover, whereas the empiricist in Wolff allows that some emotions have cognitive value, the rationalist tends to devalue the emotions. Sadness may perceive incompleteness, but in a confused way. It might achieve the clarity of locating its object or it might not. This is demonstrated by melancholics, whose sadness is indiscriminate. Even clear sadness is inferior to a distinct cognition of incompleteness, for whilst sadness might be clear about where its object is, it cannot fully conceptualise it.

Although emotions cannot furnish us with fully conceptualised cognitions, they play an important role in our mental economy. When they point clearly to an object they create a will. They tell us promptly and clearly why certain things matter to us. Without them we would have no motivation. Dysfunctional emotions prevent us from acting purposefully. It is important to keep the psyche in good order. We do not risk weakening our emotions if we investigate their workings. Conducted properly, introspection, such as the philosopher performs, can be useful. Most of the time we have no need to do it. In difficult situations, however, such as debates about competence or when the proper order of our emotions is disrupted, the deeper knowledge to which a philosopher aspires is needed.

Rational psychology

Empirical psychology is concerned with everyday experience (*WGW* I. ii.106). Rational psychology is a *philosophy* of mind. Just as philosophy is the science of what is possible, so rational psychology is the science of what is possible in respect of mind (*WGW* II.i.13). Its principles are derived from three disciplines: ontology, cosmology, and empirical psychology (*WGW* II.vi.2–4). Ontology provides the concepts of being *in abstracto* and cosmology those of being in actuality, by means of which rational psychology investigates what the soul consists of. What cosmology is to ontology, empirical psychology is to rational psychology: it furnishes the empirical particulars from which rational psychology develops its theories and against which they are tested. In practice, Wolff does not maintain the clear distinction between the empirical and the rational: much of his empirical psychology is not empirical at all, and the discussions of the cognitive faculties in the rational psychology largely repeat what was said in the empirical psychology. The distinction seems to be that empirical psychology treats the mind's operations, and rational its essential being: what substance it consists of and on what grounds it can be said to be immortal. This was what Kant saw as being the (problematic) heart of Wolffian rational psychology in the 'Paralogisms' section of the *Critique of Pure Reason.*

Rational psychology is designed to prove that the soul is immortal. The argument is of little philosophical interest, but of some historical importance. As Leibniz stated in the *Monadology*, the soul is a simple substance (*LPW*, p. 179). Simple substances, having no parts, cannot have anything taken away from them. Thus the soul's immortality is proved by an analysis of the concept of simplicity. The simplicity or unity of the soul becomes a central tenet of Wolffian psychology. This seems to contradict the division of mind into faculties. In order to reconcile these two principles, Wolff limits them both. The soul's simplicity is not material integrity, but a single source of power. The expressions of soul radiate from one focal point, as it were (*WGW* 11.vi.37–40). (Kant's 'transcendental unity of apperception' is a descendant of Wolff's argument.) In empirical terms, the soul's power underlies the activity of cognition. This limitation is intended to separate the competence of the soul's unitary power from that of its faculties. The faculties represent the formal conditions of cognition; they explain why certain types of cognitive acts are possible. The soul's power, on the other hand, explains why they actually occur. The soul's power is the efficient cause of cognition, the faculties its formal conditions.[22]

Wolff defines the soul's force as its power to create representations (*WGW* 11.vi.45). This follows Leibniz's definition of the monad as a mirror of the Universe. Wolff parts company with Leibniz, however, on the question of the soul's relation to the world. Leibniz insisted that monads were windowless; Wolff believes that the soul interacts with the world. Leibniz's monads have had windows put in.[23] The final part of Wolff's psychology deals with the problem of how we can conceive of the world acting on the soul. The idea of the soul's 'representative force' hardly clarifies things beyond suggesting that the process of representing is spontaneous. Ultimately Wolff equivocates, arguing that we can only affirm the undeniable fact that the mind and body cooperate harmoniously. We are left believing both that the physical world acts on our minds by creating material impressions and that our mind works from a central internal point to create representations of the world. In effect, two systems exist in parallel: a physical body that acts mechanically, and a mind that duplicates the physical body, but is the product of a spontaneous mental force. The world acts on us, and we on it, through the physical body, yet we apperceive our sensations on a model of the body that our mind has spontaneously created. This dualistic model recalls Descartes's division of substances into *res extensa* and *res cogitans* and the various unsuccessful attempts to reconcile the two. It survived late into the eighteenth century and re-appears, in moderated form, in the psychologies of Ernst Platner and Johann Gotlieb Fichte.

Baumgarten, Meier, Sulzer, Mendelssohn

Wolff's psychological legacy was taken up by his first followers. Georg Bernhard Bilfinger (1693–1750) devoted a substantial part of his *Dilucidationes philosophicae de Deo, anima humana, mundo, et generalibus rerum affectionibus* (*Philosophical Clarifications Concerning God, the Human Soul, the World, and the States of Things in General,* 1725) to a set of Wolffian 'psychological theses'.[24] Alexander Gottlieb Baumgarten (1714–62) divided his *Metaphysica* into four parts of which the third, and easily the longest, was psychology.[25] As Wolffianism became the leading philosophy in both Protestant and Catholic Germany, so psychology became part of the philosophical repertoire. It proved more enduring than Wolff's metaphysics. In the 1790s the young Kantian philosophers, who had rejected Wolff's metaphysics, were still lecturing on Wolffian psychology.

The legacy was, however, ambiguous. Rational psychology faced backwards towards the seventeenth century. Other aspects of Wolff's psychology found unexpected new applications during the eighteenth century. The theory of 'dark ideas' lay behind early conceptions of the unconscious. The theory of a unitary mental power became the natural ally in psychology of a fashionable vitalism in the life sciences. The doctrine of faculties was, as we have seen, susceptible of two different interpretations. The more obvious and literal view had a scholastic flavour that was uncongenial to eighteenth-century empiricists, who thought it merely framed definitions for things that did not exist. But there was also a naturalistic interpretation, according to which our cognitive behaviour fits into our developmental environment: the faculties perform tasks that are necessary for us to succeed as human beings. This harmonised with mid-century theories of environmental determinism, such as Montesquieu's 'climate theory' of politics and Linnaeus's geographical account of speciation. Wolff's emphasis on material ideas was in tune with the rehabilitation of the senses after 1750. His idea of a Newtonian science of psychometrics and his reluctance to commit himself to Leibniz's doctrine of pre-established harmony made him palatable to many empiricists. The

German tradition of philosophical aesthetics began with Wolff's pupil Baumgarten and was continued by the mid-century Wolffians Georg Friedrich Meier (1718–77) and Johann Georg Sulzer (1720–79). Finally, the philosophy of Kant is unthinkable without Wolff's legacy, not only because Kant saw it as his task to dismantle and rebuild Wolffian metaphysics, but also because Kant's procedure was itself in some ways Wolffian.

Wolff's legacy was more positive and complex than has traditionally been acknowledged. German philosophy in the eighteenth century was a series of innovations grounded in Wolff's system. The first of these filled a gap. Wolff saw dark ideas as a cognitive deficit, an absence of knowledge (*defectio perceptionum*). As they had no cognitive content, they were not analysable by reason. This implied that there was no cognitive value in the sensuous representations that constituted art, a subject that Wolff had not addressed. His pupil Baumgarten classified art as a new species of 'lower' cognition, to which he gave the name 'sensitive representations' (*repraesentationes sensitivae*).[26] He derived the term *sensitivus* from Wolff's ethics, where a 'sensitive appetite' is one that originates from a confused idea of the good. That is to say, sensitive representations can be true, though it is not clear why they are so. Baumgarten supports the truth-claims of art whilst still distinguishing between artistic and intellectual knowledge.

Sensitive representations are the foundation of cognition and are rationally analysable. On both points Baumgarten contradicts Wolff, but on both he is able to appeal to Leibniz. In the *Monadology* Leibniz argued that dark ideas should not be ignored (*LPW*, pp. 180–1). Because our minds reflect the Universe, there is much cognitive material of which we are not aware.[27] Whereas Wolff saw dark ideas as an absence, Baumgarten (following Leibniz) saw them as an untapped reservoir of cognitions. This first appeared in Baumgarten's *Metaphysica* in the notion of a 'ground of the soul' (*fundus animae*) of which we are not fully conscious.[28] Sensitive representations must also be rationally analysable. As Leibniz had argued, clear and distinct ideas are the highest of a series of classes of knowledge that reaches down to obscure ideas. The distinctions between these classes are based on the degree of accuracy and completeness with which they enumerate the characteristics of an object. In this sense, just as there is a science of analysing higher classes of ideas, so there should also be a science of the senses, which Baumgarten terms *gnoseologia inferior*.[29] The two features of sensitive representations that make them apt for art in particular are that they are vivid and 'rich' (*vielsagend*). A new science of sensitive representations, *aesthetica*, analyses these aspects of art.

In the 1750s the style of philosophical writing began to change. Although Wolff had pioneered the writing of philosophy in German, scholarly convention still preferred long Latin books with a complex architecture and scholastic style of argumentation. Georg Friedrich Meier, a pupil of Baumgarten, is a transitional figure. His *Anfangsgründe aller schönen Wissenschaften* (*Foundations of All Polite Sciences*, 1748) aims at Wolffian comprehensiveness.[30] Its second part is a psychological aesthetics, which follows Baumgarten in defending and expanding Wolff's system. Meier added treatises on the thinking matter debate, wit, the affects, animal psychology, and sleepwalking, all marginal phenomena for Wolff.[31] At the same time, Meier argued that psychology must remain within metaphysics and not form an empirical discipline on its own: a retreat from Wolff's progressive position.[32]

Meier's *Gedancken von Schertzen* (*Thoughts on Jokes*, 1744), with its enticingly empiricist title, appears to open up a new field for psychology, but the promise is disappointed, for its aim is a systematic theory of wit.[33] He proceeds in the traditional manner, distinguishing types of humour and positing mental faculties for each one. The faculties of acuity (*Scharfsinnigkeit*) and wit (*Witz*) are defined. Again, Meier signals a retreat, since he takes a negative view of intuition and consigns it, somewhat melodramatically, to 'the realm of darkness' (*das Reich der Finsternis*). Intuitions only have cognitive value when we attend to them: 'attention is . . . the hand with which the soul grasps a dark idea in its ground, lifts it up and thus brings it into the light of day'.[34] The aesthetic has no cognitive value of its own.

For Meier, as for Wolff, faculties are either cognitive (*Erkenntnisvermögen*) or appetitive (*Begehrungsvermögen*). Developing Wolff's claim that aspects of the psyche might be measurable, Meier suggests that the strength of sense perceptions could be measured, the goal being to discover what sorts of sensations have what effects on the psyche.[35] Ultimately it would be possible on this basis to establish the natural laws that rule the affects (*Gemüthsbewegungen*). In practice, however, Meier makes no more progress along this road than Wolff. His attempts at empirical psychology cleave tightly to Leibniz–Wolffian metaphysics. In his animal psychology he sticks closely to faculty psychology. Animals have all the faculties except reason. They have imagination, creativity (the buildings of spiders and bees), rudimentary language, and morality.[36] All in all, the animal psychology adds little to what Leibniz had said on the subject in the *Monadology*.

In his 1758 essay *Versuch einer Erklärung des Nachtwandelns* (*Attempt at an Explanation of Sleepwalking*), Meier argues that sleepwalking is a middle state between waking and sleeping. There is no clean break between the two, for, as Leibniz showed, 'nature never leaves a gap'.[37] As we fall asleep, our attention gradually diminishes, but our mind is never entirely inactive. The imagination continues to create images, although these are inventions (*Erdichtungen*), not representations (*Einbildungen*). Sleepwalking is a vivid form of dreaming. Our sensations reflect reality, but only in fragments. This explains why sleepwalkers are able to perform extraordinary feats, such as walking fearlessly along rooftops. Normally we would find this difficult because our sensations would make us aware of the drop on either side. The sleepwalker's sensations are confined to the peak along which he or she walks; as a result, neither fear nor uncertainty are experienced.

Meier is not interested in the subjective experience of sleepwalking, because in Wolffian psychology dreams are not an orderly picture of reality and cannot tell us anything meaningful. They can, however, shed light on the ways in which our psyche becomes disorderly. According to the doctrine of material ideas, the working of the imagination is a physiological process. A disorderly imagination can thus be a sign of a disorderly body. The physiologist Johann August Unzer (1747–1809) advocated a medical diagnostic function for dreams that looks back to Hippocrates.[38] Stimuli of many different kinds can cause dreams. Ernst Anton Nicolai argued that sexual dreams can be caused by the pressure of the bladder on the nerves leading to the gonads, which become excited and communicate the idea of sex to the mind.[39] Pierre Villaume gives a similar explanation for a recurrent dream in which he arrives at church to preach with no trousers on. He supposes that the bedclothes have fallen from the bed and the feeling of cold legs has given rise to the idea of going out without trousers. Villaume argues that dreams not only reveal the state of the body, but also that of the mind. In dreams the mind is caught with its guard down, and the psychologist can glimpse its hidden workings: 'if any condition of our soul is able to decipher the secret laws of its activity, then dreaming is it'.[40]

Around the middle of the century Wolffian psychology began to move further towards British empiricism. The most notable of the next generation of psychologists, Johann Georg Sulzer, began his career as a Wolffian and, in his basic philosophical commitments, remained one. However, his work clearly shows the influence of British empiricism. His first major publication, *Kurzer Begriff aller Wissenschaften und andern Theile der Gelehrsamkeit, worin jeder nach seinem Innhalt, Nuzen, und Vollkommenheit kürzlich beschrieben wird* (*Brief Definition of All Sciences and Other Parts of Learning, in which Each is Briefly Described According to its Content, Use, and Perfection*, 1745), had the twin Wolffian aims of systematicity and comprehensiveness, but later he abandoned this style in favour of the more modern medium of the popularising essay. His main interest was not metaphysics, but aesthetics.

In the *Brief Definition* Sulzer follows Wolff. Ontology is the science of extended objects, and 'pneumatology' (*Pneumatologie*) that of spirits. Human spirits are covered by psychology, which can be an empirical science: 'one proceeds as physics does with corporeal things, which one can understand by means of experience and experiment. One could therefore call this part of psychology experimental [psychology].'[41] This provides important knowledge about the soul, but requires great skill, for the phenomena 'are . . . so obscure and occur so suddenly that they can very easily escape our attention'.[42] Following Baumgarten's *fundus animae*, Sulzer argues that events in the 'ground of the soul' are sometimes detectable from the traces they leave elsewhere. We should pay attention to 'the dark areas of the soul (if one may so speak) . . . where it acts through very unclear and dark ideas'.[43] Sulzer pays more attention to 'dark' ideas than his predecessors, noting that 'dark ideas can have very considerable effects, and the soul can be occupied with a matter of great weight without having a truly clear knowledge of it'.[44] The 'dark' side of our mind can have quite different purposes from the conscious mind and can make us act in ways we would rather not:

These are the affairs hidden in the innermost recesses of the soul, which now and again suddenly make us act and speak, without any cause and in an indecent manner, and make us unthinkingly say things that we would undoubtedly wish to hide.[45]

As these ideas underlie all cognition, analysis of them might reveal where our conscious ideas come from and why we are able to perform complex cognitive actions intuitively. It would also be rewarding to have extraordinary psychic phenomena, such as premonitions, mental disturbances, and madness, recorded 'in special reports' – a project that Carl Philipp Moritz would begin in the 1780s.[46] Sulzer thus develops a conception of psychology that would be recognisable to psychologists of the nineteenth century. Yet he remained a Wolffian, and his empirical contributions are very much of their time. In an essay on representation and sensation Sulzer argues that the group of faculties that Wolff had bundled together as cognitive faculties in fact consists of two distinct groups, one rational and the other sensitive. The two are opposed to each other. The sensitive faculties convey a sense of self. They represent to us the condition of our own psyche and body. The rational faculties deal in abstract cognitions. When we attend to them, we become 'an abstract being that connects with nothing in the world'.[47] Any other operations that we carry out in the meantime – reflex actions and the ordinary functioning of our senses, for example – are performed without any awareness: 'when [a thinking person] does anything that is not related to reflection, he does it like a machine and unthinkingly'.[48] (We have seen a similar idea in Plotinus.) Equally, when we attend to our sensitive faculties, we cannot think. In this sense the two sides of our self are opposed to one another. This might seem a revolutionary idea that introduces a dynamic and dispersed concept of the self. By implication, it gives rationality and sensation equal power. However, seen in the context of the Rationalist tradition, it is simply an extension of Wolff's doctrine of material ideas, which has the senses competing with reason for our attention and, on occasion, winning.

Sulzer is wedded to Wolff's ontology of the soul, as his 1771 essay on the subject shows. Underlying all mental activity is a single power. Activity makes us constantly hungry for new representations. This has similarities to Locke's view that our minds are driven by 'uneasiness', but Sulzer is in full agreement with Leibniz and Wolff that the basic activity of the mind is the production of representations. (Indeed, by explaining aesthetic experience in terms of uneasiness and not pleasure, as Baumgarten had, Sulzer might be said to have returned to a more Wolffian course.) Activity might appear to cease when we are asleep because our attention falls away. Dreams confirm its continuing activity and confute Descartes's claim that consciousness is coextensive with mind. The force that underlies mental activity is immaterial and therefore not subject to change or mortality. We are back with Leibniz's immaterial, universe-representing monads.[49]

Moses Mendelssohn (1729–86) can be considered the last of the Wolffian psychologists. He retained Wolff's faculty theory and in his 1767 adaptation of Plato's *Phaedo* defended the traditional arguments for the unity and immateriality of the soul. Mendelssohn's was the version of rational psychology that Kant demolished in the *Critique of Pure Reason*, after which rational psychology effectively disappeared. His empirical psychology was also Wolffian, with nods to Shaftesbury and Locke.[50] In the sixth of his *Briefe über die Empfindungen* (*Letters on Sensibility*, 1755), loosely based on Shaftesbury's *Moralists*, he eulogises Leibniz, Wolff, and Locke together.[51] The aesthetics of tragedy that he developed with Lessing, though their premises were Wolffian, were influenced by Du Bos's

Réflections critiques sur la peinture et la poésie (*Critical Reflections on Painting and Poetry*, 1719).

The *Letters on Sensibility* are a response to Sulzer's aesthetics. Mendelssohn takes the Wolffian view that the affects exist to draw our attention to what is or should be of interest to us. Sulzer argued that our pleasure and displeasure in aesthetic experience is an expression of the mind's ease and unease respectively. Ease is a function of freedom, unease of constraint. Nature gives the mind ease, presenting it with a manifold object with which it can freely engage. Art gives a greater ease by presenting a manifold encompassed in a unity. Mendelssohn takes issue with this view because it appears to leave beauty and perfection – the latter crucial to the Wolffian system – out of the equation. Mendelssohn incorporates Sulzer's position into a Wolffian account of beauty. Retaining the idea of unity in multiplicity from Sulzer, he frames this in Baumgarten's theory of perfection.[52] The emotions aroused in us by aesthetic experience alert us to the perfection of the objects represented. The problem with this theory is that much aesthetic pleasure has nothing to do with perfection, in the Wolffian or indeed any other sense. In his *Réflections critiques*, Du Bos had listed aesthetic experiences that seemed to involve pleasure in imperfection. Tragic drama, supposedly the noblest form of literature, provided egregious examples. This exposed art to Plato's charge that it was morally neutral, which was particularly damaging for Wolffian writers on aesthetics. The problem was addressed in an essay by Friedrich Nicolai that initiated a debate on tragic drama between Mendelssohn and Lessing. As Lessing pointed out, an account such as Sulzer's – or for that matter Aristotle's – at least had the merit of locating aesthetic pleasure in the subject, so deflecting the charge that imperfection might be beautiful in itself. There is a sense in which all passions are pleasurable.[53] Prompted by this idea, Mendelssohn wrote his *Rhapsodie; oder, Zusätze zu den Briefen über die Empfindungen* (*Rhapsody; or Addenda to the Letters on Sensibility*), which distinguishes between the the representation of a perfect object, and the subjective perfection of a representation. In the latter case, when we grasp an artistic object in its multiplicity and unity, the representation will be perfect without the object itself necessarily being so. The perfection resides in our subjective attitude. We might experience feelings of fear and pity at the deaths of innocent victims in tragic drama: our representation of this imperfect object is perfect because it contains the appropriate affects. Mendelssohn's argument depends on a distinction between being struck by an impression of an object and experiencing the affect that accompanies it, an analogue in aesthetics to Wolff's principle of the duality of perceptions.[54]

LESSING

There can be no doubt that Lessing, who read widely and enjoyed close contact with some of the major figures of German Enlightenment philosophy (notably Mendelssohn and Sulzer), was aware of these ideas. At school his favourite teacher was a Wolffian.[55] He retained an abiding interest in Leibniz, to whose original texts the new editions by Raspe (1765) and Dutens (1768) gave access, the former including the previously unpublished *New Essays*, in which Leibniz spelt out his doctrine of *petites perceptions*.[56] Henry Allison has found evidence of Lessing's use of this idea in his theological writings of the 1770s, in the notion of an intrinsically rational content (theology) being at first enclosed within obscure instinctual forms.[57] The essay fragment 'Daß mehr als fünf Sinne für den Menschen sein können'('It is possible that humans have more than five senses') develops Leibniz's doctrine further. It is also clear that Lessing knew about the development of psychological theory after Leibniz. The debate on the tragic emotions, to which we have just referred, provides clear evidence of his engagement with Wolffian psychology. The central question is what emotional responses are proper for an audience of tragedy and, specifically, what is the relation between, and the relative importance of, fear, admiration, and pity. Lessing thinks pity a more appropriate response than either fear or admiration. Writing to Nicolai in November 1756, Lessing argues that fear only prepares the way for pity, and admiration only sustains it. Pity for the tragic hero will be grounded more firmly if it is accompanied by admiration, whereas admiration without pity is morally empty. Admiration and fear cannot be ends in themselves: pity is the only emotion worthy of a dramatist's attention.[58] Indeed, Lessing takes the rather odd view that fear and admiration are not independent emotions at all.[59] This owes something to Wolffian psychology. Lessing describes pity as being susceptible to improvement, as if it had cognitive content, whereas fear and admiration are merely means to initiate and bring an end to pity.[60]

The influence of Wolff's psychology is more clearly visible in the *Hamburg Dramaturgy*, where Lessing employs Wolffian concepts at key points in the argument. For instance, in number 70 he criticises the notion of a crudely mimetic art on the grounds that even our everyday experience of the world involves an active element. Thus a crudely mimetic theatre would ignore an important part of our nature:

> The main thought is this: it is both true and not true that comic tragedy . . . imitates nature faithfully; it imitates one half of nature and neglects the other half entirely; it imitates the nature of phenomena without paying the slightest attention to the nature of our sensibility and mental powers.
>
> In nature everything is connected to everything else . . . But with its infinite multiplicity nature is a spectacle only for an infinite mind. In order that finite minds might have some share in the enjoyment of this spectacle, they must acquire the faculty [*Vermögen*] of setting limits to multiplicity, which it does not possess; the faculty of isolating and of directing its attention [*Aufmerksamkeit*] at will.
>
> We exercise this faculty at every moment of our existence; without it there would be no existence for us; for all these diverse sensations [*Empfindungen*], we would sense nothing at all; we would constantly be prey to the present impression; we would dream without knowing what we were dreaming. (*LW* IV.557)[61]

At such an important stage of the argument, immediately preceding his formulation of the broader purpose of tragedy, the references to Wolffian concepts such as attention are unlikely to be merely the residue of Lessing's debates with Mendelssohn. Rather they suggest a habit of thought that is likely to find expression elsewhere in Lessing's work.

We would not expect the characters of Lessing's dramas to speak in technical philosophical terminology. However, there is some evidence for Lessing's creative exploitation of Wolffian psychology. We can start with an obvious case. In Act I, Scene vii of *Miss Sara Sampson*, Sara recounts to Mellefont a nightmare that she had the previous night:

> Exhausted by crying and lamenting – my only occupations – I sank back onto the bed with half-closed eyelids. Nature wanted a moment's recuperation to collect fresh tears. But I was still not quite asleep when all at once I saw myself on the steepest part of a cliff. You walked ahead of me, and I followed you with faltering, anxious steps, which were now and again fortified by a glance that you cast back at me. Suddenly I heard a friendly call from behind me, commanding me to stand still. It was the voice of my father – miserable me! Can I never forget him? Ah! If his memory perform an equally cruel service, if he cannot forget me either! – Yet he has forgotten me. Solace! Cruel solace for his Sara! – But hear me, Mellefont; as I was turning towards this familiar voice, my foot slid, I wobbled, and was about to fall into the abyss, when, just in time, I felt myself held back by a person who was similar to me. I was about to pay her the most passionate thanks, when she drew a dagger from her bosom. I saved you, she cried, in order to destroy you! She reached out with her armed hand – and ah! I awoke at the stab. (*LW* II.19)[62]

The dream heightens the confrontation between Sara and Mellefont, because it presents Sara with a clear image of her moral dilemma. In one sense the figure who rescues her only to stab her might be thought to represent her own conscience alerting her to danger: that is how she interprets it (*LW* 11.18). In another sense the dream prefigures the later action, in which Marwood – a figure who is similar (*ähnlich*) to Sara insofar as she has been led on by Mellefont, and who prefigures Sara's possible fate as an unmarried mother and social outcast – tries to separate Sara and Mellefont and finally kills Sara. The dramatic purpose of the dream could then be understood in a Leibnizian sense. The present is heavy with the future, and the future is accessible to us in dreams.

The details of the dream also show the influence of Wolffian theories. Wolff repeatedly says that in empirical psychology everything is a matter of degree. Mental states are not absolutes; they are positions on a graduated scale. Sara introduces the dream by describing herself as still partially conscious when the dream begins. This was the view of Wolffian psychologists such as Meier, who in his 1758 *Attempt at an Explanation of Sleepwalking* argued that sleepwalking was an intermediate state between waking and sleeping (see p. 30). This idea is reinforced by Sara's description of herself lying down with half-closed eyelids, which also suggests an intermediate state. The dream happens when Wolffian psychology predicts it should: when waking sensations are dimmed, but the mind is still active though only partly conscious. Another Wolffian touch is Sara's description of her dream sensations. Meier argues that our dream sensations reflect reality, but only in fragments. Sara describes a series of partial sensations of a scene, in which the senses give isolated and separate sensations but not a full experience of reality: she sees Mellefont in front of her, she feels unsteady on her feet, she hears a voice she imagines to be her father's, she feels herself held back by the 'similar' person, and feels the stab of the dagger. This corresponds to the Wolffian view that dreams present a fragmented reality, as our attention, which would normally integrate experience, has fallen away.

Sensibility

In 1756, inspired by his debates on tragedy with Mendelssohn, Lessing undertook to translate Hutcheson's *System of Moral Philosophy* into German. He was already familiar with Shaftesbury. Some of the psychology of *Miss Sara Sampson*, written the previous year, must also be attributable to the influence, probably mediated through the fashionable drama of Sensibility, of the British tradition of moral sense psychology. The central issue of the play is the moral value of our intuitions. Sara's dream reflects her character and situation. She is a young woman of sensibility who has forsaken the protection of her family and finds herself in a strange environment. This is reflected in the descriptive elements of the dream: her situation is precarious and frightening. Mellefont, whom Sara expected to protect her, is evidently unable to do so. He simply walks in front of her, leading her, it is implied, into danger, and she follows uncertainly and anxiously. It is clearly the dream of an anxious, guilty person. But above all it is the dream of a young woman. In 'bourgeois tragedies' of this kind the action centres on the problematic transition of the young woman towards marriage. The woman emerges from the protection of her family and is momentarily exposed to the attentions of predatory males. In each case, for similar reasons, the woman is unable to fend for herself. This is due to a conception of women as being constitutionally weak at certain points. Women are susceptible to dreams and intuitions. The extreme sensibility of Lessing's women is portrayed as being grounded in their nature. Ernst Platner explains this physiologically: women possess 'a soft and unresponsive brain, though sometimes sensitive to physical pain'.[63] The softness of the brain tissue is symbolic as well as real; it symbolises women's sensitivity and their openness to dreams and intuitions. Sara's dream takes place in the intermediate state between waking and sleeping when, in psychological terms, the mind is not occupied with clear representations and is susceptible to dark ideas.

However, the main ground for distinction between psychological types is social, not sexual. Sara and Mellefont disagree about the interpretation of the dream. She understands it as a reminder of her moral failings. The 'accusing voices' of her conscience have been reinforced by her 'shattered imagination', and the resulting 'torments', though products of the imagination, are not merely imaginary (*LW* 11.18–19). Mellefont dismisses the dream as 'the terrifying fabric of a meaningless dream' (*das schreckliche Gewebe eines sinnlosen Traums*), by which he implies a view of dreams as associative chains of ideas linked randomly and meaninglessly. Again, in Act iv, Scene i, Sara speaks of her intuitive resistance to beguiling thoughts of future happiness: 'What a flattering idea! I'm falling in love with it myself and can almost forget that within me still something stirs that will give it no credence. – What is it, this rebellious something?'(*LW* 11.64).[64] Mellefont dismisses the presentiment as mere anxiety. Marwood takes a similarly sceptical view in her attack on Mellefont's love for Sara in the form of a satirical medical diagnosis. Like Mellefont, she thinks the emotions are mechanical (Act II, Scene iii). Thus, in matters of psychology a distinction emerges between *empfindsam* characters (Sara, Sir William, Waitwell, Norton) and rationalistic characters (Marwood and Mellefont, although Mellefont has sentimental traits too). This is explained by an argument between Mellefont and Norton in Act IV, Scene iii: Norton pointedly remarks that he expected to find Mellefont 'in sheer ecstasy' about the prospect of marriage. In Mellefont's reply upper-class reserve sneers at plebeian enthusiasm:

MELLEFONT: Only the rabble get excited when luck smiles at them once.
NORTON: Perhaps because the rabble still has its feeling, which in the nobility
    has been spoilt and weakened by a thousand unnatural ideas. But I see
    something other than moderation in your expression. Coldness, indecision,
    aversion– (*LW* II.67)[65]

Norton thinks that Mellefont's life among the upper classes has rendered him unfeeling. In Act IV, Scene ii, Mellefont seems to support Norton's point when, after persuading Sara to ignore her intuitions, he reflects on the prospect of marriage. During his dissolute period he rejected the institution of matrimony, whereas now, prompted among other things by Norton's criticisms, he sees that his earlier view was a habituated delusion, 'accursed fantasies that have become so natural to me in my life of indulgence' ('vermaledeite Einbildungen, die mir durch ein zügelloses Leben so natürlich geworden', *LW* II.65). Mellefont's libertinage, with its condescending and mechanistic view of intuitions, reveals itself to be a form of false consciousness, a self-reinforcing self-deception. Mellefont and Marwood earn the wages of sin because their duplicity rebounds on them. Both deceive others and then themselves with a rationality that is unmasked as a self-interested denial of moral feeling. By contrast, Sara's 'martyrdom' vindicates the truth-value of intuitions and sensibility.

Psychology and dramatic language

Similar features can be found in *Nathan the Wise* and *Minna von Barnhelm*. Recha is portrayed as exceptionally *empfindsam* and prone to dreams and intuitions. Daja describes Recha's condition following the fire in a way that resembles Wolffian psychology. The mental effects of the fire conform to the theory of material ideas: 'Terror still trembles through her every nerve' ('Noch zittert ihr der Schreck durch jede Nerve', line 65). (The theory that neural activity consisted in the resonance of the elastic nervous fibres had been popularised by Hartley in his *Observations on Man* of 1749.)[66] Because Recha's nerves continue to vibrate, fits of imagination interrupt her normal patterns of thought. Whenever these occur and whatever thoughts are in her imagination, the idea of fire appears: 'Her fancy's coloured by fire / In every brushstroke' ('Noch malet Feuer ihre Phantasie / Zu allem, was sie malt', lines 66–7). In a state of shock, Recha now hovers between waking and sleeping:

> Sleeping it wakes,
> And waking her spirit sleeps, one moment
> Barely animal, the next more than an angel.[67] (67–9)

We have seen that Meier and the other Wolffians conceived of dreaming as an intermediate state between waking and sleeping. Recha's waking condition is somnolent and unresponsive, so that she seems 'barely animal', having no sensations or instincts. The other state is an active, somnambulistic state in which Recha seems to have prophetic powers and appears 'more than an angel'. In support, Daja reports an incident that had occurred the same morning:

> This morning she lay
> Late with eyes shut fast and was as dead.
> Suddenly she rose and cried: 'Hear! Hear!
> The camels of my father, they are coming!
> Hear! His own gentle voice!' And then
> Her eyes opened once more, and her head,
> Deprived now of her arm's support, slumped back
> Onto the pillow.[68] (70–7)

Recha's dream might merely be an extreme case of *empfindsam* intuition such as Minna exhibits in predicting a positive outcome to her search for Tellheim in *Minna von Barnhelm* (Act ii, Scene i; *LW* 1.624–5). The sensitive young woman, optimistic by nature, has an instinctive faith in the providential order of the world. But here, as in *Miss Sara Sampson* the providentialist message is given a degree of realism by the inclusion of unnecessary psychological details. Recha's perception derives from a specific, isolated sense, in this case the imagined sound of Nathan's arrival. She is in a state of heightened imaginative activity – Daja speaks of her 'over-excited brain' (*überspanntes Hirn*, line 215) – brought on by nervous trauma. She seems to hover between waking and sleeping. Dark ideas occur arbitrarily to her imagination, freed as it is from the control of the integrative attention. What matters here is the relative force of the impressions, as Wolff had argued. Because Recha's visions are not drowned out by waking stimuli – when awake Recha is unresponsive and 'barely animal' – they are especially vivid.

Recha's ideas of the Templar are the product of the faculty of creative imagination. Her memory of the fire has been reinforced and embellished in her imagination by association with other ideas. She links the Templar with the idea of a personal guardian angel, in which she has been encouraged by Daja, who is keen for Recha to express her (as Daja imagines) true Christian identity. Scene ii of Act I is largely taken up with Nathan's attempt to disabuse Recha of this association and replace what he sees as Christian enthusiasm (*Schwärmerei*) with common-sense humanism. However, this proves problematic, both practically and ethically. For one thing, Nathan himself appears to have encouraged Recha's belief in a guardian angel, when it suited his purposes to do so (206–9). Also, in order to rid Recha of her enthusiasm Nathan must exploit her suggestibility and fearfulness, by suggesting that the Templar might be dying. Predictably, Recha merely replaces one 'delusion' with another (364–7). Associating the Templar's distressing disappearance with Nathan's absence on business, Recha imagines that, like Nathan, the Templar may simply have gone away on his travels – a delusion that is clearly more upsetting to her than the delusion that he was her guardian angel, but that in Nathan's eyes is less harmful. But in trying to dispel Recha's intuition, Nathan is repeating the error of Mellefont, who dismissed Sara's dream as 'the terrifying fabric of a meaningless dream'. And his motivation, though less dangerous than Mellefont's, is arguably not pure. Nathan is motivated by possessiveness, as well as by a love of truth and a desire to protect Recha. To him Recha is emphatically 'my Recha', 'my child', and he is terrified of losing her. He reasserts his influence on her, in place of the baleful influence of Daja, in order to continue to possess her. It is only in Act IV, Scene vii that Nathan realises the extent of his possessiveness and that, if he is to remain Recha's 'father', it will not be by his concealing the truth from her but because she *wants* him as a father.[69]

A similar challenge faces Minna, like Nathan an agent of Enlightenment confronted by obstinacy and prejudice. Minna exploits Tellheim's obsession with honour to show him how irrational he is being, but her trick of posing as an outcast backfires. The unforeseen consequence of her vengefulness is that Tellheim discovers that Minna has acquired the ring from the Wirt and, wrongly but understandably, assumes she had intended to break off their betrothal. Here Minna's prospects of winning Tellheim back reach their lowest ebb, and the situation is rescued only by the chance arrival of the Graf von Bruchsall, to which Tellheim responds by leaping to Minna's aid, thus allowing her to show him the true identity of the rings. Although he is now enlightened about her intentions, he has not been cured of his obsession with honour. Indeed, it is precisely this that causes him to leap to her defence. Like all of the other characters in the play, with the possible exceptions of Werner and the garrulous Franziska, Tellheim is psychologically flawed and remains so.

If Tellheim is not reformed, then it is not because Lessing is not interested in character development, for in *Nathan the Wise* the Templar clearly evolves towards maturity, and the change comes from within. At the end of the play he is no longer the contrary character of Act II, Scene v, who is mollified only when Nathan tricks him into adopting a position that appears contrary to Nathan's but in reality is not. In Act II the Templar discovers Nathan's true humanity. But this is only one half of the journey to enlightenment. The Templar needs to discover his true self before the action can be resolved. In Act II he is still impulsive. As with Recha, Nathan uses that impulsiveness to his own ends, but the impulsiveness rebounds on Nathan when the Templar goes to the Patriarch. The Templar's maturity is first signalled by his ability to enlighten himself in Act v, Scene iii, and it is expressed in a soliloquy that is one of Lessing's most psychologically imaginative pieces of writing. The Templar is worried that Nathan is angry with him and, as he waits anxiously for Nathan to appear, he interrogates himself:

> Hm! – but then
> I'm also somewhat
> Aggravated. – What put me in this mood
> Against this man? – Even when he did say yes,
> He didn't turn me down! And Saladin
> Has taken it upon himself to work
> On him. So then, am I more truly,
> Deeply Christian than he's Jewish?
> Who really knows himself? How could I grudge
> The petty theft he took occasion
> To rob the Christians of? But what a theft!
> No petty theft this creature! – Creature?
> Then whose? Surely not the slave's who beached
> The block on life's bare shore and disappeared?
> The artist's then, who saw the godly shape
> Veined in the cast-off block and sculpted it.
> Recha's father is and always will be
> Not the Christian who sired her, but a Jew.

Hm! – ich bin doch aber auch
Sehr ärgerlich. – Was hat mich denn nun so
Erbittert gegen ihn? – Er sagte ja,
Noch schlüg er mir nichts ab. Und Saladin
Hat's über sich genommen, ihn zu stimmen.–
Wie? sollte wirklich wohl in mir der Christ
Noch tiefer nisten als in ihm der Jude? –
Wer kennt sich recht? Wie könnt ich ihm denn sonst
Den kleinen Raub nicht gönnen wollen, den
Er sich's zu solcher Angelegenheit
Gemacht den Christen abzujagen? – Freilich,
Kein kleiner Raub, ein solch Geschöpf! – Geschöpf?
Und wessen? — Doch des Sklaven nicht, der auf
Des Lebens öden Strand den Block geflößt
Und sich davongemacht? Des Künstlers doch
Wohl mehr, der in dem hingeworfnen Blocke
Die göttliche Gestalt sich dachte, die
Er dargestellt? – Ach! Rechas wahrer Vater
Bleibt, trotz dem Christen, der sie zeugte – bleibt
In Ewigkeit der Jude. (3232–51)

The self-interrogation develops into a kind of verbal association, suggested by the unforeseen connotations of *Raub* and *Geschöpf*, in which the Templar produces words guided not by reason but by the imagination's laws of association. As Wolff argued, the imagination is beyond rational control, but as the later Wolffians were beginning to see, the imagination could lead to truth.

'Emilia Galotti'

If Lessing's earlier dramas seem to represent a static struggle between the claims of feeling and reason, in *Nathan the Wise* and, above all, *Emilia Galotti*, we witness a psychological process at work. The process, as described by Leibniz, Wolff and others, is that whereby the obscurity of dark perceptions emerges, sometimes haphazardly, into the light of rational cognition. Monika Fick has argued that the plot of *Emilia Galotti* represents the tragic causality of confused perceptions.[70] For instance, the mind of the Prince, like that of the Templar, works associatively, but its arbitrariness feeds an authoritarian will. From the moment when the name of Emilia Bruneschi brings to his mind Emilia Galotti, his will is directed along the path of desire. He complains of having risen too early, which has made him irritable and easily distracted, so that the association created by the name Emilia has a profound effect (*LW* 11.129). His unease is immediately evident. When a chamberlain informs him that Gräfin Orsina is in the city, he accidentally shows his displeasure ('So much the worse – better, I mean') – a good example of the kind of social malapropism that Sulzer described.[71] Conti's arrival promises to take the Prince's mind off Emilia, but when Conti exits briefly, the Prince's mind returns to Emilia via thoughts of Orsina's portrait:

Her picture! – So be it! – Her picture in any case is not herself. – And maybe I shall find in the picture again what I no longer see in the person. – Though, I do not want to find it again. – This bothersome painter! I should not be surprised if she bribed him. – And what if she did! If another picture, painted in other colors on another background, – will let her take her place once more in my heart: why, I really think I would not mind. When I loved her I was always so lighthearted, so gay, so free from care. – Now I am the opposite of all that. But no; no, no! More at ease or less at ease; I am better this way.[72]

Ihr Bild! – mag! – Ihr Bild ist sie doch nicht selber. – Und vielleicht find' ich in dem Bilde wieder, was ich in der Person nicht mehr erblicke. – Ich will es aber nicht wiederfinden. – Der beschwerliche Maler! Ich glaube gar, sie hat ihn bestochen. – Wär' es auch! Wenn ihr ein anderes Bild, das mit andern Farben, auf einen andern Grund gemalet ist, — in meinem Herzen wieder Platz machen will: – Wahrlich, ich glaube, ich wär' es zufrieden. Als ich dort liebte, war ich immer so leicht, so fröhlich, so ausgelassen. – Nun bin ich von allem das Gegenteil. – Doch nein; nein, nein! Behäglicher, oder nicht behäglicher, ich bin so besser. (*LW* 11.131)[72]

The passage furnishes a good example of Lessing's use of Wolffian psychology to represent his characters' thought processes. The Prince attempts to reconcile himself to Orsina's presence and imagines that he might love her again. In doing so, he inadvertently returns to thoughts of Emilia. The thought of Orsina's *Bild* suggests the proverbial phrase *jemands Bild im Herzen tragen*, which he applies to Emilia. As in the Templar's soliloquy, a play on words represents the speaker's associative imagination.[73]

Similarly, the Prince seems to dominate the thoughts of Appiani, Odoardo, Claudia, and Emilia. Emilia is troubled by the feelings (*Empfindungen*) aroused in her by the Prince at the Grimaldis' *vegghia* and is disturbed by 'something' (*etwas*) that sits behind her in the church, even before she is aware that it is the Prince (*LW* 11.150). Odoardo is convinced that the Prince hates him, whereas actually the Prince speaks favourably of him. Odoardo wants to justify his anti-courtly stance, and in doing so seems to have developed an obsession with the Prince: witness the bizarre curse he utters in Act v, Scene ii (*LW* 11.193). Claudia's attitude to the Prince is problematic in a different way. She admires him so much that she denies he poses any threat to her daughter (*LW* 11.153). Like Odoardo, she is justifying a position, in her case in favour of the court. Her attitude, just like Odoardo's, leaves her unable to control the Prince's influence over the family. The Galotti parents both suppose that they have the measure of the Prince when in reality they do not.

Appiani has the same associative habits as the Prince. When he meets Emilia on the morning of their wedding, both are disturbed: Emilia by her encounter in the church; Appiani, unknowingly, by the Prince's power. Emilia recounts a dream in which the stones in her jewellery turn to pearls, which conventionally stand for tears. Like Sara's dream in *Miss Sara Sampson*, it prefigures the future in Leibnizian fashion. Claudia, like Mellefont under the influence of an upper-class ethos, trivialises the dream. Dreams are insignificant echoes of our everyday thoughts, she argues, and this one reflects Emilia's love of pearls. Whereas Emilia obediently makes a show of being satisfied with this, Appiani dwells on the dream with a strange brooding intensity. He admits that he ought not to be so melancholy on a day that is 'pregnant with so much happiness' ('schwanger mit so viel Glücklichkeit', *LW* 11.154), alluding to Leibniz's argument in the *New Essays* that the past is pregnant with the future.[74] He excuses himself on the grounds that his mind is fixed on negative thoughts: 'But once the imagination is keyed to unhappy visions –' ('Aber wenn die Einbildungskraft einmal zu traurigen Bildern gestimmt ist –', *LW* 11.155). Claudia presses him as to the cause of his mood. His explanation both invokes and, in its halting steps towards the truth, exemplifies the principle of association, by which the imagination links one idea to another arbitrarily:

APPIANI: Yes, it is true that I am unusually sad and gloomy today. But consider, madam: – being one last step away from the goal or not having started out yet, is actually the same thing. Since yesterday and the day before yesterday, all that I see, all that I hear, all that I dream has argued this truth. This *one* thought attaches itself to every other thought that I am made to have and that I want to have. – What is that? I do not understand it. – . . . One thing leads thus to another! – I am angry – angry at my friends and angry at myself – . . . My friends insist as a matter of course that I inform the prince of my marriage, before it takes place. They admit that I do not owe it to him, but respect towards him forbids every other course. And I was weak enough to give them this promise. I was just planning to drive to the palace.[75]

Appiani's anxiety expresses itself in melancholy. Had Appiani been strong and contradicted his friends, the gloom would not have taken hold. Ironically, it is lifted by the appearance of Marinelli, who provokes Appiani and gives him a second chance to assert his will. As he observes once Marinelli has left: 'That did me good! It made my blood surge. I feel different and better.'[76] However, the reactive, passive–aggressive 'surge' that Appiani enjoys in his confrontation with Marinelli is hardly the 'surge of joy' (*freudigere Aufwallung*) that Emilia had asked for on seeing him so downcast in Scene 7. Indeed, Appiani's act of will is of the wrong kind (anger instead of joy), is too late (he should have asserted his will against his friends), and is, as it transpires, dangerously misplaced, for it provokes Marinelli in turn to arrange Appiani's murder. By a complex chain of psychological cause and effect, Appiani falls victim to a melancholic failure to assert his will.

The play's main psychological theme is the conflict of the will and the imagination. It is most acute in Emilia, and only she is able to see it clearly. In response to Claudia's assurance that not wanting to sin guarantees a clear conscience, Emilia insists that she feels complicit in the Prince's licentiousness.[77] It is not that she suffers from an overheated conscience, but that her experience has taught her the need to confront one's own feelings with a resolute act of will. Whenever the will is constrained and our sensitivity beguiled, moral defeat threatens. This sense of helplessness is amplified by her inability to escape from the Prince in church. Her position prevents her from moving and asserting her will. All that remains for her is to try, by sheer mental effort, to act as if the Prince were not affecting her (*LW* 11.151). But she is not equal to the struggle. Once the Prince's words have a hold on her imagination, her perception is confused, and the echo of the Prince's words follows her home (*LW* 11.151). Claudia explains the auditory illusion as a product of fear. (She clearly wants to prevent Odoardo finding any more reasons against their residing in Guastalla.) Emilia does not experience fear of the Prince. The true source of her anxiety is her knowledge of the Prince's power to speak to her feelings. As she insists to Odoardo in Act v, a young woman equipped with sensibility is easy prey:

What we call brute force is nothing: seduction is the only true force. – I have blood pulsing in my veins, my father, blood that is as youthful, as warm as anyone's. And my senses are senses too. I vouch for nothing. I will be responsible for nothing. I know the house of the Grimaldi. It is a house of pleasure. Only one hour there, under the eyes of my mother; – and there arose within me such diverse passions as weeks of the strict discipline of religion could scarcely calm.[78]

The awareness of the susceptibility of the will to assault by the sensible imagination is what so affects her in Act II, Scene vi. Claudia's insistence that Emilia not reveal to Appiani the complicity of her senses then prepares the way for her later reaction to her kidnapping. The feeling of powerlessness gives rise to uncharacteristic indignation, when Odoardo tells her that she is to be taken to the Grimaldi house by her captors, 'as if we had no will'.[79] This is a reproach not so much to the Prince and Marinelli, as to Odoardo and Claudia: to Odoardo for showing no force of will in the face of her capture and to Claudia for selfishly dominating her will earlier. In agreeing to be silent about events in the church, Emilia subordinated her will to her mother's like a dutiful daughter.[80] The play thus gives ample evidence both of the truth of intuitions and of the psychological necessity of asserting the will.

WIELAND'S 'SYMPATHIES' AND 'HISTORY OF AGATHON'

Wieland's work, like Lessing's, integrates elements of British psychology into a Wolffian framework. His *Sympathien* (*Sympathies*, 1755) was a product of the fashion for Sensibility. Wieland's interest in Sensibility was philosophical. Shaftesbury's *An Enquiry Concerning Virtue* (1699) was translated into German in 1747.[81] Wieland was particularly attracted by Shaftesbury's idea of Sympathy, the 'natural Affection' that is responsible for our sense of virtue and our common humanity. Shaftesbury is invoked in the *Sympathies*, alongside Plato, as a teacher of 'nature and virtue' (*Natur und Tugend*, WAA 1.ii.460). He is the model philosopher. Most moralists do more harm than good because they are too stern (WAA 1. ii.489). Philosophy should enable us to feel our natural affections, through which we recognise beauty and virtue. God has created a world that is beautiful and good: in learning to see this we will also learn to love our fellow men, instead of simply loving ourselves.

Wieland's conception of sympathy brings together feelings, interests, and virtues. We are naturally equipped with a set of drives and feelings. These are not to be confused with animal drives: like Shaftesbury, Wieland rebuts the Hobbesian notion that natural man is a beast (WAA 1.ii.448). A bundle of moral, aesthetic, and cognitive faculties – such as love of one's fellow man, a sense of beauty, and 'an ever active urge to imitate the virtues of God' – human drives are intrinsically moral.[82] In addition to Shaftesbury's, other influences are evident in the *Sympathies*, most notably Platonic asceticism, expressed for instance in the idea that the visible world is a shadow of an invisible divine world (WAA 1.ii.450).

Another Platonic idea is that our souls progress through a series of incarnations that form an upward movement towards spirituality. This recalls Socrates' discourse in the *Symposium* (WAA 1.ii.476).

The Shaftesburian and Platonic elements are welded to a Leibnizian psychology. Despite his scepticism about Leibniz's metaphysics, Wieland sees that through Leibniz, Sensibility can be harnessed to Providentialism (WAA 1.ii.480). The sympathy of souls constitutes a separate, non-physical world in parallel to, but different in character from, the phenomenal world. This is also true of the mind. Much of our mental activity is unconscious. Our *petites perceptions* are hidden, but reflect the Universe, and because the present is pregnant with the future, they allow us some (fore)sight of truth. We exist in two worlds: empirical reality and cosmic harmony. Harmony looms large in the *Sympathies* (WAA 1.ii.468). The soul is an entelechy (WAA 1.ii.476) that has within it its final purpose of moral perfection and communion with God in heaven (WAA 1.ii.478). Thus the Earth is the 'nursery of heaven' (*Pflanzschule des Himmels*, WAA 1.ii.468). Most of the time, though, the truth is not available to us.

If the Leibnizian theory of the soul coheres relatively well with Shaftesbury's idea of sympathy, Wolffianism is less at home. Wieland read Wolff when he was fifteen. He subsequently read and absorbed the other Wolffians. The clash of Wolffian and Shaftesburian elements is as much a matter of tone as of content: against the 'seraphic' tones that prevail in the *Sympathies* the common sense of Wolff's 'rational thoughts' jars. Feelings (*Empfindungen*) are not enough: we also need the Wolffian rationality of 'a couple of clear concepts' (*ein paar deutliche Begriffe*, WAA 1.ii.484). Reason is what separates man from animals (WAA 1.ii.460). Wieland had sent his didactic poem 'Die Natur der Dinge' ('On the nature of things') to Meier. In the section that deals with animal souls, Wieland eulogises Meier's work on animal psychology:

> O Meier, whom with joy the clever Germans read,
> From whose wise mouth there flows but pure Platonic mead,
> The edifying truth how clearly you have told
> That even the lowly cow has an immortal soul.

> O Meier, den mit Lust das kluge Deutschland liest,
> Von dessen weisen Mund platonscher Honig fließt,
> Wie deutlich hast du uns die Möglichkeit gelehret,
> Daß sich auch in dem Vieh der Seele Wert vermehret.[83]

Wieland's attempt to turn Meier's animal psychology into verse is embarrassing, assuming that it was not intended as parody. The

Sympathies combine Shaftesbury's idealism and Wolffian rationalism in a similarly fraught marriage.

Wieland's *History of Agathon* has traditionally been read as the first German *Bildungsroman*. The novel follows the young Agathon's development as he learns to find his way in the world. It ends (or, if indeed it is a *Bildungsroman*, should end) with him reconciled to reality and finding a niche in which he can flourish. Along the way he is tested and tempted to abandon his idealism. The novel is structured by a dualistic framework consisting of the opposed world-views of Agathon himself and the sophist Hippias. However, the *Bildungsroman* model implies that Agathon is more naïve than he really is. Agathon is already fully formed when we meet him. Although an outcast, he is fundamentally sure of himself, having enjoyed a successful political career in Athens that ended through no fault of his own. When Hippias buys him as a slave, he is confident enough to resist Hippias' (transparent) attempts to change him. Even before he is cast out on the series of adventures that the novel subjects him to, he is already a man of the world.

The *Bildungsroman* is necessarily psychological, and *Agathon* more so than most, as the opening of the novel emphatically tells us. Agathon ('the good') has been separated from his childhood sweetheart Psyche ('soul'). The good needs to be reunited with the soul; the essential harmony and goodness of humanity have to be demonstrated. The ultimate prospect is of a community of good souls in the manner of the *Sympathies* or Leibniz's City of God, even if this cannot be fully realised on earth.[84] The competing philosophies of Agathon and Hippias are largely psychological in nature. They offer explanations of how people can know the world and what motivates them. Hippias' philosophy is based on French materialism. Various sources have been identified, including Helvétius, La Mettrie, Malebranche, and Montesquieu.[85] All beliefs, he argues, including our moral values, are constructs. Our real interest and what motivates us, if we are honest, is pleasure, specifically the gratification of the senses. Agathon is a Shaftesburian-cum-Platonic idealist.[86] He claims that we have an innate sense of what is right that is no less truthful than our sense of pleasure. The first debate between them results in stalemate. Hippias fails to persuade Agathon to abandon his idealism. He therefore challenges Agathon to prove that idealism is tenable in the real world. Agathon must strive to realise his potential; Hippias will show him that he is really more interested in the gratification of the senses.

In the critical literature most attention has been paid to Hippias' psychological theory, it being assumed that Hippias is right about how humans ordinarily behave. According to this view, the novel is a study in empirical psychology and traces the influences on Agathon's development. The novel shows how a character is formed by his 'milieu'. In his *Versuch über den Roman* (*Essay on the Novel*, 1774) – in large part a description of *Agathon* – Friedrich von Blanckenburg argued that the novel should show us 'the development of its hero' against a realistically represented backdrop, so that the reader can see 'all the circumstances . . . whereby and in which [the hero] has become what he is'.[87] *Agathon's* narrator repeatedly reminds the reader of the novel's (pretended) realism. This is a 'history' (*Geschichte*), and not a fanciful romance (*Roman*). However, the narrator's protestations are to some extent counterproductive, and intentionally so. The milieu is patently unreal: a fancifully reconstructed classical Greece based on historical figures whose lives were obviously different from that of Agathon. The narrator ironises the very idea of a realist portrayal of the interaction of psyche and milieu:

The intention of the author was . . . that one might be able to grasp very clearly how a man like this – born like this – brought up like this – with such and such capacities and dispositions – with this particular combination of the aforementioned – after experiences, entanglements and alterations of such and such a kind – in such and such conditions of fortune – in this place and at this time – in this society – in such and such a climate – on such and such foodstuffs (for this also has a stronger influence on wisdom and virtue than many moralists imagine) – on this diet – in short, under such circumstances as those in which he has thus far set Agathon and will continue to do so – such a wise and virtuous man has been able to exist.[88]

The playfulness undermines the idea that *Agathon* is a straightforwardly realist novel and an exemplification of environmental determinism. Much of the 'reality' presented in the novel is unstable. The competition to decide whether Agathon or Hippias is right is asymmetrical, for Hippias is allowed to intervene to skew reality his way. Agathon is not just contending with reality; he is contending with a reality artificially distorted by Hippias to resemble his image of the world. The competition is also skewed in Agathon's favour by the fact that Hippias is a failure before it begins. He carries an ironic epithet ('the wise Hippias'), which of course begs the question. He has earned material comfort, but not respect. He is interested in Agathon because he has no successor, whether because no-one wants to be like him or he does not like anyone who wants what he wants. (The *Sympathies* make the point that being sceptical is simply putting yourself in a position above other human beings.) Indeed, his first aim is not to test Agathon, but to make Agathon like himself: he proposes the test only after he realises how hard this will be.

Agathon's psychology is equally problematic. At first he appears to have the narrator's support. Agathon and Psyche are reunited by chance on a pirate ship where Agathon is a captive and Psyche, disguised as a boy, the captain's slave. Their meeting is described in terms of the sympathy of their souls:

Agathon answered the glance of this young slave with an attentiveness in which pleasant amazement gradually gave way to ecstasy. And these very motions revealed themselves also in the delightful face of the young slave; their souls recognised one another in the very same instant and seemed, to judge by their looks, to flow into one another, before their arms could embrace and their ecstatically trembling lips cry out – Psyche – Agathon. They were silent for some while; what they felt was beyond expression, and what did they need words for? The use of language ceases when souls are in direct contact with one another, directly look at and touch one another, and in an instant feel more than the tongues of the muses themselves could express in whole years.[89]

The narrator is clearly behind the lovers, but the ironic exaggeration is plain to see.

If the novel is to describe Agathon's interaction with his milieu, then the narrator will have to take a view on how the interaction functions, and this is bound to side the narrator with Hippias' materialism or Agathon's idealism. The early scenes suggest a compromise. The narrator uses Wolff's dualist model, which is both materialist (the doctrine of material ideas) and idealist (the spontaneity of reason). This emerges in some subtle descriptions of psychological processes, especially the tension between Agathon's sensitivity and his enthusiasm. In a clear pointer to the theme of enthusiasm, Agathon is found by a group of frenzied maenads. They take him for their god Dionysus, but soon return to their senses:

But the most immoderate enthusiasm has its limits and eventually gives way to the dominance of the senses. Unfortunately for the hero of our story these senseless ones gradually recovered from their ecstasy, in which their imagination had presumably utterly exhausted itself, and began to notice more and more human traits in the man who had been transformed in their eyes by his unusual beauty into a god.[90]

Their enthusiasm is presented according to a Wolffian model. In enthusiasm the imagination detaches itself from the senses. This is why the narrator describes their recovery in terms of the mind coming once more under their dominion. Without the senses, the imagination will function for a time, but soon exhaust itself (*abgemattet*), because it has no more material. As the women return to their senses, their representations gradually become more distinct and they begin to notice more of Agathon's human characteristics. This conforms to Wolff's definition of distinct ideas as containing a full enumeration of their object's characteristics. Between dark ideas and clear and distinct ideas there is a sliding scale: the narrator describes the women grasping Agathon's humanness gradually (*immer mehr*).

A similar description occurs after Agathon is separated from Psyche. In a long interior monologue he begins to doubt his principles. His life comes to resemble a dream, in which reality is chaotically jumbled:

How dream-like this all is, where the enthusiastic imagination, without regard for sequence, likelihood, time, or place, leads the benumbed soul from one adventure to another, from the crown to a beggar's cloak, from delight to desperation, from Tartarus to Elysium? – And is life a dream then, a mere dream, as vain, as unreal, as insignificant as a dream? [91]

The imagination is enthusiastic in dreams because it is not guided by nature. It is without sequence: the representations it presents to the mind are connected randomly. It has no relation to likelihood because the common sense we acquire by perceiving nature is not available to it, and so it cannot determine what is likely and what is not. The most important components of our common-sense perceptions are time and space, which provide the structure for the contents of experience. While the soul is 'benumbed' by sleep, the imagination can do what it likes. Accordingly it presents Agathon with rapid and implausible changes of state. The dream, seen in this Wolffian way, is insignificant indeed. Soon Agathon regains control:

Here Agathon regrouped for a while; his spirit, which was enmeshed in doubts, strove to work itself free, until a fresh look at the majestic natural scene around him set off another train of ideas in his mind. [92]

This exemplifies the Wolffian view that the order in our mind is given to it by the order of the world around us. It is the naturalistic Wolff: our mind is adapted to cope with the world in which it lives; it works most effectively when it cleaves to nature. Now the 'train of ideas' compiled by his imagination is quite different from the dream. It is nature and makes sense.

Wolffian psychology has two aspects. Our ideas come from sense perceptions, but the activity of apperceiving ourselves as subjects of experience is spontaneous. The narrator of *Agathon* follows Wolffian psychology in some detail. As well as yielding the subtle descriptions of psychological processes that make the novel so successful, this also results in an equivocation between idealism and materialism, which is heightened by a persistent streak of irony. This is just as essential to the novel as the narrator's observation of psychological detail, for as well as being a novel of development, *Agathon* is also a partly serious, partly playful philosophical novel of unreconciled opposites. Agathon is the idealist who overshoots human reality, and Hippias the realist who undershoots human ideality. Quite where 'real reality' lies in between these two positions is, of course, not clear.

LORETTE WILMOT LIBRARY
NAZARETH COLLEGE

CHAPTER 3

Melancholy Titans and suffering women in Storm and Stress drama

THE CONTEXT OF STORM AND STRESS PSYCHOLOGY

A local phenomenon centred on Herder and Goethe in Strasbourg and Frankfurt, the Storm and Stress movement produced twenty or so plays that turned German literary aesthetics on its head and gave psychology a cultural prominence that it had not hitherto enjoyed. There was little new about the psychology of Storm and Stress drama. Some of its most striking characteristics – physicalism and the rehabilitation of the lower faculties, for instance – were already evident in, for example, Sulzer. The increased emphasis on the physical was prompted in part by the philosophical commitments of Herder and his friends and in part by the new aesthetics of the 'original genius' and the fashion for Sensibility imported from Britain. This saw creativity psychologically, as a product of the innate spontaneity of mind. Combined with Rousseau's critique of civilisation, it implied that the artist should reject convention. Poetry should itself be natural and represent nature as it was, not as our system of morality had distorted it. Goethe heralded Shakespeare's characters as 'Nature! Nature! Nothing so much nature as Shakespeare's people.'[1] Naturalistic characterisation meant showing the human predicament as it is, whether in activity or affliction, whether taking arms against convention or suffering its slings and arrows. The two pre-eminent character types of Storm and Stress drama, the independent robust man of action (*Kraftkerl*) and the suffering woman (*leidendes Weib*), are products of this desire for naturalistic characterisation.

The *Kraftkerl* is intended to represent human spontaneity at war with civilisation. An extreme individualist, he is opposed to the Enlightenment ideal of universal reason but also removed from the levers of political power. Goethe's Götz von Berlichingen, Guelfo in Klinger's *Die Zwillinge* (*The Twins*), Julius in Leisewitz's *Julius von Tarent* (*Julius of Tarento*), and Ferdinand in Schiller's *Kabale and Liebe* (*Intrigue and Love*) are disenfranchised and recognise that they are so. In revolt against a politically powerful authority, the *Kraftkerl* renounces politics entirely. By way of compensation, he lurches into violent self-assertion. The playwright might exculpate his hero by showing how circumstances drove him to violence, but there is no wider moral or political rationale for the hero's actions, except perhaps the idea of spontaneity itself.[2] Storm and Stress dramas are not especially concerned with the political rights and wrongs of revolt; they represent the psychology of revolt, especially melancholy and self-absorption. Melancholy becomes a response to an intolerable world. If not wholly rational, it is at least an understandable, even heroic form of rebellion.

More clearly than the *Kraftkerl*, the *leidendes Weib* symbolises the dissatisfactions of eighteenth-century society, exposed as she is to male sexual predation, the constraints of a stratified society, and unfeeling bourgeois Christian morality. Psychology is important because she is portrayed as preternaturally sensitive to threats, slights, and suggestion, and consequently prone to melancholy or madness. These characters all suffer derangement: Margarete in Goethe's *Urfaust*, the Lady Ambassador in Klinger's *Das leidende Weib* (*The Suffering Woman*), Evchen in H. L. Wagner's *Die Kindermörderin* (*The Infanticide*), and Marie and Gustchen in Lenz's *Die Soldaten* (*The Soldiers*) and *Der Hofmeister* (*The Private Tutor*) respectively. The *leidendes Weib* represents the psychic damage done by society to the sensitive bourgeois person.

A further implication of naturalistic characterisation was that new ways of representing psychology were needed. The mode of representation must be appropriate to what it represented. Herder believed that French theatre and its German imitators gave 'a third-hand portrait of feeling, but never or rarely the direct, primary, unvarnished stirrings, as they seek after and finally find words'.[3] Language must be put in the service of Sensibility, even if this meant portraying language as inadequate, or disrupting it in contravention of classical and Enlightenment aesthetics. Storm and Stress drama mobilises elements of literary expression – imagery, diction, sentence structure, gesture – to represent mental states performatively. Rather than have characters describe what they are feeling, the playwrights of Storm and Stress form language into a sign-system of unconscious meanings.

DESCRIPTION AND PERFORMANCE

The performative use of language to represent states of mind can be found in Greek and Roman literature and in Elizabethan and Jacobean theatre.

However, a fully conceptualised awareness that language could be used in this way first emerged in the eighteenth century. It was a product of the union of two ideas: original genius and associationism. Associationist critics of Shakespeare, such as Alexander Gerard in *An Essay on Genius* (1774), developed the idea that part of Shakespeare's genius was his ability to empathise completely with his characters and to express this empathy in the shape of language.[4] For Shakespeare criticism, this approach seemed to offer considerable gains, explaining apparently irrational imagery and previously insoluble textual problems. In German drama prior to the influence of this trend, emotions conform for the most part to a neo-Aristotelian conception of tragedy. Lessing took Aristotle's notion of *catharsis* to mean that tragedy should be a school for sympathy. When we sympathise with a tragic character, we practise the emotions that will make us better human beings. This may promote emotions, but it also subordinates them to an ethical imperative. This is why the characters of Lessing's dramas tend, on the whole, to represent their emotional states by describing them. Consider the speech in which Emilia tries to persuade her father that she must not be handed over to the Grimaldis:

What we call brute force is nothing: seduction is the only true force. – I have blood pulsing in my veins, my father, blood that is as youthful, as warm as anyone's. And my senses are senses too. I vouch for nothing. I will be responsible for nothing. I know the house of the Grimaldis. It is a house of pleasure. Only one hour there, under the eyes of my mother; – and there arose within me such diverse passions as weeks of the strict discipline of religion could scarcely calm.[5]

At the emotional climax of the play, Emilia must display her sensibility to her father. But her emotions are contained within a reasoned discourse, the purpose of which is advocacy: the speech is a calculated act of persuasion. Emilia's emotions do not *make* her speak in this way. Before she can speak her emotions are rationalised. This corresponds broadly to the Wolffian view of emotions as unclear, simple ideas about the causes and effects of pain and pleasure. Emotions tell us what is good and bad for us, but in an unclear way, which reasoning must clarify. To be sure, this does involve a degree of realism about motivation. Wolff believed that psychological factors must be integrated into ethical reasoning. But ultimately emotions are part of that reasoned discourse. Consequently Lessing's dramatic speech tends to describe rather than perform them.

Practical considerations of actors' capabilities reinforced this tendency. Lessing's dramatic psychology drew heavily on the novels of Richardson, where tears had only to be described, not acted. Lessing could not expect his actors to generate high emotion from a cold start, within the measured, reasoned discourse that was the prevailing mood of Enlightenment theatre. His solution was to provide his actors with long speeches in which they could build up gradually to a high pitch of emotion. He called this his 'Clarissa style', after Richardson's novel.[6] It consists of descriptions of emotions that the actor can use to approach the emotions themselves. Even the enacting of emotions, therefore, takes place in an atmosphere dominated by their description.

In Goethe's Storm and Stress dramas, influenced by Herder's aesthetics, the representation of otherwise hidden mental states through the production of language is already fully formed. Margarete's song 'Es war ein König in Thule' ('There was a King of Thule') is a brilliant example of this. On the level of Margarete's consciousness, we witness her singing a simple popular ballad. On an unconscious level, the song expresses her pathetically unrealistic hope that a socially superior man such as Faust might be faithful to her out of wedlock. Through the (pseudo-)naïve ballad form Margarete unwittingly performs a desire that she cannot speak. Goethe did not altogether abandon the habit of describing instead of performing emotions. It was too much a part of the fashion for Sensibility out of which Storm and Stress emerged. It also met particular dramatic needs that continued to exist. At some points Goethe's characters talk about emotions in a way that is clearly intended to be inauthentic. This is the case with Clavigo in Act v of the drama:

CLAVIGO: Dead! Marie dead! The torches there! Their sad companions! It's an illusion, a phantom of the night that scares me, that holds a mirror before me, in which I am to foresee the result of my betrayals. – There is still time! Still! – I tremble, my heart dissolves in fright! No! No! You shall not die. I am coming! I am coming! – vanish, spirits of the night, who obstruct me with fearful terrors. (*He advances towards them*)[7]

Marie is indeed dead, and Clavigo's emotions come too late to be meaningful. His running commentary on them – as if he were trying artificially to create emotions to correspond to the tragic situation he finds himself in – expresses his remorse. In this respect Clavigo is like Faust, whose hesitancy to commit himself to Margarete is fateful and whose moment of hesitancy is similarly marked by talk about emotions that expresses remorse at failing truly to feel them.

Awareness of the difference between performance and description, such as Herder voiced, posed the further question of how to portray emotional immediacy. One set of techniques employed the disruption of 'normal' language by means of interruptions, misunderstandings, incompleteness, and other methods.[8] An extreme form of this performative language occurs in Klinger's dramas. His characters are little more than vehicles for emotions.[9] They show no psychological development: they cannot, because they are incapable of speaking rationally about their emotions. Changes of mood are abrupt and unprepared. Klinger's dramas lack almost entirely the reasoned discourse that in Lessing's dramas frames and gives significance to emotion. Their chief structural principle is the bald juxtaposition of opposed feelings, which provoke one another in turn by a sort of psychological dialectic. By way of illustration, we might contrast the function of verbal repetitions in Klinger's and in Lessing's dramas. Klinger's characters repeat words in order to maximise their emotional expressiveness:

GUELFO: What does it all help if I strike my brow with clenched fist and howl with the winds – shout and curse, and in the process only build castles in the air, houses of cards! The boy is caressed, kissed, loved by father and mother, and my figure in the whole account is a miserable zero. Guelfo! Guelfo! – Nothing sounds more foolish as when I call out to myself. Guelfo! Hey there, Guelfo! (*He stamps*)

GUELFO: Was hilft das nun all, wenn ich mir mit geballter Faust vor die Stirne schlag' und mit den Winden heule – droh' und lerme, und bey alledem nur Luftschlösser, Kartenhäuser baue! Der Junge wird gekos't, geleckt, geliebt, von Vater und Mutter, und ich steh' allenthalben in der Rechnung ein garstiges Nichts. Guelfo! Guelfo! – Nichts lautet närrischer, als wenn ich mir selbst rufe. Guelfo! He dann Guelfo! (*Stampft*)[10]

Repetition has two effects. An idea is repeated in a string of synonyms or near synonyms in order to intensify its sense and so magnify the sublime terror that accompanies it. Also, a word is repeated to make it seem ridiculous and empty, to create a melancholic sense of futility. In Lessing's plays by contrast, repetition signifies intellectual engagement, the turning of a matter round in the speaker's mind, in an attempt to find a way out of perplexity:

PRINCE: Her picture! – So be it! – Her picture in any case is not herself. – And maybe I shall find in the picture again what I no longer see in the person. – Though, I do not want to find it again. – This bothersome painter! I should not be surprised if she bribed him. – And what if she did! If another picture, painted in other colors on another background, – will let her take her place once more in my heart: why, I really think I would not mind. When I loved her I was always so lighthearted, so gay, so free from care. –

Now I am the opposite of all that. But no; no, no! More at ease or less at ease; I am better this way.[11]

The Prince repeats the word 'picture' because he is looking for a way out of his romantic entanglements. He examines it until it yields the answer that appeals to him. Repetition progresses the argument of the drama.[12]

CONTINUITY AND CHANGE IN PSYCHOLOGY AROUND 1770

The psychological ideas available to playwrights did not change greatly between 1750 and 1770. Melancholy, sensibility, uneasiness, the associative and productive imagination, dreaming and sleepwalking as middle states between sleeping and waking, madness as an excess of the productive unconscious uncontrolled by reason – these core ideas remained more or less constant. In the 1770s the creeping movement away from Wolffian psychology and towards French and especially British models becomes noticeable. This expresses itself in mental physicalism and, as a result of the weakening of Wolff's rationalist framework, the idea of the organic, self-regulating mind. As alternatives to Wolff's philosophy gained ground, emotions came increasingly to be seen as natural states of the psyche. Instead of containing unclear information about our proper goals, emotions reflected one's general well-being. They were seen as working by physiological or psychological rules.

Changing theories of dreaming illustrate the shift towards organic psychology around the middle of the century. For Leibniz, dreams provide us with more or less clear intimations of rational truths about the Universe. Enlightenment writers on dreaming tend to focus on dreams that contain prophetic truths or exhibit unusual linguistic or mathematical powers.[13] The later eighteenth century rejected prophetic dreams. Goethe sternly warned Herder that the dream-interpreting indulged in by Herder's wife Caroline and Charlotte von Stein was empty and damaging:

The dreamworld is ever a false lottery, where countless losing tickets are mixed up with at best tiny wins. One becomes a dream, a lottery oneself, if one engages seriously with these phantoms.[14]

The supposed prophetic power of dreams could, in any case, be given a naturalistic explanation.[15] As the Leibnizian view of dreams became less common in German philosophy after the 1760s (despite the resurgence of interest in Leibniz after the publication in 1765 of the *New Essays*) dreams were increasingly held to reflect the dreamer's personality and circumstances. In Gerstenberg's *Ugolino*, as Ugolino and his three sons are starved to death in the tower, the youngest, Gaddo, dreams of a lavish banquet. There is no providential meaning in this dream: Gaddo himself will die of starvation, and his brothers and father will perish too. The dream simply reflects the nature of the dreamer. Gaddo is a young boy, led more by his body than his mind, and he dreams of the satisfaction of physical cravings. The explanation of the mental state comes not from the teleological orientation of the psyche towards reason, but from the mind's own autonomous psycho-physiological laws.[16]

The shift to an autonomous, organic conception of mind was more or less complete by around 1770. Its component theories were on the whole not new. Physicalism dates back to antiquity and was the contested premise of the eighteenth-century 'thinking matter' debate.[17] Much Enlightenment psychology had a physical conception of memory. Goethe reports an anecdote about Albrecht von Haller: 'It is said of Haller that when he once fell down stairs on his head, after he had got up he recited the names of the Chinese Emperors in order to test whether his memory had suffered.'[18] Haller was concerned that the blow to his head might have damaged the ideas in his memory. More adventurously, it could be argued that the language faculty had a physical location in the brain. Moritz's collaborator C. F. Pockels cites an instance, recorded by Linnaeus, of a Swedish academic who had suffered a stroke. At first he was unable to speak; later, having recovered his power of speech, he remained unable to use proper nouns. The very specific nature of his aphasia suggested that particular mental faculties were indeed located in particular areas of the physical brain.[19] Storm and Stress writers used physicalism widely and enthusiastically. Herder speaks, in 1769, of psychology as a physics of mind.[20] In *Erkennen und Empfinden* (*Knowing and Feeling*, 1778 version) Herder argues for an unbroken continuity between all forms of consciousness, from sensation to rationality.[21] Genius, in particular, seems amenable to physical explanation. For Storm and Stress writers genius, as well as being unconscious, is a physiological-cum-psychological quality. Herder argues that a precondition of genius is being 'a person with drives and sensations in perfect condition'.[22] J. F. Abel locates genius in the responsiveness of the nerves. Lavater finds it in the extraordinary elasticity of the mind.[23]

As in Storm and Stress aesthetics, British influence was crucial. Elements of British psychology had been present in German faculty psychology from early in the century, but the influence of Locke, Hartley, and others grew steadily towards a peak in the 1770s. Locke's concept of 'uneasiness' was adapted by Moses Mendelssohn into its opposite, ease (*Behaglichkeit*), the state of satisfaction resulting from the moderate satisfaction of the senses. For Mendelssohn the perception of beauty occasions an attuning of 'the fibres of the brain' (*Gehirnfasern*), which results in a feeling of contentment.[24] Locke's idea that sense experience satisfies a craving became known in Germany from the 1760s. When in Leisewitz's *Julius of Tarento*, Julius asks 'how shall I still my hunger for feelings?', he is using a metaphor that derives from Locke.[25]

German Anglophilia reached its peak in the 1770s, along with the cults of Shakespeare and Ossian, the idea of 'original genius', and other psychological notions that were transmitted in new translations of English and Scottish writings.[26] The Anglophile tendency was also liberal. Physicalism served a political purpose. It made psychological cause and effect more explicit and more immediate: to express psychological effects in physical terms was to give them greater emphasis and in particular to stress the damage that could be done to the mind. Damaged mental states could be portrayed as the deformities caused by a harmful environment. In this way, for Storm and Stress writers psychology became a more radical version of Peter Gay's 'strategic science'.[27] The examples of Herder and Schiller will illustrate how a physicalised psychology might function as a vehicle of cultural and social critique.

In 1769 Herder set out his opposition to Faculty Psychology in the fourth *Critical Thicket*. This was the psychological starting point for his ruminations on educational theory in his travel journal of the same year. His psychology in this period was founded on sensationist 'climate theory' and a nativist approach to faculties. Our mental powers are innate, but how well and how healthily they express themselves depends on the quality of the stimuli that they receive from the environment. The influence of environment starts in infancy:

With every sensation [the infant] is as if woken from a deep dream, so as to remind him the more vividly, as if by a powerful shock, of an idea that his situation in the Universe is now causing. In this way his powers develop by means of external stimulus.[28]

Our faculty of judgement is also formed by the environment, particularly during childhood. Children are more impressionable than adults, because they have softer and more malleable brains. The quality of learning during childhood determines how we will see the world: 'the first impressions in the soft wax of our child's soul give colour and form to our judgements'.[29]

Herder's project for a new school curriculum reflects this. Education should provide vivid stimuli that will interest children in their surroundings. The content of lessons should derive from the ordinary world. This will provide the objects on which the child's developing faculties can practise. Herder rejects the traditional abstract Germanic method of teaching (*HWS* IV.445). Traditional methods are stultifying; they inhibit proper development and a fruitful relationship to the child's surroundings. In particular Herder criticises the primacy of Latin in schools, which 'takes away courage, genius, outlook on the whole [world]'.[30] That is to say, Herder's psychological theory shows how an imperfect teaching regime can have harmful effects on the child and, implicitly, on culture as a whole. Herder's larger target here is the rationalistic, Latinate culture of mid-century Germany that he believes has stifled the natural genius of the Germans.

As for Herder, so for the young Schiller, physicalism and a direct relation between mind and body yield an explanation of psychological damage, and this has an implicit cultural-critical purpose. At the Karlsschule Schiller was taught two broadly physicalist psychological approaches by J. F. Abel and J. F. Consbruch. The philosopher Abel taught a British- and French-influenced sensationism. Consbruch lectured on mind–body interaction in the tradition of the German 'philosophical doctor' (*philosophischer Arzt*).[31] Medical students at the Karlsschule were encouraged to explain disease in terms of mind–body interactions. Schiller's second medical dissertation, *Versuch über den Zusammenhang der tierischen Natur des Menschen mit seiner geistigen* (*Essay on the Connection of the Animal and Spiritual Natures of Man*), contains a section entitled 'Geistiger Schmerz untergräbt das Wohl der Maschine' ('Spiritual pain undermines the well-being of the machine'). Schiller explains that Plato called passions the fevers of the soul. 'The convulsions', he continues, 'seed themselves quickly throughout the whole frame of the nervous system, bring the vital powers into a discordancy that destroys their bloom, and unbalance all the machine's actions.'[32] As Wolfgang Riedel has shown, this theory is the model for parts of a description by Schiller of the suicidal depression suffered by his fellow-student Grammont. Grammont's depression was caused, Schiller suggests, partly by physical and partly by spiritual damage. Severe abdominal pains made his spirits low, and this was exacerbated by the malignant influence of Pietism and metaphysics. The latter made him doubt common sense, the former made him hypersensitive and prone to overgeneralisation and emotional reasoning:

Pietist enthusiasm appeared to have laid the foundation for the whole of the ensuing illness. It sharpened his conscience and made him extraordinarily sensitive to all objects of virtue and religion, and it confused his ideas. The study of metaphysics finally made him suspicious of all [claims to] truth and pushed him over to the other extreme, so that, having previously exaggerated religion, he was now drawn by his sceptical brooding to the brink of doubting its fundamental principles.

This wavering uncertainty of the most important truths was too much for his excellent heart to bear. He strove for conviction, but in trying to find it wandered off onto a false path, sank into the darkest doubts, despaired of happiness and the Divinity, believed himself to be the unluckiest man on Earth. All this I have elicited from him in our frequent exchanges, as he never concealed any aspect of his condition from me.[33]

Schiller claims to base his diagnosis on conversations with Grammont. The diagnosis also bears a striking resemblance to a case described by Abel several years later in a collection of case histories. This describes a pendular swinging between Pietism and atheism, whereby faith creates unreasonable expectations that are dashed and lead to atheism.[34] This model derived from seventeenth-century English Latitudinarianism, which saw enthusiasm and atheism as related. A liberal impulse is also discernible, for it supposes that the damage is done by the tyranny of beliefs that do not admit of rational questioning. Schiller adds to the basic pendular model a further pernicious influence – metaphysics – thinking most probably of the dominant Wolffian school. This, together with the unhealthy conscientiousness encouraged by Pietism, compounded Grammont's illness and depression. Seen in this light, Schiller's account of Grammont's depression has a cultural-critical dimension, blaming Grammont's illness on an oppressive cultural system.

SENTIMENT

By emphasising the action of the environment on the psyche, physicalism provides an appropriately dramatic, sometimes hysterical language for the passion-play of the mind, heart, and nerves that is Storm and Stress drama. Storm and Stress writing insists on the primacy of sentiment. Feeling is the primary determinant of our mental life. It is the chief means by which we are motivated, in both active and passive senses. Feelings drive us to act: as the *empfindsam* philosopher-hero of Leisewitz's *Julius of Tarento* observes, 'Love is the great mainspring' (*Liebe ist die große Feder*).[35] Feelings are also the channel through which the world affects us and determines what we are. The *empfindsam* hero is constantly exposed to the world and susceptible in particular to appeals to his or (more often) her sentiments. The mere mention of love is often enough to melt the *empfindsam* hero's heart. Julius only needs to make allusion to a past love – 'love's shadow', as he puts it – and the Abbess is moved to admit him to see Blanca in her imprisonment.[36] Similarly, in Schiller's *Fiesko*, the direct appeal to a sentimental response is used by Verrina and his co-conspirators when they try to win Fiesko round to the republican cause. They arrive at Fiesko's palace armed with a painting of the Virginia story, which they unveil with a grand pathetic flourish. Once they have left him, Fiesko feels the drug begin to work and his sentiments begin to well up: 'What a turmoil in my breast! What mysterious flight of ideas–' ('Welch ein Aufruhr in meiner Brust! Welche heimliche Flucht der Gedanken–'). The turmoil is caused by the clash of two opposed sets of feelings, republican pathos and tyrannical ambition, between which Fiesko oscillates. The scene ends with the victory of republican feelings: 'To win a crown is *great*. To cast it away is divine. (*Decisively.*) Fall, tyrant! Genoa be free, and I (*softening*) your *happiest* citizen!'[37] Verrina's strategy of appealing to Fiesko's emotions enjoys only brief success, for soon Fiesko reverts to type. That is not to say that the strategy of appealing to sentiment was unrealistic, but that it could only be a short-term strategy, for Fiesko's emotional world is too changeable to provide a stable base for his political life. He tries on republican pathos like a new outfit to see how well it suits him, but republicanism speaks less sweetly to his vanity than tyranny.

Mere mention of key sentimental words – sympathy, love, friendship, brotherhood, harmony – can sometimes be enough to swing an argument. It is not just that Storm and Stress writing is committed to sentiment as a cultural banner to be paraded more or less routinely in set-piece displays of feeling. That is the impression that is sometimes conveyed. But this is only to be expected in drama: in the crucible of dramatic conflict core values are showcased, contradicted, and even partially undermined. The non-dramatic texts of Storm and Stress, by contrast, present a fairly uniform picture of the primacy of sentiment. In Lenz's comedy *The Private Tutor*, sex is problematised and the ubiquity of sexual motivation seen in a critical light, whereas in his *Philosophische Vorlesungen* (*Philosophical Lectures*) the thought that sex underlies everything is treated as a given. The sexual drive is 'the mother of all our feelings' ('die Mutter aller unserer Empfindungen').[38]

The aim of Lenz's lectures is to domesticate our sexual nature and make it morally safe. The need for this moral rearguard action stemmed from a crux of eighteenth-century ethics, which Storm and Stress shared with the sentimental wing of the Enlightenment. The rehabilitation of feeling brought with it the need to guard against its immoral associations. This could be done by taking a stern view of licentiousness. The drama of Sensibility portrays its villains as libertines: Mellefont and Marwood in *Miss Sara Sampson*, the Prince in *Emilia Galotti*. Storm and Stress drama does the same. Mellefont, Marwood, and the Prince have descendants in Fiesko and Franz Moor, the libertine villain of Schiller's *Die Räuber* (*The Robbers*). The strategic need to damn licentiousness is evident in Schiller's treatment of Franz's psychological theories. Franz believes in the mind–body interaction that Schiller himself used in the Grammont case. Franz's theories derive in part from Abel, Schiller's favourite teacher. However, it is clear that Franz and all his works are conclusively damned. Franz's cynical belief that only sense-experiences matter is presented as a sign of his libertinism. That the theories happen also to be true, in terms of the drama, creates a further complexity. Admittedly his theories are the reasoning behind the plan to shock his father to death, which fails, but the failure is Franz's, not that of his psychological theories. Old Moor *is* shocked to death eventually by the news that Karl is the robber captain. Where Franz failed, Karl succeeds. Franz's materialism and atheism make him keen to taunt Pastor Möser, but this rebounds on him in visions of hell-fire and torment. He finally commits suicide in a fit of paranoia, proving his theories right by his own demise. Where Franz failed with his father, he succeeds in shocking himself to death. Libertinism is shown to be self-destructive. Franz's psychological theories are left in the awkward position of being theoretically right and morally wrong.

In libertine figures the rule that sentiment must be obeyed is observed in the breach. The lack of sentiment is a sign of a denatured character. Franz describes himself as cold and wooden, a sure sign of the calculating libertine. Libertines might try to protect themselves against detection with masks, both figuratively, in the sense that they hide their motives, and literally. *Fiesko* begins with a *bal masqué* at which the masks hide both identity and feeling. A favourite eighteenth-century courtly entertainment thus provides a nice psychological symbol, and because it is Fiesko's party, we associate the mask and deception in general with him. The mask becomes a symbol for Fiesko's unclear motivation. By the same token the removal of a mask signals the authentic expression of feelings: Leonore takes off her mask to express distress at Fiesko's faithlessness (*NA* iv.13). Disguise is also symbolic. When in Leisewitz's *Julius of Tarento* Guido kills his brother Julius, the brothers and their accomplices are disguised (*SuD* 1.603). This symbolises the brothers' denial of their natural brotherly affection and the closing of their hearts to one another.

Different categories of person experience different degrees of senti-ment. The main factors determining this are age, social status, and sex. Sentiment prefers youth. The figures on the Storm and Stress stage with whom the audience is expected to identify are almost exclusively young adults. Young adults are people of feeling and the older generation less so. Some Storm and Stress writing has a systematically Rousseauian attitude to age, whereby sentiment declines as age increases. Gerstenberg's *Ugolino* shows three brothers: Gaddo aged six, Anselmo twice his age, and Francesco a young adult. The long and equal gaps between their ages allow Gerstenberg to represent them as quite distinct types with conflict-ing responses to the miserable situation in their tower prison. Gaddo is led by his physical needs; he dreams of food, as is apt for a six-year-old. Anselmo, the teenager, is a more problematic character. We can see in him the beginnings of male competitiveness, but also a complete lack of the responsibility that will come with adulthood. Francesco, the eldest brother, plays the young sentimental lead and has a well-developed sense of duty to his family. Ugolino, the father and experienced man of affairs, has a heart hardened by reality. His attitude to life is fixed and determined by one thing: his feeling of guilt. This makes him fatalistic, where his sons Anselmo and Francesco see the possibility of escape. (Gaddo is too young to understand the situation.) Youth, then, is the age of openness and possibility. The young mind is a more open, albeit also a less focused, mind. This can be contrasted with the Enlightenment view, which sees passions as inchoate ideas and children as inchoate adults. For Gerstenberg childhood has its own particular value. Goethe's Werther values children in their own right and is ridiculed for it.

In social matters, Storm and Stress is sympathetic to the bourgeoisie and the landed country nobility, and opposed to the court aristocracy. In Schiller's *Intrigue and Love* the President is cynical about the feelings of Luise and Ferdinand. Matters are complicated by the fact that Ferdinand only looks like an *empfindsam* male lead. He speaks a florid emotional language and accuses Luise of a lack of feeling when she wants to end their relationship for the sake of her family, but he applies much laxer standards to himself. Whereas she is supposed to sacrifice her family for his sake, he is prepared to believe that she has another lover. There is a deep irony here. Ferdinand attacks what he sees as Luise's loss of feelings for him by claiming the sentimental high ground of 'fiery love' (*feurige Liebe*) against the 'cold duty' (*kalte Pflicht*) of her scruples (Act III, Scene iv). He accuses her of being untrue to Sensibility. But the accusation has an unintended meaning that damns him instead of her. Elsewhere in the play, fire is shown in its destructive aspect and is associated with the courtly habits of exploitation and false show that Ferdinand affects to disdain.[39] In Act III, Scene ii, von Kalb describes the forthcoming opera in which the self-immolation of Dido will be represented by a whole village being burnt to the ground (*NA* v.51). Dido's passion, portrayed no doubt in high *empfindsam* style for the entertainment of the idle rich, will end in a conflagration that destroys the work of plebeian hands. Likewise Ferdinand's fiery love will destroy the *bürgerlich* Miller family. This is prefigured in Act II, Scene ii, when the maidservant Sophie explains to Lady Milford that most of those made homeless by a recent fire are either working as their creditors' slaves or dying in the ducal silver mines (*NA* v.30). Ferdinand's behaviour and language implicitly undermine his claim to love Luise. The strongest emotion in Ferdinand is not love but jealousy, and the increasingly lurid expressions of his passion for Luise suggest a desire to control and dominate her. It might not be overly sceptical to say that Ferdinand is exploiting Luise as part of a protest against his father and the court.[40] The speed with which he turns to intrigue in order to get even with his father suggests that, far from being a principled *empfindsam* rebel, he is a chip off the old block and a natural intriguer. Like his father, he has usurped a role that is not legitimately his, but in this case it is the role of the man of feeling. It would indeed be the ultimate mark of the aristocratic courtier if he were able cynically to fake sentiment.

Gender tends to be more complex, though it is still possible to see a broad psychological typology. A common distinction is between male activity and female passivity. Female characters typically function as the objects or the instruments of males. In *Julius of Tarento* Blanca is the recipient of Julius's and Guido's affections, whilst Cäcilia is the instrument of Duke Constantin's plans to reconcile the brothers. This is a norm in the 'bourgeois tragedy', and to some extent it simply reflects social facts, but there is also evidence of a belief that the social fact of male dominance is grounded in the psychological pseudo-fact of male activity. It is not just that women are made to behave passively by society: they are represented as being intrinsically less active. Clearly this is an indefensible habit of thought, and it might be said to epitomise the limitations of Enlightenment psychological essentialism. However, we should not over-look the moments when the idea of female passivity is used, albeit paternalistically, to make a progressive point. Often the dramas show that whilst society might think that women's passivity excuses men's abusive treatment of them, in fact it does not. The passivity of women is used to show how abusive men are. Equally, the qualities associated with passivity – receptiveness, understanding, sentiment, sympathy – are valued highly, to the extent that male characters are sometimes judged on the basis of their ability to emulate women.

Sentiment, as well as being the channel through which the feeling individual is affected and damaged by the world, is also a strength. Its chief benefit is cognitive, for instance as a means of detecting evil. In Act II of Goethe's *Götz von Berlichingen*, as Weislingen rides into Bamberg, where he will be ensnared by Adelheid, his horse shies and refuses to enter the city. The quaintly primitivistic implication is that the horse instinctively recognises that its (and its master's) interests would be best served by keeping away from Adelheid (*WA* 1.vii.59). The horse is not rational and its consciousness not split, as its master's is. It cannot contradict its instincts and therefore cannot be wrong. The image of rational rider atop instinctive horse might even be interpreted psychologically as a model of the relationship of conscious and unconscious. Similarly, the sentimental young bourgeois single women of Storm and Stress drama are often gifted with an intuitive sense of evil. Amalia can see through Franz Moor's plans, whereas his father cannot. Margarete sniffs out the true nature of Mephistopheles, whereas Faust smells nothing, and in the final prison scene she senses Faust's coldness – a result of his association with Mephistopheles (*WA* 1.xxxix.315). Emilia Galotti suspects the evil intentions of the Prince rather more shrewdly than do her vain mother and gloomy, self-obsessed fiancé Appiani.

Storm and Stress drama believes more firmly in the truth of unconscious or irrational intuitions than does, say, Lessing. Dreams can give access to hidden truths, as can moments of fantastical imaginative insight. They can also have a different, more naturalistic kind of truth, when they project the dreamer's or the fantasist's own desires. In *Julius of Tarento*, Julius projects his desire, when, looking at a portrait of Blanca, he sees pearls rolling down the canvas that seem to signify her sadness at their separation (*SuD* 1.557). This is perhaps a sign of the strength of his sentiment. It is not literally true, in the sense that Margarete's presentiments of an evil presence in her bedroom are true, but it is true in the naturalistic sense of being an authentic expression of strong feeling.

The contrast of activity and passivity also relates to political attitudes, usually to the effect that tyranny is associated with the active principle and democracy (or at least opposition to tyranny) with the passive. Again the purpose is primarily to represent the natural, sensitive state of humanity as the oppressed victim of an unnatural, harsh regime. Fiesko's musings on the relative virtues of tyranny and republicanism use the language of sentiment to represent the latter. Tyranny may be 'great', but republican sacrifice would be 'divine'. As Fiesko edges towards favouring tyranny, his speech becomes 'more hurried'. Republicanism is slow, contemplative, but firm. Fiesko voices republican statements after the stage directions '*after a contemplative pause, firmly*' ('*Nach einer nachdenkenden Pause, fest*') and '*softening*' ('*sanft geschmolzen*', *NA* IV.64). Similarly, in *Julius of Tarento* Duke Constantin's heart melts (*zerschmilzt*) when he is talking to his son Julius (*SuD* 1.600), an unfamiliar affect for a tyrant. Typically tyrants know no feelings; they are isolated from human contact for, as Machiavelli and Marinelli, his fictional counterpart in Lessing's *Emilia Galotti*, argue, princes cannot have friends (*LW* 11.139–40). The Prince in *Julius of Tarento* makes the same point (*SuD* 1.593). In its new *empfindsam* context this old political wisdom turns into an argument against absolutism. Lessing's Prince stands outside the normal web of sentiment and sympathy that binds humans together and keeps them human. His actions have nothing to restrain them, and they become tyrannical. This is part of a general psychologisation of politics. Tyranny is seen as a product of unbridled male individualism. The Prince's tyranny in *Emilia Galotti* is the political effect of a psychological cause. It is the Prince's self-love that makes him both able to justify his pursuit of Emilia as a replacement for Orsina and unable to focus on his responsibilities. The immediate effect is that he is about to sign the death warrant that Camillo Rota brings him without even looking at it. The ultimate effect is the death of Appiani, killed in an act of revenge because the Prince delegated his dirty work to Marinelli, and of Emilia. The play offers another, lesser example of the consequences of irresponsible indulgence of male impulses in the case of Appiani, concerned more with his own melancholic state of mind than with Emilia. This leads him to misinterpret his gloomy intuitions or to fail to act properly on them. It is a tragic example of how the politics of the court are typified by the misdirection of dangerous male responses.

Appiani had intended, after his marriage to Emilia, to live on his country estate away from the court and the centre of political power. Court politics represents a hostile environment from which Appiani with his bourgeois sympathies feels excluded. The country seat, where he will live with his bride of an independent-minded, non-courtly family, distant from the immorality of court, is an idyll in contrast to court politics. In the same way, Appiani's analytical, introspective, sentimental manner is the opposite of the trivial, flippant, ingratiating manner of Marinelli. Appiani thus appears to give confirmation to Wolf Lepenies's interpretation of the eighteenth-century culture of melancholy as a kind of compensation for the bourgeoisie's exclusion from political power. The same could be said of Werther, excluded from socially meaningful activity, and driven to invent a counter-culture of the heart and feelings.[41]

It is certainly true that members of the German bourgeoisie were excluded from political and social power. The situation was even worse than in France, for there at least high public office could be purchased, whereas in Germany the lack of a title usually meant a bar for life. However, Lepenies's compensation theory of melancholy tends to confuse the real German bourgeoisie with their fictional representatives. It presumes that melancholy was merely a culture, not an emotional reality. What these examples show is that eighteenth-century melancholy was a natural symbol for political disenfranchisement. It stands for and acts as a continual reminder of social injustice and political exclusion. Moreover, to say that melancholy was fashionable in the late eighteenth century is not to say it was not also real. Storm and Stress writers clearly believed in the reality of melancholy. Scepticism about melancholy is expressed only by disingenuous, untrustworthy characters. Marinelli's comment on Appiani's choice of bride – 'You will laugh, Prince. But such is the fate of men of sentiment' – suggests that it is the cynical Marinelli, not the melancholic Appiani, who is false.[42] In Wagner's *The Infanticide* Magister Humbrecht reports that Evchen is pining for von Gröningseck and that in her melancholy condition her favourite reading is Young's *Night Thoughts*. Von Gröningseck's reaction is to worry, although not as empathetically as one might wish, that she might kill herself, not because of her melancholy, but because of the effect of the reading material: 'God have mercy on her! – If I had to read a single page of that, I'd be capable of doing an Englishman and hanging myself by my garter'.[43] Von Gröningseck's cultural horizon is French, and he is simply too superficial to understand Evchen's suffering. His suggestion that her melancholy might have been artificially induced by the books she has been reading is meant to strike the audience as heartless.

What sometimes gives the impression that melancholy is inauthentic is the amount of pleasure it gives melancholics. In Lenz's playlet *Der Engländer* (*The Englishman*), the lead male, Robert Hot, is suicidal by inclination from the beginning of the play. This symbolises his independence of mind, but also represents a dangerous brinkmanship of the emotions, a melancholic attachment to darkness and emptiness. For the Storm and Stress hero, feelings of pain and pleasure are closely related. Werther's celebration of ecstatic communion with nature is exactly the obverse of his morbid fear of a chaotic Universe. The transition between the two, in the letter of 18 August, is something quite intangible, a sudden perceptual shift that turns joy into terror: 'It is as if a curtain has been drawn from across my soul, and this stage of infinite life is transformed before my eyes into the abyss of the eternally gaping grave.'[44] In Lenz's story *Der Waldbruder* (*The Forest Hermit*), the melancholic Waldbruder seems to take considerable pleasure in his own misery: 'To die for the world that knew me as little as I wished to know it – O what melancholic delight there is in that thought.'[45]

Psychologists have observed that those genuinely suffering from depression can feel a proprietorial attachment to their low moods. The pleasure taken by eighteenth-century melancholics in their melancholy does not mean that their melancholy is inauthentic. The close connection of pleasure and pain in Sturm und Drang drama should instead be read as an insight into the psychology of melancholy. Earlier in the century the view was that pain and pleasure were opposites. Similarly Enlightenment aesthetics saw beauty and ugliness as the two ends of the aesthetic spectrum. The aesthetics of Storm and Stress, on the other hand, sees ugliness as an aesthetic virtue in some circumstances, by virtue of its power or sublimity. The Storm and Stress conception of tragedy is a clear example of this. For Lenz, in his *Anmerkungen über das Theater* (*Notes on the Theatre*), the aesthetic power of tragedy lies in its 'bitter sweetness', its giving pleasure through the portrayal of pain.[46] The value of emotions lies in the emotions themselves, not in any cognitive benefits they might confer. A feeling of happiness is still happiness, regardless of whether it is really doing us any good: we want emotions more than we want the truth. Emotions thus often take on an addictive quality. In Goethe's *Die Leiden des jungen Werthers* (*The Sorrows of Young Werther*), Werther is clearly addicted to his own emotions. His vision of happiness – the delusion that Lotte loves him – may only be a delusion, but if it tells him what he wants to hear, he will not contradict it. The novel represents this as a problem: Werther's addictive personality is criticised implicitly by the events it leads to, and explicitly by Lotte, who tells him off for drinking too much (*DjG* iv.162). Similarly, in Lenz's *The Englishman*

Robert Hot speaks of his being cured as a loss: 'this clarity that surrounds me and takes from me forever the dear darkness that made me so happy'.[47] Addiction is a common trait among Lenz's characters. In *The Private Tutor* Pätus is addicted to coffee.[48] In Klinger's *The Suffering Woman* von Brand is addicted to love. Love causes him 'seethings of the blood' (*Wallungen des Bluts*) and sets off chains of associations in him from which he cannot or does not want to free himself.[49] His sensibility is, as he says, drunk on love.[50] One consequence of addiction to emotions is that the addict fears a state in which the feelings will 'dry up'.

The emotional life attains and thus represents a kind of independence. Melancholy is often linked to a new and more liberal politics. Repeatedly in Storm and Stress writing the melancholic is portrayed as a victim of absolutist tyranny, whether because oppression or exclusion has made him melancholic, or because the melancholy mind can feel and represent suffering when the contented mind cannot. Guelfo's friend Grimaldi in Klinger's *The Twins* is an example of the latter. He was robbed of his beloved by the Prince, and now in his melancholy his thoughts are dominated by the idea of victimhood.[51] It is not so much that his fate has made him melancholic, but that his melancholy is a dark glass through which the darkness of his world is more clearly visible. What he has suffered occupies his whole mind. Female characters tend to show psychic disturbance as a result of being abused. A hypertrophied conscience that wreaks terrible revenge on the heroine is a mark of victimhood. This is the case for the 'suffering women' of Storm and Stress drama: Evchen Humbrecht, Margarete, Luise Millerin, the Gesandtin in Klinger's *The Suffering Woman*.

Before we consider the portrayal of women as sensitive victims, we should remember that on occasions even sexually predatory males can be racked by conscience. Sexual fulfilment carries the possibility of self-loathing. Von Gröningseck recalls how beautiful Evchen looked the moment after he had raped her, when normally '[even] the greatest beauty disgusts us' (*uns die gröste Schönheit aneckelt, SuD* 11.561). Post-coital ennui thus turns into a feeling of guilt that will steadily grow as the play progresses and ultimately turn von Gröningseck into a morally responsible person. As with much of the detail of Wagner's play, this idea was probably inspired by Goethe's *Urfaust*. Faust's great monologue 'What is the joy of heaven in her arms' (*Was ist die Himmelsfreud in ihren Armen*) represents a problematic phase in his relationship with Margarete. They have slept together, but the relationship is still private and illicit, in part because of the mismatch of their social backgrounds, and in part because

Faust is an outcast from society after the events in Auerbachs Keller. The monologue reflects Faust's guilt:

> The promise of a night of heavenly bliss,
> The thrill, the warming passion of her kiss
> Cannot relieve my miserable plight.
> I am accursed, a homeless refugee,
> An aimless outcast driven relentlessly
> Like a cascading torrent over rock and precipice,
> Raging and seething into the abyss.
> And in a peaceful meadow by that stream
> She lived her simple life, her daily round
> And all the childish thoughts that she could dream
> In that small world were safely hedged around.
> And I, whom God has cursed,
> Was not content to thunder
> In a foaming rage and burst
> The tumbling rocks asunder.
> I had to undermine that girl's tranquillity –
> That was the sacrifice that hell required of me.
> What must be done, let it be quickly done;
> Now, Devil, help me end this agony.
> My fearful destiny and hers are one,
> And she is doomed to share my fate with me.[52]

> Was ist die Himmels Freud in ihren Armen
> Das durch erschüttern durcherwarmen?
> Verdrängt es diese Seelen Noth?
> Ha bin ich nicht der Flüchtling, Unbehauste
> Der Unmensch ohne Zweck und Ruh
> Der wie ein Wassersturz von Fels zu Felsen brauste
> Begierig wüthend nach dem Abgrund zu
> Und seitwärts sie mit kindlich dumpfen Sinnen,
> Im Hüttgen auf dem kleinen Alpenfeld
> Und all ihr häusliches Beginnen
> Umfangen in der kleinen Welt.
> Und ich der Gott verhasste,
> Hatte nicht genug
> Daß ich die Felsen fasste
> Und sie zu Trümmern schlug!
> Sie! Ihren Frieden mußt ich untergraben,
> Du Hölle wolltest dieses Opfer haben!
> Hilf Teufel mir die Zeit der Angst verkürzen,
> Mags schnell geschehn was muß geschehn.
> Mag ihr Geschick auf mich zusammen stürzen.
> Und sie mit mir zu Grunde gehn. (1412–32)

In *Faust I* the speech occurs before the relationship is consummated, and as such can easily be mistaken for an image of the 'Faustian condition'.[53] But in their original position, after the consummation, it is clear that the lines are an expression of Faust's post-coital self-loathing (*das durch erschüttern durcherwarmen*). *Seelen Noth* suggests pain and anguish, not some Faustian restlessness. The language is violent (*Begierig wüthend*), and the term *der Gott verhasste* nicely conveys the sort of magnifying overgeneralisation to which melancholics are prone. Characteristically he hates himself and then turns that hatred out against the world (*Du Hölle wolltest dieses Opfer haben!*), as if by accusing Mephistopheles he might shake off the miasma. That denial of responsibility finally turns guilt into an impersonal 'fate'.

The contrast with Margarete's experience of guilt is striking. In the cathedral she feels the world accusing her. Like Faust she experiences a magnification of reality. The Latin of the mass with its grim message of total vengeance (*nil inultum remanebit*) would be savage enough, but for added effect Margarete is terrorised by the threats of a German-speaking Evil Spirit. The medieval Latin of the requiem, incomprehensible to Margarete, is translated by the Spirit into the amplifying and particularising medium of the demotic. The Spirit magnifies her experience of guilt, a guilt that turns inwards, not outwards like Faust's.

The primacy of sentiment overrides reason and rational self-interest. Gesture and behaviour can betray emotion. When in Wagner's *The Infanticide* von Hasenpoth tries to find out whether the rumour is true that von Gröningseck has 'had' Evchen, the insistence with which von Gröningseck claims the rumour is untrue proves to von Hasenpoth the opposite (*SuD* 11.560). A guilty conscience can work unconsciously and express itself in dreams. In Lenz's *The Private Tutor* Gustchen dreams that her father pulls his hair and pokes his eyes out with remorse, because he thinks that she is dead.[54] Conscience is often physicalised. Margarete's guilt assumes physical form when she faints. Sometimes guilt leads to horrific self-destructive acts, the violence of which reflects both the power of guilt and the direct, unmediated nature of emotion in general. In *The Englishman*, Robert Hot in his desperation 'runs into a wall with his head and sinks to the floor'.[55] In *The Robbers* Karl Moor is described in a stage direction as 'running into an oak tree'.[56] This specific form of self-harm was recognised as belonging to a melancholic illness. The Viennese physician Leopold Auenbrugger, famous for discovering a new method of diagnosing pulmonary illness, defined it evocatively as 'silent mania' (*die stille Wuth*).[57] A passage in Klinger's *The Suffering Woman* suggests that this was widely recognised to be the likely outcome of melancholy. The ambassador's wife, at risk of being driven insane by a guilty con- science, warns that she will end up committing suicide by smashing her head open (*SuD* 11.56). The manner of this self-harm has a simple logic. It is a perverse form of treatment: the bodily seat or cause of the mental pain is to be 'treated' physically, even if the treatment involves destruction. So in *The Private Tutor* Läuffer's self-mutilation should be read not as a pseudo-religious act of contrition for seducing Gustchen, but as the psychological effect of his socially reinforced feelings of guilt. In this way social disapproval is inscribed on the body of the guilty party. In the case of the infanticide Evchen Humbrecht, the social exclusion of the unmarried mother is inscribed on the body of her baby. The threat of social disapproval, first arrogantly trumpeted by her father the butcher, then confirmed by the washer-woman Frau Marthan, drives her mad with guilt. She loses control and stabs her child in the head with a pin (*SuD* 11.600).

SUGGESTION

The traditional meaning of suggestion is the influence on a person's behaviour of ideas (or, under hypnotism, commands) of which the person is not conscious. Suggestion was not conceptualised in this form until quite late in the eighteenth century. In less distinctly conceptualised form, however, suggestion was ubiquitous in the second half of the eighteenth century. Enlightenment sensationism provided a basis. Locke's rejection of innatism put a tremendous burden on the ability of the mind to learn: all ideas that might previously have been ascribed to innate knowledge must now be shown to have been learnt. As we could not in most cases be conscious of having learnt these – most people do not remember acquir- ing their ideas of morality, beauty, and so on – they must have entered the mind unconsciously. The German psychological tradition was espe- cially fertile ground for the idea of suggestion. After the publication of Leibniz's *New Essays* in 1765, his monadic notion of the soul, according to which knowledge emerges into consciousness from a condition of 'pre- consciousness', enjoyed new influence. The Hippocratic tradition of healing by psychic influence, still powerful in Germany, gave a medical reason for accepting suggestibility.

The Sensibility of the 1750s onwards emphasised the suggestibility of the sensitive imagination. We have seen one good example of this in Lessing's *Nathan the Wise*, where Recha unconsciously reproduces Daja's belief in angels, much to Nathan's annoyance. In this case suggestion works because the ideas come from a trusted, authoritative figure. We believe things that we are told by authorities because believing is part of the routine of obedience. More damagingly, in Goethe's *Urfaust* Margarete lives in an atmosphere of superstitious submission to the Church's authority. The Church turns the teaching of the Bible into a set of popular superstitions that are designed to terrify and subjugate. Margarete's mother hands the jewels over to a priest because she believes that 'ill-gotten gold / Corrupts the heart, ensnares the soul' (*ungerechtes Gut / Befängt die Seel, zehrt auf das Blut*, 678–9). These words are an adaptation of a biblical text, which Goethe would have known in Luther's translation, *unrecht Gut hilfft nicht* (literally: 'ill-gotten gains do not help'; Proverbs 10.2). In putting into Margarete's mother's mouth a lurid exaggeration of Luther's plainer text, Goethe is trying to characterise the popular superstition that he, a product of Enlightened Protestantism, associates with the Catholic Church. The same process is at work in the scene 'Cathedral'. Margarete hears the already intimidating Latin of the requiem mass translated by an Evil Spirit – which represents the internalised voice of the superstition that spoke through her mother – into terrifying threats of damnation and physical torment. Margarete is thus driven to the state in which she kills her child by an atmosphere of terror sponsored by the authority and prestige of the Church.

In his *Traité des systèmes* (*Treatise on Systems*, 1749) Condillac argued that those who espouse philosophical or theological systems tend to convince us to believe in the systems by virtue of their personal or professional prestige.[58] Ultimately this is why the moral stories told by philosophers and priests come true: not because they describe reality, but because we trust the people who tell them and then, having internalised the stories, we act them out. Extra-marital sex or liaisons between men and women of different social classes do lead to disaster. The reason they do so is that people internalise the stories that figures of moral authority tell them and act as if these stories were independently true. The power of suggestion is witnessed by its capacity to help certain (not otherwise true) stories about society to become self-fulfilling. Society enforces its norms through people's suggestibility. Suggestion is often the source of the guilt experienced by female characters. Their hearts tell them to love, but social norms, which they have internalised, tell them that they must hate themselves for it. In the final act of Wagner's *The Infanticide* Frau Marthan tells Evchen about an illegitimate son who tried to cut his mother's head off with a knife (*SuD* 11.596–8). Frau Marthan believes he was just a sinful child who wanted money from his mother that she did not have. Evchen interprets the story differently. The boy was driven mad when someone drunkenly told him he was a bastard and his mother was a prostitute. The different interpretations reveal different outlooks. Evchen's version reveals her as racked by guilt. She interprets the story as if the mother's loose morals were to blame and so imports her view of herself as a fallen woman into the story. In this relatively unthinking way her behaviour expresses the strict morality that her father has impressed upon her. Evchen's experience is based, of course, on Margarete's in Goethe's *Urfaust*. Margarete internalises society's condemnation of the unmarried mother. She goes mad and kills her child because she is terrified by what she hears.

In Klinger's *The Suffering Woman* guilt at leading the Gesandtin astray causes von Brand to suffer from delusions: 'Everywhere she's creeping after me. For three nights after the other I've seen her in winding sheets; she gestures at me, making signs – I'll surely despair of this if it continues.'[59] The Gesandtin's guilt at betraying her husband and children is more desperate and more graphically realised. Looking at the stars she draws a personalised meaning from the poetic cliché of the stars' innocence:

Ah! I cannot look at the heavens any longer, the beautiful wide heavens. You chaste, harmonious stars! Innocent! Dear Brand, why do the poets say 'chaste stars'? – holy expression . . . You chaste stars, pale, silver moon! shine, shine, you shine down worry into an unchaste woman's soul.[60]

The idea of guilt is arrived at apparently by accident, by an arbitrary chain of associations. The guilt was already there, imprinted in the psyche by society and waiting to be triggered by an abritrary event. Finally it drives her mad. She is haunted by 'images that chase and hunt' of the husband and children she has betrayed.[61]

Less directly, a story that is not at first believed can resurface and make itself true because events *appear* to confirm it, even if in reality they do not. In Lenz's *The Private Tutor* Läuffer is made to believe that he is an unfit human being. This culminates in his castrating himself, which symbolises his view of his own inadequacy. The immediate significance of the castration is as an act of self-punishment; it has the added 'benefit' of prophylaxis. But it also points back to the words with which the play opens. Läuffer tells us his father's view of his career prospects: 'my father says I'm not up to being a secretary' (*mein Vater sagt: ich sei nicht tauglich zum Adjunkt*).[62] Läuffer believes that the problem lies in his father's purse rather than his own supposed inadequacy. Yet his bad experiences and the traumatic guilt he feels for Gustchen's pregnancy cause his father's view of him to come gruesomely true. The castration symbolises his father's relegation of Läuffer to a socially inferior role.

Sometimes life imitates art, when the stories told about society are drawn from novels. Female characters seem especially prone to believe and internalise what they read in sentimental novels, in particular Richardson's *Pamela, Clarissa,* and *Sir Charles Grandison. Pamela* portrayed its heroine breaking down social barriers and successfully marrying above her station. The prospect of these heroines becoming role models for young German *Bürgerstöchter* was worrying because the aspirations they created were unrealistic for the vast majority of women. The glass ceiling that prevented bourgeois women marrying aristocrats remained largely intact. The aspiration to marry well might, it was argued, have the effect of making young women despise their own class.

The chief danger is the charm and fecklessness of aristocratic men. In Lenz's *The Soldiers*, the Countess complains that it was reading *Pamela* that made Marie susceptible to Desportes's advances.[63] In *The Infanticide* the guilty von Gröningseck makes this connection. When Evchen cries foul, he tries to make her see reason, appealing to the realities of ancien régime society: bourgeois women do get into trouble with aristocratic men; the best thing they can do is suffer in silence. Evchen continues to complain, calling von Gröningseck a 'devil in an angel's form' (*Teufel in Engelsgestalt*). Her persistence in claiming some hold over him now that they have had intercourse, as well as her use of a melodramatic phrase, draw from him the sneering put-down: 'You've been reading novels, it would seem.'[64] In *The Suffering Woman* we learn of the dangers of reading both English and German novels. The effect of reading Richardson is to 'spoil' young women by giving them ideas above their station. To a woman who reads these novels, no man whom she would have a realistic chance of marrying would seem good enough; and in any case none of them would marry her now. The Magister tells Suschen her mother's example should serve as a lesson: 'Then she read a book, they call it Grandison, it turned her head; she got the novel-fever, the blasted Grandison-fever.'[65] '*Grandison* fever' is a delusion that the world is or ought to be as sentimental novels portray it. The less realistic 'romances' can also give young women ideas. In Schiller's *Intrigue and Love* we first see Luise returning from church carrying a book, which is not, it appears, the Bible. Ferdinand and Luise have been reading novels, and her father Miller suggests this reading matter has given her ideas above her station:

The girl gets all sorts of Devil's drivel into her head, and then finally, with all that maundering around in Fool's Paradise, she can't get back home any more; she forgets, she is ashamed that her father is Miller the Fiddler . . .[66]

Understandably Wieland is also felt to be unsuitable reading for women. In *The Suffering Woman* Louise wants to read to the Gesandtin from *Agathon*, but the Gesandtin thinks that Wieland is partly to blame for her fall:

I don't want to hear another word about him, not another word about * *. A woman's eye ought not to look in it. If God had protected me from it, I'd never have gone so far with Brand.[67]

Lenz, on the other hand, defended novels. In *The Forest Hermit* it is suggested that reading novels does not influence people. Honesta says of the Waldbruder's bizarre behaviour 'that the reason for it lies in his heart, and that he would have become what he now is even without Werther and Idris'.[68]

Suggestibility might even have positive effects if what damages can also heal. Positive images in music and art were conventionally thought to reinforce certain moods and kinds of behaviour, and this reinforcing effect could be used therapeutically.[69] In *The Twins* Grimaldi plays fortissimo on the piano to reinforce Guelfo's anger and calm his nerves.[70] The positive effect of art is a recurrent theme of Leisewitz's *Julius of Tarento*. The staged presentation to Constantin of a garland of flowers by a farmer melts Julius's heart (*SuD* 1.585); Constantin says that even a fake show of unity by the warring brothers would cure his anxiety (*SuD* 1.588); a picture of Aeneas and Anchises, representing the ideal of filial piety, calms Constantin's anxiety (*SuD* 1.601). Not that any of these representations has the power to resolve the play's central problem of the competitiveness of Julius and Guido. As it turns out, they are palliatives.

Leisewitz's attitude reflects a generally sceptical or pessimistic view of therapy in the latter part of the century. Most therapies practised at the time were physiological. They were based on the theory of the humours and involved correcting imbalances between the four 'spirits', by means of blood-letting, diet, temperature regulation, and various other means. Although these theories and their associated remedies remained dominant, increasingly during the second half of the century they were criticised as ineffective and brutal. In their place a new cognitive approach developed, which was closer to the spirit of the Enlightenment and promised to cure mental illness by adjusting behaviour. The new approach is reflected and criticised in Lessing's comedies, although not so much on psychological grounds as because the ways of Providence are labyrinthine. Storm and Stress drama problematises cognitive therapy for different reasons. For the moment we should note three positive outcomes from cognitive therapy in Goethe's writing of the 1770s. An activity cure is prescribed for Werther; he takes a job, and for a while work distracts him from his melancholy. By engaging with reality he overcomes his tendency to avoid things he fears. The cure is, of course, short-lived, yet, although Werther writes mockingly of it (*DjG* IV.147), it does provide some respite and hope. In *Der Triumph der Empfindsamkeit* (*The Triumph of Sensibility*) the cure of Mandandane is entirely successful. She is infatuated with the sentimental Prince Oronaro, who in turn worships a model of her. She is cured of her infatuation when she sees how the Prince, given a choice between her and a dummy, chooses the dummy. The shock of recognising reality cures her (*WA* I.xvii.72). A more complex case of cognitive therapy is enacted in *Lila*, where after a series of false starts (which illustrate late Enlightenment attitudes towards therapies for mental illness) Lila is cured by means of the manipulation of her imagination. As the benevolent doctor Verazio explains, the old style of physiological 'cure' is not what he has in mind: 'We are not talking about "cures" or quackery here. If we could heal the imagination with the imagination, we would create a masterpiece.'[71] The treatment would be a masterpiece because it would exhibit a beautiful (and dramatically effective) economy of means, but also because it would succeed where the traditional physical interventions had failed. The alternative is the quackery of the traditional, brutal therapies. Cognitive therapy, on the other hand, the practice of 'curing imagination with the imagination', represents a gentler and more humane therapy, treating the patient as a feeling person and not an object. Made melancholic by her husband's absence, Lila is traumatised by a letter erroneously announcing his death. She lapses into a delusional state and 'walks abroad at night in her fantasies', an imagined, fairy-tale world of ogres and demons.[72] The treatment consists in her family acting out this fantasy world in front of her and leading her gradually out of it and back to reality.

The fact that the scenarios of both *Lila* and *The Triumph of Sensibility* are at bottom unrealistic tells us something about the status of this kind of therapy, from Goethe's not unrepresentative perspective at any rate. The successful cure seems to belong to a comedy world, a world in which idealistic experiments succeed. But such successes went against the grain of the novelistic reality of, say, *The Sorrows of Young Werther*. In the real world of contemporary medicine and psychology there was a lack of effective psychic cures. Developments in medical knowledge of the physiology of the nervous system, and pre-eminently the work of Haller, opened up new fields of clinical observation. However, improvements in diagnostic accuracy were not matched by new therapies and, as seems to be the fate of modern medicine, progress bred only higher expectations.

'CROOKED TIMBER'

The poor outcomes of therapy are symptoms of a more general scepticism about human nature. The chief expression of this scepticism is a psychology of innate drives. Drives are outside reason's control. We may try to regulate our behaviour, but our drives are more powerful than reason. It often seems that the most likely means of curbing aberrant behaviour is not by reasoning, but by opposing one drive with another. In the most extreme examples of Storm and Stress drama, Klinger's plays, we witness the brute antagonism of opposed emotional states; reason barely registers. For most of the dramatists, reason does feature, but only as the loser in a fruitless struggle against drives. In Lenz's view, expressed in the *Philosophical Lectures*, the sex drive is beyond control, and this is the source of tragedy in his dramas: witness Läuffer in *The Private Tutor* and Desportes in *The Soldiers*.[73] In the former case, the sex drive is finally domesticated and Läuffer marries, as befits a comedy, although the brutal means used to curb his sex drive belongs rather to tragedy. In the latter, Desportes's urges have tragic consequences.

Paradoxically the pessimistic attitude to drives seems to have been a consequence of Rousseauian idealism about human nature, and like sensitivity and suggestion this had a political dimension. The natural qualities of humanity, such as our sensitivity or our survival instinct, also have negative aspects, such as suggestibility and competitiveness. But these only become negatives in circumstances that make them so. Competitiveness is perhaps the most prominent drive and central to the pessimism of Storm and Stress. In *Ugolino* Anselmo competes with his older brother Francesco; *Julius of Tarento* contains the opposed brothers who compete with one another, the sentimental Julius and the martial Guido; Klinger's *The Twins* and Schiller's *The Robbers* show an envious younger brother in competition with a more fortunate or gifted older brother. The constellation of the competitive brothers is also present in Klinger's *The Suffering Woman*. It is an ancient literary theme, of course, from Cain and Abel onwards, but it is particularly common in Storm and Stress drama.

The ubiquity of fraternal competitiveness is explained by two factors in combination, a psychological and a political one. Psychologically, competitiveness was seen by many in the eighteenth century as a natural propensity of men in particular. One might even say that for Storm and Stress competitiveness is the male counterpart to female sensitivity. Competitiveness supplied an explanatory model for 'conjectural history', those fashionable hypothetical accounts of the development and spread of civilisation.[74] The spread of populations might be the consequence of competition or rivalry within an original population. This would lead to conflict and, either to avoid conflict or as the result of conflict, one part of the population would emigrate to found a new civilisation. This kind of rivalry would be likely in those societies that were unable to resolve conflict by political means. In an open society, rivalry would be dissipated. So in Mandeville's *Fable of the Bees* and Adam Smith's *The Wealth of Nations* the natural competitive energies of society are channelled into economic activity. But the liberty to turn competitiveness down profitable channels is precisely what is lacking in Storm and Stress drama. In their paternalistic and hierarchical societies there is no forum in which competition can play itself out. Competitiveness tends instead to be bottled up until it explodes. Violent expressions of competitiveness are symptoms of political frustration. Explosions of hysterical behaviour and mindless violence in Storm and Stress dramas are not as empty as they might seem. The destructive male is often also a victim of a closed society. His violent competitiveness, like female suggestibility, symbolically represents a set of social and political complaints.

A common constellation is rivalry between father and son, which can take extreme forms. In Lenz's *The Englishman* Robert Hot cries 'Away with fathers!'[75] There might also be an element of envy or jealousy: the son envies the father's power. At the same time, there is little antipathy on the part of the older generation towards the younger, which shows that this is not a Freudian scenario. Where such antipathy occurs, in Klinger's *The Twins* or Leisewitz's *Julius of Tarento*, it is usually simply a matter of one child being preferred to another. Old Guelfo prefers Ferdinando to the young Guelfo because Ferdinando is the older son and more compliant. Constantin prefers Julius to Guido because he is more peaceful. Old Moor prefers Karl to Franz because he is the first born and has good looks and charm. What fathers dislike is awkward sons, not sons as such, in the same way as what tyrants dislike is awkward subjects.

Related to competitiveness is contrariness. The underlying structure of Klinger's play *Sturm und Drang* (*Storm and Stress*) consists in one mood provoking or aggravating another.[76] In this regard Klinger is the opposite of Lessing. For Klinger the timber of humanity is seriously crooked. Contrariness is a fundamental propensity, which goes so deep as to defy reason's efforts to correct it. Lessing, on the other hand, presents us with successful cases of behavioural therapy in which contrary people are made rational. Character faults can be ironed out by the use of 'reverse psychology'. The 'therapist' simply encourages the 'patient' to do the opposite of what the therapist wants her or him to do, knowing that the patient is contrary and will in fact do the opposite of what she or he is encouraged to do; that is, exactly what is in her or his and the therapist's real interests. On recognising how a spirit of contrariness alone has led to this result, the patient will see that contrariness is against her or his best interests. That, at least, is the theory, and in Lessing's *Nathan the Wise* Nathan puts it into practice by manoeuvring the Templar into agreeing with him by first allowing the Templar to criticise the exclusivity of Judaism (and thus Nathan's own Jewish identity) before showing him that the criticism makes them allies in humanity (Act II, Scene v). This kind of reverse psychology can work in the utopia of *Nathan the Wise* or in the very sparsely defined worlds of Lessing's early comedies. It is less successful in the post-Seven Years' War German reality of *Minna von Barnhelm*, where Minna wins Tellheim back but does not persuade him that he was wrong to place so much emphasis on honour.

In Storm and Stress drama, ploys using reverse psychology always fail, because the stubbornness of the melancholic hero is more powerful than reason. In *The Twins* his father suggests that Guelfo is a bastard in order then to be able to stage a dramatic, remorseful renunciation and win Guelfo over; the ploy fails miserably.[77] In *Julius of Tarento* Constantin devises two plans to end the enmity between Julius and Guido. As its source is Guido's jealousy, Constantin first plans to have Julius fall in love with another woman (*SuD* 1.568). Predictably Julius is not interested and the plan fails. Constantin's second plan is to redirect the sons' competitive urges. He announces a competition to renounce love. Again, predictably this only causes the brothers to desire more fiercely to outdo one another.

The resistance to manipulation that these scenarios demonstrate makes a clear point. Manipulation of emotions is tyrannical and not part of a modern and liberal society. The contrast we drew earlier with Mandeville and Adam Smith applies again here. In Storm and Stress drama, competitive instincts will not converge productively because the political circumstances will not allow them to. It may be doubtful though whether Guelfo, the outrageous hero of Klinger's *The Twins*, would find a home in any society. He is an extreme case of the melancholic *Kraftkerl,* incapable even of taking his doctor's advice.[78] Yet in general Rousseau's argument holds good: heroic greatness comes about in spite of society, not because of it; the heroes of antiquity were criminals, as Plutarch showed. Occasionally the politics of Storm and Stress drama do wander off in the direction of this radical libertarianism where no laws means no criminals. But the main purpose of portraying the conflict between the melancholic *Kraftkerl* and the manipulative tyrant is to show that hierarchical societies do not work. When shock therapy (of the kind that works in Goethe's fantastical comedy *The Triumph of Sensibility*) is tried in Lenz's *The Forest Hermit* and *The Englishman,* it fails. 'Top–down' remedies, the sign of a hierarchical society, do not work.

CHAPTER 4

Empirical psychology and classicism: Moritz, Schiller, Goethe

WEIMAR CLASSICISM AND THE GERMAN PSYCHOLOGICAL TRADITION

The classicism of Moritz, Schiller, and Goethe was the main channel through which eighteenth-century psychology fed into the nineteenth century in Germany. This might seem a strange claim. It is often argued that Goethe's classicism was a reaction against the 'pathological' Storm and Stress. His negative attitude to *Werther* in the 1790s is well known. Hans-Jürgen Schings has argued that Schiller's classical aesthetics belonged to the rationalist tradition of criticism of melancholy.[1] In his review of Bürger's poems Schiller claimed that melancholy was not a proper subject for poetry.[2] The reality is more complex. In a letter to Schiller of March 1801 Goethe wrote that empirical psychology was 'where we poets are in actual fact at home'.[3] Moritz, Schiller, and Goethe came – more or less independently, but via a similar route – to the view that classicism was a cure for melancholy. Moritz and Goethe identified closely with Rousseau, whose *Confessions* began to appear in 1782. Around this time Moritz began to compile his autobiography, which eventually fed into the psychological novel *Anton Reiser* and the project of a journal of psychological case histories. Goethe began to experiment with biographical and autobiographical modes in the early 1790s, after befriending Moritz in Rome. Schiller's experiments in empirical psychology in the 1780s were prompted by the psychology taught at the Karlsschule by J. F. Abel. Schiller read Moritz's journal and was sympathetic to Moritz's aesthetics, if not to the man himself, when they met in Weimar in 1789.

Moritz and Goethe exercised a considerable influence on the development of psychological theory in the nineteenth century in Germany. Although Moritz himself was virtually forgotten in the nineteenth century, the tradition of the case history was continued by Schiller's teacher J. F. Abel, Moritz's collaborator C. F. Pockels, I. D. Mauchart (who dedicated his collection to Moritz), C. F. Heynig, C. C. E. Schmid, and, in Britain, Alexander Crichton. In the next generation there followed J. C. Reil, J. C. Hoffbauer, and C. D. Nasse. A continuous line of descent leads from Moritz via these writers to psychoanalysis and modern clinical psychology. Goethe was a stimulus for some of the most influential nineteenth-century German theorists of 'depth psychology'. Schopenhauer, the first systematic theorist of the unconscious, drew his conception of anxiety in *Die Welt als Wille und Vorstellung* (*The World as Will and Representation*) from the idea of *Sorge* in *Faust I*. Carl Gustav Carus developed a Goethean theory of the unconscious in his *Vorlesungen über Psychologie* (*Lectures on Psychology*, 1831) and *Psyche* (1846). Carus and Goethe became friends in 1821, drawn together by their work on comparative anatomy and a shared interest in the visual arts. Goethe provided Carus with some key ideas and showed a close interest in Carus's psychology: he was reading the *Lectures on Psychology* two weeks before his death in March 1832. Freud's reception of Goethe is well known. Goethe served Freud as a source of apt illustrative quotations, but there are also strong thematic affinities to Goethe in Freud's writing, especially to *Faust*. Jung was also anxious to coopt Goethe and used *Faust* to define his own brand of analytical psychology against Freud's.[4] The importance of Weimar classicism for the German tradition of psychology should not be underestimated.

ROUSSEAU'S 'CONFESSIONS'

Rousseau wrote the early books of the *Confessions* during an unpleasant war of words in late 1766 and early 1767. In the autumn of 1765, in response to an offer of assistance from Hume, Rousseau had left for England. The relationship with Hume soon buckled under the weight of Rousseau's paranoia. In the ensuing row, charges were levelled against him that brought the whole conduct of his life into question. It made sense, then, for him to respond in the form of an apologetic autobiography, a modern version of Augustine's *Confessions*.[5] Because of where the charges came from, the *apologia* had to meet certain philosophical standards. Rousseau writes that he intends to make his mind transparent to others. Clearly it is already transparent to him; the *Confessions* do not pretend to be an exercise in self-discovery. Others, though, are obviously misled by received opinion. It is to counter this that he will lay his mind bare to his readers by making all the evidence available indiscriminately. The reader will then be able to judge for himself what sort of a person

Rousseau is and how his experiences have formed his character. The mature Rousseau, with all his neuroses and paranoia, will be explained as the sum of the younger Rousseau's experiences. The method is genetic; it follows the hidden determinants of the present back to their sources in the past.[6] This is explained in a long apology at end of Book IV:

I never promised to present the public with a great personage. I promised to depict myself as I am; and to know me in my later years it is necessary to have known me well in my youth. As objects generally make less impression on me than does my memory of them, and as all my ideas take pictorial form, the first features to engrave themselves on my mind have remained there, and such as have subsequently imprinted themselves have combined with these rather than obliterated them. There is a certain sequence of impressions and ideas which modify those that follow them, and it is necessary to know the original set before passing any judgements. I endeavour in all cases to explain the prime causes, in order to explain the interrelation of results. I should like in some way to make my soul transparent to the reader's eye, and for that purpose I am trying to present it from all points of view, to show it in all lights, and to contrive that none of its movements shall escape his notice, so that he may judge for himself of the principle which has produced them.

If I made myself responsible for the result and said to him, 'Such is my character', he might suppose, if not that I am deceiving him, at least that I am deceiving myself. By relating to him in simple detail all that has happened to me, all that I have done, all that I have felt, I cannot lead him into error, unless wilfully; and even if I wish to, I shall not easily succeed by this method. His task is to assemble these elements and to assess the being who is made up of them. The summing-up must be his, and if he comes to wrong conclusions, the fault will be of his own making. But, with this in view, it is not enough for my story to be truthful, it must be detailed as well. It is not for me to judge the relative importance of events; I must relate them all, and leave the selection up to him. That is the task to which I have devoted myself up to this point with all my courage, and I shall not relax in the sequel.[7]

Rousseau wants to be seen to be making a principled methodological decision, and so he outlines a developmental psychology according to the canons of empiricism. But the apparently principled decision hides a polemical intent.[8] He insists that if the reader, despite having so much evidence at his disposal, fails to understand the mature Rousseau's behaviour, then it can only be the reader's fault. Rousseau gives the reader so much rope to hang him with that the reader will be too embarrassed to do so. Rousseau also cleverly emphasises the parsimony of his philosophical method. This is to be psychology in the best tradition of British empiricism. He dismisses innatism. All psychopathology is caused by the environment, not by nature.⁹ By an elegant and no doubt intended irony, his method resembles the empirico-sensationism of Hume and the other *philosophes*: Rousseau admits of no psychological a priori by means of which he might be accused of smuggling his own prejudices into the story. He can claim to be as Humean as Hume himself.

The theoretical reflections are interesting in their own right, but do not say much about the psychological mechanisms by which his character is supposed to have been shaped. In practice, the narrative is fairly transparent. Youthful experiences are presented in terms of the simple causal mechanisms of Enlightenment psychology. Experiences create feelings of pain and pleasure. Our natural inclination is to minimise the former and maximise the latter. Our pain-minimising and pleasure-maximising actions constitute our behaviour and in due course solidify into character. New experiences affect us by interacting with our existing habits according to the principles of the association of ideas. Working within this parsimonious Enlightenment tradition, Rousseau explains how the books he read as a child (above all Plutarch) affected him by attractive example. This created his provocative republicanism and adoption of the label 'citizen', his victim-complex, his lack of tact and of any awareness of appropriate behaviour, his love of role-playing, and his masochism.¹⁰ At the same time as he was moulded into a defiant republican, he was also made into a sentimentalist, thanks to a positive experience that is made doubly attractive by its contrasting with a later negative one. As a young child he was loved and indulged by family and friends, especially his aunt Suson, with whom he claims to recall spending happy hours and from whom he gained his love of music. These idyllic beginnings contrast with the alienation and exclusion that he would experience later, and this no doubt helped to tinge their memory with sentiment and nostalgia for rural life. They also created in him an impulse diametrically opposed to his republicanism, namely a desperate desire to please. Rousseau tells us that Mlle Lambercier, sister of the parson at Bossey where he was sent for his education, mothered him, and he dreaded the thought of displeasing her. When Mlle Lambercier eventually beat him for the first time, the punishment seemed relatively mild compared to her disapproval. As in Geneva, so in Bossey the young Rousseau met with examples of love and authority that he found hard to tell apart. The result was a thoroughly confused attitude towards punishment:

Since Mlle Lambercier treated us with a mother's love, she had also a mother's authority, which she exercised sometimes by inflicting on us such chastisements as we had earned. For a long while she confined herself to threats, and the threat of a punishment entirely unknown to me frightened me sufficiently. But when in the end I was beaten I found the experience less dreadful in fact than in anticipation; and the very strange thing was that this punishment increased my affection for the inflicter.[11]

Still more bizarre was that the punishment gave him a sexual thrill, so much indeed that afterwards he found himself wanting to misbehave in order to attract another beating.

The early books of the *Confessions* are a masterpiece of the analysis of complex behaviour down to its causes. The simplicity of the method has a polemical purpose. The detail of the young Rousseau's experiences is related as if it were a mass of pure, unworked raw material, and the causal mechanisms that generate the end result remain simple. Rousseau wants to be seen to have reduced his philosophical commitments to a parsimonious minimum – a sound tactic in a philosophical culture that despised theories and systems. By passing muster with the empiricists, Rousseau's methodological parsimony lends credence to his claim to be fundamentally honest and innocent. In fact the structure of the *Confessions* is anything but simple. Rousseau uses a number of techniques to lend atmosphere and colour, chief among which are symmetry and alternation between dark and light episodes.[12] It is this which expresses the conflict within the young Rousseau. This keynote of his character is sounded within the first few pages of Book 1, in a memorable rhetorical flourish:

Such were the first affections of my dawning years; and thus there began to form in me, or to display itself for the first time, a heart at once proud and affectionate, and a character at once effeminate and inflexible, which by always wavering between weakness and courage, between self-indulgence and virtue, has throughout my life set me in conflict with myself, to such effect that abstinence and enjoyment, pleasure and prudence have alike eluded me.[13]

MORITZ

Moritz's life imitated Rousseau's in several respects, at first coincidentally, later consciously.[14] Both suffered from depression and 'hypochondria', which they traced back to similar life experiences. Like Rousseau, Moritz was exposed to Pietistic Christianity and edifying spiritual autobiographies. Both had to leave home for their education and lodge with strangers where they suffered unjust punishment that affected their attitude to authority. From a young age Moritz had to work in order to support himself. His social position was perhaps more marginal than Rousseau's, but he developed the same strong desire to be accepted in polite, cultured circles. The route to acceptance was education, to which both assigned a high value throughout their lives. Both were examples of a late-eighteenth-century type: the well-educated poor man with aspirations and a desire for recognition. They aimed for acceptance not just by cultured bourgeois society, but by the leading figures at the centre of Enlightenment culture. Under the pull of this aspiration, the story of the social ascent from humble beginnings to celebrity acquires the kind of dramatic contours that we see in Rousseau's *Confessions* and Moritz's *Anton Reiser.*

In *Anton Reiser*, Moritz gives a pitiful and starkly objective account of the atmosphere of his family home, in which he suggests that it was Pietism that made him chronically melancholic. It certainly provided him with an impulse to reflect on the condition of his soul. Pietism had developed a strong culture of self-observation documented in several Pietist autobiographies that Moritz encountered in his youth. Another distinctive aspect of Pietism was the emphasis it put on good deeds. This provided a link to the Enlightenment's ideal of educating the self and 'improving' society. Thus Moritz was following a Pietist tradition when he saw himself as a practical *Aufklärer* on a mission to shine the light of reason into the recesses of the mind.

Moritz's early career as a teacher took him into the orbit of Rousseau's pedagogical theories. At Basedow's Philanthropinum in Dessau he was exposed to the Rousseauian view that children should be allowed to develop freely in a natural environment, away from the harmful influence of civilisation. Moritz took against the dogmatism of the Dessau theorists, but in his *Unterhaltungen mit seinen Schülern* (*Conversations with his Pupils*, 1780) the influence of Rousseauian principles is still clear. This work is a collection of educational materials, including some fictive and morally improving conversations between teacher and students on matters such as natural religion. In these there is a pronounced similarity of tone and subject to the *Vicaire savoyard* of Rousseau's *Emile*.[15]

The other literary product of Moritz's time in Dessau was a diary, which formed the basis of the *Beiträge zur Philosophie des Lebens* (*Contributions to the Philosophy of Life*, 1780). The *Contributions* take their cue from the Pietist tradition of self-observation established in the autobiographies of Spener, Francke, and Zinzendorf, and continued by Haller and Lavater. The perspective is that of one observing his mental states as indicators of progress along the path of life. For the Pietists the path led towards spiritual oneness with God. In Moritz's *Contributions* the observational perspective and the trajectory of the path are those of Pietism, but the goal is the completely secular one of his own happiness and mental well-being.[16] This is why the *Contributions* are more personal than Pietist autobiography and at the same time more public. There is no question of the self being united with others in a common goal; the mind is its own world, not God's. But because the goal of Moritz's life-path is not a Pietist notion of God, Moritz's notion of happiness is not penned in by confessional boundaries. Nor was he the first German to secularise self-observation. By the middle of the eighteenth century there were the beginnings of a secular tradition, for instance in J. G. H. Feder's *Grundlehren zur Kenntnis des menschlichen Willens* (*Fundamental Doctrines in the Knowledge of the Human Will*).[17] Feder was a 'utilitarian eclectic' philosopher. The mainstream of Wolffian psychology, by contrast, did not recognise self-observation as a form of empirical psychology. Thus although there were beginnings, self-observation did not have a secure foothold in secular German thought before Moritz.

Some aspects of the *Contributions* foreshadow Moritz's later theory of empirical psychology, for instance their classical ethics. Their aim is to offer 'observations of oneself for the improvement of others' (*Beobachtungen über sich selbst zum Besten andrer Menschen*, *MW* iii.8). The method is distanced, dispassionate self-observation; it is necessary to shelter from the 'whirlwind' (*Wirbel*) of one's desires and attain disinterestedness, 'to play the cold observer for a while, without being in the least bit interested in oneself' (*um eine Zeitlang den kalten Beobachter zu spielen, ohne sich im mindesten für sich selber zu interessieren*, *MW* iii.9). The self-observer must think about himself 'cold-bloodedly' (*kaltblütig denken*, *MW* iii.14); the desired condition is 'coldness and serenity' (*Kälte und Heiterkeit*). So the correct observational stance contains its own therapeutic value: the mind that achieves cool self-observation is on the way to classical serenity. More specifically, the dispassionate stance is an Epicurean response to anxiety, designed to counter excessive hopes and fears.

Other aspects of the *Contributions* are typical of the psychology of the time. The work presents a conventional view of melancholy. The greatest enemies of a healthy mind are 'inertia' and 'inactivity' (*Trägheit, Unthätigkeit*, *MW* iii.15). We must keep our minds active. The mind is powered by a single source of activity or 'fundamental force' (*Grundkraft*).[18] It is likely that Moritz derived his idea from Tetens, who identifies the *Grundkraft* with our activity (*Tätigkeit*). For Moritz, the *Grundkraft* manifests itself in our mental life's constant ebb and flow between opposed emotions, such as pain and pleasure, hope and fear. This must be kept in regular motion (*MW* III.22–3). The specific contribution of self-observation is to identify and record the cognitive distortions that occur in melancholy and hypochondria. The *Contributions* already show signs of the acute psychological observation of his own melancholy that makes *Anton Reiser* remarkable. Moritz observes the pleasure he takes in his feelings of victimhood: 'There is great delight in the thought that one is suffering a wrong' (*Es liegt eine große Wonne in dem Gedanken, Unrecht zu leiden, MW* III.40). This is why our imagination nurtures ideas of victimhood that may have no basis in reality. In these situations we are enjoying our as yet unsatisfied desire for revenge (*unbefriedigtes Rachbegier, MW* III.71). We feel proprietorial towards our victimhood because vengeful emotions have distorted our thinking. Somewhat disappointingly this insight leads to a conventional eighteenth-century rationalist psychology, according to which cognition is always at risk from the emotions. By contrast, in his later, more fully worked-out psychological writings – the *Magazin zur Erfahrungsseelenkunde* (*Magazine for Empirical Psychology*) and *Anton Reiser* – Moritz treats the relation between emotion and cognition more organically. Emotion and cognition are implicated in one another: the emotions influence cognition, as Descartes and the Enlightenment had taught, but also distorted cognitions give rise to maladaptive emotions.

Moritz's plan for a broader study of psychology took shape between 1780 and 1782. In June 1782 he published an exploratory essay *Aussichten zu einer Experimental-Seelenlehre* (*Prospect for an Experimental Psychology*), in which he outlined his idea for the *Magazine*. He had already begun to collect materials for the journal when he was teaching at the Graues Kloster (*MW* III.97). If, as the new Rousseauian pedagogical theory maintained, education must be made to suit the child and not the child to suit the education, then a teacher ought to be able to read his pupils' characters well (*MW* III.87). Moritz had practised by writing character sketches of his pupils. The idea for the journal may have been prompted by his reading of Herder. Among other names he mentions as predecessors of the project is that of Rousseau, whose *Confessions* appeared in the same year (*MW* III.89).[19]

The *Prospect* essay is a trailer for the planned journal. Justifying his theoretical presuppositions, Moritz emphasises theoretical parsimony. The journal will collect data, not theorise on the nature of mind. In arguing this, he was not following Rousseau's *Confessions*, which he had not yet read, but tapping into a common Enlightenment vein of empiricist and anti-systematic thought. Specifically he seems to have drawn on British empiricism, mediated by Herder and the Berlin *Aufklärer*, and on the *Encyclopédie*. Rousseau is not a direct influence at this point, but Moritz's reference points are similar to Rousseau's.[20]

A theory of mind will only be available to us once a mass of data has been accumulated, in which human nature will be reflected: 'This would become a universal mirror in which the human race could view itself' (*Das würde alsdann ein allgemeiner Spiegel werden, worin das menschliche Geschlecht sich beschauen könnte, MW* III.90). In the meantime contributors must resist the temptation to add their own reflections to the reports they contribute to the magazine. At present, the system of morality on which we might ground such reflections is only provisional. Once the data are collected, a theory of mind will present itself to us automatically through the natural contours of the data:

The system of morality that we have can only ever be considered an approximate outline that means we don't have to work completely in the dark: but one must take this system as flexibly as possible, only fixing a few points down, and not attempting to draw lines from one point to another, but waiting until these lines practically draw themselves.[21]

One source of material will be accounts of childhood. (Here Moritz might have Rousseau in mind.) Objectivity is vital. Contributors must be 'cold observers' (*kalte Beobachter*) of themselves (*MW* III.92). At the same time they must pay 'attention to seemingly trivial detail' (*Aufmerksamkeit aufs Kleinscheinende*; *MW* III.93). In all of this, 'coldness and serenity of spirit' (*Kälte und Heiterkeit der Seele*) are needed (*MW* III.94).

In this way a fuller picture of how childhood experiences condition character will emerge. Mark Boulby has suggested that the psychological ideas in the *Prospect* essay derived from the Göttingen sensationist Michael Hißmann, one of the chief advocates in Germany of Hartley's view that all of our ideas are formed by association.[22] Moritz's views also have similarities with Lichtenberg's, which would further support a connection with Göttingen and Britain. Like Lichtenberg, he offers a radically empiricist account of ideas. All our ideas are only the expression of us as individuals. They reflect our personal experience. The negative corollary of this, which Moritz, unlike Lichtenberg, does not mention, is that there is no hope of convergence on a single set of ideas. Moritz could not travel as far along the road to scepticism as Lichtenberg. A positive corollary of this sensationism – which Moritz was keen to stress because it lent support to his project – is that a collection of such individuals' perspectives would combine to produce an encyclopedia of human thinking (*MW* III.87).

In the *Prospect* essay Moritz defines empirical psychology as an experimental science. He took the title *Experimental-Seelenlehre* from Johann Gottlob Krüger's book of the same name (1756). Krüger examined the relation of mind to body and had a settled view of how mind and body interacted, by a system of physical influence. Moses Mendelssohn, Moritz's mentor, advised Moritz to drop this title. An approach like Krüger's implied a closed scientific system and an agreed (and dangerously materialistic) view of mind–body relations. This would contradict the agnostic position Moritz had taken on the relation of data to theory. Moritz agreed. Later in 1782 he republished the essay under a subtly altered title, *Vorschlag zu einem Magazin der Erfahrungs Seelenkunde* (*Proposal for a Magazine of Empirical Psychology*). This emphasised the collecting of empirical data rather than the experimental testing of a materialist hypothesis. Mendelssohn further suggested that Moritz organise the *Magazine*'s contents under the four headings devised by Marcus Herz (*Gs* 1.i.3). These again implied a more pragmatic approach than Krüger's. Mental phenomena in general would come under the heading 'Study of the nature of the soul' (*Seelennaturkunde*). The treatment of abnormal mental states was termed 'Study of diseases of the soul' (*Seelenkrankheitskunde*). The study of the signs whereby mind communicated its contents, such as physiognomy, Moritz called 'Study of the signs of the soul' (*Seelenzeichenkunde*), and the study of how to promote good mental health and prevent mental illness was to be known as 'Dietetics of the soul' (*Seelendiätetik*, *Gs* 1.i.3). With its title from Mendelssohn and categories from Herz, the *Magazine* was certain to be approved by the inner circle of the Berlin Enlightenment.

'Gnōthi sauton'; or, 'Magazine for Empirical Psychology'

The *Magazine* was published by August Mylius in Berlin 'with the support of several friends of truth', as the title page has it. The first issue appeared in 1783, the last in 1793, each year's volume consisting of three parts of approximately 120 to 150 pages. Moritz was the sole editor of the first four volumes. In 1786, finding he had less time, he accepted an offer of help from Carl Friedrich Pockels, a contributor to the *Magazine* since 1784. Moritz and Pockels are named as joint editors of volumes V and VI, although for much of this time Moritz was in Italy and did not see the issues published in his name. During his absence

Pockels maintained the *Magazine*'s format but changed its tone. A hard-boiled rationalist, Pockels was less tolerant than Moritz of paranormal phenomena. Moritz took such reports at face value and looked for naturalistic explanations; Pockels preferred to dismiss them as misreported. On Moritz's return, the relationship with Pockels broke down. Pockels claimed ownership of the *Magazine*, arguing that without his intervention it would have collapsed. However, Moritz had the support of Mylius and was reinstated as the sole editor, whilst Pockels moved on to publish a rival serial, *Denkwürdigkeiten zur Bereicherung der Erfahrungsseelenlehre und Characterkunde. Ein Lesebuch für Gelehrte und Ungelehrte* (*Anecdotes for the Enrichment of Empirical Psychology and the Study of Character*, from 1794). After volume VIII Moritz again found himself short of time. For the next two volumes he enlisted the philosopher Salomon Maimon. As a Wolffian in the process of making the awkward transition to the new philosophy of Kant, Maimon was not fully in sympathy with Moritz's anti-theoretical editorial policy. In volumes IX and X Maimon's theoretical essays began to edge out the empirical data, and by volume X, to which Moritz did not contribute, the *Magazine* had fully embraced the distinction between the 'higher' and 'lower' cognitive faculties that characterised Wolffian and Kantian theories of mind. This was the last volume of the *Magazine*: it ceased publication in 1793, with Maimon claiming that it had fully served the purpose of collecting data for which it had been founded.[23]

Recent research has tended to reaffirm Moritz's empiricism. Bennholdt-Thomsen and Guzzoni have concluded that in comparison with the successor journals of Mauchart, Pockels, and Heynig, Moritz intellectualises and moralises very little.[24] Its empiricism was what made the *Magazine* worth imitating. Förstl, Howard, and Angermeyer have rediagnosed the cases reported in the *Magazine* using modern psychiatric definitions. Their conclusions confirm the *Magazine*'s value in two ways. Moritz's objective reporting of data makes rediagnosis simple. The data are easily transferable between different theoretical frameworks. Secondly, epidemiological analysis of Moritz's data proves consistent with the results of modern studies. The distribution of different psychoses in the population by age, gender, and social status is the same as we find today. For example, the patients in Moritz's cases of organic psychosis have a higher mean age than in those of functional psychoses; and a relatively low proportion (16 per cent) with 'schizophrenia' are married.[25]

The *Magazine* deserves to be considered properly empirical. However, even if material is presented neutrally, it still has to be organised. Moritz has a set of criteria that decide what gets into the *Magazine* and what does not, and these in turn imply a theory of mind. An analysis of the contents of the *Magazine* reveals twelve basic categories of material. These are: character sketches of young people from a teacher's point of view, sketches of adult character types in the tradition of Theophrastus, reports of unusual dreams, cases of hysteria, cases of paranoia and 'hypochondria', the effects of delirium on the imagination, the cognitive behaviour of deaf mutes, accounts of language use and language learning, criminality resulting from negative life-experiences, suicides, premonitions, and death-bed thoughts and attitudes to death. All of the reports in the *Magazine* can be assigned to one or more of these twelve categories.

In the first place the categories show Moritz's pragmatic concerns as an educationalist and theorist of language-teaching. Beyond this, he shares the preoccupations of psychology in late-eighteenth-century Germany. Moritz uses five models of psychological explanation. The first comes from the 'moral medicine' (*moralische Arzneikunst*) of writers such as Krüger, according to which abnormal states of mind give rise to medical conditions and vice versa. The second is the associationism that originated with Locke, Hartley, and Hume, and became popular in Germany in the 1770s. This can be used to explain the content of dreams and premonitions, and the cognitive distortions present in 'hypochondria'. Thirdly, Moritz uses the Leibniz–Wolffian notion of dark ideas, which can explain how intuitions arise that have no obvious relation to our conscious states. Fourth is the Rousseauian model of developmental psychology, according to which mind is a developing organism that only thrives in a healthy natural environment. This comes into its own in cases of criminality, where environmental factors can be seen to have prevented the healthy development of mind. Finally, Moritz preserves vestiges of the ancient theory of the four temperaments. This model lies behind some of Moritz's character sketches, which are based in part on modifications of types such as the phlegmatic or the choleric.

Despite his disavowal of theoretical reflection, Moritz could not withstand the temptation to give a commentary on the data. This appears in a series of reviews of the reports in volumes I to III. In addition volume I contains a theoretical preface, and volumes VII.3 and VIII.3 feature short essays on mysticism and self-delusion. In these Moritz develops a fully fledged psychological theory. In the introduction to volume I he claims that a healthy mind is one that is balanced between activity (*Tätigkeit*) and imagination (*Gs* 1.i.31–8). This is based on the idea that mind is a mixture, or *krasis*, to use the ancient Greek term, of qualities. A good mixture is one that has balance or harmony. (Moritz may have taken this from Shaftesbury or from Tetens's attempt to mediate between Locke and Leibniz.)[26] These qualities denote innate forces or tendencies; they describe how the mind acts in relation to the world. The world is given to us in simple material ideas. Before these appear in consciousness, they are formed into composites by association. The resulting ideas are, to all intents and purposes, fixed (*Gs* 1.i.36). If fixed in the wrong way or if somehow inaccurate, the *Seelenarzt* will need to alter them (*Gs* 1.i.37). The chief means by which he does this is strengthening our idea of cause and effect. By constantly rehearsing patterns of cause and effect, we gain power over other principles such as similarity and contiguity. This corrects the cognitive distortions that have persuaded us either that the world is not subject to us and what we do has no effect on it (as melancholics believe) or that the world has complete and malevolent power over us ('hypochondria'). The treatment restores a healthy relationship between self and world (*Gs* IV.i.4–5). It gives our innate activity a chance to reassert itself against the associative imagination.

Another example of the imagination running wild is mysticism, to which Moritz devotes more space in the *Magazine* than we might expect of a member of the Berlin Enlightenment (*Gs* VII.iii.75–6). Here his psychological theory connects with a broader cultural project. His treatment of mysticism, dreams, and premonitions contrasts strongly with the 'Revisions' (*Revisionen*) written by Pockels in volumes V to VI. Pockels takes a militantly rationalistic line. Premonitions that seem to give support to mysticism can only be the result of misreporting by stupid or malicious people. Moritz accepts the reporting of premonitions in good faith. He engages sympathetically with mysticism, not because he believes that its contents are true, but because he sees it as a natural product of innate human powers.

'Anton Reiser'; A Psychological Novel

Moritz began writing *Anton Reiser* as a case history for the *Magazine*. This accounts for the novel's not being *durchkomponiert*. It is a series of episodes, told in different styles and varying degrees of detail, and without much attempt to establish a continuous narrative thread or mood. Moritz's writing habits were chaotic, and he had to write *Anton Reiser* fast. His priority was to produce material for the *Magazine*'s four-monthly deadlines. The considerable quality of Moritz's writing lies not in structure, but in individual passages of great frankness, lucidity, and psychological insight.[27] Moritz did not write the novel according to a received model. It is not a direct descendant of the Pietist tradition of autobiography; that particular influence had already been played out and fully secularised in the *Contributions to the Philosophy of Life*. More immediate influences included Rousseau's *Confessions* and *Emile* (also important for *Andreas Hartknopf*, 1786, and *Fragmente aus dem Tagebuche eines Geistersehers* (*Fragments from the Diary of a Ghost-Seer*), 1787), Hartley's associationist psychology, and Goethe's *Werther*.[28]

The novel tells the story of Anton's growth into manhood. Its theme, advertised by the subtitle 'A Psychological Novel' (*Ein psychologischer Roman*), is his chronic and severe mental illness, as well as miserable poverty and repeated social humiliations. In eighteenth-century terms, Anton suffers from melancholy. The symptoms include inertia and lassitude, delusions, dissociation from reality, morbidity and suicidal moods, paranoia, anxiety, and aggressiveness. Some of these were associated with melancholy in the eighteenth century; others – delusions, paranoia, and aggressiveness – did not form part of its normal definition. All of them are now recognised in the diagnosis of severe clinical depression. At the same time, there is little of the positive side of melancholy that one expects to find in the eighteenth century. Anton does not indulge in thoughts of pleasing sadness or wistfulness, as Werther does. If, in Susan Sontag's words, 'depression is melancholy minus its charms', Anton suffers from depression.[29]

The narrative follows Anton's biography chronologically, focusing on his experiences and the factors that cause him to react as he does. There are indications that the narrator thinks of Anton as having a naturally melancholic character. But the narrative structure is predominantly causal; his melancholy is a consequence of his experiences. The causal explanations are the same as those of the *Magazine*. Four explanatory strategies stand out. First there is the environmental or behaviourist style of explanation that we saw in Rousseau's *Confessions*: the impressions Anton receives condition his cognitive behaviour and create his character. His family home provided the optimal conditions for producing a melancholic child. His parents' extreme religiosity, loveless marriage, lack of praise for Anton, their poverty, Anton's humiliating experiences at school: all of these combined to make him anxious for his well-being and prone to fits of deep gloom. Particularly damaging was the bad atmosphere created by his parents' frequent arguments:

In his earliest youth he never tasted the caresses of fond parents, was never rewarded after some small effort by a smile.

When he entered his parents' house, he entered a house of discontentment, anger, tears, and complaints. These first impressions have never been erased from his soul, and have often filled it with black thoughts that no philosophy could drive away.[30]

Anton's mother was prone to melancholy herself and nurtured a victim-complex, which she may have passed on to Anton. Both tended to see themselves as victims of injustice and actively to seek out punishment in order to confirm their self-image. The parallels with Rousseau are obvious, though probably not a result of any direct influence. Moritz's account reads more authentically than Rousseau's. In Anton victimhood is not dramatised; the fact that he enjoyed and sought out punishment is a bleak and sad fact:

Perhaps [his parents'] marriage might have gone better if Anton's mother had not had the unfortunate habit of feeling insulted, and *wanting* to feel insulted, even when no such thing was intended, in order to have grounds for feeling offended and downcast and feeling a certain self-pity which gave her a kind of pleasure.

Unfortunately, she seems to have passed on this affliction to her son, who still often struggles vainly against it.

Even as a child, when everyone got something, and his share was put in front of him without anyone saying it was his, he would sooner leave it untouched, even though he knew it was meant for him, simply in order to feel the sweet sense of suffering injustice and to be able to say: 'Everyone else has got something, and there's nothing for me!' Since he felt imaginary injustice so deeply, he could not but feel real injustice all the more deeply . . .

Anton could often spend hours pondering and weighing up reasons in the most meticulous way, about whether a chastisement received from his father was just or unjust.[31]

The stylistic flatness and twisted sentence structure add to the authenticity, where Rousseau's poised and polished rhetoric suggests the opposite.

The effect of this environment is to make Anton's imaginative side prevail over his active side. Hobbled by the conviction that he is one of life's victims, he cannot act to improve his situation. Instead he escapes into an imaginary world that is increasingly dissociated from reality. Just as Rousseau had created a world out of books, so Anton pieces together elements of novels and philosophical and religious tracts. His Pietist father disapproves of the worldliness of Anton's reading, so that added to the imaginary escape is the danger associated with 'forbidden reading' (*Verbotene Lektüre*). The pleasure of reading is combined with the prospect of the pain of punishment. Thus, in a further parallel with Rousseau, Anton's emotions come to oscillate between euphoric highs and dysphoric lows. He alternates between wanting to be loved by his parents, and fearing and loathing them for ruining his life (*MW* 1.41).

The second explanatory strategy is associationism. This accounts for how ideas are connected in the imagination and stored in the memory. The imagination does not compose ideas according to rational criteria. An experience will not necessarily be ordered in a chronological series or linked to other experiences whose meaning is the same. These are possible outcomes, but other equally likely ones include associating experiences on the basis of their similarity, even a trivial one, or because we rightly or wrongly perceive them to be causally linked, as is the case in several of the childhood experiences in Rousseau's *Confessions*. Because of the power of our associative imagination to link experiences in this way, it becomes an article of faith for late-eighteenth-century psychological writers that apparently insignificant aspects of our experience may not be so insignificant after all. Rousseau justified his approach in this way. The narrator of *Anton Reiser* reports Anton's experience of dependency on his benefactors in painful detail, and he feels the need to make the same apology:

This catalogue of Reiser's free meals and the persons who provided them is by no means so unimportant as it may seem at first glance: it is of such petty-seeming circumstances that life is made up, and these have the strongest influence on a person's disposition.[32]

In the *Prospect* essay Moritz had argued for the importance of detail. The *Magazine* carried out this programme, with a series of contributions on recollections of childhood. In *Anton Reiser*, the detail explains Anton's *idées fixes*, which are the product of our associative imagination and are responsible for the sometimes dangerous gap between imagination and reality. Goethe's Werther had an imagination so powerful that he was able to create the world anew. Anton is Werther's poor cousin; Moritz's novel is, like Goethe's, a story of the 'sufferings of imagination', but without the social status and charm.[33] Anton's imaginary world compensates for his unhappiness. This includes a private theology. The Pietism of Madame Guyon teaches Anton the importance of 'inner prayer'.[34] He learns from her to see the baby Jesus everywhere around him (*MW* 1.49–50). Taking this literally, as children do, he imagines Jesus as a small boy and himself pushing Jesus around with him in a wheelbarrow. Elements of the other books he reads combine with Guyon's ideas. The Bible, the *Acerra philologica* and Fénélon's *Télémaque* contribute ingredients. The result was, the narrator says, 'the strangest combination of ideas that perhaps ever existed in a human brain'.[35]

The narrator's third strategy is continually to remind the reader of the imagination's dark side. Moritz retains the Enlightenment's distinction between higher and lower cognitive functions. The imagination is a lower faculty; it creates a picture of the world that is prone to illusion and distortion. Anton imagines that he is the victim of unjust punishment, a martyr. This and his other core beliefs about himself correspond only partly to reality. In order to make them correspond better, he reinforces his feeling of martyrdom by punishing himself. In imitation of the early Christians, he harms himself deliberately: 'Sometimes . . . he actually began to prick himself with pins and torment himself in other ways, in order thus to become similar to the holy saints, since he had plenty of pain already.'[36]

To victimisation by society Anton adds the displeasure of his private God. When he fails to live up to the standards set by Madame Guyon, like the Pietist autobiographers before him he imagines that God is displeased with him (*MW* 1.53). This is a further expression of his positively enjoying 'the sweet sense of suffering injustice' (*MW* 1.55).[37] Used to seeing himself as a victim, he expects to be treated as one, and so at school he expects to fail, to be punished, and to be treated as a bad child:

. . . for a while a kind of depression and despair actually made him into a bad boy . . . The idea that his dearest wishes and hopes had gone awry, and that the career leading to fame that he had begun was now closed for ever, gnawed at him incessantly, without his always being distinctly conscious of it, and drove him to all manner of misbehaviour.[38]

When he suffers a setback, instead of understanding it as a challenge or as a piece of bad luck, he treats it as further confirmation of his victimhood. He finds no pleasure in the world outside his own imagination (*MW* 1.138). He avoids other people, who are, he believes, only trying to hurt him, and prefers his own company (*MW* 1.152). Eventually this sense of victimhood becomes so powerful that it robs him of his motivation, and he succumbs to a profound depressive 'paralysis of [the] soul' (*Seelenlähmung*).[39] His beliefs about the world centre on the ideas of emptiness and pointlessness. As his lower faculties cause cognitive distortions in his higher faculties, he develops a philosophy designed to confirm his feelings of pointlessness. But by actively reinforcing his depression, he becomes the main cause of his own unhappiness; he is his own tormentor. From this, as all those who suffer from severe depression will at some time come to believe, there is only one escape:

One evening he was walking sadly and gloomily along the street – it was already twilight, but not dark enough to prevent his being seen by some people, the sight of whom he found unbearable, because he thought he was an object of their mockery and contempt.–

The air was cold and damp, with a mixture of rain and snow falling – all his clothes were wet through – suddenly there arose in him the feeling *that he could not escape from* himself.–

And with this idea he felt as though a mountain were weighing on him – he tried to struggle free by force, but it was as though *the burden of his existence* were crushing him.–

That he had to *get up with himself, go to bed with himself,* every single day – he had to drag his detested self along at every step.–

His consciousness, with the feeling of being *contemptible* and *discarded*, was just as burdensome to him as his body with its feeling of wet and cold; and at that moment he would have taken off his body as willingly as his wet clothes – if a longed-for death had smiled at him from some corner.–[40]

It is not only a matter of the lower faculties creating cognitive distortions, as the Western Christian and Rationalist traditions have taught. That is only one side of the story. The narrator's fourth strategy is to show that cognitive distortions lead to maladaptive emotions. A disordered mind can disturb well-ordered passions. One instance of this is Anton's fear of death. He envisages death as the end of all sensation and consciousness. In itself that might not be so bad, but Reiser's problem is that he paradoxically imagines himself experiencing that loss of consciousness. The consequence is that when he hears of a death that corresponds to this idea of being locked in total blackness, it causes an attack of panic. The trigger is the news of an accident, in which a miner had fallen down a mine shaft and smashed his head open in the dark below:

Anton [thought] of a complete cessation of thinking and feeling, and a kind of annihilation and being deprived of oneself, that filled him with horror and terror whenever he imagined it vividly. From then on he also had an intense fear of death, which caused him many sad hours.[41]

This is an accurate description of morbid panic attacks. Subject to these cognitive distortions, Anton suffers bouts of depression triggered by experiences that appear to confirm his negative beliefs. His beliefs about the world help to disorder his emotional life: having a distorted image of the world makes him more depressed.

The novel thus presents two aspects of Anton's depression. It describes a depression caused both by negative thought patterns and by maladaptive emotions, which interact to form a vicious circle. By adopting both approaches – the Wolffian view that passions disorder the mind, and the late Enlightenment's view that cognitive distortions disturb our proper emotional functioning – Moritz creates a fully organic psychology. Indeed one might venture to say that *Anton Reiser* contains the first fully organic and accurately reported account of what current medicine calls severe clinical depression. The novel makes an ungainsayable case for considering Moritz a significant figure in the history of psychological theory.

'Fragments from the Diary of a Ghost-Seer'

It is strange to find that some writers on Moritz consider the *Magazine* to have been a failure.[42] Its ten-year run was quite long by the standards of new journals of the time. It spawned a number of imitators and is the root of the modern psychological case-study. It is true that Moritz's empiricist position came under attack, first from Pockels, and a second time from Maimon. But it is not true to say that the *Magazine* failed because Moritz's empiricism was in itself inadequate or because Moritz had no model of what made a healthy mind. The *Magazine* and *Anton Reiser* show one facet of Moritz's psychology. To find the other facet, his theory of what makes a mind healthy, we have to look to his *Fragments from the Diary of a Ghost-Seer* (1787).

During work on the *Magazine* and *Anton Reiser*, Moritz was developing a systematic philosophical outlook, which issued in his essay *Über die bildende Nachahmung des Schönen* (*On the Creative Imitation of the Beautiful*; 1788). Psychology fed into aesthetics. Like many upwardly mobile Germans in the late eighteenth century, Moritz saw the acquisition of a classical education as a way of bettering himself. The latter part of his short writing career was dominated by his efforts at devouring and processing this classical culture. The first signs of his classicism are in the *Fragments*. Written between 1782 and 1786, they purport to be the musings of a reclusive mystic, freemason, and 'soul doctor' (*Seelenarzt*), Sonnenberg. The book's purpose is not to carry its readers to any particular intellectual goal; it is to reveal the mind of a man. The thoughts ramble in no obvious direction, and are at certain points rather eccentric and 'hypochondriac' in their pursuit of hobby-horses. If there is a unifying theme, it is a psychological one. As a *Seelenarzt* Sonnenberg can reflect on his own pathologies, in a way that Reiser could not. The fiction of Sonnenberg's diaries serves to integrate Moritz's interests into a more or less systematic whole.

The psychology of the *Fragments* is familiar from the earlier *Contributions* and the introduction to the *Magazine*. Mind is a unitary object, powered by a single 'thought power' (*Denkkraft*). Its underlying characteristic is activity (*Tätigkeit, MW* III.276). Mental health consists in the proper balance between activity and sensitivity. But there is a new element in the psychology of the *Fragments*. In the introduction to the *Magazine* Moritz argued that activity is a cure for melancholy. In the *Fragments*, by contrast, activity represents a danger. The mind can become too active, too creative, and lose its hold on reality. Too much activity leads to 'hypochondria'. We forget that there is much that we cannot know; we begin to fill the gaps of our ignorance, to speculate on unanswerable questions, to 'expatiate in boundless futurity', as Johnson's *Rasselas* puts it.[43] The cure for this is resignation, which acts as a brake on the mind's activity. Through resignation we acknowledge that there are gaps we cannot fill and things we cannot control. Acknowledging our limitations makes us more realistic and more effective: 'Whoever directs their efforts at success with the greatest degree of resignation will surely have the greatest success', says Sonnenberg.[44] The idea of resignation probably derives from Rousseau's *Emile*, a book that Sonnenberg cherishes (*MW* III. 282). Rousseau argues that there is a natural, instinctive resignation that stops animals struggling pointlessly against obstacles or makes a sick body conserve its energy for fighting disease. In the process of civilisation humans have lost instinctive resignation and must now re-learn it. Though weaker than natural resignation, learned resignation is still vital for our mental and social well-being.[45] Sonnenberg sees it as a precondition of happiness. For a *Seelenarzt*, whose job is to show others how to be happy, it is essential:

A person who wishes to communicate happiness and contentment to others must first become completely happy and content himself.– But he can only become so by means of the moderation of his desires and a complete resignation.[46]

This idea comports well with the empiricist methodology of the *Magazine*. There Moritz advocated 'coldness and serenity' (*MW* III. 14). People who would heal their 'hypochondria' must become objective observers of their own inner life. Objectivity is part of the therapy. Resignation likewise implies a distanced and objective assessment of our goals and our capacity to reach them. It is as if, in order to achieve something, we must renounce any interest we might have in it.

The theory of resignation presumes that maladaptive emotions are connected to, and can be treated through, our cognitive behaviour. It also comports with the central idea of Moritz's aesthetics, disinterested pleasure.[47] Moritz draws a contrast between approaching art with desires and interests, and approaching it disinterestedly. The successful artist will not allow his work to be dominated by any interest he has in it. Art should please its consumers despite and not because of their interest in it. Anton Reiser is an example of an unsuccessful artist. He wants something from art; it satisfies a need in him. Another example is Goethe's Werther. Anton and Werther fail as artists because they never achieve mastery of an object; they treat art as a projection of their subjectivity.[48]

What defines Moritz's mature psychology is a contrast between two conditions: melancholic or 'hypochondriac' self-absorption and the healthy objectivity of the 'cold gaze'. The same contrast is present in his classicism. The ancients wisely acknowledged that humans have limitations, that selfhood is not all-encompassing. Apollo, patron of doctors, had the motto 'Know yourself' (*Gnōthi seauton*) carved on the gates of the Temple of Apollo at Delphi. Moritz used this as the title of his *Magazine* because, as well as containing a valuable medical truth, it embodies the classical ideal of objectivity. To know oneself is to know who and where one is. It is not an invitation to become self-absorbed. On the contrary, it is an injunction to be sober and realistic. At the same moment, independently of Moritz, Goethe was using the Delphic motto in a similar way. In the poem 'Dedication' (*Zueignung*, 1784) a vision of poetry appears and enjoins the poet to cast off his 'hypochondriac' self-absorption and recognise that he is a part of a larger whole: 'Know thyself: live with the world in peace' (*Erkenne dich, leb mit der Welt in Frieden!*, line 64).

SCHILLER

In Chapter 3 we saw the beginnings of Schiller's interest in psychology under the tutelage of J. F. Abel (see p. 62). *The Robbers*, written whilst Schiller was still at the Karlsschule, has some affinities with Moritz's empirical psychology. In a preface to the first edition Schiller describes the Moor brothers thus:

Here criminality is unmasked together with all its inner workings . . . I have tried
to sketch an accurate living portrait of a monstrous character of this kind [i.e.
Franz], to tease out the complete mechanics of his criminal mentality . . . Next to
him stands another [i.e. Karl], who might perhaps prove no less disconcerting to
my readers . . . A remarkable person, a person of substance, equipped with all the
power to become, according to the direction this takes, either a Brutus or a
Catiline. Unhappy circumstances decide in favour of the latter and only after
monstrous errors does he achieve the former.[49]

Karl's career as a robber is the result of bad luck. By setting the two
brothers next to one another and writing as if both belonged to a single
class, Schiller suggests a dangerous moral equivalence. Good and evil are
separated only by contingency. In this sense, *The Robbers* can be viewed as
a thought experiment in empirical psychology. A pair of twins is followed
from birth to death. Although the environment of their childhood was in
most respects the same, in some it differed. Old Moor did not treat Franz
and Karl equally. He praised Karl's qualities, said he was destined for
greatness (*NA* III.13–14), and allowed or encouraged him to act out
heroic episodes from Plutarch (*NA* III.87). Karl, Franz tells his father,
'was the apple of your eye'.[50] The servants loved Karl and preferred him
to Franz. Daniel used to let Karl ride his father's favourite horse (*NA*
III.97). Franz, meanwhile, was discouraged, criticised, and ridiculed as
'that everyday dullard, that cold wooden Franz, and all the other names
that the contrast between the two of us so often prompted'.[51] Karl finds
it easy to befriend and to trust others and inspires their loyalty. The fact
that he was loved as a child makes him confident that other people can be
trusted to respond sympathetically. Franz, who was not loved, finds
people untrustworthy and is prone to paranoia. All those who come into
contact with him either distrust or fear him. He was born ugly, but not
immoral. He has come to immorality through a process of learning,
which we can imagine as follows. He resents nature for giving him an
ugly face and so does not trust nature to have given him normal feelings.
From dismissing the possibility of natural feelings in himself, it is a short
step to dismissing their reality in others. Moral sense is therefore unnatural for Franz; he sees it as a cultural or social construct. In the powerful it
is an expression of their power; in the weak an expression of their
weakness.

That is not to say that Franz experiences no emotions. Schiller knows
that perverted rationality is not what makes villains. This emerges from a
comparison with Shakespeare's *Richard III*. The key idea that Schiller
borrowed from Shakespeare was that cunning and Machiavellian politics

were a response to social exclusion. However, Franz is not nearly as effective a politician as Richard. Richard charms Lady Anne Neville into his bed, having killed her husband, but Franz makes absolutely no headway with Amalie. When he resorts to force, she outwits him. His cunning must also compete with his own 'lower faculties' (*NA* III. 76). In Shakespeare's play, Richard is brought down by fate and his ambition. Franz, by contrast, is brought down by his suppressed feelings. In trying to usurp Karl's primacy, Franz suppresses his moral sense and acts instead according to what he thinks is his self-interest. Because he does not listen to his moral sense, he is not prepared for it when it speaks of his guilt. The violence of the final crisis is the result of his neglect of his feelings. His suicide is the revenge of his suppressed feelings on his reason.

'Intrigue and Love'

In *Über die ästhetische Erziehung* (*Letters on Aesthetic Education*) Schiller explores the 'antagonism of forces' in the psyche (*Antagonism der Kräfte, NA* xx.326).[52] In his plays the antagonism emerges in a battle between the higher and lower faculties that leads to instability and moments of crisis, in particular when suppressed feelings take revenge on hubristic reason.[53] In the early plays the moments of crisis are marked by violence; less so in the later, 'classical' plays. Schiller's study of Kant in the early 1790s did little to change his underlying concerns; rather it entrenched his belief in the tragic aspect of human duality. According to Wilkinson and Willoughby, Schiller believed that, by separating the will from the lower faculties, Kant ran 'the risk of fostering a will so aggressive that it either emasculates natural impulse or provokes from it a counter-aggression of the most primitive kind'.[54] This is similar to the revenge of feeling on reason in Franz Moor, and it is ideal subject matter for Schiller's preferred form of revenge drama, in which the intrigues of a hubristic political rationality are avenged by moral feeling.

Opposed to the 'antagonism of forces' is an ideal of the harmonious mind, which Schiller represents symbolically, taking Leisewitz's *Julius of Tarento* as his model. Leisewitz's play repeatedly alludes to arguments for the harmony of mind and body, probably inspired by Moses Mendelssohn's reworking in *Phädon* (1767) of the *harmonia* argument from Plato's *Phaedo*.[55] This holds that the relation of a lyre to the harmonious sounds it makes is analogous to the relation of mind to body. (Schiller had discussed the idea in his medical thesis.)[56] In Leisewitz's play this forms the backdrop to a tragic split between sentiment and political rationality represented by Julius and Guido, which destroys the harmony of the state. Schiller uses the idea of shattered harmony at a crucial moment in *Intrigue and Love*. In Act III, Scene iv, Luise announces to Ferdinand that she must renounce him. He reacts violently: '*Ferdinand, in his distraction and fury, has seized a violin and tried to play on it.– Now he rips the strings apart, smashes the instrument on the floor, and bursts forth in loud laughter.*'[57] Ferdinand's smashing the violin can be seen as a transferred act of violence against Miller himself. It also symbolises the destruction of universal and psychic harmony, as is clear from the context, for Ferdinand smashes the violin in response to Luise's claim moments earlier that their liaison, should it continue, would 'rend asunder the seams of the bourgeois world and bring the universal and everlasting order down in ruins'.[58] The violin represents that 'universal eternal order' that Luise claims will be destroyed by being literally smashed on the ground.

Although he is not fully conscious of it, Ferdinand is also enacting the crisis in his own mind. Ferdinand's jealousy is violent and vengeful. As we saw in Chapter 3, he attacks what he sees as Luise's lack of feeling by contrasting the sentimental high ground of his 'fiery love' with the 'cold duty' of her scruples (see p. 67), but the accusation has an unintended meaning that damns him instead, for elsewhere in the play fire is associated with the courtly life that Ferdinand affects to disdain. Until now Ferdinand has been guided by the rationality of revolt against the court and has acted the role of a man of feeling. The collapse of this scheme exposes a split in his personality, which the smashing of the violin represents. At first he is silently angry and tries to divert himself by picking up the violin. As he cannot get a tune from it, he tears the strings (that part of the instrument tuned to produce harmony) and then smashes it on the ground. Finally he breaks into a fit of scornful, misanthropic laughter that echoes his father's 'biting laughter' (*beißendes Lachen*) at Luise's expense in Act II (*NA* v.42). The crisis is a sudden explosion of emotions that is so out of proportion because it is itself a form of revenge: a revenge of the emotions against reason. The episode as a whole is a psychologised version of tragic *nemesis*, in which revenge expresses itself through the 'lower faculties'.

Although Schiller sees the antagonism of feeling and reason as a feature of the psyche's constitution, he also believes in the possibility of their being brought back into harmony. In this respect Schiller's early philosophy belongs to the same tradition as Wieland's and Shaftesbury's. Schiller's, though, has a strongly medical flavour. He sees violent psychic crises as part of the natural, self-regulating economy of the body. In the

Philosophische Briefe (*Philosophical Letters*) he has Julius claim that 'Scepticism and free-thinking are the paroxysms of fever in the human mind and must, precisely by virtue of the unnatural shock they cause in well-organised souls, ultimately help to secure good health.'[59] Crisis is a stage on the way to cure. In the *Philosophical Letters* Julius uses scepticism to bring about a curative crisis. In the tragic dramas *The Robbers* and *Intrigue and Love*, by contrast, political rationality causes a crisis that leads to death.

'Don Karlos' and the prose writings of the 1780s

Schiller's relationship with Moritz began badly and never fully recovered.[60] In 1784 Moritz published a highly critical review of *Intrigue and Love*, in which he found fault with the psychology of Schiller's plays. In a second review, he argued that Schiller had not explained how Franz Moor came to be such a monster or how Ferdinand von Walter was capable of such a violent fit of jealousy. Coming from the psychologist Moritz the criticisms carried weight. Schiller and Moritz met the following year in Leipzig, in an attempt by the publisher Göschen to engineer a rapprochement between two of Germany's most promising writers. Although they appear to have parted on good terms, Schiller never warmed to Moritz. When Moritz visited Weimar in the winter of 1788–9, on his way back from Italy, Schiller repaid him for the reviews of *Intrigue and Love* by criticising Moritz's *Magazine*. The mass of case-histories was depressing. It needed a broader outlook and a more positive message; Moritz should end each volume by drawing out the lessons of the cases and showing that human nature was not so fragile after all. In his turn Moritz pointed out some similarities between Schiller's story *Der Verbrecher aus verlorener Ehre* (*A Criminal through Lost Honour*) and *Anton Reiser*. Schiller's criminal Wolf fails to win approval in society and so seeks it outside society by turning to crime. Anton's drift to the margins is also a response to rejection. The categories that society uses to classify us cast us in roles that we have to live up to if we are to win approval. Wolf becomes a criminal because he is called a criminal (*NA* xvi. 10–11).

This was a perceptive point, though Moritz was wrong if he meant to imply that Schiller had borrowed his ideas. It was more a case of convergent development. Schiller's interest in empirical psychology continued in the mid 1780s. Early in 1783 he began work on *Don Karlos*, at first conceiving of Karlos as 'a fiery, noble, and sensitive youth'.[61] Soon Karlos became darker and more pathological. A plan of 1785 refers to

Karlos's 'unusual melancholy'.[62] A version of Act I was published that year with a stage direction that uses gesture and scenery to create a picture of melancholy:

KARLOS *comes slowly and lost in thought out of a dark grove, his racked figure betrays the struggle in his soul; on occasions he cautiously stands still as if listening out for something . . . Sadness and anger alternate in his gestures, he runs violently back and forth and finally collapses exhausted on a bench.*[63]

The priest Domingo complains that attempts to dispel this mysterious sorrow (*räzelhafter Gram,* line 21) have failed. Karlos alludes several times to a secret, in hysterical images, and Domingo concludes: 'You torment your heart with empty / Groundless fantasies' (*Sie peinigen Ihr Herz mit leeren / grundlosen Phantasien,* lines 283–4). Karlos thinks they are anything but groundless: he is convinced that he is being watched and conspired against (lines 284–97).

For the first complete edition of the play, published in 1787, Schiller removed the pictorial stage direction, preferring to enact Karlos's melancholy in words. Its first cause was a lack of parental affection. His mother had died in childbirth, and his father seemed not to love him:

> CARLOS (*reflects and passes his hand over his forehead*):
> O noble sir – I have such awful luck
> With mothers. What I did as my first act
> Upon my entrance in this world – was kill
> My mother. . .
> And my new mother – what has she done for me
> But rob me quickly of my father's love?
> My father scarcely loved me save for this:
> The merit due me as his only child.
> Now she gives him a daughter – Oh, who knows
> What slumbers hidden in the mist of time?[64]

The lack of a father's love makes matters worse. (This was the sort of strong psychological motivation that Moritz had missed in the earlier plays: a lack of parental affection was one of the explanations for Anton Reiser's melancholy.)[65] Karlos feels resentful towards his father for treating Karlos as his heir, not his son: 'But I don't know what father means – I am / The son of a king' (*Ich weiß ja nicht, was Vater heißt – ich bin / Ein Königssohn,* lines 220–1). The personal symbolises the political. Karlos's psychological problems come to stand symbolically for the condition of a tyrannically ruled people: a failure as his son's father, Philipp is hardly likely to be a good father to his people.

Karlos cannot reveal more than this to Domingo. Only when the Marquis of Posa gives him an opportunity to unbutton, do we hear the full, grim story. Unloved by his father and having lost his birth-mother, Karlos had thrown himself at Posa and put Posa in his debt, as he now reminds him:

> CARLOS: So deep
> Is my descent – and I am sunk so low –
> I must remind you of our early years,
> And in the name of childhood days I must
> Entreat you to repay debts long forgotten,
> Debts that were made when we wore sailor suits –
> When you and I were just unruly boys,
> Grown up together in such fellowship
> That nothing bothered me except to see
> Myself eclipsed by what you were – and so
> I then resolved to love you without measure,
> Because I lacked the strength to be like you.
> So I began to pester you with ev'ry
> Variety of tender brother-love.
> Your proud heart gave me cold return for this.
> How often I stood there – you never saw –
> And hot and heavy teardrops hung upon
> My lashes when you would skip over me
> And clasp far lesser children in your arms.
> Oh, why just them? I would cry out in pain:
> Am I not good to you with all my heart?
> But you, you knelt down there so cold before me.
> That was, you said, quite proper for a king's son. . .
> I never did deserve such treatment from you.
> You could disdain, despise the love I proffered
> But never drive me off.[66]

This is an inventory of melancholic symptoms: he has a low opinion of himself; he sees other people in highly moralised, black-and-white terms; he pities himself; he feels deep sadness; he perceives slights to his character where none are meant; he is angry and resentful. In order to win Posa's love, he does exactly what we might expect a melancholic with a victim-complex to do: he tries to put Posa in his debt by volunteering to take a punishment that was meant for Posa. Posa had hit the Queen of Bohemia in the eye with a shuttlecock, and Philipp had promised the culprit punishment for the offense 'and even if it were / Done by his son himself'.[67] Karlos picks up the cue, admits to the crime, and takes the punishment – a physical beating and public humiliation. In doing so

Karlos is also enacting before the eyes of Posa and the court the loveless relationship he thinks he has with his father. Posa is not only in Karlos's debt; he must also pity him.

Karlos now reveals his secret love for the Queen. Posa is shocked, but not shocked enough for Karlos, who demands that Posa agree 'that on the circle of this earth / No misery exists that's close to mine'.[68] Karlos invites Posa to punish him. The cognitive distortions are again typical of melancholy: exaggeration, mind-reading ('do not think you can spare me: I know what you're really thinking'), and the pathetic inflation of his love into a world-threatening catastrophe:

> World custom,
> All nature's order, and the law of Rome
> Condemn this passion. My pretension strikes
> Most frightfully against my father's rights.
> I know that – but no matter, I still love.
> This leads to madness or to execution.
> I love without all hope and sinfully –
> In mortal terror and in fear of death –
> I see that – oh, no matter, I still love.[69]

Imagining the consequences of a sin he has not yet committed and inflating his love for his stepmother to true incest between blood-relatives, Karlos is hardly encouraging Posa to help him. Yet now he asks Posa to arrange for a few minutes alone with the Queen. Posa's hesitant reply elicits another melodramatic outburst:

> MARQUIS: And what about your father?
> CARLOS: Unhappy man! Why must you mention him?
>   Tell me about the terrors of my conscience,
>   About my father do not talk to me.
> MARQUIS: Then do you hate your father?
> CARLOS: No! Oh, no!
>   I do not hate my father – but such fear
>   And sinner's apprehension seizes me
>   At the mere mention of this fearful name.
>   How can I help it that love's tender seeds
>   Were crushed by servile care and training when
>   My heart was still so young. I was already
>   A six-year old before I gazed upon
>   That awful man, the one who, so they told
>   Me, was my father. Early on a morning
>   When he had just subscribed four sentences
>   Of death it happened. After that I saw

Him only when a punishment was to
Be given me for an offense. My God!
I feel I am becoming bitter –[70]

That Karlos can recognise his own bitterness is progress. He seems to have a fairly clear, though still overwrought idea of what went wrong with his childhood. But there is not complete clarity even here. The image of a terrifying, bloodthirsty father is part of Karlos's problem. (Posa will reach a more balanced view of the King.) By dwelling on his childhood, Karlos has given free rein to his natural inclination to brood:

Like furies from the pit there follow me
Most awful dreams. My better self despairs,
And struggles with a host of monstrous plans;
Through labyrinthine subtleties my mind
In its most wretched contemplation moves
Until, when at the very edge of the
Declivity, it stops.[71]

Overly 'subtle' thinking is another symptom of melancholy: a tendency to dwell on and devote irrationally large amounts of mental energy to sceptically dissecting and hypothesising about events.

Alongside *Don Karlos* during the mid 1780s Schiller was producing work aimed at a broader reading public. In the story *A Criminal through Lost Honour* Schiller followed the fashion for psychological case-histories à la Moritz. The story was probably written in 1785, but the material on which it was based went back to Schiller's time at the Karlsschule. Similarities with *The Robbers* suggest that Schiller already knew the story in 1780. He may have learned of it from Abel, as the bandit Schwan, the model for Schiller's Wolf, had been arrested by Abel's father. Two years later Abel himself published a version of the story in the second volume of his Moritz-inspired *Collection and Explication of Remarkable Phenomena from Human Life.*[72]

It is the story of the bandit Wolf's 'silenced conscience' (*verstummtes Gewissen*; *NA* XVI.23), which is drowned out by louder and more urgent voices. In an apologetic preamble Schiller argues that although we might think ourselves different from Wolf, this difference would seem smaller, were we able to see what went on in Wolf's mind and catch his thoughts in the quieter moments before he acts, when he is as 'cold' as the reader. What if we could trace these thoughts back to their sources in 'the constitution and disposition of things surrounding such a person up to the point at which the accumulated kindling catches fire in his inner being'?[73] The job of the story-teller is to show how actions are the products of 'the *changeless* structure of the human soul' acted on by 'the *changeable* conditions that determined it from without'.[74] The narrator thus becomes an empirical psychologist, and the reader is forced to recognise that the criminality of a Wolf is not so far removed from his own life, so that 'it no longer surprises [the reader] that in the very same bed where otherwise health-giving herbs grow the poisonous hemlock also flourishes'.[75] These introductory deliberations, reminiscent of the prefaces to the first edition of *The Robbers*, aim to turn the qualitative difference between the reader and Wolf into an empirically quantitative one and to undermine the reader's feeling that he is superior to Wolf.

The most significant feature of Wolf's upbringing was that he lost his father early in his childhood (*NA* xvi.10). This meant that a large burden fell on his shoulders. Like Franz Moor, Wolf was also physically ugly:

Nature had neglected his body. A small, unremarkable figure, curly hair of a disagreeable black, a flat nose and swollen upper lip, which was in addition deformed by a blow from a horse, gave him a revolting appearance that scared all women away from him and provided the wit of his friends with rich material.[76]

In order to wrest the affections of a girl from a better-looking competitor Wolf resorts to poaching (*NA* xvi.10–11). (This recalls the constellation Franz-Amalie-Karl.) After a series of spells in gaol, Wolf happens upon the gamekeeper in the forest, whom he murders, so finally breaking his links with society. Cast adrift, he chances on a band of robbers and is offered its leadership by popular acclamation. Intoxicated by his apparent popularity (and wine) Wolf accepts. His first rosy impressions of the band's brotherliness and honour are soon disappointed (*NA* xvi.23). The price on his head makes his relationship with the band uneasy. He decides to reform, but his attempts to re-enter society are frustrated, and finally he is arrested on his way to enrol in the Prussian army.

As well as the similarity to *Anton Reiser* which Moritz observed, Schiller's general aim is similar to Moritz's. Schiller was already familiar with the empiricist tradition of psychology, but by 1785 Moritz's *Magazine* was becoming well-known and influential. Forensic psychology was one of the categories of case Moritz published. He believed that psychological analysis would aid in the objective judging of criminals. In this respect Schiller's aims are in harmony with Moritz's. The same goes for his method. Schiller has the same idea of narratorial 'coldness' as Moritz and refers to psychology in the story's preamble (*Seelenkunde*, *NA* xvi.9).

He assumes that this is the sort of story that is suitable for psychological study and that his readers will see it in this way. Empirical psychology has evidently become part of the cultural landscape.

The other significant narrative that Schiller wrote while working on *Don Karlos* was the novel *Der Geisterseher* (*The Ghost-Seer*), begun in 1786. The literary model for the novel was the sub-genre of the 'novel of enthusiasm' (*Schwärmerroman*), which treated religious enthusiasm from a rational perspective.[77] In Wieland's *Don Sylvio von Rosalva* (*Don Sylvio of Rosalva*), for instance, the enthusiast hero is gradually guided away from his belief in the supernatural towards common sense. The main psychological interest of Schiller's novel is its treatment of religious melancholy (*NA* xvi.103). The novel's hero, the Prince, undergoes a process of education that aims to correct his religious melancholy by exposing it to scepticism, but the educator turns out to be a malign influence. The novel seems to advocate the central ground of a rational theology, between two dangerous extremes. One is a form of religious belief in which God is a terrifying tyrant and any lapse from strict observance brings terrible consequences. (The Großinquisitor who scares the humanity out of Philipp at the end of *Don Karlos* also represents this position.) The other extreme is scepticism and atheism. Both of these can cause religious melancholy, and both can be found in the same person. The religious melancholic moves in a pendular fashion between scepticism and rigorism. This was the fate of Franz Moor. Schiller had encountered pendular religious melancholy in Grammont, his fellow student at the Karlsschule.

As with Franz Moor and Grammont, so too in *The Ghost-Seer* the experience of scepticism leads to a crisis. Falling increasingly under the spell of the shadowy Armenian, the Prince becomes a sceptic concerned only with power – another Franz Moor.[78] In his early life the Prince had been a 'religious enthusiast' (*religiöser Schwärmer*, *NA* xvi.46). Brought up in an oppressive religious atmosphere, he had developed an intense fear of God:

A dogmatic and servile upbringing . . . had impressed terrifying images into his tender brain, from which he was never able fully to free himself his whole life long. Religious melancholy was a hereditary disease in his family; the education given to him and his brothers was appropriate to this disposition; the people to whom he was entrusted were chosen from this point of view, that is to say they were either enthusiasts or hypocrites . . . Our prince's entire youth had this same black nocturnal form . . . All of his ideas of religion had something fearful about them, and it was precisely terrifying and rough impressions that would first take hold of his imagination and stick in it the longest. His God was a vision of terror, a punitive being; his worship was a servile trembling or a blind devotion that stifled any strength and courage. All his childish and youthful inclinations, to which a tough body and blooming health gave all the more powerful force, were obstructed by religion; it was in conflict with everything that his youthful heart adored; he knew it never as a boon, only as a scourge of his desires. And so there gradually took fire in his heart a silent resentment against it, which made the most bizarre mixture with the respectful faith and blind fear in his head – an aversion to a Lord before whom he felt repugnance and respect in equal measure.[79]

Brought into the orbit of the Bucentauro, a secret society of free-thinkers, he now turns into a radical sceptic. The consequence is moral degeneration, and this prepares him in turn for the sensuous lure of Catholicism. In this way the Prince returns to the fearful religiosity of his youth (*NA* XVI.104). If the malign influence of the Armenian is the catalyst for the Prince's descent, what makes the descent so rapid is his own unbalanced character. Like Karlos, the Prince has been brought up to be a melancholic, and he shows the same cognitive distortions as Karlos – a tendency to exaggerate, a susceptibility to the easy, all-embracing answers that faith and cynicism provide.

Schiller's response to Moritz's 'On the Creative Imitation of the Beautiful'

It is already apparent in *Don Karlos* that the highly visual and energetic style of the early dramas is giving way to a more classical, objective style. There would be no more instructing actors to waft perfume over the stalls or smash their heads against trees. Objectivity also meant liberating poetry from the tyranny of mood. Poetry can represent mood, but should not be dominated by it. Moritz's *On the Creative Imitation of the Beautiful* (1788) was perhaps the most significant external influence on the development of Schiller's classical aesthetics. Moritz provided Schiller with a compelling statement of the autonomy of the aesthetic realm. In 1791 this was supported by the weightier authority of Kant's *Critique of Judgement*. After this Kant's influence occluded Moritz's, although in a course of lectures on aesthetics that he gave in the winter of 1792/3 Moritz still loomed large. Moritz contributed something to Schiller's aesthetics that Kant could not: this was the idea that achieving objectivity in art involved overcoming psychopathologies.

Moritz's criticisms of *Intrigue and Love* reflected his own movement towards classicism. In the same year his essay 'Versuch einer Vereinigung aller schönen Künste und Wissenschaften unter dem Begriff des in sich Vollendeten' ('Attempt at a unification of all the creative arts and sciences in the concept of the totality') appeared in the *Berlinische Monatsschrift*.[80] Moritz argued that the work of art should be 'complete in itself' (*ein in sich Vollkommenes*). It should not depend for its effects on any other interest the artist or his audience might have. This was Moritz's first step towards *On the Creative Imitation of the Beautiful*, in which he developed his idea of the autonomy of art more fully. When Moritz visited Weimar in the winter of 1788/9, he brought with him a copy of the new essay, which he had drafted in Rome with Goethe's help. Goethe promoted it with a selection of extracts in Wieland's *German Mercury* (*Teutscher Merkur*), although Goethe's support probably made Schiller suspicious of the visitor. Moritz acknowledged that his study of aesthetics had improved his mental condition. Schiller wrote approvingly of this to his future sister-in-law Caroline von Beulwitz: 'His philosophical studies have had a happy effect on his mind and rescued him from a terrible spiritual condition, as he himself admits. His mind has won a victory over his hypochondria through strenuous thinking.'[81] The following month he wrote to Caroline and Charlotte that Moritz's essay possessed for him 'absolute truth' (*absolute Wahrheit*; *NA* xxv.203). Weimar (Goethe excepted) was less enthusiastic. Herder and Knebel disliked Moritz and criticised his essay for its 'cold' classicism. Schiller rode to Moritz's defence against Knebel. Whilst he found Moritz's apparently slavish imitation of Goethe distasteful, Moritz was at least copying a good model and, as Schiller wrote to Caroline using a phrase straight from *On the Creative Imitation of the Beautiful*, 'imitation is a lower form of perfection'.[82]

Schiller's review of Gottfried Bürger's poems, written in 1790/1, contains the first fruits of his reading of *On the Creative Imitation of the Beautiful* and, *in nuce*, the key ideas of his classical aesthetics. He begins by sketching poetry's capacity to harmonise human faculties, which at present are fragmented:

With the isolation and separate working of our mental powers that the extended sphere of knowledge and separation of the professions make necessary, only poetry is able to bring into harmony once more the separated powers of the soul – head and heart, intelligence and wit, reason and imagination – and once again to restore the wholeness of a human being in us.[83]

Bürger expresses emotions subjectively and does not give them the objectivity that is needed if they are to provide suitable nourishment for our reason and so unite all our faculties:

Most of all one misses the art of idealising in Herr B[ürger], when he represents feeling . . . For [his poems] are not merely representations of this particular (and very unpoetic) spiritual condition; rather they are obviously the *offspring* of the same. The sensibility, reluctance, melancholy of the poet are not merely the *object* that he sings of, they are unfortunately the *Apollo* that inspires him. . . a poet should beware writing whilst in the midst of pain. . . He may create from the gentle and distant memory of. . . but never from immediate domination by the feeling that he wants to create a beautiful sensuous representation of. . . Ideal beauty is categorically only possible with freedom of spirit, with autonomy, which negates the dominance of passion.[84]

Schiller employs two arguments. The first is that melancholy is not an appropriate subject for poetry, because on its own it cannot provide sufficient interest for all of its reader's faculties. In particular it does not address our faculty of reason, and that is a grave deficit, for reason wants to be active, not melancholically passive. (This relates to the idea that the underlying force of mind consists in activity, an idea which Moritz uses in *On the Creative Imitation of the Beautiful.*) The second is that a poetic representation of a mood, and a poem created under the same mood, are two quite different things. Whilst the former might in some circumstances count as beautiful – bearing in mind the strictures against melancholy as a subject for poetry that we have just noted – the latter cannot count as beautiful under any circumstances. The melancholy poet is ill-equipped to create beautiful representations of melancholy. What he will produce will be a product of melancholy instead of a representation of it.

The first criticism of Bürger is similar to the point Schiller made about Moritz's *Magazine*. When a poem expresses strong and disturbing emotions, its reader will be in need of a countervailing mood of serenity. The individual psychopathologies need to be framed by a general anthropology, as it were. It is the latter point that dominates Schiller's argument. The poet must be able to distance himself from the emotions he is writing about:

Only the serene and peaceful soul can give birth to a totality. The struggle with external conditions and hypochondria, which utterly paralyse every mental faculty, are the last things that should be allowed to burden the mind of a poet who is going to disentangle himself from the present and soar freely and boldly up into the world of ideals. No matter how fiercely the storm rages in his bosom, his brow should be wreathed in clear daylight.[85]

Whether or not this is fair on Bürger, it is a significant development for Schiller. The melancholic heroes of his dramas would now be set within a larger framework. Sentiment would no longer be the yardstick against which characters were measured. The classical Schiller would continue to make melancholy a central feature of his work, but as a psychopathology that needs to be described, diagnosed, and cured. Schiller's aesthetics, like Moritz's, represent an attempt to cure melancholy by means of a kind of cognitive therapy. The aesthetics of Weimar Classicism aims to show that there is a way out from beneath the dark cloud.

'Wallenstein'

One of *Wallenstein*'s ironies is that whereas its hero believes himself to be one of 'Jupiter's fair children, born in light', his behaviour is that of a saturnine melancholic.[86] When Illo accuses him of temporising and of justifying this with astrology, Wallenstein angrily brands Illo as saturnine:

> You know no better than you speak. How often
> Have I explained it to you! Jupiter,
> Bright-shining god, was set when you were born;
> These secrets are beyond your understanding.
> In earth to burrow is your place, blind like
> That subterranean god who lit your way
> Into this life with grey and leaden beams.
> Common and earthly things you may perceive,
> May shrewdly see the links that lie at hand;
> In this I trust you and believe your words.
> But what in mystery is woven, what
> Great secrets grown and shaped in Nature's depths –
> The spirit ladder, from this world of dust
> Ascending by a thousand rungs to reach
> The stars, and trod by countless heavenly powers
> Pursuing up and down their busy ways –
> The circles within circles, that draw close
> And closer yet upon the focal sun –
> These things the unclouded eye alone can see
> Of Jupiter's fair children, born in light.[87]

Wallenstein's behaviour tells another story: *he* is the brooding, dark, pessimistic one who 'burrows' in the Earth and 'shrewdly see[s] the links that lie at hand'. In this fantastical speech alone he shows enough cognitive distortions to be classified as a melancholic: he expresses his anger through the idea that important rules have been broken, implies that he can read Illo's mind, and thinks in black-and-white terms.

Melancholy was a common feature of accounts of Wallenstein before Schiller, and it was central to Schiller's conception of the character from the earliest phase of his work on the play. The astrological material, on the other hand, was a late addition, designed to reinforce and make more explicit the underlying strain of melancholy. A further distinctive touch came from empirical psychology. Wallenstein's life-experiences are brought into play as explanations for his melancholy. One of these is the miraculous fall recounted by Gordon and Buttler. Even before this event Wallenstein was distinguished from his peers by his solitariness and brooding:

> GORDON: It must be thirty years ago. Already
>   The youth of twenty strove with fearless courage,
>   Grave was his spirit, far beyond his years,
>   Bent only upon greatness, like a man's.
>   With silent mind he moved amongst our number,
>   His own society; the childish pleasures
>   Of other boys could hold no joy for him;
>   But often he would suddenly be seized,
>   And wondrous, from the secrets of his breast,
>   A ray of thought would beam, a shaft of wisdom,
>   And we would gaze upon each other wondering
>   If madness, or a god had spoken from him.[88]

Earnest, silent, secretive, and then suddenly brilliant – Wallenstein is a melancholic genius in the tradition of the pseudo-Aristotelian *Problem* XXX. The fall from a second-storey window accentuates his melancholy by giving him a sense of his own uniqueness:

> BUTTLER: Yes, that was where he fell two storeys' height,
>   When in a window bay he fell asleep,
>   And picked himself up quite unharmed again.
>   And from that day they say there could be seen
>   The signs of madness in his mind and bearing.
> GORDON: More grave and pensive he became, indeed,
>   And turned a catholic. His wondrous rescue
>   Worked wondrous change in him. He felt that now
>   He bore a favour and a charm of freedom,
>   And bold as one who knows he cannot stumble
>   He danced upon the swaying rope of life.[89]

A superstitious sense of mission motivated his conversion to Catholicism and sent him climbing to the heights from which he now threatens to fall, a textbook Aristotelian tragic hero. This is the source of the most significant distortion in his cognitive behaviour. He failed to recognise his fall for what it was – a bizarre accident. So he repeated the ascent, thinking that he was immune from the fall that typically accompanies hubris. This is why the story of the *Fenstersturz* echoes his wife's account of his fall from imperial favour at Regensburg in Act III, Scene iii. The Herzogin is trying to allay Thekla's fears:

> Your lot will be more peaceful.– Yet we too,
> I and your father, had our happy days;
> Our early years I still recall with joy.
> Then still he strove ahead with cheerful vigour,
> A brightly-warming fire was his ambition,
> Not yet this flame that rages all-consuming.
> The Emperor still loved him, trusted him,
> And all that he attempted brought success.
> But from that fateful day at Regensburg,
> That brought him tumbling from his lofty height,
> A lone and wayward spirit came upon him
> And black suspicion clouds his open mind.
> His calm is gone, no longer can he trust
> His own glad strength, or fortune's ancient favour,
> But turns his heart towards those gloomy arts
> That never brought fortune to their adepts.[90]

The fall from favour reverses the effects of the fall from the window, denting Wallenstein's faith in himself and making him pessimistic and fatalistic. This account – surprisingly late in the play – explains the bass note of Wallenstein's character: his melancholy makes him unable to act. Rather than acting he indulges in pointless brooding, such as the grandiloquent but inconsequential monologue of Act I, Scene iv, in which, like Hamlet weighing existence against suicide, he ponders whether we can ever really determine our actions. At the end of the monologue he persuades himself that he is still innocent: that is, like Hamlet he finds reasons to continue to temporise. His dependence on astrology symbolises his inability to motivate himself. When he tries to act, distorted ideas lead him astray. Generalising from the miraculous fall from the window, he believes that he is destined to succeed. The fall at Regensburg complicates this: the sense of destiny is joined by low spirits, irritability, and an anxious restlessness. He is convinced that he is right, because everybody else is wrong. His sense of his infallibility now expresses itself in bouts of reactive aggression such as his lecture on astrology to Illo.

Wallenstein's belief that he is surrounded by knaves and fools is not altogether wrong. In his dealings with the Austrians Wallenstein is the victim as well as the aggressor. This was how Wallenstein appeared to Schiller the historian in his *Geschichte des dreißigjährigen Kriegs* (*History of the Thirty Years' War*): 'Wallenstein did not fall because he was a rebel;

rather he rebelled because he fell.'[91] To emphasise this, the Imperial conspiracy against Wallenstein is the first issue addressed in *The Piccolomini*, and it appears as early as *Wallensteins Lager* (*Wallenstein's Camp*), when the Capuchin Friar, an agent of the Catholic Empire, vilifies Wallenstein's army for sparing the Swedes and for being lazy, rapacious blasphemers. His real target is Wallenstein, whose conversion to Catholicism is presented by the Capuchin as a token of his treachery, a slur repeated by the Imperial legate Questenberg in his debate with Wallenstein in *The Piccolomini*.[92]

Wallenstein is cast in the role of a traitor before he becomes one. The debate with Questenberg shows his desire to win approval. Seeing the legitimate avenues close, his desire for approval turns to unlawful means. Like Wolf in *A Criminal through Lost Honour*, rejected by legitimate authority he turns into authority's scourge.[93] The portrayal of Wallenstein thus bears out the claim Schiller makes for the art of drama in the play's prologue:

> [Art will] see man encompassed by the press of life
> And lay the greater share of blame and guilt
> Upon ill-fortune written in the stars.[94]

The irony is that Wallenstein's ill-starred fate turns him into a melancholic who believes literally in the power of the stars.

The later dramas

If after *Wallenstein* Schiller's psychological interests receded into the background somewhat, this was not because he had become a critic of melancholy. It had more to do with the Kantian moral theory that both fascinated and repelled him and left less room for psychological considerations, except where they form the inclinations that Schiller's heroes have to overcome in performing their self-destructive duty and attaining a tragic moral sublimity. At the same time, the violent revenge of the lower faculties is toned down. Schiller's concern is still with the harmonisation of our two natures, but mind and body are to be reconciled on mind's terms.

Empirical psychology continues to feature in the dramas' expositions. In Act 1 of *Maria Stuart* Mortimer's early experiences are used to explain his mature psychopathologies. Mortimer is close in one respect to the Prince in *The Ghost-Seer*, for his childhood experience destabilised his attitude to religion. He grew up in 'the Puritans' sombre prayer meetings'.[95] When he experienced Catholicism on his Grand Tour, the visual appeal of the beauties of Rome was like a liberation from prison (lines 454–6). His conversion was thus a pendular swing from the extreme asceticism of English Puritanism to the extreme luxuriance of Roman Catholicism, and it made a fanatic of him, superstitious and obsessed by a personal mission. He describes his reaction to hearing that Maria has been entrusted to his uncle as a personal revelation:

> I traced
> the hand of Heaven in the circumstance:
> I felt that destiny had picked me out
> To be your rescuer and liberator.[96]

Mortimer has some of the same symptoms as Karlos and Wallenstein: in particular a tendency towards selective generalisation. From the fact that the news of Maria's being held captive by Amias Paulet reached him soon after his conversion he drew the false conclusion that he had been chosen to rescue her. This chance incident grew into the belief that he was the chosen instrument of heaven. Youthful idealism is distorted into a morbid desire for martyrdom (654–60). This obsession with martyrdom leads to his suicide, a common fate of the religious melancholic.

Die Braut von Messina (*The Bride of Messina*) shows a similar interest in the psychology of childhood experiences. In a series of dark hints, the play raises questions about the upbringing of the feuding brothers. Their mother Isabella says their father was 'feared' (line 34) and sought to control the young brothers with 'awful justice of impartial sternness'.[97] The Chorus hints at dark deeds in the family's history. The brothers' father had stolen his own father's intended bride, so setting a dangerous example for his sons. The Chorus concludes the story of the Duke's usurpation of his father's marriage bed (966) with the suggestion that worse secrets still remain to be uncovered: 'horrible deeds without name, / Black crimes are concealed by this house'.[98] The suggestion is, perhaps, that the Duke committed patricide.

The brothers' home life was soured by their father's melancholy and their parents' difficult marriage. Isabella disapproved of the Duke's Arab astrologer, who compounded his unpopularity by interpreting the Duke's 'strangely wondrous dream' (*seltsam wunderbarer Traum*) to mean that his baby daughter would destroy the royal house. The Duke ordered that the baby girl be killed, an act that Isabella was able secretly to prevent. She could not visit the girl, however, because her husband nurtured dark and paranoid suspicions:

> The very sight
> Of her dear face that I so burned to see
> I had to forego, in fear of the strict father
> Who was devoured by restless pain
> Of jealousy and brooding dark suspicion
> And planted spies behind my every step.[99]

Even though he is dead, Isabella feels the effects of her husband's melancholy. When Don Manuel is reluctant to reveal his bride's name, Isabella compares him to his father:

> *He*
> Always loved to hide himself in webs
> Of his own making, keep his counsel
> Shut fast in his impenetrable mind.[100]

Secretive, brooding, tyrannical, and a believer in astrology, the Duke is another Wallenstein. Some of his melancholy has rubbed off on his sons. They suffer from rapid mood swings, which makes their reconciliation early in the play possible but also unlikely to last. The fragility of the reconciliation is signalled by their complete lack of self-knowledge. They fail to acknowledge the true causes of their conflict and self-pityingly portray themselves as the victims of a conspiracy of their subordinates. Reconciled, the brothers part passionately, but not without resuming their earlier violence, directed this time not at one another but at the 'faithless' world around them (497). Don Cesar, younger and more passionate, gives voice to the mixture of extreme emotions that seems to characterise the male members of the family:

> The feud is dead and buried now between
> Me and my dear beloved brother. I proclaim
> As my mortal enemy and antagonist,
> To be hated like the very gates of hell,
> Whoever rekindles the extinguished flame
> Of this our feud and brings it back to life.[101]

With the image of fire – a favourite double-edged metaphor of Schiller's – Don Cesar unintentionally implies that the flame of their old conflict is not entirely dead and is waiting to break out again. The violence of the oath ensures that when love turns back into hatred it will be fatal. This hostage to fortune is made all the more ironic by the fact that it is his once hated, now beloved brother whom Don Cesar has in his ignorance sworn to hate.

'The Maid of Orleans'

In his dramatisation of the legend of Joan of Arc Schiller departed from the historical tradition by making Johanna an active combatant, rather than the non-combatant figurehead as earlier accounts portray her. Her military success is grounded in a renunciation of her womanhood.[102] In submitting herself to the needs of the moment, Johanna also denies her individuality and silences her conscience. The moral problem emerges when she meets Montgomery, in an episode based on Achilles' slaying of Lycaon in *Iliad* XXI. Achilles kills Lycaon in such a way as to incline us to have pity for him, despite his lack of mercy. Both he and Lycaon are mortals; both will die on the battlefield; Achilles is simply playing his part in the bitter story of the mortal hero.[103] Johanna emphasises the differences between herself and Montgomery. She lacks mortal fallibility:

> Do not invoke my sex!
> do not call me a woman! I have no sex. Like spirits
> bodiless, not subjected to the world's ways of loving,
> I have no sex, nor does this armour hide a heart.[104]

Her denial of her own bodily nature returns to haunt her. Immediately after she has killed Montgomery, she recognises the unnaturalness of what she has done:

> My soul melts into pity and my hand draws back,
> as if it was encroaching on some holy shrine,
> from violating the young bodies of my foes.
> I shudder at the very sight of naked steel,
> but when the need is there, there is also the strength,
> and in my trembling hand, the sword unerringly
> moves of its own accord, as if it were alive.[105]

Her words imply an opposition between her body, which expresses moral sentiment by shuddering, and the unfeeling spirit that guides her.

In the subsequent encounter with Lionel, the spirit deserts Johanna and her body takes revenge on her mind. She rips off Lionel's helmet, but as she exposes the bodily object of her gaze, it disarms her.[106] Her body, which had threatened to collapse in the face of Montgomery, now does so: 'JOHANNA *raises the sword against him with a sudden movement, but lets it fall again as she catches sight of his face.*'[107] The sword, symbol of her

masculine role, now hangs limp and ineffectual. The awakening of sexual
feelings makes her powerless. There was an intimation of this when she
killed Montgomery and she saw his 'blooming' (*blühend*) body; now she
is undone by Lionel's 'blooming' male form. Unable to kill him, she saves
his life by encouraging him to escape before the French arrive. As he
leaves, he takes the sword from her, reasserting his masculinity and
confirming her femininity. La Hire and Dunois arrive in time to catch
Johanna as she collapses in an all-too-feminine faint.

In the next scene the faint is modulated into a melting swoon. Outside
the celebrations of French victory, Johanna reflects uneasily on her
changed feelings in a lyrical mode that has thus far been foreign to her.
The lyrical voice is answered by the sound of '*a soft melting melody*'
offstage (*eine weiche, schmelzende Melodie*, IV.i.2550). In *Über die ästhetische Erziehung* (*Letters on Aesthetic Education*), Schiller contrasts two
complementary forms of beauty, 'melting beauty' (*schmelzende Schönheit*)
and 'energetic beauty' (*energische Schönheit*). The effect of melting beauty
is 'releasing' (*auflösend*), restoring our balance when we are 'over-tensed'
(*angespannt*, Letter 17, NA xx.364). The cause of tension may be 'the
compulsion of thought' (*der Zwang von Begriffen*, Letter 17, NA xx.365).
Melting beauty brings relaxing release from the tyranny of concepts
or laws: 'the man one-sidedly dominated by law, or the spiritually
tensed man, will be released and set free'.[108] Johanna has been 'over-
tensed' by the 'compulsion' of her mission to free France. Her sub-
ordination to the Spirit deprived her of natural emotional and physical
experiences. Now, after killing Montgomery and failing to kill the Black
Knight and Lionel, she is being released by the experience of melting
beauty. She had a foretaste of this melting beauty when she felt her soul
'melt' with pity before Montgomery (*In Mitleid schmilzt die Seele*, II.
viii.1680). Understood thus, Johanna's faint at the end of Act III is a
symptom of a crisis; it is not weakness so much as the feelings taking
revenge on reason for the latter's subjection of them to 'the compulsion
of thought'. Like Ferdinand's fit of jealousy, it is the lower faculties'
revenge on hubristic reason, and it gives rise to a need for further moral
development.

Schiller's plots have some features in common. A usurper tries to assert
his or her legitimacy and to manipulate others by means of some
form of political rationality – deception in Ferdinand's case, self-denial
in Johanna's. In overpowering the feelings and the moral sense, reason
brings about a crisis, and the lower faculties go into rebellion.
Often the process occurs in one character: Franz Moor's deceits and his

rationalisation of psychosomatic interaction return to haunt him in paranoid ravings about hell-fire. Alternatively, the functions of reason and feeling can be assigned to two or more characters. The emotionally driven Don Karlos is used by Posa for political ends, but the soundness of Karlos's moral feeling frustrates Posa's planning. Wallenstein treats his allegiance to the Emperor as a matter of political rationality, only to have his own subordinates follow feelings that lead them away from him and, most damagingly, to see Max and Thekla become so emotionally involved that they rebel against his rule. Elisabeth's and Maria's attempts to resolve their respective problems by manipulation founder on the emotions of those they would manipulate.

This was also the sense of Schiller's response to Kant's ethics. Kant's ethics involved compulsion and fear.[109] But compulsion only serves to make enemies of the lower faculties. Schiller used this argument in his aesthetic and philosophical writing to show how the repression of the lower faculties by reason represents one of the historico-cultural problems that we must overcome. In the *Aesthetic Education,* he talks of 'the nefarious influence exerted . . . by a preponderance of rationality . . . this violent usurping of authority by ratiocination'.[110] Schiller attributes the characteristics of activity and passivity to spirit and matter respectively. Material is passive (*leidend*) and the intellect is active (*tätig*). Our task is to reconcile them. There are times when Schiller seems to agree with Kant that it is the lower faculties that pose the greater threat, for instance writing to Körner in 1792: 'The so-called *lower* mental powers are like sleeping lions that one often does better not to wake, because they cannot easily be shut up again.'[111] There are also moments in the *Aesthetic Education* when, whilst trying to seem impartial, he portrays the lower faculties in a negative light. In Letter 27, for instance, he speaks of the mind's 'degrading kinship with matter'.[112] 'Degrading' here belongs to an implied quotation: from the perspective of mind, which wants to be free, its association with matter is dishonourable. For us, who are a combination of matter and mind and who must try to harmonise the two, it cannot be so: the higher and lower faculties must be equally worthy partners. However, there is still a whiff of negativity in Schiller's treatment of the lower faculties. One might infer this from the statement in Letter 19 of the *Aesthetic Education* that reason cannot in reality be overcome by the senses; it can only appear to be, in cases where through neglect it fails to assert itself (*NA* xx.370). In the same spirit Schiller compares reason to Zeus, who would not deign to join battle before Troy in person (*NA* xx.330). One might say that higher and lower faculties are engaged in a dialectical process whereby the lower must in the end reaffirm the hegemony of the higher. This is because the dialectic comes about within a metaphysical framework in which the higher faculties have priority.

Schiller sees the 'antagonism of forces' as a tragic fact of the psyche's constitution. His mature work continues to document the dangers of melancholy and psychic imbalance and the possibility of the restoration of health through crisis. After the French Revolution he became both more restrained in his dramaturgy and less prepared to prescribe violent revolutions as cures. Whilst he disliked Kant's moral rigorism, he had to follow Kant in giving the final say to reason. There are moments in the later plays when we see the revenge of the lower faculties threaten to become immoderate, but these are to be read as warnings. What little violence is wrought on reason by the lower faculties rarely has that disproportionate quantity that true revenge has. In general, the lower faculties, in subverting reason, are dancing to the tune of a higher rationality.

GOETHE'S CLASSICISM

In the week before Goethe was due to sail from Naples to Sicily in March 1787, his anxiety about the crossing made him consider abandoning the trip and returning to Rome. Characteristically, he chose at this moment of uncertainty to draw the balance of his life. His thoughts turned to another compulsive worrier:

Sometimes I'm reminded of Rousseau and his hypochondriacal misery, and yet I can understand why such a fine character as his could become so distorted. If I did not feel such interest in the natural world and could not see that in this apparent confusion there are a hundred observations that can be compared and ordered just as a surveyor checks a number of individual measurements by taking a line through them, I would often have to consider myself mad.[113]

Like Moritz, Goethe saw Rousseau as a spiritual cousin and felt he shared Rousseau's tendency towards 'hypochondria'. A temperament like Rousseau's might infer from the variety of phenomena that nature was chaotic. Science showed that the world had structure; it anchored Goethe to reality. The same argument occurs repeatedly in the diary that he kept in Italy. Science, anthropology, the study of ancient art and architecture, the influence of the Italian climate and way of life: all of these have a therapeutic effect on him and promise him rebirth as a new person. In

Italy Goethe imagines himself progressing towards a goal. Geographically his goal is Rome, intellectually it is an objective understanding of nature and society; aesthetically, a new plasticity of form; psychologically, an end to 'hypochondriac' hopes and fears.

The idea of Goethe's Italian rebirth is formed from two elements. The first is epistemological and can be defined as objectivity and openness to sense impressions. Early in the journey Goethe writes that he aims at 'the complete divesting of all pretension' by having 'faith in the ability of [his] eye to see'.[114] By 'pretension' he means preconceived assumptions about the meaning of things. Objectivity, on the other hand, means a condition of passive receptivity towards sense data. Although the eye is to be passive, active engagement is needed to make it so. He 'must first educate [his] eye, accustom [himself] to seeing'.[115] An objective relation to things has psychological benefits. It gives him 'an entirely new elasticity of mind'[116] and 'good humour', so that 'free from any tension [he has] the highest pleasure and good observation'.[117] Both the therapeutic method and the desired condition exhibit the 'coldness' that Moritz and Schiller were also advocating.

The second element in Goethe's rebirth sets the virtues of vision against the vices of the imagination. The imagination offers the promise of understanding, but only seeing can fully realise the promise (*WA* iv. xiii.47–8). As well as being less vivid, the imagination is unreliable, responding too easily to our hopes and fears and often telling us not what is the case but what some unspoken desire wants to be the case. In place of a Wertheresque emotional investment in hopes for his own future fulfilment, which could so easily flip over into a fear of emptiness, Goethe now advocates philosophical calm and objectivity. This is coloured by his reading of Lucretius, who said of Epicurus that 'he set a limit to desire and fear' (*De rerum natura*, vi.25). This meant abandoning religion. Although Goethe was prepared (chiefly for reasons of tact) to acknowledge that religion was a comfort to others, he sided with Lucretius in limiting his own pretensions to present reality, as he wrote to Stolberg:

If for myself I more or less follow the teaching of Lucretius and limit all my pretensions to the sphere of life, still it always greatly pleases and refreshes me when I see how, for tender souls, motherly nature also has more tender notes and resonances sounding in her undulating harmonies and in so many ways allows mortal man a taste of the eternal and immortal.[118]

These two arguments – the epistemological argument for empiricism and the Epicurean ethical teaching about hopes and fears – form the intellectual core of Goethe's classicism. The first yields an argument for classical form: wholeness, simplicity, and closeness to the earth.[119] Classical form is 'objective'; it corresponds to or grows out of what objectively is. The second is a set of ideas derived from ancient moral philosophy, chiefly the Epicureanism of Lucretius and the other Golden Age Latin poets. The highest human goal is happiness, defined as fulfilment of one's needs in the absence of care. We can achieve happiness by means of moderation and by accepting our physical and mental limitations. We can banish care by renouncing the excessive hopes and fears generated by religion. Goethe's classicism thus has a twofold relation to psychology. First it is concerned with the role and status of the intellect, which must have a proper balance of activity and receptivity. It must be active with regard to the feelings, because the dominance of feelings over the intellect is one of the enemies of objectivity, and it must be receptive with regard to the world, so that the sense organs are left to do their job of forming an accurate picture of things. Second, classicism is a protection against the cognitive distortions that cause 'hypochondria' and melancholy. This new understanding of melancholy is one of the main themes of Goethe's writing in the 1790s and a conspicuous feature of his work on *Faust* in the years 1797 to 1801.

Goethe's response to Moritz's 'On the Creative Imitation of the Beautiful'

Before he left for Italy Goethe revised *The Sorrows of Young Werther* for a new edition of his works. The fresh confrontation with Werther lay behind his negative comments on imagination in the Italian diary. In the new edition he set out to give a more objective account of Werther's melancholy. Sceptical additions to the editor's report on Werther's last days and an entirely new parallel story telling of the fate of a love-sick farm-boy distance Werther from the reader and emphasise his pathological side – not that the first edition, which Goethe at the time described as the 'story of a disease' (*historia morbi*)[120], presented an entirely attractive picture of its melodramatic, querulous, and self-pitying hero. In the first edition the key to Werther's melancholy was the power and independence of his imagination. In the revised editor's report this is presented in the language of associationism. Pre-empting the Italian diary's emphasis on seeing and the pleasure Goethe takes in the Italian sunlight, the editor comments that not even the fair weather could lift Werther's spirits:

The beautiful weather had barely any effect on his low spirits, his soul was stifled and oppressed, images of melancholy had taken possession of him, and there was no change in his spirit other than from one painful thought to the next.[121]

Werther's problem is that he cannot simply see. Seeing is always overtaken by imagining, his vision confused by his 'pretensions'. He cannot see landscape; he can only see a reflection of his own moods. The consequence is that he becomes frustrated with painting.

The position Goethe had reached in the revision of *Werther* and the Italian diary coincided with Moritz's development, and their meeting in Rome catalysed the classical and anti-Wertherian aesthetic theory of Moritz's *On the Creative Imitation of the Beautiful*. Werther saw art as the expression of his emotional urges and insisted that the proper criteria for judging art were subjective. Moritz in turn provided Goethe with a clearer view of these faults and a means of remedying them. By means of an analysis of the concept of beauty, Moritz argues that art must be a self-satisfying whole and cannot therefore be the instrument of any external purpose or interest. It also follows from the 'wholeness' of art that it should properly be judged in formal terms, for its constituent parts contribute only to the being of the whole. Art cannot be judged in terms of realism. Having established this, Moritz offers an account of how the dilettante falls short of the true artist. Beauty appeals to us because it speaks to a drive towards wholeness that resides in our 'power of activity' or 'creative power' (*Tatkraft, Bildungskraft, MW* 11.558–61). Many of us, however, possess more sensitivity than creativity. If we have enough sensitivity to appreciate beauty, but insufficient *Bildungskraft* to create it, we may become unhappy, for every experience of art will confront us with our failure (*MW* 11.565). The problem arises when in such individuals sensitivity mistakes itself for creativity:

The more complete our faculty of sensibility is for a particular species of beauty, the more it risks deceiving itself, mistaking itself for imagination and in this way destroying its peace with itself through a thousand failed attempts.[122]

We feel beauty but we cannot reach it, and we experience this failure as a theft (*MW* 11.576). This has two similarities with Goethe's new understanding of Werther. The first is that melancholy can be caused by an (imagined) experience of loss or act of violence against oneself.[123] For sensitive but uncreative people it is as if the beauty they can feel but not create has been stolen from them. They tend as a result to react with defensive aggression to any real or perceived slight – hence Werther's irritable aggression towards things or people who contradict him. The second is that the melancholic is not the artistic genius that the tradition of pseudo-Aristotle and the Renaissance imagined; the melancholic is more likely to be a failed artist. Melancholy might, in fact, be the result of artistic impotence. Hence Werther's failure as a creative artist could be behind his melancholy.

The fragment published in 1808 under the title *Briefe aus der Schweiz. Erste Abteilung* (*Letters from Switzerland. First Section*) purports to be a series of letters written by Werther during a journey in Switzerland before his infamous sorrows. Implicitly the letters offer an explanation for his later melancholy. The main theme is his desire to become an artist, and by the end of the fragment it is clear both that he will be frustrated and that his frustration will have deeper consequences, for the reasons given by Moritz. The first letter introduces the theme of the difference between imagining and seeing. For Werther, seeing is no more intense or powerful than imagining. He recognises that the scenery should do something for him: 'This wonderful presence excites my spirit within, rouses me to activity, and what can I do, what do I do? I just sit down and write and describe.'[124] The experience of natural beauty does not awaken his creativity. He is on the road to becoming a highly sensitive, but frustrated dilettante. The result is a series of unsuccessful attempts at creating art, such as Moritz's essay describes. When he sees a landscape painting, he is filled with frustration and physical unease (*WA* 1.xix.201). In a parlour game, in which each player has to produce an extempore poem, Werther freezes and has to be helped out by his friend Ferdinand. Now recognising that he must submit himself to a proper training, he has Ferdinand pose naked. Werther succeeds in drawing him, but the most striking effect of the episode is to make Werther drool over Ferdinand's body; this has more to do with sexual frustration than with art. Accordingly Werther decides to hire a young girl to pose naked for him, so that he can pair his pictures of Ferdinand with a suitable partner. She undresses, while he simply stares. She lies down and seems to go to sleep:

Finally a passionate dream seemed to disturb her, she sighed deeply, changed her position with a jolt, muttered the name of a lover and seemed to stretch her arms out towards him. 'Come!' she finally called with clearly audible voice, 'come into my arms, my friend, or I really will fall asleep.'[125]

Here the fragment ends, leaving Werther standing before his model impotent both as an artist and a lover.

Religious melancholy and Epicurean anxiety in 'Faust'

The first example of religious melancholy in Goethe's writing is in the poem 'Prometheus' (1773), which is usually read as a combative expression of a form of atheism, namely the Epicurean view that the Gods are not worthy of being worshipped by us. According to Epicurus, ignoring the Gods will help us to reach a state of untroubled calm (*ataraxia*). Prometheus, however, is anything but calm. The story behind his anger is given in a confession from his youth. As a child he had been a passionate believer, which he describes in unmistakably Pietistic language. His high expectations of communion with Zeus were disappointed, for Zeus slept through his prayers of thanks and gave Prometheus no relief from his anguish. His reaction is to travel to the opposite extreme and become an angry sceptic. The poem portrays a riven consciousness, the result of a faith that has been disappointed.

Werther is a similar case, for he expects too much and makes the mistake of thinking that if he worships the world, it will reward him with more intense feelings. Disappointed, he turns into a blasphemer, casting himself in the role of Christ sacrificed for the sake of a fallen world. The structure of the novel is of a series of alternating moods of enthusiasm and desperation, euphoria and dysphoria. The letter of 18 August presents this oscillation in a condensed form. The first half of the letter is an ecstatic hymn to nature, the second a fit of morbid panic, in which Werther portrays nature as 'a monster forever devouring, regurgitating, chewing and gorging'.[126] The two halves of the letter are symmetrical, for, as Werther writes at the beginning of the letter, 'the source of Man's contentment' (his imagination) has become 'the source of his misery'.[127] The letter pivots on a sudden shift in his mood and hence in the colour that his imagination projects onto the world.

Goethe's earliest conception of Faust, given form in the great opening monologue, was of a religious melancholic oscillating between enthusiasm and pessimism. The first monologue is constructed as a succession of alternations between despair at his physical and spiritual confinement, and elation at the prospect of freedom and discovery. As Faust contrasts the attractions of magic with the frustrations of scholarship, these alternations appear in a compressed form:

> And so I've turned to magic lore;
> The spirit message of this art
> Some secret message might impart.
> No longer shall I sweat to teach

> What always lay beyond my reach;
> I'll know what makes the world revolve,
> Its inner mysteries resolve,
> No more in empty words I'll deal –
> Creation's wellsprings I'll reveal.[128]

Enthusiasm, disappointed by reality, is unveiled as an excess of high spirits. The result is a bitter pessimism that also undermines itself, for if empty bitterness is all that rationality can give, then surely it would be better to be irrational. So the pessimist turns back towards enthusiasm, and the pendulum begins its cycle again.

Faust's melancholy is easily diagnosed. His mood is low and his spirits depressed most of the time. He complains of physical symptoms in the form of inexplicable pains and a heightened, anxious awareness of his heartbeat:

> And still you wonder why this pain
> Constricts your heart and hems it in,
> Why agonies you can't explain
> Sap all life's energies within.[129]

He experiences feelings of worthlessness and low self-esteem (17–22) and diminished pleasure in things that he might otherwise be expected to enjoy, such as the acquisition of knowledge (17). He also shows the same cognitive distortions as we saw in Schiller's Karlos and Wallenstein. He pretends to foresee his fate; he draws sweeping negative conclusions that go far beyond the evidence on which they are based; he ignores the positive information about his circumstances in favour of the negative; he reasons emotionally; he moralises, using excessively precise and demanding notions of how people should behave. Most characteristic of Faust, however, is a cognitive distortion that has been termed dichotomous or bipolar or 'black-and-white' thinking.[130] This is the tendency to see the world in extreme dualistic terms. University teaching is absolutely pointless; magic will reveal absolute truths. Book-learning is deathly, nature a panacea. His study is a prison, the outside world free. Words are empty, feelings full. To treat these thoughts as symptoms of melancholy is not to say that there is no truth in them. On the contrary, all of what Faust says has a kernel of truth in it. It is his manner of treating that truth – exaggerating, overgeneralising, moralising, selectively abstracting, catastrophising, thinking in black-and-white terms – that marks him as a melancholic.

When Goethe returned to *Faust* in Italy, he was less sympathetic to the idea that the quest for knowledge led to melancholy. On the contrary, the structure and discipline provided by natural science had saved him from the 'hypochondria' that afflicted Rousseau. This is reflected in Faust's monologue addressed to the Earth Spirit (*Erdgeist*), which Goethe probably wrote in Rome in 1788. Faust proclaims that the Earth Spirit has given him insight into how nature is organised. All beings, including humans, belong to a single series, and nature coheres. So Faust's knowledge is not 'cold amazement' (*kalt staunender Besuch*, 3223). It is intimate; the animals are his 'brothers'. From Faust's glowing account of these ideas it is clear that science is being offered as a cure for his melancholy. Goethe wanted to paint a positive picture of Faust's thirst for knowledge. But the more intellectually respectable he became, the more difficult his alliance with Mephistopheles would be to justify. The idea that Faust's restless craving could be fully satisfied ran directly counter to Goethe's conception of *Faust* in the 1770s and indeed any previous version of the Faust legend. The solution at which Goethe arrived when he resumed work on *Faust* in 1797 was to alter the character of his melancholy. Retaining the pendular dynamic of his moods, the new material that filled the gap between the debate with Wagner and the scene with the student deepened Faust's melancholy and added two new elements to it. One was the Epicurean concept of *cura* ('care', 'anxiety'), which Goethe drew from Lucretius and the other Golden Age Roman poets and used frequently in the 1790s.[131] He also had Faust reflect, on two occasions, on his earlier life, and reveal the cause of his melancholy to be religion, in the manner of 'Prometheus'. These additions served to make the alliance with Mephistopheles psychologically intelligible and at the same time protected Faust's scientific ambitions from contamination by that alliance.

In Epicurean philosophy *cura* is the main obstacle to the good life.[132] Its chief cause is fear of death. This goes very deep in the psyche and can affect behaviour unconsciously, creating a generalised feeling of anxiety. This is why Lucretius pairs *cura* with *metus* ('fear'): anxiety and fear go hand-in-hand.[133] *Cura* makes us cling to life in too desperate a manner, which can lead to immorality, crime, aggression and, in turn, religion.[134] Religion has a central position in the argument as both a cause and a consequence of fear of death. Religion causes fear of death because it thrives on images of punishment in the afterlife. It is a consequence of fear of death in the sense that it offers empty and illusory relief to the fearful and can camouflage the immorality of the ambitious, who pretend to be pious in order to seem moral. Only if we liberate ourselves from religion and overcome our fear of death, can we achieve the state of freedom from disturbance in which true happiness lies.

Fear of death is ubiquitous in Faust's language.[135] It is sometimes explicit, sometimes present by association, in images of worms, dust, mould, confinement, and the opposed concepts of the wet (life) and the dry (death). In the *Urfaust* material the theme is not fully developed. In the additions of the 1790s, it becomes explicit. Faust interprets his rejection by the Earth Spirit as a kind of death.[136] Looking around him, he sees the signs of death in his moth-ridden, dust-coated study and the grimace of a skull (656–67). Surrounded by intimations of mortality, he laments the power of care (*die Sorge*):

> Once our imagination boldly sought
> To reach eternity; but now a tiny scope
> Is all it needs. The swirling tide of time has brought
> An end to all our joy and all our hope.
> Deep in our hearts is lodged the worm of care,
> It works its secret pain and worry there.
> In ever-changing guises it appears,
> Gnaws at our peace of mind and turns our joys to tears,
> As house and home, as child and wife,
> As fire or flood, as poison or as knife;
> We tremble at the things that never harmed us yet,
> And what we never lost we bitterly regret.[137]

> Wenn Phantasie sich sonst mit kühnem Flug
> Und hoffnungsvoll zum Ewigen erweitert,
> So ist ein kleiner Raum ihr nun genug,
> Wenn Glück auf Glück im Zeitenstrudel scheitert.
> Die Sorge nistet gleich im tiefen Herzen,
> Dort wirket sie geheime Schmerzen,
> Unruhig wiegt sie sich und störet Lust und Ruh;
> Sie deckt sich stets mit neuen Masken zu,
> Sie mag als Haus und Hof, als Weib und Kind erscheinen,
> Als Feuer, Wasser, Dolch und Gift;
> Du bebst vor allem was nicht trifft,
> Und was du nie verlierst, das mußt du stets beweinen. (640–51)

Reality accretes around our ideals, and this accumulation of 'foreign matter' (*fremder Stoff*, 635) brings with it care. At any rate this is how Faust interprets his predicament, in a moment of Schillerian melancholy.[138] He seems to be complaining about the cares of everyday life, but of course it makes no sense for the unmarried and childless Faust to complain about 'house and home . . . child and wife'.[139] These are just the visible marks of an anxiety that is deeper and has other origins. Care is 'secret'; the forms it takes say nothing about its true cause, which is, as Faust says, hidden 'deep in our hearts'.

The idea of a deep, generalised anxiety that disturbs peace and pleasure derives from Book III of *De rerum natura*. This is how Knebel translated the equivalent passage of Lucretius:

> . . . die Schrecken des Orkus;
> Jene, welche von Grund aus trüben das Leben der Menschen;
> Alles mit Todesfarbe beschwärzen, und nie dem Gemüthe
> Reine Freude vergönnen, noch ungestörete Wollust.[140]

. . . the fear of Acheron . . . which blasts the life of man from its very foundations, sullying everything with the blackness of death and leaving no pleasure pure and unalloyed.[141]

Knebel was translating Lucretius, with Goethe's help, at the same time as Goethe was working on *Faust*. For Lucretius, fear of death insinuates itself into our unconscious and gives rise to such a hatred of life that despite their fear of death men will commit suicide. People forget that the source of their anxiety is death and sink into a hatred of life that is more immediate to them than their fear of death. Similarly, Faust sees only the visible manifestations of care and speculates that its sources are 'secret'. Then he half persuades himself that death would be a route to new adventures. But the truth of his condition is beyond rescue by such ponderings, which are in any case the product of his condition, not its cure. Suicide could only be a vain act of denial of his fear of death, in the course of which Faust would, by the grimmest of ironies, only reaffirm it by suffering the fate described by Lucretius. He becomes obsessed with defying the Christian threat of hell-fire, but he cannot keep control of the poetic vision that his desperate euphoria creates:

> Now is the time to act, and by your action show
> That man is fit to stand at the immortals' side,
> And not to quail before that gloomy cavern, where
> Imagination damns itself to torment and despair;
> Press on towards that passage from which none returns,
> Around whose narrow mouth all hell-fire burns.[142]

His imagination paints hell in vivid colours. The image of confinement ('narrow mouth') suggests that he is afraid of death, although he will not acknowledge it.

Strangely for one who affects to disdain religion, he is rescued from suicide by the Easter Chorus. To explain this, he offers a spiritual autobiography, similar to that of Prometheus. In his youth Faust had reacted to 'the loving kiss of heaven' with 'a thousand burning tears' (*der Himmels-Liebe Kuß . . . unter tausend heißen Thränen*, 771, 777). Then, when he had faith, prayer was a 'fervent joy' (*brünstiger Genuß*), even if a solitary one. That is to say, like Prometheus, Faust in his youth was a Pietist. In the next scene, walking out of town with Wagner, he gives a similar account of the time when he and his father had dispensed medicine during the plague:

> Here deep in thought I've often sat alone
> In agony of mind, with fasting and with prayer.
> So rich in hope and strong in faith I thought
> To force God's will, and heaven I besought
> With pleas and tears and pious abstinence
> To put an end to that vile pestilence.[143]

For the first time in a treatment of the Faust story he is portrayed as having been a believing Christian.[144] In these two passages he acquires the biography of a religious melancholic: his melancholy – the wild oscillation between optimism and pessimism, the unconscious fear of death, the anxiety, the decision to commit suicide, the sadness, the dissociation from reality – is the consequence of a disappointed faith.

This resolves the question of how Faust could be driven into the alliance with Mephistopheles. At the beginning of the wager scene Faust is again in a morbid frame of mind. He complains of his confinement and of the restlessness and anxiety that ruin all his pleasures (1544–5). Life becomes odious, death would be welcome (1554–71). As he confesses to Mephistopheles, he has been suffering from poor sleep and bad dreams, common symptoms of melancholy:

> And even when night falls, and on my bed
> Fearful and uneasy I must lie, I find
> No welcome rest to comfort me – instead
> Wild dreams will come to haunt my anxious mind.[145]

Reminded of his abortive suicide, Faust expresses his hatred of life in a riot of curses, ending with a splenetic rejection of the Christian virtue of patience (1606). His anxiety and restlessness, fed by strange, half-understood fears, and his chafing against the self-denying ordinances of Christianity, make him utterly desperate.

This low point is the condition for his entering into the wager, the ultimate expression of his melancholy. The anxious restlessness that made life odious to him resurfaces in his vow to be constantly active. As his side of the wager Faust offers tireless, restless striving ('Striving with all my power': *Das Streben meiner ganzen Kraft*, 1742). This is the opposite of what Lucretius prescribes, corresponding rather to his description of the man who suffers from fear of death and with restless toil (*mit rastloser Arbeit*, III.61) and tireless striving (*mit unermüdetem Streben*, II.12) throws himself into life. He may commit suicide, or he may strive to amass the wealth that he thinks will protect him from death. In either case he disregards morality:

Often from fear of death mortals are gripped by such a hate of living and looking on the light that with anguished hearts they do themselves to death. They forget that this fear is the very foundation of their troubles: this is what harasses conscience, snaps the bonds of friendship and in a word utterly destroys all moral responsibility.[146]

Ja, aus Furcht vor dem Tod', ergreift oft also die Menschen
Bitterer Lebenshaß, und der Haß des himmlischen Lichtes,
Daß sie sich selber den Tod mit traurigem Herzen beschließen;
Nicht bedenkend, es sey dieselbige Furcht nur die Quelle
Ihres Kummers; nur sie verletze die Schaam, das Gewissen,
Breche der Freundschaft Band, zerstöre was heilig und recht ist. (III.79–84)

Faust's wager culminates in a commitment to be permanently dissatisfied:

If I should bid the moment stay, or try
To hold its fleeting beauty, then you may
Cast me in chains and carry me away,
For in that instant I will gladly die.[147]

To accept the present for what it is would represent failure. It would be a sign of inertia and self-satisfaction. He would have to have been gulled into merely being happy. This is the opposite of the Epicurean ethic, which advocates calm and freedom from disturbance by hopes or fears for the future. In Epicurean terms, Faust is committing himself to be forever a victim of care.

Goethe based Faust's formulation of the wager on a passage from Rousseau's *Les Rêveries du promeneur solitaire* (*Reveries of the Solitary Walker*). The hypochondriac Rousseau is reflecting on the incapacity of humans ever to be fully contented:

Everything is in constant flux on this earth. Nothing keeps the same unchanging shape, and our affections, being attached to things outside us, necessarily change and pass away as they do. Always out ahead of us or lagging behind, they recall a past which is gone or anticipate a future which may never come into being; there is nothing solid there for the heart to attach itself to. Thus our earthly joys are almost without exception the creatures of a moment; I doubt whether any of us knows the meaning of lasting happiness. Even in our keenest pleasures there is scarcely a single moment of which the heart could truthfully say: 'Would that this moment could last for ever!' And how can we give the name of happiness to a fleeting state which leaves our hearts still empty and anxious, either regretting something that is past or desiring something that is yet to come?[148]

In echoing this idea of Rousseau's, Faust is committing himself to a life lived in denial of the present moment, a life lived forever under the shadow of the future or the past, a life perpetually beset by hopes and fears. It is a life lived in a constant state of anxiety.

Having brought Faust close to suicide and driven him into the wager with Mephistopheles, Care reappears shortly before Faust's death in Act v of *Faust ii* in the form of a spectral 'grey woman' and gives a description of her typical victim that tallies with Faust's life and character. The wager's emphasis on restless activity is echoed here. The 'unstoppable roll' (*unaufhaltsam Rollen*) described by Care is what Faust wanted from the wager, when he proclaimed, 'Let's plunge into the . . . roll of events' (*Stürzen wir uns . . . ins Rollen der Begebenheit!*, 1754–5). The 'invigorating discontent' (*erquickende[r] Verdruß*, 1767) that Faust expected from the association with Mephistopheles now recurs in Care's words as 'ill re-invigoration' (*schlecht Erquicken*, 11484). More generally Care makes people deny the present and attend only to the future (11465), just as Faust had vowed to do. Care is an externalisation of the spirit of frenetic, amoral striving in which Faust entered into the wager. Care is the cause both of her victim's compulsive restlessness with all its disastrous conse-quences for those around him, and of his moral blindness. Any activity undertaken by her victims will at best be fruitless. Faust seems to admit that this has been his fate in the account of his life that he gives Care, where the emphasis is more on frenetic and ephemeral activity than on any lasting achievement (11433–4). Care's description of her victim corres-ponds in detail to what Faust has done since the wager and in the scenes immediately before her appearance.[149] It also prefigures his final hours, for Care's victim 'attends only to the future / and so is never finished' (*ist der Zukunft nur gewärtig, / Und so wird er niemals fertig*, 11465–6), just as Faust will enunciate his grand vision of a future society that will never come about, because the work is not progressing. Horace describes *cura* as 'dark' and 'corrupting', and Goethe's Care characterises herself in terms of darkness and wrong-doing (11455, 11458, 11478). She makes people aware only of the future, whereas Epicurus promised to free us from hopes and fears. She makes people behave in contradictory ways, both paralysing them (11485) and making them move erratically and restlessly (11481). Propelling this chaotic movement are psychological needs that the victim of Care does not understand. The source for this is Lucretius's account of how 'hunting cares' (*curae sequaces*) pursue the rich man no matter how far or fast he moves.[150] Had he devoted himself to an understanding of the nature of the Universe, he would have found peace and comfort; instead his illusory worries have made him alternately frenetically active or somnolent:

And will *you* kick and protest against your sentence? You, whose life is next door to death although you still live and look on the light. You, who waste the major part of your time in sleep and, when you are awake, are snoring still and dreaming. You, who bear a mind hag-ridden by baseless fear and cannot find the commonest cause of your distress, hounded as you are, pathetic creature, by a pack of troubles and drifting in a drunken stupor upon a wavering tide of fantasy.

Men feel plainly within their minds a heavy burden, whose weight depresses them. If only they perceived with equal clearness the causes of this depression, the origin of this lump of evil within their breasts, they would not lead such a life as we now see all too commonly – no-one knowing what he really wants and everyone for ever trying to get away from where he is, as though travel alone could throw off the load. Often the owner of some stately mansion, bored stiff by staying at home, takes his departure, only to return as speedily when he feels himself no better off out of doors. Off he goes to his country seat, driving his Gaulish ponies hotfoot, as though rushing to save a house on fire. No sooner has he crossed its doorstep than he starts yawning or retires moodily to sleep and courts oblivion, or else rushes back to revisit the city. In so doing the individual is really running away from himself. Since he remains reluctantly wedded to the self whom he cannot of course escape, he grows to hate him, because he is a sick man ignorant of the cause of his malady. If he did but see this, he would cast other thoughts aside and devote himself first to studying the nature of the universe.[151]

Faust's activities may have more tangible consequences, but they are no less escapist. That is clear from the wager. The move from academic life to restless activity was an escape. The anxiety that made the escape seem necessary has followed him continuously ever since (11428–9), no matter how fast he has 'raced through the world' (*durch die Welt gerannt*, 11433).

Returning to *Faust I*, it is possible to see how the idea of *Sorge* relates to the work's overarching theological framework. With the wager made and Faust offstage preparing for the start of his adventures, Mephistopheles crows triumphantly over the trap he has set for Faust. It has traditionally been assumed that Faust's striving is what saves him, for in the 'Prologue in Heaven' the Lord presents striving as an admirable characteristic. Yet it is in fact Mephistopheles who provides the cue for the Lord's description of Faust's 'dark compulsion' (*dunkler Drang*, 308): 'His fevered mind is in a constant ferment. / [He is] half-conscious of his folly.'[152] Mephistopheles provides both an organic metaphor ('ferment': *Gärung*) with which the Lord will express Faust's harmonious relation to the Universe and the notion that humans have a semi-conscious purpose. The Lord picks up the cues, so that there is a surprising unanimity in the *Prologue in Heaven* concerning Faust's psychological make-up. The core of Faust's being is in harmony with creation; it is a stable, continuous drive towards a half-recognised goal, blindly purposeless yet functionally purposive, like the growth of a plant. Equally, from a Mephistophelean viewpoint it is what makes Faust restless, dissatisfied, and destructive. Striving is dark and riddled with error: a force, not a plan. In this sense Mephistopheles is partly justified in ridiculing human reason, which, he says, is just a means by which humans can be even more beastly to one another.

Although this theological framework is not the final word on the psychology of *Faust*, for nineteenth-century, post-Idealist students of Goethe the picture was clear. Faust embodied a fundamental urge or drive that was common to humans but present in Faust to an exceptional degree. This is rooted deep in the core of their being and defines their humanity. Its tendency might be towards the clarity of the divine or the rational or the spiritual, but in empirical persons it is 'dark' and unconscious – perhaps it is even identical with the unconscious which Schopenhauer and Carus would uncover. In any case, it is continually frustrated by the empirical world. Life is a struggle towards self-expression, and Faustian striving distils the spirit of this struggle to its essence. In a political sense, Faust came to be identified with the national aspirations of the German people. Psychologically he came to represent the objectified unconscious, the core idea of the German tradition of depth psychology.

CHAPTER 5

Idealism's campaign against psychology

The two decades following the publication of Kant's *Critique of Pure Reason* in 1781 saw a succession of attempts to redefine the fundamentals of philosophy. To some this 'Revolution of the Spirit' seemed as radical as the political revolution across the Rhine: Friedrich Schlegel adventurously claimed that the French Revolution, Fichte's *Wissenschaftslehre* (*Theory of Science*) and Goethe's *Wilhelm Meisters Lehrjahre* (*Wilhelm Meister's Apprenticeship*) were 'the greatest tendencies of the age'.[1] Its impact on German psychology was complex. The Idealists disliked the way psychology tended to analyse concepts down to their sensuous elements and to divide the mind into discrete faculties. Either way, it denied the unity of mind and therewith the basis of ethical autonomy. The Idealists' own theories of cognition were designed expressly to make psychology redundant. Despite short-lived successes, this endeavour largely failed. For practical and institutional reasons it proved impossible for the Idealists to make a clean break with the tradition of psychology. Idealist philosophy was deeply marked by its contact with psychology: like it or not, the Idealists' theories of cognition depended in important ways on eighteenth-century psychology. Moreover, for philosophical reasons the prospect of a clean break was a chimera. In the long term the effect of Kant's attempt to eradicate psychology achieved the opposite. In attempting to drive psychology out of philosophy, Kant drove it into science, whence, now armed with the weapon of scientific method, it mounted a reinvasion of philosophy, which has had profound consequences for its subsequent history. By this unintended route, Kant can be said to have laid the foundations of nineteenth-century German scientific psychology.

According to Kant's own arguments in the *Critique of Pure Reason*, psychology ought not to have been affected by the new philosophy. The question that gave Idealism its impetus was the question that had been asked many times in the eighteenth century: what does the mind bring to experience? Kant's answer was that the mind brings a subjective epistemic framework that guarantees the truth of empirical knowledge. His chief concern in the *Critique of Pure Reason* is with the status of this epistemic framework, and not with any effects that it might have on the content of our empirical knowledge. The framework was to be neutral with regard to the contents of knowledge. As he states in its introduction, if the *Critique of Pure Reason* has any effect on knowledge, it is a negative one: the *Critique* serves 'not to extend, but to purify our reason'.[2] The new philosophy disallows the use of reason to generate knowledge on its own. It should have no effect on the contents of any empirical psychological theories. However, Kant believed that empiricism was wrong in supposing that conceptual knowledge was the product of sense impressions alone. He labelled Locke's empiricism 'physiological', meaning that it treated concepts as if they could be dissected down to their sensuous origins. Kant, by contrast, believed that there was an a-priori element in conceptual knowledge, that this a-priori element was not psychological, and that therefore psychology had to be banished from the theory of cognition.

For institutional reasons, however, Kant and his followers found it impossible to make a clean break with the Enlightenment tradition of psychology. Such was the weight of Wolff's authority that as university teachers of philosophy the Idealists were obliged to lecture on psychology, and they took the content of this psychology wherever they could find it. Moreover, Kant and the earliest post-Kantians were not born Kantians. By and large they converted to Kantianism from Wolffian rationalism. For these reasons, some Wolffian philosophy, including its psychology, was carried over into Idealism. This is most obvious in the case of Kant himself, but the same is broadly true of his successors: their published works show the influence of Wolffian psychology in a variety of ways.

Even where Kant's campaign to drive psychology out of philosophy was pursued, far from doing any long-term damage to psychology, it strengthened it, contrary to Kant's intentions. Kant claimed that psychology would never be a proper science. In response to this, the heirs of the empiricist and Wolffian traditions sought to establish psychology on the same footing as physics by taking up Wolff's idea of 'Psycheometria'. The result was the invention of psychophysics and the beginnings of psychology as a laboratory science. The other unplanned offspring of Idealism was a *naturphilosophisch* psychology, which led from Schelling via G. H. von Schubert, Schopenhauer, and C. G. Carus to the depth psychology of Freud and Jung. This tradition took up Kant's notion of a transcendental self from which all empirical expressions of self mysteriously emanate, and reinterpreted it as an unconscious, physiological self, even though this directly contravened Kant's ruling that the self was ultimately unknowable.

However, this later legacy of Idealism was not initially apparent. In the preface to his *Psychology* A. C. A. Eschenmayer, a disciple of Schelling, complained that recent philosophy had not favoured psychology, which had been 'until now neglected, or rather [it was slumbering] little noticed in the shadow of philosophy.'[3] The Danish *Naturphilosoph* Henrik Steffens was more direct: 'Since the great revolution initiated by Kant, [psychology] has been forced out of speculative philosophy.'[4] The present chapter focuses in the first place not on Idealist psychology, but on the implications of Idealist theory of knowledge for psychology. It aims to explain how Kant's Copernican Revolution in philosophy set out to exclude Enlightenment psychology; what consequences this had for the attitudes of his followers Fichte, Schelling, Hegel, and the Early Romantics, and how, by intended and unintended ways, Idealism made way for new forms of psychological theory.

KANT

Kant's view of psychology was complex. At times he seems to have tolerated empirical psychology, albeit not as a science; at other times he appears to have thought that psychology should be banished. In *De mundi sensibilis atque intelligibilis forma et principiis* (*On the Form and Principles of the Sensible and Intelligible World*, 1770), for instance, he states that empirical psychology deals with the 'phenomena of the internal sense' (*phaenomena . . . sensus interni*, KAA 11.397), a definition little different from Locke's.[5] Nearly thirty years later he expressed the same view in his *Anthropology*: 'In psychology we examine ourselves according to the representations of the inner sense.'[6]

At the same time Kant raises doubts about psychology's scientific status. In the *Metaphysische Anfangsgründe der Naturwissenschaft* (*Metaphysical Foundations of Natural Science*) he argues that Locke's empirical psychology – he also calls it a 'physiology of the inner sense' (*Physiologie des inneren Sinnes*, KWW IV.383; A381) – is incapable of becoming a natural science (KAA IV.471).[7] There are two reasons for this. In the first place, it is not quantitative (KAA IV.471). Secondly, a science must be objective in the sense that its object of study is independent from and unaffected by the methods used to analyse it. Kant argues that this is not true of psychology either as self-observation of the inner sense – in which the act of observing alters what is being observed – since the observed inner sense is itself doing the observing; or as observation of other people, who are aware that they are being observed and consciously or unconsciously reflect this in their behaviour (*KWW* x.401). Empirical psychology therefore has only anecdotal status.

More damagingly, Kant believes that empirical psychology invades areas where it does not belong. Psychological data must not be used as material in other branches of philosophy. In the prize essay 'Über die Fortschritte der Metaphysik' ('On the Progress of Metaphysics'), he insists that psychology must stay within limits: 'For the human perspective, psychology is no more than and can never be anything other than anthropology, i.e. knowledge of human beings only insofar as they know themselves as objects of the inner sense.'[8] So for instance the spontaneous productive imagination has nothing to do with the empirical imagination, which is responsible for synthesis: the latter does not belong to transcendental philosophy, but to psychology.[9] Similarly, there must be no psychological arguments in ethics.[10]

Kant's actual aim is not the philosophically modest one (professed at the beginning of the *Critique of Pure Reason*) of purifying the sciences and the branches of philosophy by keeping each within its proper limits. There is a more fundamental reason for Kant's strictures on psychology, and this stems from the dualism that underpins his philosophy. Writing to Marcus Herz in 1773 he acknowledged that he finds the question of the relation of mind and body a hopelessly difficult one; it is a 'subtle investigation and to my mind for all time a fruitless one'.[11] Similarly, in the preface to the *Anthropology* he argues that there is no hope of ever establishing a physical basis for mind:

Whoever broods over the natural causes in which e.g. the faculty of memory may be grounded can (so Descartes) ratiocinate this way and that about the traces of impressions left in the brain that sensations leave behind, but must concede that he is a mere observer of this play of his representations and must leave nature to do her work, whereas he does not know the nerves and fibres of the brain or understand how to apply them to his purpose: so that in the end all theoretical speculation about this is hot air.[12]

Kant could argue with some justice that psychology had not yet advanced to the stage of being able to say anything useful about the physiology of mind (although there was a good deal more empirical data available than he suggests, had he been interested in it). His conception of mind is such that he cannot see any point in pursuing this kind of research. Fundamentally, he believes that the dual nature of man makes physiological psychology a waste of time.

The role of psychology in the 'Critique of Pure Reason'

The *Critique of Pure Reason* aims to construct a firm metaphysical foundation for experience as it was conceived in common sense and science. Kant knew that he was facing in two directions. He had to resist the corrosive empiricism of Locke and, in particular, its sceptical version in Hume. At the same time he had to dismantle and rebuild the rationalism of Leibniz and Wolff. Both of these philosophies seemed to Kant, in their different ways, unable to account for experience. Empiricism could not explain how we were equipped to receive experiences. Rationalism was unable to explain how our cognitive apparatus knew where to locate its objects.

For Hume our everyday picture of the external world is constituted by our imagination, which fills in the gaps, as it were, between sense impressions. Sense impressions are linked to or 'associated' with one another by the imagination according to certain empirical rules, such as causation, likeness, proximity, and so on, which have no demonstrable objective reality. This caused serious difficulties in the two principal areas of Kant's philosophical interest, science and ethics. In science, Hume's empiricism undermines causality, which ceases to be an objective reality and becomes a subjective construct. The danger that Hume poses to ethics stems from this enhanced role of the imagination. For Hume, the way our experience is constituted is a function of psychological laws. If the self is determined by psychological laws, then there can be no free-will and, on Kant's reasoning, no morality. German Idealism gets its distinctive flavour from Kant's strong notion of free-will. In the 1760s he had read Rousseau and been deeply impressed by the latter's insistence on the primacy of ethics.[13] Repeatedly in Kant's writings one finds the assertion that morality is more important than knowledge and that the domain of the ethical (or 'practical' – *praktisch*) must not be contaminated by the scientific (or 'theoretical' – *theoretisch*). Thus in the preface to the *Grundlegung zur Metaphysik der Sitten* (*Foundations of the Metaphysics of Morals*) Kant writes of his intention 'to develop a pure moral philosophy, which is cleansed of anything that might be empirical and belong to anthropology'.[14] The threat of a scientific psychology is that it will replace free-will with natural necessity. The task of the *Critique of Pure Reason* is to protect free-will from this, whilst at the same time establishing the continuity and objectivity of experience. It must both guarantee the scientific concept of causality *and* fence off the self from its consequences.

Kant's defence of science proceeds by arguing that Hume's account of experience is insufficient. For any experience at all to be possible certain necessary conditions have to obtain which, once we accept them, take us beyond Hume. This also has a constructive aspect, for just as we can say that empiricism's account of experience is insufficient, so too can we work back from sense impressions to what must be necessary for us to have them in the first place. Empiricism had falsely resolved experience down into atomistic sense impressions. For Kant, there is no experience without concepts, and these concepts are formal structures that cannot be determined by analysing the constituent elements of our ideas into more primal ideas and finally into sense impressions. Thus it was a further corollary of this argument that metaphysics – the science of objective concepts – had to be re-established.

In re-establishing metaphysics Kant faced the task of cleaning the Augean stables of rationalism. He saw that rationalism had operated with an illegitimate conception of reason. Leibniz believed that his entire metaphysical system could be derived from the law of sufficient reason. In this sense, for rationalism facts of experience have no purchase on scientific truth; science does not need experience. This was intolerable because it was incompatible with Kant's Newtonian ideal of experimental science. Kant's response was to insist on a 'Principle of Significance', a criterion for assessing whether concepts are meaningful.[15] According to this principle, concepts can be meaningful only if they are at least potentially applicable to experience. A concept that can have no field of application in experience is a meaningless chimera:

Thus all concepts and with them all principles, however *a priori* they may be, are nevertheless related to empirical intuitions, i.e. to *data* for possible experience. Without this they have no objective validity at all, but are rather a mere play.[16]

Empiricism had boiled experience down into sense impressions; rationalism had made experience redundant. The errors of empiricism and rationalism were the inverse of one another. Kant expresses this insight in an often quoted formulation: 'Leibniz *intellectualized* the appearances, just as Locke totally *sensitivizes* the concepts of understanding.'[17] The symmetry of rationalism and empiricism connected with Wolff's duality of concepts. Concepts must be a fusion of content and form. They need the material provided by sense impressions and the form provided by subjective ideas. Without this – that is to say if there were no field of experience for the application of concepts and if concepts did not contain rules for their use – then concepts would be meaningless: 'Thoughts without content are empty, intuitions without concepts are blind.'[18]

However, the dismantling of rationalism turned out to be rather easier than the reconstruction of metaphysics, and although the *Critique of Pure Reason* begins with arguments against Hume and ends with arguments against Leibniz, this is the reverse of the order in which Kant worked out his arguments. Kant claimed that he was woken from his dogmatic slumbers by Hume. The awakening was a realisation that Hume's sceptical version of empiricism had disastrous implications for metaphysics. Kant's answer came some time later: he saw that the threat of Hume's scepticism might be warded off by an argument deriving from rationalism. This argument – that a claim to knowledge only makes sense if certain necessary framework conditions apply – has two aspects. On the one hand it is a weapon against scepticism. It sets up propositions about the conditions necessary for knowledge such that, if the sceptic denies these conditions, he contradicts his own scepticism. (This kind of transcendental argument was familiar to Wolff and the Enlightenment rationalists.) It also furnishes support for some basic metaphysical concepts, such as causality. However, the status of the transcendental argument is itself open to question. It cannot be empirical, because then it would be subject to the sceptical challenge that it might not obtain universally. Equally, it must not allow that its concepts have content, or else it would generate knowledge from reason alone and re-open the door to full-blown rationalism. Accordingly Kant repeatedly insists on the limited scope of his claims. Transcendental arguments should show what is formally necessary for us to have experience – that is, the recognitional ability to use concepts – and no more.

Much of the early part of the *Critique of Pure Reason* is concerned with defending the possibility and defining the nature of metaphysical propositions or 'judgements'. These judgements can be illustrated by the analogy of propositions in geometry, which are 'synthetic a-priori' judgements, that is they are not merely analytic (defined as propositions the denial of which necessarily involves the denier in a contradiction), nor do they need to be validated from experience. Kant's new slimmed-down metaphysics consists in such 'pure concepts of the understanding' (*reine Verstandesbegriffe*) or, following the terminology of Aristotle's logic, 'categories'. The first part of *Critique of Pure Reason* culminates in a demonstration that it is legitimate to use these categories.

Kant thinks that two kinds of demonstration are necessary: a subjective or transcendental and an objective or metaphysical demonstration. The subjective deduction shows that thought must occur by means of these categories. The objective deduction shows what these categories must be; it is an 'exhaustive inventory' compiled according to a principle that will guarantee the list's completeness. We will not be concerned here with the objective deduction, which attempts to deduce the complete list of categories from what Kant supposes to be the pure forms of propositional thought. The subjective deduction, on the other hand, explains how it is that the world of appearances necessarily presents itself to us, through the categories, in such a way that our mental faculties can grasp it. This part of the argument took up a great deal of Kant's effort, to the extent that its imperfections demanded a complete revision for the second edition of the *Critique*. Even this second version did not satisfy Kant, for he continued to produce further, more concise versions up to 1794.[19]

The aim of the subjective deduction is twofold. Its primary aim is to show that there is a unity of experience. Kant believes that he must show how it is that the 'many' of sensation becomes a 'one' in consciousness through the operations of our faculties, specifically memory and imagination, controlled by the understanding. The subjective deduction is a piece of psychological demonstration. Ultimately, on the terms of Kant's own argument, this part of the deduction is untenable, for it treats empirical states of affairs (our memory, imagination and so on) as the transcendental and therefore non-empirical conditions of experience, as Kant's contemporaries were quick to recognise.

The key idea in the deduction is 'synthesis'. Synthesis is defined as 'the act of bringing together mental representations and comprehending their multiplicity in a cognition'.[20] This is the job of the imagination. It receives data which it forms into what we actually experience. Imagination precedes the application of concepts: it is, as it were, 'blind' (*KWW* III.117, B103/A78) and unguided by the understanding. (In this sense Kant's conception of the imagination follows a long tradition of seeing the imagination as a fundamental though unconscious process.) The third stage in cognition, after sensation and synthesis, is the application of concepts to experience by the understanding. With this final stage, experience – the way in which the world of appearances is presented to us – is given. There are thus three stages in experience: sensation, imagination, understanding. Insofar as Kant distinguishes between these three stages in terms of their objects, he is part of the eighteenth-century tradition of Faculty Psychology, which divides the mind into a hierarchy of cascading faculties, each with different responsibilities. The distinction between reason (defined as the faculty of logic) and understanding (the ability to use concepts) came to Kant directly from contemporary psychology.[21]

Against this it might be argued that the theory of cognition set out in the subjective deduction is not an argument about any individual person's experience, but about the necessary features of experience in general. It is not an empirical psychology but a 'transcendental psychology'.[22] The relation between this 'transcendental psychology' and empirical psychology is the same as the relation between the a-priori conditions of knowledge and knowledge itself. Transcendental psychology prescribes the conditions within which empirical psychology functions. It gives us the specification that our cognitive apparatus must meet if it is to carry out cognitive tasks.[23] If Kant is nonetheless to be accused of psychologism, then this is at the most a weak form of it.[24] For transcendental psychology gives a very limited range of prescriptions to empirical psychology.[25]

However, the charge of psychologism remains. For one thing, most of the time Kant is not explicit about what the 'possible experience' posited by the transcendental argument really is, if not possible human experience. Reading between the lines, the answer seems fairly clear. For all Kant's claims that his argument concerns the principles and not the empirical facts of experience, for the Enlightenment humanist Kant experience is not a pure abstraction, not any conceivable cognitive system. Kant was not describing a computer. He was describing a human mind, a *Gemüt*. In so doing he was engaging in a debate about psychology.

Kant's psychological theories

One of the catalysts of the *Critique of Pure Reason* was Johann Nikolaus Tetens's *Philosophische Versuche über die menschliche Natur und ihre Entwicklung* (*Philosophical Essays on Human Nature and its Development*, 1777).[26] Tetens argued that the formal properties of mind determine knowledge. Two of Tetens's arguments were particularly important for Kant. These were Tetens's tripartite division of mental faculties, whose influence we have seen on the subjective deduction, and his conception of the imagination's active role in cognition. Tetens demonstrated the active role of the imagination with the example of the wing of Pegasus.[27] The point at which the wing is joined to Pegasus' equine body is a non-existent entity. There is nothing in experience that joins a horse's body to a wing. The idea of the joint, then, is not composed by association from the idea of a horse's anatomy and idea of a winged creature's anatomy. Tetens is thus able to confute the empiricist idea that the imagination does not really conceive of this thing as a new entity and instead creates it by means of the combination of prior experiences. On the contrary, argues Tetens, this is a clear case of the imagination creating something that is not in our experience. Thus there are cases where imagination is prior to perception.

Kant also conceives of an active role for imagination in making a unity out of the manifold of experience. He goes on to make a bold claim: 'No psychologist has yet thought that the imagination is a necessary ingredient of perception itself.'[28] The difference between Kant and Tetens and what constitutes Kant's originality is that he sees this active role of the imagination as necessary for ordinary thought. But the ability of the imagination to produce these 'schemata' is mysterious: 'This schematism of our understanding . . . is a hidden art in the depths of the human soul, whose true operations we can divine from nature and lay unveiled before our eyes only with difficulty.'[29] Kant's conception of the schematism applies a familiar idea from eighteenth-century psychology – that the imagination is unconsciously productive – to everyday cognition.[30] This kind of reliance on psychological arguments is evident throughout his writings. Like other German university philosophers of his day, Kant lectured on empirical psychology. These lectures can be reconstructed from his students' notes, and what emerges is essentially Wolffian psychology, although Kant presents the doctrine in a more approachable, colourful, and empirical way than most of his Wolffian contemporaries.[31] Nonetheless, in his psychology Kant remained wedded to Wolffian rationalism. His only published work on a psychological theme, the *Anthropologie in pragmatischer Hinsicht* (*Anthropology in Pragmatic Perspective*) is, in its texture and structure, no more and no less than a piece of rationalist psychology. Its first part, the 'Anthropologische Didaktik' ('Anthropological Didactics'), is divided into three parts, corresponding to the cognitive, the sensory, and the appetitive faculties. These are sustained throughout the work. This may be because a three-faculty structure of mind corresponds to the threefold structure of the critical philosophy as a whole. The cognitive faculties have nature as their object, and this is the subject of the *Critique of Pure Reason*. The *Second Critique* sets out the laws of what we should want, the objects of our appetitive faculties (*Begehrungsvermögen*). In the *Third Critique* Kant defines the rules that govern our feelings of pleasure and pain, our aesthetic responses to objects of nature and art.[32] In any case, Kant was following a pattern established by Tetens.

Whereas the *Critique of Pure Reason* establishes a transcendental psychology, the *Anthropology* gives the empirical determinations of our faculties.

The pragmatic character of the *Anthropology* consists in its describing the proper and improper use of the faculties, their 'weaknesses and ailments' (*Schwächen und Krankheiten*) as well as their empirical nature. Thus the second part, the 'Anthropologische Characteristik' ('Anthropological characteristics'), is in the form of a characterology. It describes the set of behavioural signs that indicate a person's inner states, according to the venerable tradition of the theory of temperaments. It helps us to distinguish the melancholic temperament from the phlegmatic, the choleric from the sanguine. What it does not do, though, is explain the mechanisms that produce the different temperaments. Part of Kant wants to remain equivocal about this, like a good empiricist. So, for instance, he maintains that it is not decided whether it is the blood, the humours, or the nerves that create character (*KWW* x.626–7). But part of Kant is a schematic rationalist who, just as he wants to be sure that he has completed the table of categories in the *Critique of Pure Reason*, insists that the system of the four temperaments is complete and admits of no exceptions. Hence the diagram shown in Figure 1 (*KWW* x.632). This diagram is meant to represent the actual relation between the four temperaments, which Kant insists are absolute and never mixed. Goethe observed that this cannot be based on experience: at best it is an idealisation, at worst unpleasantly dogmatic (letter to Voigt, *WA* IV.xiii.347). The theory of the temperaments belonged to an ancient psychological tradition (although it was not uncommon in rationalist Germany), and if it is surprising to find these ideas in Kant, then we should remember how Kant turned his back on the 'physiological' method of Locke and the British empiricists. Rejecting that modern analytical approach made Kant more prone to fall back on archaic theories. For all the revolutionary effects of the *Critique of Pure Reason*, Kant was in some respects a conservative philosopher. If the epistemic structure of rationalism died with Kant, then much of its content survived.

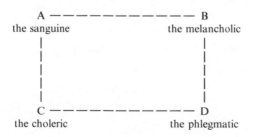

Figure 1

Some of the psychological arguments that he took from the Wolffian tradition can be excised from his work without leaving deep scars. But there are also commitments that go deeper. The evidence of his indebtedness to the Wolffian tradition can be found on almost every page of Kant's works, and not just on the surface. Kant's preference for the psychology of rationalism above that of empiricism is built into the very structure of his thought. He wants above all to protect the 'noumenal' status of the thinking self – the self as something that must be thought but cannot be known. The transcendental argument involves us saying that we must think the self as the subject of our cognition but that we cannot know it as such.[33] We can only know the self as a phenomenal object, for otherwise we would contravene the Principle of Significance, which holds that concepts must be capable of relating to empirical contents. However, the doctrine of Transcendental Idealism, which claims that the thinking I is unknowable, leaves the relation of known to unknown unclear. What, then, is the status of the 'transcendental unity of apperception', if it is both responsible for thought and yet not subject to the categories and thereby phenomenal? The self would appear to lie behind the categories and the categories to face in one direction only: away from the self. That way leads to Idealism proper. Kant's position on the status of the transcendental self cannot survive being pressed any harder. His position on the doctrine of Transcendental Idealism is hardly less fragile, for, to put it crudely, it is not clear in what sense arguments about the necessary conditions for things can be independent of the existence of the things whose conditions they purport to determine. At times Kant himself shows some uncertainty on this. In the preface to the first edition of the *Critique of Pure Reason* he states that the analysis of the conditions of thought is 'a search for a cause for a given effect [i.e. our cognition] and therefore resembles to some degree a hypothesis'.[34] This is far from the final certainty of a transcendental argument, which ought to admit of no exceptions. Kant immediately retracts the statement, saying that he will show that it is in fact not hypothetical. Kant was unsure about the cogency of the subjective deduction of the categories. The reception of the *Critique of Pure Reason* by his contemporaries justified his fears.

FICHTE

In Thomas Love Peacock's satirical novel *Nightmare Abbey* the philosopher Mr Flosky, 'a very lachrymose and morbid gentleman', who 'plunged into the central opacity of Kantian metaphysics, and lay *perdu*

several years in transcendental darkness', who even christened his eldest
son Emanuel Kant Flosky, speaks of his own philosophy as 'transcendental psychology'.[35] Much of the early reaction to the *Critique of Pure
Reason* focussed on psychological issues. The Wolffian rationalists thought
that Kant had merely rewritten Faculty Psychology. The empiricists also
found a psychology in the *Critique of Pure Reason*, and they used this
to show that Kant's transcendental argument did not move beyond
empirical reasoning. As for the Kantians, it was the issue of psychology
that split them into an Idealist and a realist faction, the former, led by
Fichte, developing Kant's arguments away from psychology, the latter, led
by Fries and Schmid, repositioning Kantianism as a scientific theory of
mind.

The first impulse was given by the sceptic Fritz Jacobi, who argued that
the transcendental self was incompatible with the category of causality.
The *Critique* clearly needed the idea that sense impressions are caused by
objects. Without it experience could have no material, but with it the
transcendental self could not be defended. Jacobi nicely summarises the
problem in terms of his own uneasy experience of reading the *Critique*:

I must admit that this circumstance caused me not a little delay in my study of
Kantian philosophy, with the consequence that for several years in succession I
had to begin the *Critique of Pure Reason* over again, because I was continually
confused by the fact that I could not enter the system without this premise [i.e.
causation], and could not remain in the system with the same premise.[36]

If we think of the transcendental self as lying behind the empirical self,
there must be a relation between the two, and this must be thought of in
terms of the categories, as they are exhaustive and hence there can be no
other way to conceive of the relation. But if the transcendental self is
thought of in terms of the categories, then it must be empirical, for the
categories can only be applied to empirical objects. If so, Kant's transcendental self turns out to be empirical after all, and Kantianism unravels
into what Jacobi calls Spinozism.

Fichte's reception of the *Critique of Pure Reason* was conditioned by his
earlier encounter with Kant's ethics and Jacobi's supposition of Spinozism.[37] Following the arguments of the *Critique of Practical Reason*, philosophy had to be freed of all connection with psychology. Other interpreters of
Kant, such as Karl Leonhard Reinhold, had sought to underpin Kant's
system with a solid foundation, but this, according to Jacobi, led to
Spinozism. Fichte's answer was to claim that realism about the world
flows with unimpeachable logic from a primal, but utterly unjustifiable,

dogmatic decision. Reinhold still appeared to cling to the realist view that the self was ultimately knowable, whereas Kant had argued that it was not. If we were conscious of the sources of the self – in particular the sources of the moral will – then we must be able to give an account of this consciousness that was not empirical. Fichte's aim was, in short, to ground the categorical imperative in a non-empirical theory of the self. The I (*Ich*) – the absolute subject which conceives of representations, subjects, objects, and so on – must be posited in order for what is opposed or 'opposited' to it to be thought at all: 'The absolute subject, the I, is not given by empirical intuition; but posited by intellectual intuition, and the absolute object, the Not-I, is what is opposed to it.'[38] By arguing in this fashion Fichte can claim to be following the anti-psychological spirit of the *Critique of Pure Reason*. Reason, the medium of the absolute subject, now occupies the originary point and is completely independent, as Fichte proclaims in the introduction to the *Wissenschaftslehre* (*Theory of Science*):

What then ultimately is the content of the Theory of Science in a word? This: reason is absolutely independent; it exists only for itself; but its subject is also only itself. Hence all that reason is must be grounded in reason itself and explained by means of reason and not by something outside it to which thing, outside itself, it could not attain without giving itself up. In short: the Theory of Science is Transcendental Idealism.[39]

In order for us to know anything, we must first posit the empirically unknowable self. Only then can the empirical non-self be known. The *Ding an sich* as absolute subject is the prerequisite of all empirical knowledge. But if the self is empirically unknowable, as what do we think the self? Clearly not as a thing, for that would be to say that the self is at least notionally determined, and what is determined cannot have primal reality: 'anything to which passivity (*Leiden*) is ascribed and thus not activity is something that has been effected (an effect, and therefore dependent on another real thing and without its own primal reality)'.[40] Fichte is keen to distance the self from any suggestion of passivity: we can only think the self as absolute spontaneity and as undetermined by any prior reality. The language of activity and passivity (*Tun* and *Leiden*) suggests a psychological argument. It suggests faculties or powers acting on one another. Fichte is, as we have seen, determined to avoid this. In this spirit he defines the self not as an entity, nor even as a state, but as an action (*Thathandlung*). This serves to link the self not to the psychological realm of mental states, but to the ethical realm of the will. The activity of the *Ich* is 'action turning in on itself' (*in sich zurückgehendes*

Handeln, FGA 1.iv.216). The actions are actions of self-positing (*setzen*). Writing to Reinhold in 1795, Fichte insists on the distinction between his own transcendental conception of the self and the psychologism of which he thinks Reinhold guilty:

Now this original *positing*, and *oppositing*, and *dividing* is NB not *thinking*, not *intuiting*, not *sensing*, not *willing*, not *feeling* etc., rather it is the *whole activity* of the human mind, which has no name, which never appears in consciousness, which cannot be *conceived*, because it is that which is *determinable* by all particular acts of the mind (such as *create consciousness*) but in no way is *determined.*[41]

The primal point in Fichte's philosophy is that at which 'the I posits its own being'.[42] From this an opposition arises. The self has created something that is not itself, the Not-I (*Nicht-Ich*) or object. This is the beginning of the dialectical process in which we, as thinking beings, are all engaged, the process of ejecting objects from the self and creating a duality, which is underpinned by the deeper unity of the self. Objects are created and finite, the subject is the creator and infinite. The interplay of the limited and the unlimited – the self's attempts to project its unlimitedness onto limited objects, its return to the self and its further acts of objectification – all of this is the work of the spontaneous imagination:

This communication of the I in and with itself, in that it posits itself as both finite and infinite – a communication that at the same time consists in a conflict with itself and thus reproduces itself, inasmuch as the I wants to unite things that cannot be united, trying one moment to assume the infinite into the form of the finite, the next to posit it outside of the same, and in the same moment trying once again to assume it into the form of the finite – this is the faculty of *imagination.*[43]

In a sense then, Fichte, like Kant, returns to the Enlightenment's notion of the pre-rational creative imagination. For Fichte, however, the structure of the imagination cannot be determined along psychological lines. The imagination has a logical structure, not an empirical one. The faculties of Faculty Psychology are furnished with the logical functions of positing and 'oppositing'.

The practical task of philosophy is training in self-observation. The motto of the *Theory of Science* might thus be interpreted as a modern version of the Delphic motto 'know thyself' (*gnōthi seauton*), though in a sense directly opposed to Goethe's and Moritz's: 'Attend to yourself: turn your gaze away from all that surrounds you and towards your inner self – is the first demand that philosophy makes of its student.'[44] Whereas the

Critique of Pure Reason sits in judgement over the powers of reason, the *Theory of Science* sets out the process through which the intelligence must go to prescribe its own laws.

Thus far Fichte adheres to Kant's conception of Transcendental Idealism as purifying and not extending reason. It follows from the architecture of Fichte's philosophy – the separation of a foundational 'doctrine of knowledge' (*Wissenschaftslehre*) from the diverse branches of 'practical' philosophy – that the *Theory of Science* ought not to determine the contents of theoretical philosophy.[45] However, it plainly does. Fichte argues for a particular conception of the self. The self is equipped with various drives (*Triebe*) that effect logical actions, such as the self's drive to realise its own infinitude. This would be harmless, except that it leads to a particularly virulent form of the mind–body problem. If the self's drives and its relation to the body are of a logical nature, it is hard even to say where a mind–body interface might be located. In his *Grundlage des Naturrechts nach Prinzipien der Wissenschaftslehre* (*Foundations of Natural Law*, 1796–7), Fichte posits the existence of two distinct but parallel bodies, the *Leib* and the *Körper*. The *Leib* is the rational body, the bodily extension of the self. The *Körper* is the empirical body that is affected by the world. The mediation between *Leib* and *Körper* occurs through two species of matter, 'subtle' (*subtil*) matter and 'crude' (*roh*) matter. (Fichte took this conception of two forms of matter from Platner's broadly Wolffian *Anthropology*, where it performs a similar role.)[46] The will determines subtle matter (*FGA* 1.iii.372). The primacy of the will is, therefore, preserved. Also preserved is the distinction between man and animal. For Fichte, an animal is an organism, whereas man is, primally at least, absolutely nothing. Man is utterly 'undetermined':

Every animal *is* what it is; only man is originally nothing at all. What man is to be he must become and – since he is to be a being for himself – must become it by himself. Nature has completed all of its works, except that she withdrew her hand from man and entrusted him to himself. Malleability as such is the character of humanity.[47]

From this primal state of undetermination, two roads lead. One is the road of realism, the dogmatic assumption that man is determined by his world. The other is the road of Idealism and freedom, which posits the human will as essentially and transcendentally active. But it also leaves room for Wolffian psychology, for mental faculties whose functions are determined logically and not empirically. As with Kant, the radical epistemology coexists with the preserved remains of an earlier psychology.

NOVALIS

Novalis's Pietist leanings might have given him a more favourable attitude towards psychology than the other Idealists, and there is some evidence in his diaries and correspondence of an esoteric, private psychology.[48] However, his public views on what the status and content of psychology should properly be were shaped by his Idealist philosophy. Much of what he wrote concerning psychology is attributable to the influence of Fichte, for although Novalis and Friedrich Schlegel were intent on moving beyond Fichte and might in some respects be judged to have done so, Novalis's psychology retains clearly Fichtean features. Fichte had suggested that the choice between idealist and realist ontologies was arbitrary. As Novalis puts it: 'Judging oneself according to things or things according to oneself – are one and the same thing.'[49] Novalis first accepted and then sought to overcome this ontological decisionism. This involved collapsing the distance between immanence and transcendence, so that, in Novalis's words, 'transcendent nature is also immanent – and so the immanent person is also transcendent – and vice versa'.[50] As in Schelling's *System of Transcendental Idealism* (*System des transzendentalen Idealismus*), transcendental philosophy and nature philosophy run parallel to one another, so mind is the key to nature and nature is 'an encyclopedic systematic index or plan of our mind'.[51] The study of the mutual constitution of the mental and the natural Novalis calls 'psychology of reality' or 'world psychology' (*Realpsychologie, Weltpsychologie*).

Again like Fichte, Novalis believes that a human possesses two bodies. One is the physical body, which acts on and is acted on by the world. The other is a spiritual body that obeys the soul. The two bodies interact by means of a 'nexus of associations' (*Associations nexus*) by means of which body affects mind. However, there is also evidence, Novalis says, of a reversed relationship (*umgekehrtes Verhältnis*), by means of which mind affects body (*NS* 11.546). The physical body works according to the laws of 'excitement' (*Erregung*). This derives, with modifications, from the Brownian medical theory that Novalis learnt from Schelling, A. C. A. Eschenmayer, and Andreas Röschlaub.[52] The idea of excitement has wider implications for Novalis as a Pietist, for an excess of excitement threatens to undermine the spiritual calm and harmony that the Pietist aims to achieve. Against this threat, Novalis devised a theory of managing and controlling the body, a 'theory of the art of living' (*Lebenskunstlehre*). Its premise is that basic bodily functions can be brought under rational control. It is not that humans should aim at an ascetic denial of the body.

Rather they should be physically self-determining: the fully developed and complete person is one who can be excitable at will, who 'has all constitutions complete with their variations in his power'.[53] That is to say, Novalis adopts Fichte's voluntarism. For Fichte philosophy starts from the attempt to 'know thyself' and aims at mastery of the whole psycho-physical self. As we gain control over our bodies, so we become free from nature and impose our will on it. Novalis tends in a similar direction, but emphasises the therapeutic benefits. By mastering one's physical system, one comes to know mind and body so well that one becomes one's own doctor.[54] Novalis has a distinctive and paradoxical attitude towards illness. Some forms of illness have a positive value. For instance, there are 'absolute' (*absolut*) and 'sublime' (*erhaben*) forms of 'hypochondria' (*NS* 11.395, 614). These, as distinct from ordinary 'minor' hypochondria, can be cultivated and practised for educative purposes. 'Hypochondria' yields 'self-knowledge of the body' (*körperliche Selbstkenntniß*) and of how the mind controls it. In its pure form this facilitates self-mastery (*Selbstbeherrschung*, *NS* 11.607). (This is, of course, the direct antithesis of Moritz's and Goethe's attitude to 'hypochondria', the conquest of which was a necessity for living in peace with one's physical nature.) The idea of mastery also explains part of the attraction of animal magnetism. We have seen how Novalis sets great store by the ability of mind to affect body and what he terms the 'reversed relation' existing between them. Animal magnetism exemplifies this reversed relation. It shows the mind setting the body – even another person's body! – in motion by means of thought alone (*NS* 111.602).

Heinrich von Ofterdingen

It might seem unfair to treat Novalis's *Heinrich von Ofterdingen* as a psychologically realistic novel. However, the novel does engage with psychological theory in a consistent way, so that its psychology can be counted realist on its own terms. This is apparent in the novel's treatment of dreaming, which reflects some of the ideas discussed in the last section. During the discussion of poetry and nature in Chapter 7, Klingsohr observes that moments of poetic inspiration are, like dreams, exhausting. Morning dreams are hard to shake off, but shaken off they must be, if one is not to fall into 'more oppressive tiredness' (*drückendere Müdigkeit*) and spend the day in 'sickly exhaustion'(*krankhafte Erschöpfung*). The idea of alternating states of tension and exhaustion derives from the Brownian view of health, according to which our body moves between two poles of tension and relaxation, the ideal being a steady middle state.[55] This is why Klingsohr uses the adjective 'sickly' (*krankhaft*), which might not otherwise seem appropriate to describe the after-effects of disturbed sleep: Brown saw an excess or lack of tension as the cause of all sickness.

The novel opens with Heinrich's dream of the blue flower, which embodies the similarity of dreaming and inspiration suggested later by Klingsohr, for the dream serves as a provocation to Heinrich to pursue his ideal of becoming a poet and also is itself poetry, that is to say the product of a freely active imagination. This is the Romantic view of dreaming that Heinrich defends in discussion with his father. The discussion presents an archetypal constellation. Young Heinrich believes in meaningful dreams; his father, a practical craftsman, thinks that dreams are 'froth' (*Träume sind Schäume*). Heinrich and his father represent a contrast between two philosophical stances – Sensibility and Enlightenment – that is familiar to us from Lessing's dramas. When the father argues that the age of miracles is gone, to be replaced, he implies, by an age of reason, he recalls another familiar debate between Enlightenment and its opponents (*NS* 1.198). Heinrich, on the other hand, argues that in dreams the imagination, which is otherwise constrained, relaxes in freedom.[56] However, Novalis does not simply succumb to the clichéd contrast of dreaming Romanticism against sober Enlightenment. Prompted by Heinrich, the father recounts a dream from his own youth and in the process begins to draw closer to Heinrich's view. When Heinrich asks whether the flower his father saw in the dream was blue, his father is at first non-committal, but then silently takes up Heinrich's suggestion into his account of the dream and talks of 'a little blue flower' (*ein blaues Blümchen*, *NS* 1.202). This might simply be conciliatory diplomacy on his part, but it seems more likely that the father is in the process of recapturing his own romantic youth and that his experience was similar to what Heinrich's will be. Besides the blue flower, the dreams have common elements and both express a psyche filled with romantic and erotic yearning. The implication is that the dream-world is shared, that there is a common, unindividuated unconscious.

As well as expressing the young man's drive towards romantic fulfilment, the dreams present a romanticised world. In the terms of Novalis's Romantic aesthetics, they express 'nature as it could be' (*die Natur, wie sie seyn könnte*, *NS* III.652). Seen in this way, the dreams express not individual psychology, but *Realpsychologie* or *Weltpsychologie*. They are metaphorical representations of movement towards union – the union between man and woman, but also a more general union of the parts of nature, a universal sympathy, like the 'wondrous Sympathy' (*wundervolle Sympathie*) that brought the world into being or the 'almighty Sympathy of nature' (*allmächtige Sympathie der Natur*) that Heinrich dreams of. Besides the tendency towards union, the dreams contain images of communication and transition: water imagery is the main vehicle of these ideas. In the dreams we see the world becoming spirit. One of Heinrich's first experiences in his dream is the sublimation of his body. He feels himself moving 'with incomprehensible lightness' (*mit unbegreiflicher Leichtigkeit*), and his sensations reach 'unheard-of heights' (*unerhörte Höhen*) of sharpness (*NS* 1.196). This may recall Novalis's Fichtean notion of the mastery of the senses: Heinrich's senses are becoming pure spirit, just as the dream-world itself shows nature being reconstituted by and on the terms of spirit.

This seems to be the tendency of the novel as a whole, as far as one can tell. In the unfinished second part of the novel Heinrich is to progress into an allegorical universe, where nature has become one with spirit (*NS* III.652). Ordinary psychology – alluded to in Klingsohr's Brownian theory of excitement – has thus functioned as a provocation. The dream excites Heinrich physically and mentally, and it prompts him to pursue his mission: it is the beginning of his education. At the same time, the content of the dream shows spirit reconstituting nature.[57] Symbolically it represents mastery, the education of physical nature by spirit. These two ideas, the theory of excitement and the 'theory of the development of nature' (*Bildungslehre der Natur*), complement one another and together form the heart of Novalis's Fichtean philosophical anthropology:

THEORY OF EXCITEMENT. All stimulus is to be merely temporal, merely *a means of education*, merely an incitement to autonomous activity.

THEORY OF THE DEVELOPMENT OF NATURE. Nature is to become moral. We are its *educators* – its moral *tangents* – its moral stimuli.[58]

THE FUTURE OF IDEALIST PSYCHOLOGY

To conclude this discussion of Idealism's treatment of psychology, we shall return to our starting point: Eschenmayer's and Steffens's remarks on the low status of psychology in Idealism. It is important to recognise that this low status was not an accidental by-product of philosophical developments in other areas. Kant had rejected the 'physiological' approach of empiricism and argued that psychology had no place in philosophy, even as a source of illustrative material. His followers went even further, denying the very meaningfulness of an empirical science of psychology. Fichte, like Kant, believed that psychology must be excluded from epistemology.[59] He saw psychology as an earlier, more primitive form of philosophical life: eighteenth-century psychologists did at least have a conception of self, but it was a crude and materialist one (*FGA* 1.ii.383), and totally inappropriate to its subject. This 'contrast of form and material' made psychology a 'philosophical grotesque', in Friedrich Schlegel's view.[60] Novalis expressed this in still stronger terms: 'So-called psychology is one of those masks that have taken over the positions in the temple where the real images of the gods should be.'[61] Schelling also saw the psychological method as leading to the denigration of man:

Psychology . . . necessarily tends . . . to demean everything noble and uncommon. . . . The great deeds and characters of the past in the marvellous existence of the ancient world appear, under the psychological knife, to be the natural result of a few quite comprehensible motives. The ideas of the philosophers are revealed as the products of a handful of rather crude psychological deceptions.[62]

It would be better, in fact, if psychology were banned altogether. It appears that, were Schelling installed in the censor's office, this is precisely what he would do.[63] Hegel agrees that psychology is inappropriate: it is fixated on materiality and gives too little attention to activity (*HGW* v.258), and it tends to have a fragmenting effect, 'so that the spirit becomes a mere aggregate of autonomous powers'.[64] He rejects out of hand all existing psychology, not however because it is primitive, but because it is decadent (*HGW* x.262). Current psychology 'is in an utterly miserable condition'.[65] Indeed, the only good book on psychology is Aristotle's *De anima* (*HGW* x.11).

The Idealist view is that if there is to be a science of man, it must begin from the premise that our whole being, even our body, is rational. This science is called anthropology, Fichte argued (*FGA* 1.iii.377–8). The reframing of the sciences of man within a more general anthropology is a typical Idealist move.[66] According to Fichte and Novalis, anthropology would take its concepts from more rational branches of philosophy such as ethics and law (*NS* 11.51). Hegel, on the other hand, would replace psychology with his own *Phenomenology of Spirit*, as he states in the advertisement for it: 'The Phenomenology of Spirit is to take the place of psychological explanations.'[67] Another possibility just dawning on the horizon is a science of psychology on an entirely new basis, namely animal magnetism, which has shown just how wrong earlier psychology was (*HGW* x.13).

The Idealist campaign against psychology did not go unanswered. C. C. E. Schmid published a response to Schelling in the *Anthropologisches Journal* (*Anthropological Journal*). Schmid claims that the Idealists are simply intellectually lazy.[68] Rather than endure the hard grind of empirical research, they extrapolate so-called empirical theories from their basic philosophical positions – a charge that has some truth in it, as we saw in the case of Fichte's commitment to Platner's theory of subtle nervous fluid. The Idealists did in fact tend to adopt theories that cohered with their positions, without much concern for the theories' basis in reality. It is hard to see otherwise why Schelling and Hegel should have been so committed to animal magnetism. Yet the Idealists' suggestions for the future of psychology were not as empty as they might now seem. The tradition of Idealist anthropology did prosper for some time to come. Gottfried Keller has his Green Henry attend a series of lectures on anthropology, not that they profit him much.[69] Schelling's *Naturphilosophie* offered possibilities, in combination with animal magnetism, as we shall see in the next section. Finally there was the quantitative approach, which Kant had identified as the only basis for a science of psychology. In doing so Kant thought he was setting an impossibly high hurdle for psychology to jump. There was, of course, a risk that someone would take Kant at his word and jump the hurdle, and this is indeed what happened. The irony is that the first to try was Kant's immediate successor in the chair of philosophy at Königsberg, J. F. Herbart.

Idealism's twofold legacy: Herbart and Eschenmayer

The two best-known psychological products of Idealism are J. F. Herbart's *Lehrbuch zur Psychologie* (*Text Book for Psychology*, 1816) and A. C. A. Eschenmayer's *Psychologie* (*Psychology*, 1816). Both products of Idealism, they represent two utterly different conclusions that could be drawn from Kant's philosophy, and they both run counter to Kant's express intentions. Herbart attempts to provide psychology with a mathematical basis, in order to circumvent Kant's strictures on its robustness, whilst Eschenmayer develops a Schellingian psychology of the absolute I, contrary to Kant's insistence that the self is ultimately unknowable.

Herbart (1776–1841) succeeded Kant in Königsberg, but under the new title of Professor of Philosophy and Psychology, which must have made Kant turn in his grave. His *Psychology* is the first of three parts of an applied metaphysics.[70] Its place in Herbart's system corresponds to the place of the *Critique of Pure Reason* in Kant's; that is to say it lays the foundation for the system as a whole. Continuing the work of Schmid and Fries, Herbart aims to turn Kant's philosophy back into psychology. In Herbart's view the 'real' Kant (as opposed to the Kant of the post-Kantians) is a psychologist in the Wolffian tradition of Faculty Psychology and his critical philosophy cannot be separated out from his Wolffian terminology: 'Kant made use of the spiritual faculties . . . and it is not easy to divest them of this form.'[71] Whilst he accepts the substance of the *Critique of Pure Reason*, Herbart wants to take psychology back beyond Kant and Wolff to Leibniz and Locke. Psychology is not to be empirical observation of the inner sense, though. That, as Kant had argued, is mere unphilosophical common sense, which can only tell us what we already know and ordinarily practice.[72] Psychology should instead be a mathematical, Newtonian science of measurable forces. In his *Hauptpunkte der Metaphysik* (*Main Points of Metaphysics*, 1806) Herbart sketches what he calls the 'elements of a future psychology' (*Elemente einer künftigen Psychologie*). These consist in a hypothetical algebra of such mental forces as 'activity'(*Tätigkeit*), 'blockage' (*Hemmung*) and so on.[73]

For Herbart, as for Leibniz, mental content consists only of representations. These representations are 'forces' (*Kräfte*); they act through time on one another in ways that can be measured empirically and expressed in algebraic formulae. Herbart's essay 'De attentionis mensura causisque primariis' ('On the measurement and primary causes of attention', 1821) sets out the mathematics of calculating the extent of attention.[74] Attention had been important to the empiricists from Locke onwards; it provided the instrument whereby the mind could achieve consciousness of sensations; equipped with attention, all that a mind needed was sensations. Herbart aims to establish formulae for quantifying its workings. These are complex and thoroughly hypothetical. He makes no attempt to give his hypotheses an experimental grounding. Nonetheless experimentation was clearly the logical conclusion of his approach, and his concept of an algebra of mental forces was taken up by subsequent psychologists. F. E. Beneke (1798–1854) advocated experimentation in psychology in his *Die neue Psychologie* (*The New Psychology*, 1845).[75] The founders of laboratory psychology in Germany – Gustav Theodor Fechner (1801–87), Wilhelm Wundt (1832–1920), and others – were influenced by Herbart (and thus also indirectly and negatively by Kant who, as we saw, thought a quantitative psychology impossible).

Eschenmayer (1770–1852) was first influenced by Kant's metaphysics of nature, but after 1797 became an acolyte of Schelling. The argument and structure of his *Psychology* sprang directly from Schellingian

Naturphilosophie. Of particular importance to Eschenmayer was the idea of triplicity expounded in Schelling's *Bruno*. In his 1797 *Ideen zu einer Philosophie der Natur* (*Ideas for a Philosophy of Nature*), Schelling applied Fichte's dialectic of the *Ich* to nature. Nature is deemed to have three levels or powers (*Potenzen*): finite, infinite, and eternal. Eschenmayer applies this triplicity to the threefold structure of mind developed by Tetens and Kant. Sensibility, understanding, and reason are the psychological analogues of Schelling's three powers.[76]

Needless to say Eschenmayer's psychology is entirely hypothetical, like Herbart's psychometrics. A summary of its structure will give a sufficient taste. The psychology is divided into three sections: empirical, pure, and applied. The first treats the physical end of feeling and comprises the subsections 'mental organism' (*geistiger Organismus*), 'bodily organism' (*leiblicher Organismus*), and 'mixed organism' (*gemischter Organismus*). Of these the first, 'mental organism', consists of an analysis of the mental faculties by chronologically ordered *Epochen*, as in Schelling's *System* (pp. 24–148). The second, 'bodily organism', reveals the threefold structure of the body (abdomen, thorax, head), of its systems (lymphatic, circulatory, nervous), and of anatomy (bones, muscles, nerves). Just as Fichte and Hegel argue that the human body is rational, so Eschenmayer hypothesises that the mind builds the body according to its own (tripartite) plan (pp. 149–219). The third sub-section, 'mixed organism' treats waking, sleeping, dreaming, animal magnetism, and visions (pp. 220–78). The second main section, 'Pure Psychology' (*reine Psychologie*), is effectively a digest of Kant's three critiques, with the familiar tripartite division into logic, aesthetics, and ethics (pp. 279–420). The final and most bizarre section, 'Applied Psychology' (*angewandte Psychologie*), is neither psychological nor applied. Rather, in a manner similar to the conclusion of the *Epochen* of Schelling's *System*, Eschenmayer pretends to derive the principles of cosmogony and astronomy from psychology (pp. 421–567).

CHAPTER 6

Romanticism and animal magnetism

The second wave of Romanticism centred on Berlin and Dresden and differed markedly from the Romanticism of Novalis and the Schlegels. Whereas the latter, even if it sometimes treated Idealism ironically, was a continuation of the Idealist project, the second wave of Romanticism took a more positive interest in psychology, which it interpreted through Schellingian *Naturphilosophie*, although, as we shall see, even this had its limits. *Naturphilosophisch* psychology tended to emphasise the role of the unconscious, inspired by Schelling's view of nature as the unconscious absolute. For a time, encouraged by German nationalism, the pseudo-science of animal magnetism became philosophically acceptable in parts of Germany. Animal magnetism enjoyed its highest popularity in the twenty years following the defeat of Prussia by Napoleon in 1806. For writers of the second wave of Romanticism animal magnetism was a specifically German science.

Johann Christian Reil (1759–1813) became influential because of his *Rhapsodien über die Anwendung der psychischen Curmethode auf Geisteszerrüttungen* (*Rhapsodies on the Use of the Psychological Method of Heading on Mental Disturbances*, 1803), in which he opposed the incarceration and physical maltreatment of the mentally ill. Writing in a 'rhapsodic' manner, Reil argued that the mentally ill should be hospitalised and treated by the 'psychological method', a therapy that aimed to reform behaviour by persuasion, training, and aversion. Reil appealed to a Romantic spirit of revolt against eighteenth-century rationalism, but there is actually little Romanticism in the psychology of the *Rhapsodies*.[1] The regime Reil proposed was closer in spirit to the Enlightenment than to Romanticism. Goethe had been promulgating a 'psychological method' in the 1770s. The *Rhapsodies* are more Rousseauian than Romantic. Reil believes that society is progressing not towards civilisation but madness

(*RR* 12). Our response is confinement and the enforcement of artificial standards of behaviour, but this is barbaric (*RR* 14). Even so, Reil aimed to make the mad rational, not to cherish madness as an alternative way of seeing the world. His therapeutic methods were, if not physically, then mentally brutal. Later he adopted a Schellingian view of natural science, but there is no evidence of this in the *Rhapsodies*. Indeed, those who have suggested that Reil belonged to the Romantic movement have misunderstood the Romantics' use of Reil. Although Reil was an important reference point and a useful source of material, the attitude implied by the Romantic writers' use of Reil is on the whole negative.

Reil studied medicine in Göttingen from 1779 to 1782, before moving to Berlin where he lodged with Marcus Herz and mixed in the Enlightenment circles attracted to Henriette Herz's salon. At first Reil was influenced by Herz and the Enlightenment tradition of the Philosophical Doctor (*philosophischer Arzt*). In *Von der Lebenskraft* (*On the Vital Force*, 1796), he takes a broadly materialist line, emphasising the influence of the nervous system on the psyche. His conception of sleep and dreams derives from Herz's *Versuch über den Schwindel* (*Essay on Fainting*, 1786).[2] The *Rhapsodies* also contain several references to the Philosophical Doctor Mauchart and recommend the training of doctors in 'psychological medicine' (*psychische Heilkunde*).[3] The influence of Moritz is also marked. Reil was continuing Moritz's work: in 1803 he argued for the establishment of a chair of empirical psychology at the University of Halle. His classification of mental illnesses derives from the French 'mad-doctor' Philippe Pinel (*RR* 309). Finally, he was influenced by elements in Kant's theory of mind. He emphasises the centrality of self-consciousness (*RR* 53–4) and accepts Kant's account of the conditioning of sense impressions by the forms of time and space (*RR* 58).

Reil's proposed treatments owe much to existing psychological literature. In the preface to the *Rhapsodies* he acknowledges that he is only an amateur and that he became interested in the subject after reading the pastor H. B. Wagnitz's *Historische Nachrichten und Bemerkungen über die merkwürdigsten Zuchthäuser in Deutschland* (*Historical Account of and Remarks on the Most Notable Asylums in Germany*, 1791–2) in which Wagnitz inveighed against the condition of some asylums (*RR* 3–6). Reil did not have extensive first-hand experience of the asylums. His material came in the main from printed sources. Moreover, his approach is not as revolutionary as it is often made to appear. The treatments are not in fact psychological, if by that is meant the use of non-physical methods alone (*RR* 28). He advocates systemic shock treatments such as cold baths and localised shocks such as loud noises. It is a behaviourist approach that assumes patients will alter their behaviour in response to sensory stimuli, that this happens because stimuli restore proper function to the nervous system, and that consciousness is ultimately constituted by the nervous system.

Like many late Enlightenment writers, Reil viewed melancholy more positively than the traditional black bile theory did.[4] The core of mind is self-consciousness (*Selbstbewußtsein*), which gives our identity continuity and without which we would only have unconnected intuitions (*RR* 53–4). Intuitions are given to us in the forms of space and time (*RR* 58). To handle these we require the faculties of reflection (*Besonnenheit*) and attention (*Aufmerksamkeit, RR* 98–111). These constitute our personality. The transactions between senses and mind are sustained by a well-balanced nervous system (*RR* 61–2). Abnormal mental states result from the nervous system being disrupted and not integrating intuitions (*RR* 63–4). This occurs ordinarily in sleep, dreams, and sleepwalking, when the nervous system ceases to operate and we are governed instead by our ganglious system (*RR* 78–9, 89, 92). If the ganglious system is dominant while we are awake, self-consciousness is diminished and personality disorders arise.

Reil sees melancholy as caused by cognitive distortions. An *idée fixe* dominates our attention and becomes the focus of our entire mental life. The other phenomena associated with melancholy, such as low moods and sadness, are secondary and contingent upon circumstances (*RR* 309). Reil gives a prominent place to the contraction of a melancholic patient's personal domain. This is experienced as a sense of loss or of unachieved goals (*RR* 311). It can be treated by persuading the patient that he or she has in fact achieved the goal in question (*RR* 329). Because the fixation excluded the patient's other intuitions and unbalanced the sense of self, removing the fixation re-establishes a sense of self.

Melancholy can cause inertia or, in extreme cases, catalepsy. Severe melancholy is therefore rarely amenable to treatment by cognitive techniques. This is where Reil's behaviourism emerges. As a rule mental illness is caused by nervous stimulation (*Erregung*) and must be treated by the same. The precise nature of the cure will depend on the character of patient (*RR* 224). Coarse people should be treated roughly, sensitive people gently. In order to facilitate later stages of treatment, the doctor must first establish his authority with the patient through fear:

At the beginning methods that create fear have the quickest effect. Even those patients who must be handled kindly require an earnest treatment in this phase in order to inspire them with respect for those who have charge of them. They resemble children who try to assert their will but soon give in when a painful obstacle is put in their intention's path.[5]

A cataleptic or someone who is fixated on an object cannot be treated by cognitive means alone (*RR* 224). The patient must be made weak and deprived of any sense of independence (*RR* 225). The journey to the asylum – Reil is not opposed to asylums as such – must be made ominous, by means of blindfolding or transportation in a sealed wagon. On arrival cannon-fire or drums should greet the patient. Even once dominance over the patient has been secured, authority must be maintained. Orders must be brief: there is no point in reasoning with a patient until the treatment is well advanced (*RR* 227). Even for sensitive patients brutal shock treatments work well: 'Tender or fearful subjects can be made obedient by means of rough instructions, threats, or the mere sight of a frightening scene.'[6] One is reminded of King Frederick William I of Prussia making his son, the future Frederick the Great, watch the execution of his friend von Katte. In Kleist's drama *Prinz Friedrich von Homburg* (*The Prince of Homburg*) Reil's shock therapy is associated with Prussian autocracy.

In 1804 Schellingian ideas began to appear in Reil's writings and from 1806/7 he became a fully fledged *Naturphilosoph*.[7] It has been suggested that his Idealism was connected to his nationalism. With the fall of Prussia in 1806, he became convinced of the need to think in a Germanic way.[8] The *Beyträge zur Beförderung einer Kurmethode auf psychischem Wege* (*Contributions to the Promulgation of a Psychological Method of Therapy*, 1808), co-edited with his Kantian colleague Johann Christoph Hoffbauer, provided Reil with a vehicle for his now Schellingian theory of mind and body. The key Schellingian ideas are the parallelism of mental and physical systems, the 'centricity' (*Centricität*) of the body's construction, and a Brownian theory of medicine.[9] These mostly bizarre and ill-founded ideas proved much less influential than the late Enlightenment thought of the *Rhapsodies*.

SCHUBERT

Like Reil, Gotthilf Heinrich von Schubert was a medic by training who was attracted to *Naturphilosophie* via medicine and had no particular interest in the Idealists' arguments against psychology. His first significant work, *Ansichten von der Nachtseite der Naturwissenschaft* (*Views of the Dark Side of Science*, 1808) arose from a series of lectures he gave in the winter of 1807/8 in Dresden to an audience that included Kleist. The mysterious title draws attention to neglected aspects of science 'that have been assigned to the realm of belief in miracles'.[10] In his autobiography Schubert says that Kleist pressed him to talk about animal magnetism, on which he had read widely and published. The lectures deal first with Schubert's favourite topics: mythology, geology, and astronomy, only later moving onto history and psychology. The structure of the work is Schellingian (and perhaps Hegelian, the *Phenomenology* having been published in 1807). Schubert sets out to tell the history of nature as the unfolding of human consciousness from the earliest religious nature-worship, through the loss of social cohesion in antiquity, to its recovery in the shape of Christianity (pp. 10–11), and finally to the beginnings of modern science. From our modern vantage point it is possible to see that history is progressing towards a higher existence. The latest developments, especially the discovery of animal magnetism and galvanism, give a true indication of the tendency of the human spirit:

Finally we will recognise in many and various phenomena the intervention of the future, higher existence in our present less complete existence, and see how the seed of a new life that slumbers deep within us clearly shows through at moments when the forces of our present life are at rest.[11]

These insights are given in dreaming, clairvoyance, and 'magnetic sleep'. Schubert embraced Schelling's notion of the organism. The individual must be seen in relation to the whole of which it is a part. Instead of the mechanistic conception of cause and effect promulgated by Newton, Schubert proposed an organic conception of action in which the force of gravity becomes 'a constant striving . . . for inner union with the whole mass of the planet'.[12] Organism also entails polarity, the other key element of Schelling's *Naturphilosophie*, for set against the whole is its opposite pole, the individual. A dialectical opposition of spirit and body underlies the realms of nature. In the vegetable realm body controls spirit; in the animal realm spirit controls body, but not itself; finally in humans the spirit controls the body and itself and gives rise to mind proper.[13] History and the development of science also pass through a dialectic. So, for instance, the earliest religions combined the ideas of love (or procreation) and death.

In psychology Schubert distinguishes between a conscious and an unconscious world. Consciousness is not able to penetrate deep reality, only phenomena. Intuitions of reality come to us in unconscious states. When consciousness is inactive, our sixth sense predominates. Schubert calls this the 'sense of commonality' (*Gemeingefühl*). With no consciousness and visual awareness, which is the primary medium of consciousness,

Gemeingefühl is sharpened. In this condition we can communicate with others regardless of distance and physical obstacles, and even with minerals.[14] In 'magnetic sleep' people are sensitive to metal ores.[15] Although the eyes are closed, the sleeper still sees with a sharp 'inner eye' that can perceive even invisible things and predict changes in his or her own body.[16] This is responsible for the sympathy between the 'somnambulist' and 'magnetiser' in animal magnetism.[17] The sleeper can 'see' the magnetiser even when the latter is out of the room. Their wills are as one.

Die Symbolik des Traumes (*The Symbolism of Dreams*, 1814) is Schubert's most interesting work psychologically, despite his claims that he does not intend to provide a theory of psychology at all.[18] It is really a semiotics of dreaming in the tradition of Artemidorus's *Oneirocriticon* (*c.* 150 CE). The psychology of *The Symbolism of Dreams* derives largely from Reil. Like Reil Schubert believes that there are two systems in body, the nervous and the ganglious. The ganglious system controls vegetative processes.[19] In waking life the nervous system is in control. In sleep the ganglious system becomes dominant. The ganglious system creates dreams, which have nothing to do with ordinary consciousness. Dreaming is a natural process. All humans dream, and in essentially the same way, so that the meaning of dreams is universal.[20] The differences between dreams arise only through our interpretation of them. Dreams are easily misunderstood because they are so condensed and hieroglyphic. The process of association that assembles them is much quicker than conscious association: 'We express in this language with some few hieroglyphics, strangely conjoined images more in moments than we are able to expound in whole hours with words.'[21] Dreams resemble 'the language of poetry and revelation'.[22] The dreaming mind is a 'cryptic poet' (*versteckter Poet*).[23] Dreams are also prophetic.

Schubert was not a particularly original psychological thinker. The main emphasis of his work is not so much psychology as Schellingian cultural and natural history. What interested Schubert about psychological phenomena was the picture they paint of the world. First and foremost a Schellingian *Naturphilosoph* and a historian of culture, as a psychologist he reworked the tradition that reaches back to Leibniz in a *naturphilosophisch* spirit.

ANIMAL MAGNETISM

The word 'mesmerism' has come to refer to a phenomenon, hypnotism, which was only a minor and incidental part of Franz Anton Mesmer's original theory. His central idea was that there is a magnetic fluid, 'a generally distributed, constant, extremely fine fluid that has in its nature the ability to take on all sorts of movement and to convey and reproduce this'.[24] This issues from the Earth, the Sun, and other bodies, and passes through organic bodies too. The smooth passage of this fluid is essential for the human body's proper functioning. Illnesses are caused by blockages in the body. These can be removed and the body returned to a healthy condition by means of manipulation, for just as a magnetised needle will always return to north when disturbed, so a body will return to health when magnetised.[25] Animal magnetism is 'a general means of healing and protecting against all illnesses'.[26] The concept of animal magnetism thus contains a physical theory about magnetic force, a medical theory about the causes of illness, and a theory of medical practice. Late in his life Mesmer also devised a theory of education and a political theory, including a plan for a democratic German constitution. Like many Romantic ideas, animal magnetism was a theory of everything.

Mesmer's ideas developed in a rather ad hoc way. As a medical student in Vienna he came under the influence of iatromechanism. This treated the body as a mechanical object subject to purely physical laws, especially Newton's theory of gravitation. His doctoral thesis argued that the body is subject to gravitational attraction via its own force of 'animal gravitation' (*gravitas animalis*). When an acquaintance of Mesmer's, Professor of Astronomy Father Maximilian Hell, alerted him to some experiments using variously shaped magnets to treat ailments, Mesmer renamed the force 'animal magnetism'. Hell and Mesmer fell out, the professor arguing that the treatment depended on using correctly shaped magnets, Mesmer denying the magnets' efficacy and claiming that animal magnetism was a property of the organism, which the doctor must manipulate by making passes over the patient's body with his hands. Mesmer's practice in Vienna became successful and lucrative; it is referred to in Mozart's *Così fan tutte*. However, his attempts to win endorsements for his theory from learned societies failed. In 1777 suspicions arose of an unhealthily close relationship between Mesmer and a young female patient, and he was forced to leave Vienna.[27]

Animal magnetism first attracted widespread attention when Mesmer established a practice in Paris in 1778. His method and the theory on which it was based tapped into the concerns of fashionable Parisian society for harmony, political liberty, and Sensibility.[28] Mesmer preferred to treat his patients in groups, seated round a *baquet* or bath of magnetised iron and water, in his exotically and mysteriously furnished rooms.

A spirit of communal sympathy was created (including modest physical contact), and patients were encouraged to reach a 'condition of crisis' (*Zustand der Krise*), usually an outburst of feeling, after which they were supposed to be cured.[29] This and the special provision he made for treating less well-off patients fostered a spirit of equality. Mesmer saw 'magnetic sleep' (*magnetischer Schlaf*) as a virtuous, natural state, in a Rousseauian sense. Magnetic sleep takes us back to a time before society or civilisation perverted us. It eradicates the differences that society has interposed between us and returns us to a state of harmony. It was in this sense that Mesmer's French and German followers named the societies they founded for the promotion of animal magnetism 'harmony societies' (*harmonische Gesellschaften*). This also explains a large part of the political attraction of animal magnetism. In the condition of magnetic sleep humans are as nature made them: 'This condition represents man as he naturally is, without being perverted by the use of the senses or by an alien influence.'[30] According to Mesmer's follower Deleuze, animal magnetism gave 'proof of the spirituality of soul . . . the dignity of man, his supremacy in the order of creation, and his moral liberty'.[31] From this perspective it is also easier to understand why Mesmer thought his theory of animal magnetism should comprise a political theory and, in the version that he dictated in 1814, a Swiss-style constitution for Germany.[32]

From Paris Mesmerism spread to the provinces. The Marquis de Puységur established it in the southeast, simplifying Mesmer's practice by dispensing with the group treatments, the mysterious décor and music, and the curative crisis. He treated patients individually, except when fair weather allowed a group to sit under a specially magnetised tree. Puységur believed that the practitioner must establish mental and physical control over the patient. The practitioner would sit facing the patient with the patient's knees pinned between his own, and would stare into the patient's eyes. This would induce a state of 'magnetic sleep' in which, in response to the practitioner's questions, the patient would be able to see into his or (normally) her own body and diagnose her illness.

In this form animal magnetism crossed to Baden in the mid 1780s.[33] In Karlsruhe it was sponsored by the Markgraf Karl Friedrich, an adherent of Swedenborgian mysticism. Its chief practitioners were the doctors Johann Lorenz Böckmann and Eberhard Gmelin. They were concerned to defend animal magnetism against the charges of charlatanry that dogged Mesmer and carried more weight in Germany than in France. Gmelin emphasised his own empirical approach, arguing that opponents of animal magnetism had been blinded by 'dogmatism' and their 'addiction to systems'.[34]

Gmelin and Böckmann set out to show by experiment that magnetic sleep was not the result of foul play. They also investigated Mesmer's theory of magnetic fluid and concluded that its evidential basis was slight. There was no evidence of the human body emitting magnetic force. There was, on the other hand, good evidence, from Galvani's experiments, that the body's tissue possessed an electric force. Böckmann and Gmelin decided therefore to follow the existing, well-founded scientific model and re-name animal magnetism 'animalised' or 'animal electricity' (*animalisirte Electricität*).[35]

Their observations of the phenomena of magnetic sleep show a concern for empirical data. Böckmann observed that in the state of 'disorganisation' (*Desorganisation*) the sleeper's senses and instincts appear to be sharper. There are no signs of will and self-consciousness, however.[36] Some senses are inactive but others achieve an extraordinary clarity.[37] Sleepers appear not to be conscious of their environment. They are only aware of the person they are 'in rapport with' and of the particular tasks that the magnetiser commands them to address.[38] In their practice, Böckmann and Gmelin encounter several examples of people who are capable of intellectual feats in magnetic sleep that they cannot perform when awake.[39] These include the ability to predict the future course of an illness, to speak another language, to 'see' the colours of objects when blindfolded. Indeed, they make similar claims for magnetic sleep to those made by Wolffians for dreaming and sleepwalking. A dependence on Wolffian psychology shows through at other points. Gmelin supposes that in magnetic sleep people have access to an otherwise 'dark sense' (*dunkler Sinn*) of their own body, their soul, and external objects.[40] Underlying Gmelin's empiricism is a metaphysical commitment to Enlightenment rationalism. He interprets the phenomenon of animal magnetism in general as a universal cement and as evidence for our position in the Chain of Being between the apes and the angels.[41]

From Baden animal magnetism was introduced to Bremen by Lavater, where its leading practitioner was Arnold Wienholt.[42] In both Bremen and Baden, however, it met with deep suspicion and was the subject of a wave of critical articles, which by the end of the 1780s served to kill off what popular interest there had been. Gmelin continued to publish reports of the cases he treated, but his was a lone voice. To the German intelligentsia, aware that the Royal Commission in Paris had found no evidence that animal magnetism worked, Mesmer's theory seemed both morally suspect and a return to the mystical, unscientific past. In one critical piece, Böckmann was compared to Paracelsus, Kircher, and van Helmont.[43]

Briefly and unexpectedly it enjoyed a period of popularity in Berlin, home of the *Berlinische Monatsschrift* (*Berlin Monthly*), which had hitherto been one of its most trenchant critics. Selle, director of Berlin's hospital the Charité, began experiments on animal magnetism in 1788, and Biester, co-publisher of the *Berlin Monthly*, wrote a broadly favourable account of the treatment. The reactionary King Frederick William II even underwent a course of magnetic treatment. When he died in 1797 and the anti-Enlightenment reaction that he had sponsored ceased, animal magnetism died too and the *Berlin Monthly* resumed its earlier hostility.

Before 1806, then, animal magnetism was not popular in Germany. It became so only when significant figures in the Berlin medical establishment, above all Christoph Wilhelm Hufeland and Reil, converted to Idealist *Naturphilosophie*. Reil was among the first appointees to the medical faculty of Berlin's new university. The collapse and occupation of Prussia required a renaissance of patriotic spirit. Idealist *Naturphilosophie* was a German achievement and therefore patriotic. (Reil died of typhus while tending the wounded at the Battle of Leipzig in 1813.) Hufeland had been exposed to *Naturphilosophie*, Brownianism, and animal magnetism during his time in Weimar and Jena, and had been opposed to all three. However, after succeeding Selle as surgeon to the Prussian royal family and director of the medical faculty and the Charité in 1801, he changed his view, eventually announcing his support for animal magnetism in 1811. He had employed the services of a practitioner of animal magnetism at the Charité for some time, Carl Alexander Ferdinand Kluge, who published an account of his practice in 1811.[44] In addition to Hufeland, Reil, and Kluge, there was a lively community of Romantics and *Naturphilosophen* in Berlin, originally attracted by the foundation of the new university and the presence of Fichte. Animal magnetism was easily incorporated into this ferment of Idealism, Romanticism, and nationalism.

In his *Über Sympathie* (*On Sympathy*, 1811) Hufeland presents animal magnetism as part of a universe in which 'all individual existence is merely a one-sided reflexion of the whole'.[45] Viewed in this way, animal magnetism has no need of Mesmer's mechanistic notions of a magnetic substance; those were Enlightenment ideas, which had now been superseded.[46] If it is not clear what sympathy is or how it works, Hufeland's detailed accounts of it do not dispel the fog. When two people are in sympathy, as a magnetiser and magnetisee are, one becomes subject to the other's 'sphere of influence' and takes on their 'form of life'. Such is the 'general law of sympathy', according to which 'between two subjects that stand in a sympathetic relationship to one another the life-form of one is conditioned by the sphere of influence of the other, and the organism that is considered the active or positive party in this relationship assimilates itself to the other and passes on its (healthy or sick) life-form to it'.[47] The magnetiser imparts his magnetic flow to the magnetisee; the relationship is one of domination. Hufeland's essay contains some examples of animal magnetism as performed by his acolyte Kluge. In the same year Kluge published his *Versuch einer Darstellung des animalischen Magnetismus als Heilmittel* (*Essay on Animal Magnetism as a Cure*), in which, like Hufeland, he treats animal magnetism as a latterday form of sympathy. Hufeland and Kluge thus represent an odd hybrid of the late Enlightenment and *Naturphilosophie*.

The central figure in animal magnetism's rise in Berlin was Karl Christian Wolfart. Having studied medicine at Göttingen and Marburg, Wolfart taught physics and medicine at the Kurfürstliches Gymnasium in Hanau before taking on responsibility for the plague cordon on the Austrian border. When this was disrupted by the campaigns of 1806, he withdrew to Hanau to write, producing among other things a disagreeable patriotic verse drama *Herman, Fürst der Cherusker* (*Herman, Prince of the Cherusci*, 1810). In 1809 he established himself in Berlin, where he became part of the cultural scene, playing host to Kleist among others, and published the journal *Askläpieion* (*Asclepieion*). The *Naturphilosoph* Lorenz Oken had persuaded Reil to propose that Mesmer be granted use of a hospital in Berlin. The proposal was turned down, but the Minister for Culture and Education, Schuckmann, agreed to the establishment of a Commission of Enquiry into animal magnetism, on which Wolfart, Hufeland, and Reil sat. Equipped with an unauthorised letter from Hufeland stating that he had been sent by the Commission, Wolfart travelled to Lake Constance to meet the ageing Mesmer. He advertised his trip in an article 'Über die Erweckung von Mesmers Lehre, und die Anwendung des sogenannten thierischen Magnetismus' ('On the origins of Mesmer's theory and the application of so-called animal magnetism'), and cited his membership of the Commission. (Schuckmann had in fact expressly forbidden the use of the Commission's name for this purpose; Wolfart and Hufeland only escaped censure by going over Schuckmann's head to Minister of State von Hardenberg, a supporter of animal magnetism.) Wolfart sounded a patriotic note:

It is the exclusive preserve of our fatherland . . . to confirm these discoveries and theories that were incomprehensible to French doctors and therefore have not been believed, and to put them beyond further doubt for posterity. It is in

Berlin, the nourisher of all good things, that this high calling will first be fulfilled.[48]

Wolfart's assumption that the Berlin Commission would find in animal magnetism's favour must have irritated Schuckmann; his patriotism, on the other hand, will have pleased Hardenberg.

Mesmer dictated his current thinking on animal magnetism and other issues to Wolfart, who published the resulting notes under the title *Mesmerismus. Oder System der Wechselwirkungen, Theorie und Anwendung des thierischen Magnetismus als die allgemeine Heilkunde zur Erhaltung des Menschen* (*Mesmerism. Or System of Reciprocity, Theory and Application of Animal Magnetism as the General Medicine for the Preservation of Man*), a bizarre omnium gatherum of physics, medicine, politics, and education. In 1817 Wolfart succeeded in being appointed to a chair for 'medical magnetism' (*Heilmagnetismus*) at Berlin's new university, at the third attempt and against the wishes of the majority of the faculty. His acolyte David Koreff was also appointed to a chair. On Koreff's recommendation two further advocates of animal magnetism were appointed by the Prussian government to chairs at the new university in Bonn: in 1818 the doctor and philosopher Carl Joseph Hieronymus Windischmann, and in 1828 the Tirolean farmer's son Joseph Ennemoser, author of a doctoral thesis on the influence of mountains on health (*De montium influxu in valetudinem hominis*). Accepted by the Berlin government and able to place its unqualified acolytes in high academic positions, animal magnetism had reached the zenith of its influence.

Wolfart's account of animal magnetism places it squarely in a Schellingian, anti-Enlightenment framework:

Only from a knowledge of the inner mechanism of the Universe, of all that exists, whatever is and will be can the true idea of so-called animal magnetism be derived, and this knowledge depends in turn on the whole theory, this being nothing other than *true philosophy of nature*, or *physics of nature* both in the spiritual and physical dimension, that is therein bound in unity.[49]

Mesmer's theory has not been fully understood because of 'blind empiricism'.[50] Animal magnetism is not a fluid or a force; rather it is a cause of movement, which we might call 'tone or tonic movement' (*Ton oder tonische Bewegung*). This 'tone' is what preserves organic life. Wolfart's notion of 'tone' originates from the Brownian theory of medicine favoured by the Schellingians. According to Brownianism, all organisms are in a condition of tension. Illnesses are the result either of too much or too little tension, that is to say all illnesses are, at bottom, one. Wolfart claims that the only cause of illness is 'a reduction in irritability, i.e. of the active reciprocation between the muscles and nerves'.[51] Wolfart follows Mesmer in giving it the name 'obstruction' (*Obstruktion*). Just as there is only one illness, so there is only one method of treatment, which consists in restoring the organism's proper 'tonic movement'.[52]

A more general application of Schellingian categories can be found in Georg Kieser's *System des Tellurismus oder thierischen Magnetismus* (*System of Tellurism or Animal Magnetism*, 1822). Kieser views animal magnetism as part of a general scheme of universal polarity. Each thing stands in a polar relationship to another. For instance, the Sun is positive and the Earth negative. The dominance of positive bodies alternates with that of negative ones. Animal magnetism occurs when the negative, earthly force dominates. Hence Kieser's title 'Tellurism' (from the Latin *tellus*, earth). Kieser credits the outline of this theory to the Schellingian *Naturphilosoph* Nees von Esenbeck.[53]

There is a certain predictability to the classification of negative or positive. Man is positive and woman negative; knowledge positive, feeling negative; day positive, night negative. Animal magnetism is associated with the Earth, woman, and night. As women are negative, one might expect them to be better magnetisers than men. Empirically this is obviously not the case, as practitioners of animal magnetism are almost invariably male and patients for the most part female. Kieser explains that men dominate women in terms of quantity (that is, strength) and therefore they channel the magnetic force better than women.[54] Thus the male will overcomes the female will. Animal magnetism is therefore an exceptional phenomenon. It occurs naturally only in dreaming and sleepwalking.[55] In sleep the 'daylight senses' (*Tagsinne*), that is the five conventional senses, rest and the 'night sense' (*Nachtsinn*) comes into play. This 'night sense' is not a specific, directional sense; it is a 'total sense' (*Allsinn*), open to the Universe as a whole.[56]

As well as setting animal magnetism in a *naturphilosophisch* context, Kieser offers information for practitioners. The following trees are good for magnetising: beech, linden, elm, ash, and fruit-trees.[57] Of the mental faculties, imagination and feeling are tellurian, but the highest expression of the tellurian mind is 'believing intuition' (*gläubige Anschauung*).[58] By means of will or faith some people are capable of magnetising themselves, which explains the phenomenon of trance sometimes reported in religious contexts.[59] The following miscellaneous conditions and accessories are helpful for magnetising: night, darkness, winter (the winter solstice, being the height of the tellurian year, is a magical time: hence Christ's date of birth), moonlight, music (especially minor chords), garlic, incense, water, iron, and mirrors (which help to focus magnetism).[60]

Kieser gives 'neurogamy' (*Neurogamie*) as one of the names of animal magnetism. It is a 'marriage of the nerves', that is to say the sensory worlds of the magnetiser and the magnetisee come together. A. C. A. Eschenmayer follows a similar idea in his *Versuch die scheinbare Magie des thierischen Magnetismus aus physischen und psychologischen Gründen zu erklären* (*Attempt to Explain the Apparently Magical Character of Animal Magnetism from Physical and Psychological Principles*). Animal magnetism gives us 'a glimpse into [the soul's] secret workshop'.[61] Certain magnetic phenomena, such as prediction, show us the imagination in elevated or liberated form (*gesteigert oder freyer geworden*).[62] Animal magnetism is a truer expression of mind than normal conscious thought. In his conclusion, Eschenmayer develops a metaphor from reproduction, similar to Kieser's 'neurogamy'. Animal magnetism is 'a spiritual reproduction through spiritual mating'.[63] The 'mating' presumably refers to the relationship between magnetiser and magnetisee. But Eschenmayer is also talking in a more abstract way. Animal magnetism transcends mere natural 'mating'. Animal magnetism transports humans onto a higher, transcendent plane; it offers a prospect above and beyond the empirical world: 'This spiritual reproduction and mating, as we see it in animal magnetism, [is] a process that moves upwards from the natural element of the reproductive organs, and in which the soul ultimately rises above its earthly life.'[64]

KLEIST

Kleist's writings show an exceptionally keen eye for the weak points of the psyche, in particular the gaps between mental or linguistic rationality and feeling, and the uncontrollable nature of the latter.[65] Sudden moments of psychic crisis are common in his stories and plays. They are often accompanied by metaphors of storms or electricity.[66] Kleist was scientifically highly literate and was especially fascinated by recent discoveries in the physics of electricity such as the Leyden jar, an early form of capacitor. The model of the psyche suggested by the Leyden jar – a build-up of emotional charge culminating in a sudden and powerful discharge – describes a typical feature of Kleist's works. Likewise the idea of a hidden and irrational psyche, which erupts violently, is typical.

What little we know about Kleist's reading does not show any evidence of an interest in psychological literature, aside from the usual fare of novels and popular philosophy. But two writers of whom Kleist was fond are significant in this regard: Wieland and Schubert. From the young Wieland, and later from Schubert's account of animal magnetism, he drew the notion of sympathy. Also from Schubert (and originally from Reil) came examples of divided psyches. As we have seen, the idea of psychic doubling comes originally from the Wolffian notion that there is a part of the mind that is not available to us in consciousness. By 1800 this had developed a positive and a negative version. In Kant's view the empirical self is always and necessarily fragmentary, for it is not itself the source of the subjective conditions that determine consciousness; these lie further back in the noumenal self and are not empirically accessible. Early German Romantics such as Novalis interpreted this in a positive, Fichtean or Schellingian sense. The noumenal self is real and can in fact be accessed, if only by non-conscious, circuitous, and unexpected routes. Kleist seems ambivalent on this point. Some evidence suggests that he did view the self as an ultimate reality, accessible to the empirical self. One route to this was provided by animal magnetism. There are also grounds for seeing the Kantian view – which Kleist probably drew from the anonymous popular novel *Der Kettenträger* (*Bound in Chains*) – in some of his works. Kleist seems to adopt both a positive view of the sympathetic unconscious and a pessimistic view of the self as split and fragile.

'Penthesilea'

The relationship between Penthesilea and Achilles is, among other things, a sympathy between kindred souls, although, given Kleist's love of paradox, the sympathy coexists with antipathy. Both are leaders in battle and are their respective armies' most powerful weapon, but they fight as individuals who lead by example, rather than as integrated members of a fighting unit. Neither is entirely in accord with the norms of their respective societies. Achilles, who is, according to the legend, the Greeks' key to sacking Troy, has to be watched continuously by a minder. Penthesilea had to be encouraged to take up leadership of her army by her dying mother Otrere, who enthused her by suggesting that she might bring Achilles back to Themiscyra. What was for Otrere a means of getting Penthesilea to accept her duty by exploiting the general feeling of excitement amongst the Amazons at the prospect of meeting the Greeks, becomes for Penthesilea the guiding rationale of her actions ('My one thought waking, one dream sleeping, was / of you!').[67] This is contrary to the law that an Amazon must not know the identity of her victim and must take whomsoever battle brings her way.

Out of harmony with their respective societies, Penthesilea and Achilles are not fully understood by their colleagues. Prothoe, though she evidently knows Penthesilea well – she realises that Penthesilea is bothered by an unfulfilled desire (669) – mistakes her blush for the result of a fall (658–60). (Similarly in *The Prince of Homburg* the Kurfürstin and Natalie mistake Homburg's sleepwalking for an illness (Act 1, Scene i): these cases show how ordinary consciousness is unable to comprehend the expressions of the true self and instead writes them off as pathological.) Penthesilea and Achilles are ambitious and proud, even hubristic. Each uses similar fate-tempting rhetorical formulas to express their determination to catch the other.[68] Their inexplicable behaviour elicits similar expressions of amazement from their respective cohorts.[69] Both are described with meteorological imagery and compared to forces of nature.[70] This is partly because of their power in battle, but also because they are subject to powerful passions that they cannot control or rationalise. They blush, are silent, suffer moments of absence.

Penthesilea is more obviously aware of being divided against herself than Achilles is. Her soul is contrary, her heart unrestrained, her feelings and behaviour foreign to her (680, 720, 747). Achilles lacks this reflective clarity, but he is also subject to two conflicting and confusing forces. They are both fighters and lovers, and since at first the situation prevents them from being both at the same time, they switch between two personas, as it were. First Penthesilea pursues Achilles with 'extraordinary anger' (*sonderbare Wut*), but when she catches him, she spares him (159–70). Later, when Achilles tries to kill her after she has saved him from Deiphobus, she smiles at him (912). Achilles' behaviour has changed too; now he hunts her as a hunting dog pursues a stag, without deliberation and reflection, but instinctively (213–20).

Achilles and Penthesilea are not simply suffering from changing moods. If that were the case, they would enjoy continuity of memory; each mood would be aware of the other. The absence of continuity of selfhood marks them as double personalities. In other respects their condition resembles animal magnetism. Penthesilea is described as 'robbed of her senses' (*sinnberaubt*); she is unaware of her surroundings (324; cf. 1100). She is equally unaware of herself. She is capable of astonishing physical feats and quite unaware of any danger to herself (300–30). The existence of a magnetic relationship between them is suggested by electrical metaphors and descriptions of their behaviour.[71]

When Penthesilea first sees Achilles she is thoughtful and her face is expressionless, until she blushes (63–71). When Odysseus speaks to her, she appears not to be listening and looks amazed, like a sixteen-year-old girl (83–90). Later, in Scene 15, she says that when she saw Achilles she was 'blinded' (*geblendet*), like a wanderer at night whose path is lit by lightning (2212–16). When she looks at Achilles a second time, it is 'with a drunken look' (*mit trunknem Blick*) and her eye is caught by his 'shimmering figure' (*schimmernde Gestalt*), that is to say his armour, which is later compared to the Sun (93, 360–2). After this, speaking to Odysseus, her cheeks are red (97). When Achilles returns from the parley, he shows similar symptoms. Only partly aware of his surroundings (493–567), he ignores Odysseus and focuses instead on his horses (537–9) and on the sight of Penthesilea in the distance (558).

Penthesilea experiences another change of personality in Scene 9. At first she is the wild, violent, sexy Penthesilea (1170–1206). Her fellows think she is mad and that the fall from her horse has unhinged her. Suddenly reality dawns on her: she blushes (1209), asks what is happening, begins to rage at herself, and then relapses into weakness and despondency (1237, 1244–1307). Another fit of raillery at the Amazon traditions and desperation at her own failure ends when she looks into the Sun, is briefly turned back into the wild Penthesilea (1320), and then resignedly accepts retreat. Crossing the river she turns to the Sun again and seeing its reflection in the water tries to dive in, but is saved and faints (1389–90).

However, as the relationship between Penthesilea and Achilles develops, with Penthesilea his captive and he pretending to be hers, the two personas begin to merge in a confused and problematic whole, symbolised by the half rhyme of 'kisses' with 'bites' (*Küsse, Bisse*). Achilles and Penthesilea become both warriors and lovers, so drawing closer to one another at the same time as making it clear that a true union is impossible. Achilles introduced the confusion of love and war in his long speech in Scene 4. He compares Penthesilea's arrows to suitors, speaks of exchanging kisses hot as bronze, and of making her his bride 'wreathed with mortal wounds' (*bekränzt mit Todeswunden*; 587–616).[72] In Scene 15 Penthesilea's Amazon and human selves are reconciled: she is both Achilles' lover and the leader of the Amazon state, able to give a detailed and rational account of its history and workings, even managing to sound at times like a Prussian civil servant.[73] When Achilles interrupts her by smiling, she starts again, in a punctilious attempt to get her speech exactly right (2033). It is therefore an apt token of the reconciliation between them that the assurance she gives to Achilles that he will find her no less a woman for the absence of her amputated right breast comes across as high comedy (2017). She acts the role of advocate of her Amazon state, but of course the whole scene is an illusion, based on the unreal premise that Achilles is her captive. Achilles himself gives pointed reminders of its unreality, which Penthesilea in her seriousness misses (2018–19, 2031–2). The scene thus resembles a familiar topic of the psychological literature: the attempt to cure a deluded fantasist by acting a charade that reveals how absurd the delusion is. Here, however, Achilles is ultimately the victim of the trick that he and Prothoe play on Penthesilea. In her deluded state she swears that she would never harm him; he believes her and makes no attempt to defend himself when they meet in single combat. But the deal he made was with her other personality; the fighter Penthesilea is unaware of it.

When Penthesilea finds out that the meeting has been an illusion and that she did not in fact capture Achilles, at first she cannot believe it and tries to persuade him (and perhaps an uncertain part of herself) that it is not so. She tries to attract him to Themiscyra, but her words now seem formulaic and empty (2281–90). The High Priestess charges her with having caused the Greek captives to be lost. Penthesilea's response is shame (2351). In this desperate state, she hears that Achilles has challenged her to single combat and accepts. Completely deranged now that her *idée fixe* of capturing Achilles is destroyed, she kills Achilles and eats him. Achilles fails to defend himself, thinking that Penthesilea, once she has forgotten her Amazon's desire to hunt him down, will be tame and will love him if he submits to her. His response to the news that she is advancing to the single combat with dogs and elephants is to say that they are as tame as she is (2548). He assumes that the Penthesilea he spoke to in Scene 15 was the real Penthesilea. Achilles is thus the victim of his own deception.

In his *Symbolism of Dreams* Schubert cites a case from Reil that appears to lie behind the violent ending of *Penthesilea*. This concerns a pregnant woman who is seized by a desire to kill her beloved husband and eat his flesh, a desire that she finally carries out. The murder appears to have been committed in full and clear sanity. Schubert concludes that it shows how closely related sexual desire and murderous desire are:

The story of a premeditated murder that an otherwise apparently rational pregnant woman had committed against her husband, for whose flesh she felt an irresistible appetite, is in Reil, p. 394. The unfortunate woman even salted the victim's flesh in order to be able to enjoy it for longer. Such observations also recall the dictum of Swedenborg, that in the other world passionate desire turns into a desire to kill one another, and the long-recognised affinity of the desire to love (carnal desire) and the desire to kill.[74]

Both Penthesilea and Achilles are embodiments of this affinity between lust and violence. Penthesilea is the more extreme, and the condition she would have to attain in order to reconcile the drives safely more unconventional and anomic, at any rate for one who truly feels. As Prothoe says at the end of the final scene:

> She fell because she bloomed too proud and strong!
> The dead oak stands, defying wind and weather,
> The gale pulls down the good wood with a crash,
> For with his fingers he can fasten in its crown.[75]

The fact that she has healthy, strong feelings and not dead ones – she really felt for her victim, unlike the other Amazons who merely followed their customs – exposed her to destructive passions. Or as Kleist wrote to Wilhelmine von Zenge in one of his examples of how to collect vivid and salutary images: 'When the storm extinguishes small fires but makes large ones even larger, to what extent can it be compared to misfortune?'.[76] On the other hand, Penthesilea observes that her misfortune is not of the health-giving kind that purifies and heals. It is a misfortune that, because of her intense and passionate character, explodes into violence:

> Suffering, they say,
> Refines and elevates the soul, but that's
> Not been the case with me, dear heart; it has
> Exacerbated me and worked me up
> Into an unimaginable rage
> Against both gods and men.[77]

The play's imagery of fire, electricity, and weather is ambivalent, potentially both healing and destructive. As the play progresses, the negative meaning of the metaphors comes to the fore. In her final speech, her 'suicide with words',[78] Penthesilea speaks of hardening the 'annihilating passion' (*vernichtendes Gefühl*) with which she will kill herself in the furnace of her misery:

> For now I will descend
> Into myself, as if into a mine,
> To dig a killing feeling out as cold
> As iron ore. This ore, I will refine it, in the burning
> Fire of my misery, into hard
> Steel.[79]

The misfortune that can purify and heal can also destroy, because it feeds on itself, like a flame creating its own draw. The play follows the logic of the split in Penthesilea's self – her 'double personalities' (*doppelte Persön-lichkeiten*), in Schubert's phrase – between the passionate inner Penthesilea and the outer Penthesilea shaped by the conventions of Themiscyra. The split becomes ever more acute as the relationship with Achilles develops. When, thanks to the trick, Achilles appears to submit fully to her and to reconcile her two personalities, he simply makes the fall from grace more damaging.

Thus the play's violent and highly distinctive psychology echoes Schubert's *Symbolism*. We consist of inner and outer selves. The inner self is grounded in the ganglious system, identified by Reil, that generates unconscious 'dark feelings'. The outer self is grounded in the sensory and intellectual system that generates consciousness. We are thus always 'double personalities'. In extreme cases the conflicting demands of our two selves can tear us apart:

The more vigorously and powerfully the outer person vegetates, the more impotent the inner becomes and withdraws back into its visual realm of obscure feelings and dreams, but the more powerfully the inner person comes to life, the more the outer person must die away. An all too ancient experience! What the one wishes for most is no good for the other, what the latter desires is poison to the former. Both natures of this strange yoked pair loudly demand their right, which neither will sacrifice to the other; one pulls one way, the other pulls the other, and man is strung between them, cursed and blessed, torn in two directions, often torn apart by the recalcitrant team; inevitably, the one at deadly war with the other.[80]

'Käthchen of Heilbronn'

Schubert records in his autobiography that during the time he spent in Dresden in 1807/8 he was pressed by Kleist to talk about animal magnet-ism. The lectures he delivered to Kleist's circle coincided with work on the ending of *Penthesilea* and *Das Käthchen von Heilbronn* (*Käthchen of Heilbronn*). Kleist's knowledge of animal magnetism probably came from Schubert.[81] The character of Käthchen, her relationship to Graf Wetter vom Strahl, and indeed the play as a whole suggest a *naturphilo-sophisch* interpretation of animal magnetism. The situation established in the secret court (*Vehmgericht*) casts Strahl in the role of magnetiser and Käthchen in the role of patient. The influence of animal magnetism goes deeper, however. If the weather imagery in *Penthesilea* becomes predictable after a while, then the name Wetter vom Strahl is comically obvious. As Jürgen Barkhoff has shown, the name is a metaphor for the emanations of 'fluid' from the magnetiser[82]. Also in its literal sense the name alludes to animal magnetism, for magnetic fluid was associated with electrical phenomena in the physical world. For instance, the *Natur-philosophen* assimilated the results of Galvani's experiments on frogs to animal magnetism. The same metaphor of lightning describes the magnetism emanating from Achilles, when the sunlight shining through a break in the clouds catches his armour (*Penthesilea*, 1033–43). Strahl's armour also features in his first encounter with Käthchen. He visited her father's smithy to have his armour repaired. In a hurry, he did not take the armour off. When Käthchen came with refreshments, she saw him in full armour and collapsed. Her father picked her up; supported by him, she stared at Strahl, who in turn measured her with a look from head to toe (*vom Wirbel bis zur Sohle*, KWS 1.435). (The passing of the magnetiser's hands over the patient's body should be from the shoulders downwards.) From this point she paid no attention to anyone else and would only talk to him (*KWS* 1.436). When he left, she walked straight out of a high window after him.

After this first meeting Käthchen remains 'in rapport' with him. She will not obey her father. Previously she had: when he asked her whether she would accept a proposal of marriage, she told him 'Your will be mine' (*Dein Wille sei meiner*; *KWS* 1.433). Now her will is subject only to Strahl's. In the *Vehmgericht* only Strahl can make her answer questions directly. Her obedience to him is as exaggerated as her disobedience towards her father. She addresses Strahl as her 'strict lord', presumably because she thinks he has issued the commands according to which she is now acting (*KWS* 1.438). She calls him her 'judge' (*Richter*): only he, and not the actual judges, can be her judge because only he commands her and can decide whether she has been obedient (*KWS* 1.441). She asks him to teach her to give the right answers, claims that her soul is transparent to him. She only gives answers when prompted by specific questions, as if her memory is not fully available to her consciousness (*KWS* 1.442, 444). The result is utter confusion. Käthchen assumes that Strahl knows why she is behaving the way she is and that it is because he has commanded her to. He has no idea of this. She repeatedly answers him with a baffling 'You know!' (*KWS* 1. 439). Yet although she behaves as though he has magnetised her and is in full rapport with her, she cannot express the fact, for her consciousness is internal to the rapport, as is always the case in animal magnetism.

It is understandable, then, that Strahl is accused of enticing Käthchen and practising black magic. Two charges were commonly made against Mesmer and his followers. The indecently close relationship between the (usually male) magnetiser and the (usually female) patient was suspicious. The fact that the patient became dependent upon the magnetiser was thought to open the door to indecent behaviour. The other charge was charlatanry and a lapse into mysticism that ran counter to the principles of the Enlightenment. Thus, in the *Vehmgericht* Strahl is in the same position as Mesmer and his followers, except that Strahl has no idea how he has created the effect and in that sense is entirely innocent. (It is essential for the meaning of the play that he should be so.) Theobald is in a similarly pressing predicament, because he has no idea how Strahl controls Käthchen. Clearly it is not just sexual, as the judges at first assume; Theobald has already excluded that. When the judges ask him by what means Strahl controls her, he says it is beyond the comprehension of his five senses (*KWS* 1.434). As we have seen, animal magnetism operates on the sixth sense and is not accessible to the other five. It is a condition of the inner ganglious person, in Schubert's terms, not the outer sensory person. When Käthchen dives out of the window, she is 'robbed of her five senses' (*ihrer fünf Sinne beraubt; KWS* 1.436).

Käthchen lacks a general consciousness and is unaware of her surroundings, so much so that she is not scared by the 'trial by fire' of the play's subtitle. Mostly her discourse is meaningless to the other characters. The first time she speaks coherently is when she brings the letter detailing the Rheingraf's attack to Thurneck. Even here she cannot say what motivated her; she was driven to snatch the letter out of Prior Hatto's hand. Of course, within the terms of the task she has apparently been given, she is coherent. (In animal magnetism patients are only aware of the particular tasks that the magnetiser has commanded them to perform.)[83] Similarly, after rescuing the picture case from the burning castle, she cannot remember how she escaped, only the location of the case and the picture. In general she appears confident, direct, and unreflective. It is probably coincidental that the confident, sure-footed and unselfconscious Käthchen von Heilbronn has the same initials in reverse order as the uncertain, self-conscious Heinrich von Kleist, but it is an apt coincidence.[84]

Strahl's behaviour reflects the paradox of his being a magnetiser without knowing it. His empirical consciousness is mistaken on almost every count, most obviously in the matter of Kunigunde. It is also in conflict with his desires. Hence he is by turns aggressive and gentle towards Käthchen, threatening her with a whip and then ensuring that she keeps warm (*KWS* 1.490). His 'true' self – the self that recognises Käthchen as his beloved – emerges only in Act III, when he is anxious to save Käthchen from the fire. The first normal conversation that Käthchen and Strahl enjoy is in Act IV, Scene ii. He approaches her as she sleeps under an elder bush. At first Strahl arms himself against the possibility that he is in love with her, arguing that it is 'the mere sympathetic tug of the heart' (*der bloße sympathetische Zug des Herzens*; *KWS* 1.503). The fact that he tries to talk to her suggests otherwise. He notes that she sleeps deeply and yet appears to dream and to talk in her sleep. This gives him an opportunity, but also enforces a kind of discipline, for in order to communicate with her he has to enter her world, even subordinate himself to her (*KWS* 1.505). The situation is similar to that between Achilles and Penthesilea, or rather the two scenes contrast, for while there is a kind of deception in both, Strahl's role-playing approaches the truth of his situation more closely than does Achilles'. The passive, conventional, feminine Käthchen is the opposite of the dominant, unconventional, 'masculine' Penthesilea.

As Strahl collects more information, the play moves towards revelation and resolution. For most of the play the truth is on another plane altogether and only accessible in a state of magnetic crisis when the five outer senses are dead and the inner *Allsinn* works. This is the meaning of Strahl's illness reported to Kunigunde by Brigitte in Act II, Scene ix. After it has reached its crisis, Strahl goes into a state of suspended animation; he appears dead. During the crisis Strahl's and Käthchen's souls meet on three consecutive nights, an idea that almost certainly came from a poem by Wieland in which a cherub appears in the dreams of two lovers on three consecutive nights to reassure them. (Brigitte reports Strahl's having seen an angel; a cherub appears in Act III to guide Käthchen through the *Feuerprobe*.) It has further been suggested that Strahl's predicament of having to choose between a right and a wrong lover echoes the situation in *Agathon*, where Psyche tells Agathon she was confident that the Priestess could not win Agathon over, because only she, Psyche, could love him 'as you would wish to be loved' ('wie du geliebt zu seyn wünschtest').[85] Similarly, Strahl says in his dream that 'the girl capable of loving him was not at hand' ('das Mädchen, das fähig wäre, ihn zu leiben, sei nicht vorhanden', *KWS* 1.469). More generally, Kleist was probably influenced by the young Wieland's conception of sympathy.[86] Wieland republished a selection of early works in 1797–8 as a six-volume supplement to his collected works. This included the Leibnizian didactic poem 'Die Natur der Dinge' ('The nature of things') in which he presented a world that consists of harmonious spirits divided from one another only by matter and where the present is pregnant with the future, like that of the *Sympathies*. Before becoming real, souls are twinned with other sympathetic souls. Once real, they can recall their being joined in dreams. If they are lucky, they find one another in life, drawn together by a 'magnetic' force.[87] In a letter to Wilhelmine von Zenge of August 1800 Kleist seems to use this notion of the convergence of souls. He suggests that Wilhelmine and he should both read Schiller's *Wallenstein*, so that their 'souls will be together in this third object'.[88]

The scenario of *Käthchen of Heilbronn* seems to be based on the idea of sympathy that Kleist drew from Wieland and on the animal magnetism that he learned from Schubert. In comparison with his other dramas and his stories this might seem an uncharacteristically positive message, an 'escape into the positive', in Jochen Schmidt's phrase.[89] The 'positive', fairy-tale character of the play is clearly signalled throughout, at times with comically emphatic signposts. Even so, there is no reason not to take the ideas of sympathy and animal magnetism seriously. It would not be possible to do so without fatally undermining the play as a whole, which is built around them.[90] In this regard the ending of the play seems quite clear. Whilst at first Strahl appears to be moving away from his true identity by planning to marry Kunigunde, it is only by coming close to her that Strahl will realise the truth about Käthchen. This is the significance of the wedding that closes the play. Strahl consciously arranges matters so that he will marry Käthchen on the very day and in the very place he was to have married Kunigunde. What would have been the very worst of endings thus turns into the very best. Indeed the play as a whole conforms to this pattern of revealing the truth from its opposite. It is a typically Kleistian idea: only by going round the imperfect world and so committing ourselves more fully to it can we come back to paradise. Aside from the neatness of replacing the wrong bride with the right, the play's ending exposes Kunigunde to a humiliating rejection. The play thus ends with the restoration of the 'natural' order: the submissive Käthchen is recognised as the Emperor's illegitimate daughter and installed as Strahl's bride, and the unnaturally assertive impostor Kunigunde is humiliated.

'The Prince of Homburg'

The Prince of Homburg portrays an officer of the Prussian army undergoing a traumatic process of education. More generally, it enacts a conflict between reason, which demands the adherence by military commanders to a fixed battle plan, and the spontaneity of feeling, which drives Homburg to enter battle before his cue and then, when he is given to believe that his commander has been killed, to pursue the Swedes in revenge. Homburg himself, bitter at being arrested for disobeying orders, sees a contradiction between the 'magnanimity and love' (*Edelmut und Liebe*; line 785) to which he is accustomed and the unfeeling rationality of the Elector who would sacrifice him for the sake of a mere law. At the end of the play he is forgiven: the Elector, giving up his plan of a dynastic marriage for Natalie, allows her to marry Homburg and rescinds the death penalty, once Homburg has subordinated his personal desires to his duty to the state. Homburg comes to this new awareness partly by chance and partly through his manipulation by those around him who want to teach him a lesson. Yet Homburg's last words suggest that he does not comprehend what has happened or the lesson he is supposed to have learnt.

As in Lessing's *Minna of Barnhelm*, however, to which Kleist's play has some marked similarities, the process of teaching gets out of hand, partly because unforeseen chance events intervene, and partly because the Elector, like Minna, acts more spontaneously and impulsively than he is prepared to admit. The Elector is far from being a model of rationality. In the first scene, he performs a cruel experiment on the sleepwalking Homburg, designed to find out 'how far he'll go', as the Elector puts it.[91] When the experiment goes wrong, the Elector leaves hurriedly and subsequently issues a face-saving instruction to the effect that Homburg must not learn of the trick. The Elector does not imagine that the death sentence he decrees for insubordination will fall on Homburg. Naturally he is surprised by events. His status is further undermined by his weaknesses as a military leader. Knowing what he knows, it seems negligent of him to give Homburg command of the cavalry. Moreover, he is personally reckless in battle, exposing himself to the enemy and falling from his horse (378–83). Hohenzollern, meanwhile, seems to think that there is some personal grievance involved in the death sentence (911–13). There is a suggestion that the Elector is envious of the younger man, although chance seems the more likely culprit for Homburg's arrest, as we have noted.

Still, the Elector falls well short of embodying a spirit of Prussian rationality. He is even a mystery to himself. Faced with insubordination and the threat of a coup by Kottbus's men, he announces that they are to have the task of executing Homburg. In reacting thus he is thinking on his feet, and the idea is a cruel one – as cruel as the trick he plays on Homburg in Act 1. However, it is evidently supposed to win our approval, as it gets the Elector neatly out of a tight situation and enables him to make the final magnanimous gesture of freeing Homburg and restoring him to his command. It is surely ironic, then, that when the Elector asks the officers whether they wish to fight alongside Homburg again – 'Having gone through the school of these last days / Will you risk it a fourth time with him?' – the word 'school' suggests a planned and orderly process of education.[92] Nothing could be further from the truth.

Yet underlying the events that serve to bring Homburg to enlightenment is a coherent pattern, if not one of the Elector's own making. The events have a focussed effect if not intention. They conspire to break Homburg's somnambulism and crush his will. As such they bear strong similarities to the methods proposed by Reil for breaking the will of a melancholic.[93] In the final scene the Elector orders that cannons be fired to wake Homburg; Reil advocates the use of loud noises such as cannon-fire or drums. On his way from prison to visit the Kurfürstin Homburg sees an open grave; Reil suggests that patients be shown the sight of something terrifying so as to make them obedient. In Act v Homburg is led in blindfolded. Reil suggests that patients should be brought blind-folded or in covered wagons to the asylum, in order to disorientate them.

Homburg is represented as an enthusiast, prone to melancholic dreaminess. The cause of his condition appears to be the *idée fixe* of glory in battle, which dominates his attention. Thus far, however, he has not achieved the glory he desires and has been the cause of two defeats in battle. The result is a sense of loss that renders him inert and prone to moments of catalepsy. His melancholic dreaminess is also associated with moments of true vision. After seeing the grave, his imagination runs wild:

> Oh look, lady, these eyes that see you now
> They want to overcast with night, this breast
> Of mine drill through with murderous bullets.
> The windows on the marketplace are booked
> That give on that bleak spectacle
> And a man today on the summit of his life
> Still viewing the future like a fairyland
> Will scent the little space between two planks tomorrow
> And a slab will say of him: he was.[94]

This is the product of a fertile imagination prompted by fear. Repeatedly Homburg has moments of imaginary vision. Elements in the dream that he recounts in Act i, Scene iv even seem prophetic. Most of its details are, admittedly, present in the previous scenes: in this sense the dream seems merely to add a magical gloss to real events. The scene he depicts is that described in the stage direction at the beginning of the act, but one detail – he describes the palace as 'radiant with gold and silver' – seems to refer specifically to the final scene, when the palace is illuminated.[95] Does Homburg's dream have the same status as Strahl's dream in *Käthchen*? In terms of its function, perhaps: it expresses Homburg's desire, projects an image of a beloved who is unknown – Homburg knows her identity is obvious, but something prevents it from entering his consciousness –, and prefigures the goal of his life. Yet unlike Strahl's dream, Homburg's is an elaboration of an actual experience. The ideas of sympathy and animal magnetism which were appropriate to the 'grand historical knightly drama' (*großes historisches Ritterschauspiel*) of *Käthchen's* subtitle are perhaps less appropriate here.[96]

Homburg's mental condition appears to change in the ways suggested by Reil. After the cannons begin in Act II, Scene ii, he is more alert, behaving with clear purpose and even aggression (470, 485–9). Yet it is far from clear that he has learnt his lesson. The excess of self-confidence that made him disobey orders in the first place, and an over-reliance on feeling do not leave him. In the final scene his dream from Act I is re-enacted. Natalie crowns Homburg with a laurel wreath as in the dream, puts the gold chain round his neck, and presses his hand to her heart, causing him to faint. He is woken by cannon-fire, but wonders whether he is still dreaming. As in *Minna of Barnhelm*, no indication is given as to whether he becomes fully conscious of what has happened. This final residue of unresolved human irrationality suggests that the 'cure' has not been successful. Instead of waking Homburg to the ordinary realities of life, the events of the play confirm him in his dreaminess. The play thus reaches a harmonious conclusion in spite of the irrationality of its characters. As a whole the final scene suggests circularity.[97] It is the same location and time of day as the first scene; the foreign flowers and the wreath and chain also recall the opening scene. The circularity is confirmed by Homburg's apparent failure to appreciate reality for what it is. Indeed, he might well conclude that the world does after all operate according to the laws of our heart and not reason. The treatment of Homburg according to Reil's methods, if not managed by the Elector then appearing to have been co-ordinated by some metaphysical instance, has some effect but does not fully reinstate Homburg's normal consciousness.

E. T. A. HOFFMANN

It seems that E. T. A. Hoffmann was familiar with the psychological tradition from a relatively early age. One of his favourite books was

Rousseau's *Confessions*, which he claimed to have read thirty times and valued for its conscientiousness.[98] In 1812 he lists the three most powerful plays he has seen as Shakespeare's *Romeo and Juliet*, Calderon's *La devoción de la cruz* (*Devotion to the Cross*) in Friedrich Schlegel's translation, and Kleist's *Käthchen of Heilbronn*, and claims that they put him in a state of 'poetic somnambulism'.[99] He already knew and valued Kleist's stories and Tieck's *Fantasus*, perhaps his favourite work of fiction. In the period immediately before the composition of *Der goldne Topf* (*The Golden Pot*), his literary breakthrough, his reading took a more philosophical turn. A diary entry of 17 April 1812 has him reading Novalis and studying Schelling (*HSB* 1056). Again, in the summer of 1813 he writes of studying Schelling's *Von der Weltseele* (*On the World-Spirit*). In August he began to read Schubert's *Views of the Dark Side of Science* with enthusiasm.[100] The following March, on hearing that Schubert's *Symbolism of Dreams* was nearing publication, he pestered Kunz for a copy.[101]

If his interest in psychological matters was initiated by literature, it was confirmed by the latest psychological theory. Crucial above all for his interest in psychology was his friendship in Bamberg with the Schellingian doctors Adalbert Friedrich Marcus, director of the local lunatic asylum, and Andreas Röschlaub, who informed him about Brownianism, animal magnetism, cranioscopy and more. He became acquainted with the standard works on psychopathology by Reil, Pinel, and Chiarugi, and read contemporary accounts of animal magnetism by Kluge and Bartels. His interest in Schelling and Schubert also dates from this period. These books, especially Kluge's *Essay on Animal Magnetism*, Reil's *Rhapsodies*, and Schubert's *Views of the Dark Side of Science* and *Symbolism of Dreams* (the latter published in Bamberg), loom large in Hoffmann's tales.

Hoffmann's treatment of contemporary psychology

What use did Hoffmann make of the psychological material he read? This is a fraught question, as we shall see, for it is tied up with deep-lying problems of interpretation. However, there are two general points that can be made in advance of a closer reading of the tales. The frame in which he set the four-volume collection of tales published from 1819 under the title *Die Serapions-Brüder* (*The Serapion Brethren*) establishes the fiction of a group of story-telling, punch-drinking friends who meet to share and discuss their stories. Together they develop a 'Serapiontic Principle' (*Serapiontisches Prinzip*) by which the stories are to be judged. Cyprian tells the story of his encounter with a mad hermit who believes he is the martyr St Serapion. When he finishes, Lothar points out that the day's date, 14 November, is the date on which the hermit Serapion died, and the saint's day of the real Serapion. This fantastical coincidence leads Lothar to elaborate on the aesthetics of Serapiontic story-telling. In ancient times poets were seers, who 'announced the wonders of a higher realm'.[102] Much modern writing, by contrast, makes us cold inside, as it has lost the idea that the poet 'has really seen what he is speaking about'. Serapion was a poet, because he believed he truly was St Serapion. However, Serapion was also mad, for he lived only in the fantastical world of his imagination. He lacked 'the knowledge of the double nature [*Duplizität*] . . . by which alone our life is in fact conditioned'.[103] Lothar now spells out how the human mind is marked by this *Duplizität*:

There is an inner world, and the mental power to see it in full clarity, in the most perfect brilliance of vigorous life, but it is our earthly lot that this very external world in which we are encased acts as the lever that sets that power in motion. Inner appearances are absorbed into the circle in which external appearances enclose us and which the spirit can only escape in dark mysterious intimations that never take shape in clear form.[104]

Lothar subsequently glosses this outer world as 'the body' (*der Körper*; *HSB* 55). As well as imprisoning the imagination, the body acts as a lever that sets the imagination moving. The inner ideas cannot escape the ambit of the outer world; that is to say, what the imagination creates is ordinarily limited to sensible reality. In this sense the imagination is the Aristotelian and Wolffian faculty that creates mental representations of our sense perceptions. However, at moments when sensible reality does not constrain it, the imagination escapes the confines of reality and presents itself to us in 'dark, mysterious intimations' that do not have 'clear form'. Lothar then enunciates the 'Serapiontic Principle' again, this time as a rule of self-criticism: 'Let each examine whether he really has seen what he has undertaken to proclaim, before he ventures to bring it to public notice.'[105] The Principle is accepted by all the friends as a yardstick by which future stories are to be judged.

Reference is made to the Serapiontic Principle several times, even in the volumes published in 1820 and 1821 (*HSB* 74, 400, 471, 709), and it is reasonable to suppose that, even if it does not directly express Hoffmann's view of his poetics, the Principle says something important about his poetic world and specifically about its psychology.[106] Cyprian boasts that he has read Pinel, Reil, and 'all manner of books about madness'.[107] The heart of the Principle is a psychological model, or rather two psychological models. One is the spontaneous imagination that accesses a world beyond the corporeal world that we ordinarily see. It is 'encased' (*eingeschachtet*) by the real world. Presumably the 'encasing' is meant to denote its being inhibited by other (rational, sensory) faculties that have priority over it.[108] In another formulation, the imagination 'is absorbed into' (*geht auf in*) representations of sense perceptions, perhaps in the sense that the number and volume of sensory representations is so great as to block out the ideas of the imagination. In both formulations we have something resembling Schubert's psychology.

The other model requires that the imagination be triggered by sense perceptions. The contents of the imagination are dependent on corporeal reality, without which the imagination could not become active. This model is the 'physiological' psychology of the main eighteenth-century tradition, which had been condemned by Kant and his followers. What we have, then, is a diplomatic attempt to make Idealist and realist models of mind cohabit. This seems intrinsically unlikely to work, because each model represents its own reality. Imagination is not just imagination: it is an 'inner world' (*innre Welt*), and in it hides what Schubert called 'the cryptic poet' (*der versteckte Poet*). On the other hand, the corporeal world is not denied reality, as it seems to be in some Idealist and Romantic writing. The Serapiontic Principle seems designed to preserve the parallel existence of two worlds, not to resolve it; it does not tell us which of the two worlds is the more real. It confirms, rather, the anthropological doubleness (*Duplizität*, *HSB* 54) which Lothar says is characteristic of humans and which Serapion himself, trapped as he was inside his own fixed ideas, could not see. The Serapiontic Principle thus identifies one of the themes of Hoffmann's tales as being our psychological doubleness and the resulting uneasy sense that we inhabit two separate worlds.

It follows from their psychological doubleness that Hoffmann's characters can be subjected to two types of psychological explanation. One is a broadly behaviourist type of explanation, which sees psychological states as responses to external stimuli. The other sees psychological states as the products of an inner process. As this is hidden in the mysterious creative imagination about which nothing can be said, the explanation is not really an explanation at all, and it requires a leap of faith to believe it. The former style of explanation, on the other hand, is external and, viewed from an Idealist perspective, shallow. The coexistence of two mutually exclusive forms of psychology is, moreover, part of a more general uncertainty as to what constitutes reality. The prosaic reality of the tales' settings coexists with fantastical or fairy-tale elements. Psychology represents one of the intersections between these two worlds. 'Physiological' psychology, if true, privileges ordinary reality and renders the fairy-tale elements illusory. The possibility of a realist psychology is discussed by the Serapion Brethren after Theodor's story *Die Automate* (*The Automat*). Ottmar complains that the story's mysteries are not resolved, but Theodor argues that this is as it should be: 'I think that the remarkable history of the speaking Turk is fragmentary in its very nature. In my view the reader's or listener's imagination only needs to get a couple of hefty blows for it then to fly off on its own.'[109] Ottmar seeks to construe Theodor's defence of the story as a personal peculiarity: Theodor used to have a taste for unfinished works and would read the second part of a book but not its first and third. Theodor says he still has this taste:

There's nothing I hate more than when in a story or novel the ground on which the fantastical world has moved is swept so clean by the historical broom that not a crumb, not a speck remains, when one goes home so completely settled that one does not even feel a desire to look behind the curtains.[110]

Theodor thus defends the tales' failure to commit to the kind of psychological closure that is entailed by 'physiological' psychology with its 'historical broom'. The justification is that the reader is to be drawn into the confusion experienced by his characters. This is the effect of the unexplained fantastic's coexisting with ordinary reality. As Ludwig puts it in *Der Dichter und der Komponist* (*The Poet and the Composer*): 'Here then is the fantastical . . . cheekily bursting into everyday life and turning everything on its head.'[111] The coexistence of the fantastic and the ordinary world is designed to disorientate the reader.[112] The presence of the fantastic necessarily casts an ironic light on ordinary reality, so that the reader's relation to reality becomes unsettled. This is a risky undertaking, as Cyprian admits in the discussion following Lothar's story *Nußknacker und Mäusekönig* (*Nutcracker and Mouse King*) but, if judged rightly, it does produce 'a certain ironising tone . . . that pricks the sluggish mind or rather steals up on it with a friendly expression like an evil rogue and tempts it off into foreign territory'.[113]

The idea of a fairy-tale world producing an ironic dissonance may well have come to Hoffmann from Schubert's notion of the 'cryptic poet whose pronouncements stand in a constant ironic contrast to the perspectives and inclinations of normal sensory life'.[114] Much of the psychological detail in the tales is also drawn from Schubert and other contemporary writers, above all Reil, Pinel, and Kluge. In attempting to cure Serapion,

Cyprian had told him of cases of *idées fixes*, which Hoffmann drew from
Zimmermann (*HSB* 22). Serapion replies to Cyprian's diagnosis by
arguing that if he were really mad then only a madman would believe
himself able to cure him, an argument that Hoffmann found in Reil (*HSB*
23). Theodor comments that he would not have risked getting as close to
Serapion as Cyprian did, since the madman might have turned violent.
Theodor's conception of violent madness derives from Pinel (*HSB* 29).
Several details in the discussion of animal magnetism at the start of
Volume II are similarly drawn from Reil, Kluge, and Schubert (*HSB*
261, 267, 268, 272, 273). In the frame at the start of Section 4, Cyprian, in
taking the formal oath of the Serapion Brethren, lists various *idées fixes*
that he could have, all of which derive from Reil (*HSB* 401).[115] When in
Die Brautwahl (*The Choosing of the Bride*) the Secretary of the Privy
Chancery is told he has had strange dreams as a result of drinking too
much, he indignantly responds that he knows perfectly well what happens
in sleep, having read Heinrich Nudow's *Versuch einer Theorie des Schlafes*
(*Attempt at a Theory of Sleep*), the dream of Scipio in Cicero's *De re
publica* (*On the Republic*), Artemidorus' *Oneirocriticon*, and the anonymous *Frankfurter Traumbüchlein* (*Frankfurt Dream Book*), the last of which
Hoffmann knew from Schubert's *Symbolism of Dreams* (*HSB* 558). In the
Fantasie- und Nacht-Stücke (*Tales of Fantasy and Night*) the situation is
similar: much of the psychological detail derives from Hoffmann's
sources. When in *Der Magnetiseur* (*The Magnetiser*) Ottmar asks to hear
about his father's dream, so that he can add, he says, to his and Alban's
experience of the phenomena of animal magnetism, he is quoting an
argument of Kluge's (*HSB* 143). Later Theobald tries to influence the rich
daughter of his guardian by standing at her bedside when she is dreaming,
copying a case reported by Kluge (*HSB* 157). In *The Golden Pot* (Ninth
Vigil) Anselmus reflects that Veronica has saved him from madness: he
had been as far gone as the man who believed himself a barleycorn, a case
reported in Reil's *Über die Fieber* (*On Fevers*, *HFN* 237–8). Hoffmann
probably took the central idea of *Das öde Haus* (*The Deserted House*) from
Kluge's account of extra-sensory perception (*HFN* 459–88). In the same
story a friend who is concerned for Theodor's sanity surreptitiously leaves
a copy of Reil's *Rhapsodies* at Theodor's house (*HFN* 474). The extraordinary phenomena reported in the story derive from Kluge, Schubert, and
Bartels (*HFN* 476). In *Das Gelübde* (*The Vow*) Hermenigilda's account of
her waking dream resembles accounts of somnambulism in Kluge and
Schubert (*HFN* 577).[116] Hoffmann probably used the same sources for the
Baron's dream-like state in *The Magnetiser* (*HFN* 143). Hoffmann's novels

reveal a similar procedure. In *Die Elixiere des Teufels* (*The Devil's Elixir*) Medardus cites ancient mysteries as evidence 'that love's highest bliss, the fulfilling of the mystery is absorbed into death', an idea drawn from Schubert.[117] In *Kater Murr* (*Tomcat Murr*) Kreisler, staring at his reflection in the lake, which he momentarily believes to be Ettlinger, cites a paranoia classified by Kluge. In fact the source is Reil's *Rhapsodies* – an uncharacteristic slip.[118] Murr is also apt to cite medical authorities, especially if he has not read them. So, telling of his inability to sleep one night, he cites Moritz, Davidson, Nudow, Tiedemann, Wienholt, Reil, Schubert, Kluge 'and others . . . who have written about sleep and dreams and whom I haven't read'.[119]

This suggests strongly that if there is any system in Hoffmann's use of contemporary psychology, it is a systematic playfulness. No single psychological theory remains valid. Psychology in general is clearly not prized knowledge that unlocks the secrets of the mind. Nor is psychological knowledge or insight given only to characters with whom the reader is encouraged to identify. The Serapion Brethren themselves are on occasion shown to disagree or be wrong in their use of psychology. Even psychological authorities such as Reil are made fun of or implicitly criticised. For instance, the local doctor who treated Serapion recommended that he be allowed to run wild in the woods, a treatment that is directly contrary to Reil's methods, but the treatment has clearly benefited Serapion (*HSB* 19–20). He has settled into a peaceful and regular way of life, and the local people have understood and cherished him. His behaviour has become completely normal, except for his harmless *idée fixe*. When Cyprian visits, his presence is an intrusion. He brings with him a layman's reading of Pinel, Reil, and 'all manner of books about madness', with which he hopes to get to the root of Serapion's *idée fixe*. Yet Cyprian does not succeed in persuading Serapion of who he really is. In fact he seems only to provoke Serapion into defiance and scorn. In this case, Hoffmann follows contemporary psychology, only to reverse its findings.[120] Indeed, Reil's insistence on the complete subjection of the patient to the doctor's will is presented as immoral. The same point is made about animal magnetism. In the tale of a magnetic cure at the beginning of Volume II of *The Serapion Brethren*, Theodor criticises 'the complete surrender of one's own self, this bleak dependence on an alien spiritual principle', which he says fills him with 'fright and terror'.[121] This fear of determinism in the form of animal magnetism is a recurrent theme.

'The Golden Pot'

The Golden Pot is the story of the student Anselmus's experience of 'the fantastical . . . cheekily bursting into everyday life and turning everything on its head' (*HSB* 90). It is a story of confusion and disorientation, effects which the reader experiences indirectly through the thoughts of Anselmus and directly through some perplexing shifts in the focus of the narrative between the ordinary life of contemporary Dresden and a magical, fairy-tale world. This fairy-tale world is the scene of a cosmic, pseudo-religious struggle between the forces of light represented by the Salamander Prince of Atlantis and his daughters, who are trying to recruit Anselmus to their ranks, and those of darkness represented by the evil Apple-Woman, who wants to prevent his recruitment. These figures have corresponding doubles in this world, the Salamander Prince's double being the mysterious Royal Archivist Lindhorst. In addition, the reader has to contend with the two contradictory types of psychological explanation that we saw in the frame of *The Serapion Brethren*. These shifts are made more disorientating by writing which, as the story lurches back and forth between the two worlds, comically exaggerates their banal and fantastical sides respectively. The doubleness of *The Golden Pot* is symbolised by the 'pot' itself which, as a magical artifact has been the cause of strife between the Salamander Prince and his brother and is to be the wedding-gift of the Salamander to Anselmus and Serpentina, but in its previous literary incarnation, in Wieland's *Don Sylvio*, was a chamber-pot.

Anselmus is an awkward, bumbling figure. This symbolises his imprisonment in the ordinary world. The world of solid objects is an obstacle to him: his first act is to knock over the Apple-Woman's basket. He represents the duality of ordinary consciousness (or the 'outer world' of the Serapiontic Principle) and the imagination or 'inner world'. Accordingly, his awkwardness lessens whenever he is moving, physically or spiritually, towards the fairy-tale world, and increases when he is moving away from it. Whilst his rational and sensory faculties are directed towards the ordinary world, the fairy-tale world speaks through his feelings, especially his imagination, which is why most ordinary people mistake it for fiction. While the others laugh at Lindhorst's preposterous account of his ancestry, Anselmus feels strangely moved by Lindhorst's metallic voice and penetrating eyes (*HFN* 142). Metal and the power of the gaze are elements in animal magnetism.[122] Listening to Lindhorst Anselmus feels himself 'shuddering internally'.[123] Lindhorst's voice is mysteriously penetrating, the language of penetration suggesting that Anselmus's inner self is being taken over by a foreign presence. Indeed, his will is being guided, if not controlled, as the will of a somnambulist is guided by a magnetiser. The daughters first manifest themselves to Anselmus in the sound of a breeze in the branches of an elder, which merges into whispering and ringing tones and then gradually becomes identifiable, if not immediately intelligible, words. Schubert's notion of the 'music of nature' (*Naturmusik*) is at work here. The poetic and magical character of the snakes manifests itself in their ability to call forth sounds that are at once musical and natural. Anselmus tries to explain these away as auditory illusions, until he is struck by an electric shock – another phenomenon associated with animal magnetism – and Serpentina appears to him. Anselmus is being 'hypnotised'.

The normality to which Anselmus returns after this experience is unbearable. He is gripped by a powerful melancholy, the details of which Hoffmann derived from Reil or possibly Chiarugi.[124] His life seems worthless; he is indecisive, gloomy, unable to feel, brooding (*HFN* 145).[125] To escape his condition he takes up the offer of a boat trip over the river with Konrektor Paulmann, possibly an allusion to Reil's prescription of cold baths to dispel an overheated imagination,[126] although when Anselmus sees the snakes in the water he seems to want to dive in in order to be with them, not to sober up. Heerbrand suggests another form of cure, also an idea from Reil: Anselmus is to work for Lindhorst transcribing some ancient manuscripts, though this cure will of course have the opposite of the intended effect.[127] Paulmann diagnoses Anselmus's problem as a case of *idée fixe* and suggests that the problem is physiological and can be cured by the application of leeches to the backside (*HFN* 135–6). This is a satirical allusion to Friedrich Nicolai's account of how he cured his fear of ghosts by the same method. It serves to suggest that the cures offered by ordinary folk are ineffective, mundane, or ridiculous.

The fantastical events experienced by Anselmus have correlates in the ordinary world. Lindhorst appears to him dressed in a long grey coat. As he strides off into the dusk followed by Anselmus, Lindhorst disappears as if by magic:

He was already drawing close to the Kosel Garden when the wind entered his wide overcoat and caused the coat tails to spread out, so that they fluttered in the air like a huge pair of wings. To Anselmus, who was watching Archivarius Lindhorst with a look of utter amazement, it was as if a large bird were spreading its wings for a fast flight. And now while the student gazed steadfastly into the oncoming dusk, a white-grey vulture soared into the air with a creaking cry;

Anselmus clearly saw that the white flutter he had thought to be the retreating Archivarius Lindhorst must have been this vulture, although he could still not understand where the Archivarius had vanished so abruptly.[128]

Did Anselmus see Lindhorst fly away? Or did his imagination conflate two ordinary things – the Archivarius's billowing coat and a large bird of prey? Anselmus tends towards the latter, common-sense explanation. However, this ordinary, psychological explanation is imperfect and leaves a gap: where did Lindhorst go?

Real experiences of the fairy-tale world can be explained away psychologically. The acts of imagination that allow people to see into the fairy-tale world have ordinary psychological correlates. Veronica's experience with the witch on the night of 23 September in the Seventh Vigil is afterwards explained as a dream prompted by an open door that let in the stormy weather. The tangible evidence of her meeting with the witch – her wet coat – can as well be interpreted to support the psychological explanation, until, that is, another piece of evidence surfaces, the small mirror hanging round her neck. In the Ninth Vigil Anselmus is tempted by Veronica and starts to be clumsy again. Only when drunk on punch can he think of Lindhorst. Indeed, Paulmann and Heerbrand also seem to believe in the fantastic when they have been drinking (*HFN* 183–5). Is this just a false belief created by the alcohol, or does the punch allow them to understand things that they cannot grasp when sober? The psychology of the ordinary world offers an explanation in parallel with the events of the magical world.

Slowly Anselmus moves into harmony with the magical world. The work of transcribing Lindhorst's mysterious manuscripts is a metaphor for the poetic nature of his development.[129] He is an unconscious conduit for the texts, for he can reproduce them but is not conscious of their meaning. The better he becomes at the work, the more mysterious is the nature of the texts he transcribes. He is, in Lindhorst's words, moving out of 'a time devoid of happiness, when degenerate man [is] no longer . . . able to understand the voice of Nature'.[130] He experiences complete sympathy with Serpentina 'as if he were so completely within the grasp of the gentle and lovely form that he could neither move nor live without her, and as if her beating pulse throbbed within him'.[131] When, on the other hand, he is close to Veronica, he feels as though his will is being subjected to hers:

[H]e could not help thinking occasionally about Veronica; indeed, it sometimes seemed as if she appeared before him and blushingly confessed how she loved him with her whole heart and how desperately she wished to rescue him from the phantoms that ridiculed and confused him. He felt at times as if some external power that suddenly interrupted his thoughts drew him irresistibly toward the forgotten Veronica, and as if he must pursue her wherever she chose to lead him, as though he were tied to her with an unbreakable bond.[132]

We have seen how in *The Serapion Brethren* Theodor criticises 'the complete surrender of one's own self, this bleak dependence on an alien spiritual principle' (*HSB* 273). Lindhorst later confirms Veronica's influence over Anselmus as that of a 'hostile principle' (*feindliches Prinzip, HFN* 193). Veronica then appears to him in a dream, recalling the common idea that it is possible to implant ideas in the mind of a sleeper; Theobald tries something similar in *The Magnetiser*. The force of Veronica's desire for Anselmus (or her desire one day to achieve high status as his wife) makes him see her and think he is in love with her. Whilst playing with her, he sees her face in the mirror as she stands behind him:

Suddenly Anselmus felt as if a battle were commencing in his soul. Thoughts and images flashed before his eyes – Archivarius Lindhorst – Serpentina – the green snake. But the tumult finally abated and this chaos was clearly converted into consciousness . . . He wondered more than a little about all those dreams, and he ultimately attributed them solely to the feverish state of mind into which he had been thrown by Veronica's love, as well as to the work he had done in Archivarius Lindhorst's room where, in addition, there were so many strangely intoxicating odors.[133]

The magical world is absorbed into ordinary consciousness, in the way that the Serapion Brother Lothar describes inner phenomena being absorbed by the outer world surrounding us (*HSB* 54). Convinced that Veronica will save him from his madness, Anselmus returns to the work of transcribing, but he cannot understand the manuscript, which to his now 'clear' consciousness looks like a piece of veined marble or mossy stone, as indeed ancient artifacts do appear to ordinary consciousness. At this point Anselmus makes a blot on the manuscript and is condemned by Lindhorst to imprisonment in a glass bottle.

In the medical books of the time the feeling of being imprisoned in a glass vessel is attested as a symptom of madness.[134] Anselmus appears not only to be inside glass; his body almost seems to be made of glass. The Apple-Woman taunts him by saying that her rat will gnaw the shelf in half, he will fall off, and she will catch him in her skirts so that he will not break his nose or the glass bottle (*HFN* 191). He shares his imprisonment with ordinary students, who do not realise they are confined. The bottle thus symbolises the limitations of ordinary consciousness, which only the poetic soul, aware of his own doubleness, can feel. The irony is that ordinary people are, by the lights of ordinary psychology, mad. Serpentina encourages Anselmus to show the Christian virtues of faith, love, and hope. Anselmus finally frees himself by his own efforts and is joined with Serpentina in her home Atlantis.

The fact that Atlantis, the mythical lost island, is Serpentina's and Anselmus's home confirms that harmony between the two worlds is irretrievably lost to ordinary consciousness and only available to the poetic soul. This is connected to the final fate of Anselmus in the ordinary world. Whilst Lindhorst continues to exist in both worlds, nothing is said explicitly about Anselmus's fate in this world. There are hints that his place is taken by the narrator, or that the narrator is in fact the 'real' Anselmus.[135] In the Twelfth Vigil the narrator appears to experience poetry in the same way as Anselmus. Both work at the same writing desk; both awake to find the evidence of their poetic activity before them in writing. This evidence is, in fact, all that the narrator, who has been drinking punch, has to prove that he did indeed write the story we have been reading. The poetic process is unclear to him. He 'sees' a vision of Atlantis, but then explains it as the work of the Salamander, that is to say as an effect of the punch (*HFN* 203). The thought that he is now banished to the ordinary world and afflicted by doubleness makes him melancholic, just as Anselmus had been in the Fourth Vigil. He is rescued from his melancholy by Lindhorst (and not, it should be noted, the Salamander). Is his poetic vision of Atlantis true, then? The end of *The Golden Pot* gives an ambivalent answer that does not fully resolve its doubleness. Poetry itself is the only 'real' thing left to prove that Atlantis exists.

'The Sandman'

Neither Idealist psychology, which leaves no hard evidence behind, nor ordinary psychology with its 'historical broom' is straightforwardly validated by *The Golden Pot*. In *Der Sandmann* (*The Sandman*) the psychological issues are similar, but further complicated by the nature of the forces involved. It is a story of confusion and disorientation again, for like Anselmus Nathanael wavers between two different explanations for his experiences. According to the rational explanation the admittedly frightening advocate and alchemist Coppelius and the Piedmontese barometer salesman Coppola are two different people. Only Nathanael's imagination has conflated them, as a result of a traumatic childhood experience. The visits of the child-hating Coppelius to his father were associated in his imagination with the terrifying figure of the Sandman.

Much of what Nathanael feared was in fact 'the phantom of [his] own self', as Klara puts it (*das Phantom [seines] eigenen Ichs, HFN* 17). Nathanael, on the other hand, believes that Coppelius and Coppola are the same malevolent person, who killed his father and on whom Nathanael must avenge himself. Further than this Nathanael's understanding cannot reach, which leaves much for the reader to explain – for instance, the grotesque switching of Nathanael's limbs, Coppola's Italian provenance, and the power of Coppola's telescope – and therefore makes the rational explanation the more probable of the two candidates.

In some respects Nathanael's account does have probability on its side, however. In particular there is the sequence of events that leads to Nathanael seeing the mechanical doll Olimpia through Coppola's telescope, which is hard to explain without assuming the hidden agency of Coppelius. While he is (too conveniently) absent, Nathanael's flat burns down, but his friends are able to save his effects unharmed – despite the fact that the fire started on the ground floor beneath Nathanael's rooms – and move them into the house facing Spalanzani's, where he is visited by Coppola. Most improbably, when Coppola escapes with Olimpia, Spalanzani calls after him by the name Coppelius. The situation of Nathanael looking from his lodgings at Olimpia through the telescope repeats the situation in which he saw Coppelius and his father at work: the detail of the parted curtains occurs in both scenes. Coppelius, it would appear, has engineered a repeat of the situation in order to drive Nathanael insane. Nevertheless, some critics have insisted that the source of Nathanael's problems is purely psychological, bolstered by Freud's notorious suggestion that Nathanael suffers from castration anxiety.[136]

The psychological approach also receives some support. As a child, after his encounter with Coppelius Nathanael sleeps and, on waking, asks whether the Sandman is still there, which suggests that the episode might have been a nightmare. But, as in *The Golden Pot*, the common-sense psychological explanation is undermined by the characters that voice it.[137] Nathanael's fiancée Klara bears a 'speaking' name: her 'clarity' is the same clarity of consciousness that leads Anselmus to reject the magical world of salamanders and witches. She possesses a 'truly clear, sharply anaytical intelligence' (*gar heller, scharf sichtender Verstand, HFN* 21), but she is also plodding and blinkered. After reading Nathanael's letter to Lothar, she does her homework, researching alchemy and chemical explosions in her efforts to prove Nathanael wrong (*HFN* 16). Her letter to Nathanael shows her limitations. She quotes Lothar's thoughts but admits that she does not quite understand what his final sentence means. This is despite their having 'fully discussed the subject of dark powers' ([*sich*] *recht über die Materie von dunklen Mächten und Gewalten ausgesprochen*), the notes of which conversation she has written up not without difficulty. The difficulty may stem from the fact that Lothar's view is ambiguous and only half supports her case:

If there is a dark power that treacherously attaches a thread to our heart to drag us along a perilous and ruinous path that we would not otherwise have trod; if there is such a power, it must form inside us, form part of us, must be identical with ourselves; only in this way can we believe in it and give it the opportunity it needs to accomplish its secret work.[138]

This is far from supporting Klara's lesson to Nathanael that 'all the fears and terrors of which you speak only took place in your mind'.[139] The 'only', which makes Nathanael's experience into a fiction, is Klara's. Lothar shrewdly says that if there is a mysterious foreign power, it will take on the shape of our own mind so as to be believed by us. This would make it hard to disprove what Nathanael claims to have experienced. Lothar seems in fact to be arguing against Klara.

Nathanael tries to accept Klara's account of his experience, but ultimately finds it impossible. The poem he writes about Coppelius seems to have a cathartic effect. Working on it makes him calm, but at the end, when Klara emerges the triumphant victor over Coppelius and cleanses Nathanael's imagination, he looks into her eyes and sees 'death that with Klara's eyes looked upon him kindly'.[140] It is implied that the 'kind' Klara and not Coppelius will kill him. Still, the poem, unread in Nathanael's pocket, seems to have drawn off the poison, at least until Klara reminds him of Coppelius, which issues in his outburst 'You damned lifeless automaton!' and the threat of a duel with Lothar.[141] Klara becomes similar, in Nathanael's mind, to Olimpia, whose eyes, seen through the telescope, appear dead.

Although Olimpia is a machine, Nathanael sees his own feelings reflected in her. Her hands are cold to the touch, and so at first is her kiss, but Olimpia can hold him tight and keep his lips on hers, so that the kiss begins to feel warm (*HFN* 31–2). Similarly her cries of 'ah!' are interpreted by Nathanael as a passionate 'yes' (*HFN* 33). His projection of his feelings onto her is confirmed as he spends more time with her. He believes they have a psychic affinity, which is understandable given that the feelings he senses in her are really his own.

After the discovery of Spalanzani and Coppelius, Nathanael suffers another breakdown, from which he recovers gradually. People are careful not to remind him of Coppelius, fearing that this would reawaken his memory of events and with it would come the 'madness' associated with Coppelius (*HFN* 38). Inadvertently Klara reminds him by directing his gaze from the tower to the strange small grey bush that seems to be approaching them, a reminder of Coppelius's bushy grey eyebrows (*HFN* 10).[142] Nathanael automatically reaches for his telescope to see the 'bush', looks at Klara instead, but thinks that he is looking at Olimpia – presumably both because looking through the telescope carries an association of seeing Olimpia and because the two have become conflated in his mind. What he sees is a 'doll' (*Püppchen*). At the same time he recalls lines from his poem about Coppelius. The confusion now is real, grounded in a multiple association, the root of which is Coppelius.

Amid the calls for help Coppelius ominously reassures bystanders that Nathanael will come down from the tower 'by himself'. A master psychologist, Coppelius knows that Nathanael's madness will end in his death and that Nathanael will fulfil his own prophecy that 'a sombre destiny has really cast a murky veil over my life which I will perhaps tear through only when I die'.[143] Coppelius's certainty may be connected with the magnetic powers of the telescope he had sold Nathanael and through which he controls his will. The use of optical instruments in animal magnetism is proposed by Kluge in his *Essay on Animal Magnetism.*[144]

Nathanael's problem is that he really is pursued by a 'dark power', Coppelius, the demonic magnetiser and creator of human automata. All of his inner life comes to revolve around Coppelius. Lothar's diagnosis is shown to be broadly correct. If there is such a dark power as Coppelius, then 'it must form itself within us into something resembling us, indeed it must become our own self' (*HFN* 16). Coppelius controls Nathanael's fate by exploiting his fears. This begins with the idea of the Sandman. Although he was old enough to know that the old nurse's story must be a fiction, Nathanael was still fascinated by this mythical creature that collects the eyes of naughty children and feeds them to its nestlings on the moon. When it chances that Nathanael witnesses Coppelius calling for eyes for an automaton, the association between Coppelius and the Sandman is fixed. Coppelius is now doubly terrifying and can play on the fear associated in Nathanael's mind with eyes, hence his appearance as a purveyor of optical equipment. The fact that the names Coppelius and Coppola allude to the Italian *coppa* (eyeball) lends an overarching and almost supernatural fitness to Nathanael's fate. He has become the victim of the eye demon, and all the stages on the route to his fate involve eyes in some form or other. The truth behind Nathanael's fate is thus a mixture of both rational psychology and the ghoulish supernatural.

CHAPTER 7

After Romanticism: the physiological unconscious

A product partly of *Naturphilosophie* and partly of the eighteenth-century tradition, a physiological psychology of the unconscious rose to prominence between 1820 and 1850. Its central idea was that there is an unconscious mind that is constituted by our physiology. Consciousness is only the tip of the psychological iceberg, as it were, whose submerged bulk, supporting and shaping the smaller conscious part, is an assemblage of drives and needs created by the physiological processes of the body. This model of the physiological unconscious is a continuation of the tradition that we have been tracing: the theory of dark ideas, the plastic imagination, the vitalistic physiology of Herder and Goethe, the Idealist and Romantic distinction between conscious and unconscious realms, the physiology of the *Naturphilosophen.* The relation of the unconscious to rationality is, as one might expect from its ancestry, ambivalent. The unconscious is rationality's enemy: it undermines reason's attempt to govern according to ideas. At the same time, the unconscious is a product of physiology and is therefore natural and intelligible. It exemplifies L. L. Whyte's claim that 'the discovery of the unconscious is the recognition of a Goethean order, as much as of a Freudian disorder, in the depths of the mind'.[1] The focus of the present chapter is on three (in other respects quite different) exponents of this form of psychology: Arthur Schopenhauer, Carl Gustav Carus, and Georg Büchner. They represent variations on the same theme. For all three, the psyche is guided by irrational impulse, but the impulse itself is part of a larger natural order that is conceived along broadly Goethean lines.

SCHOPENHAUER

Schopenhauer's *Die Welt als Wille und Vorstellung* (*The World as Will and Representation*) was published in 1818. Its roots, however, are in the eighteenth century, in a reading of Kant's *Critique of Pure Reason* schooled in the empirico-scepticism of G. E. Schulze and intended to turn Transcendental Idealism back towards the radical Idealism of Berkeley. Schopenhauer both partook of and reacted against the Idealist hypostatisation of the will. In place of Kant's 'thing in itself' (*Ding an sich*) Schopenhauer installed the will, which he redefined as the universal will to life, manifested in a body that desires to survive and procreate. Empirical, individuated consciousness is separated from this deep reality by the 'Veil of Maya'. Morality is only possible through overcoming the will to life. In a sense, then, morality is opposed to physical existence, as, arguably, it was for Kant. But morality is not Schopenhauer's chief concern. By redefining the will as the will to life and by separating individuated consciousness from reality, Schopenhauer effectively blocks the channels through which morality might flow. His philosophy thus amounts to a radical psychologisation of German Idealism. Later psychologists acknowledged this tendency. In his *Philosophie des Unbewußten* (*Philosophy of the Unconscious*, 1869) Eduard von Hartmann transformed Schopenhauer's will into the unconscious. Freud, despite his denials, was influenced by Schopenhauer.[2]

Reception of Kant

Schopenhauer made essentially the same criticism of Kant as had Schulze, who taught him at Göttingen, and Jacobi. In order to defend himself against the charge of Berkeleian Idealism, Kant says that the things in themselves are real, existing things and are the cause of our perception of appearances. They are unknowable only in the sense that we cannot know them from any perspective other than our own and thus cannot know them as they are in themselves. However, if things in themselves cause appearances, the category of causality is being employed in respect of them and outside the realm of experience, which Kant expressly forbids. Schopenhauer's solution to this problem is to grant that things in themselves are purely ideal and to deny our representations any perspective at all on reality. Kant ought, in Schopenhauer's view, to have been more Berkeleian (*SWL* 1.32).[3]

Schopenhauer takes this revision of Kant more or less for granted. It is, he says, an elementary view such as any reflective person could reach. On further reflection, we soon realise that all is representation (*SWL* 1.31). This leaves him still able to accept elements of Kant's account of experience. He agrees that sense data are conditioned by the categories of time and space. Yet he rejects the Transcendental Analytic almost in its entirety. All of the categories can be derived from space, time, and causality, and the last of these is not a category, but a given in experience. As he has dispensed with the twelve Pure Concepts of the Understanding, there is now no need for the understanding itself, and it duly disappears, its functions swallowed by intuition on the one hand and reason on the other.

Metaphysics of the will

The idea that the world amounts to representation alone, whilst true, is one-sided and the result of an arbitrary decision to extrapolate from the world's ultimate unknowability (*SWL* 1.32). Yet the very arbitrariness of the decision points towards the true nature of what exists beyond our representations. What exists is our will, that thing in us that asserts its (arbitrary) rights. The only two things that exist are my representations of the world and my will to have them (or indeed to be or do or think anything). Schopenhauer thus recasts things in themselves as will.[4] In the phenomenal world we are individuals: the representations that we experience constitute our particular perspective on the world. Ultimately we come to know the world through our body, and the body is the ground of our knowledge. This could not be so if the body were simply an object like other objects, for a representation cannot be the grounds of all other representations. In fact, says Schopenhauer, we know the body in two ways: as an object like other objects, and directly as an objectification of our will. In this latter sense the body is an aspect of the will, and not merely a phenomenon (*SWL* 1.159). All actions of the body are, therefore, expressions of the will, in Schopenhauer's sense. Equally, all acts of will express themselves through the body. Knowledge of the will is a-priori knowledge of the body, and knowledge of the body a-posteriori knowledge of will (*SWL* 1.158).

The individual parts of the body objectify the particular drive of the will that they enact. The teeth and tongue are objectified hunger; the genitalia are the objectified sex drive; the hands and feet are objectifications of the will to grip and to move respectively (*SWL* 1.159). Schopenhauer was much influenced by the work of the British physiologist Marshall Hall, whose *On the Diseases of the Nervous System* he cites frequently. In particular he is anxious to prove that actions are reflexes and are not intended. He believes that by doing so he is giving evidence for the supposition that certain acts of the body are expressions of the will to life, rather than expressions of consciously formulated intentions. Thus we have the apparent paradox of Schopenhauer removing acts from the sphere of (conscious) willing precisely in order to reassign them to the sphere of the (unconscious) will.

One of the factors that contributed to Schopenhauer's influence was his emphasis on the importance of the sex-drive. (Goethe also belongs to this tradition: his theory of organisms makes an organism's sex-drive the chief determinant of its form.)⁵ The genitalia are not controllable by reason and belong entirely to the sphere of the will. In the sense that the genitalia are in fact *opposed* to rationality, they are therefore the purest expression of the will. From this Schopenhauer concludes that, as it is opposed to the genitals and their furtherance of the cause of life, reason must, in its purest form, be dedicated to the destruction and denial of life: ·

Far more than any other external member of the body, the genitals are subject merely to the will, and not at all to knowledge . . . The genitals [are] the real focus of the will, and are therefore the opposite pole to the brain, the representative of knowledge, i.e. to the other side of the world, the world as representation. The genitals are the life-preserving principle assuring to time endless life . . . On the other hand, knowledge affords the possibility of the suppression of willing, of salvation through freedom, of overcoming and annihilating the world.⁶

This is the essence of Schopenhauer's pessimism. As thinking beings we are fated to desire our own destruction. Yet reason is forever being frustrated by the body.

Drives and anxiety

The will is by definition irrational; it is 'blind incessant impulse' (*blinder, unaufhaltsamer Drang*; SWL 1.380). It knows of no goals, no point at which it would be satisfied, no limitations on its competence. It knows only 'an endless striving' (*ein endloses Streben*; SWL 1.240). However, reason mostly veils the will. Only in physical reflexes and outbursts of passion and anger does the will express itself fully (*SWL* v.683, v.336).

Character is innate and unalterable (*angeboren und unveränderlich*) and predetermines our behaviour (*SWL* v.274). If our motivation changes, this is not because the nature of our will or longing has changed, but because the knowledge on the basis of which we determine our actions has changed (*SWL* 1.405). The same is true of the feeling of regret. Regret results not from our will changing, but from our knowledge changing and our coming to see that what we did was led by false ideas (*SWL* 1.407). Equally, the causes of emotional pleasure and pain are not physical reality but abstract thoughts (*SWL* 1.411). Pains consist in 'restrictions' (*Hemmungen*) placed on striving (*SWL* 1.425). Striving itself is also painful, for we strive to overcome or to satisfy a want. Schopenhauer expresses this last idea in a passage that shows the impact of his reading of *Faust*:

All striving springs from want or deficiency, from dissatisfaction with one's own state or condition, and is therefore suffering so long as it is not satisfied. No satisfaction, however, is lasting; on the contrary, it is always merely the starting-point of a fresh striving. We see striving everywhere impeded in many ways, everywhere struggling and fighting, and hence always as suffering. Thus that there is no ultimate aim of striving means that there is no measure or end of suffering.[7]

This echoes Faust's pessimism leading up to his abortive suicide. Like Faust, Schopenhauer observes that if we banish our pains, we only cause them to return in new shapes, each of which is an expression of our underlying want and anxiety (*Sorge*):

The ceaseless efforts to banish suffering achieve nothing more than a change in its form. This is essentially want, lack, care for the maintenance of life. If, which is very difficult, we have succeeded in removing pain in this form, it at once appears on the scene in a thousand others, varying according to age and circumstances, such as sexual impulse, passionate love, jealousy, envy, hatred, anxiety, ambition, avarice, sickness, and so on. Finally, if it cannot find entry in any other shape, it comes in the sad grey garment of weariness, satiety, and boredom, against which many different attempts are made. Even if we ultimately succeed in driving these away, it will hardly be done without letting pain in again in one of the previous forms, and thus starting the dance once more at the beginning; for every human life is tossed backwards and forwards between pain and boredom.[8]

What troubles us is not the pains themselves, but the forms that they take in our understanding. Consciousness of our pathologies is almost always false consciousness. Were we able to acknowledge the true nature of our existence, the pain would be less. However, the only way to end the cycle of false fulfilment and recurrent dissatisfaction is to renounce needs in the first place, which is all but impossible. Life is a battle between reason and the will, in which reason's only hope lies, tragically, in the denial of the will to life itself (*SWL* v.370, 378).

CARUS

Carl Gustav Carus was a polymath. Like Goethe he was active in both arts and sciences and viewed all his activities as interrelated. His interests also overlapped with Goethe's. His chief achievement was in comparative anatomy, where he is credited with having discovered the circulatory system of insects. His profession was medicine: he was a pioneer of gynaecology, as well as dabbling in animal magnetism. A ground-breaking writer on psychology, he also wrote several works on aesthetics and art, three books on Goethe, an autobiography, eleven books and articles on physiognomy, and a *naturphilosophisch* theory of nature. He was a competent painter and imitator of Caspar David Friedrich.[9]

Carus's psychological work belongs to the middle part of his career. His *Vorlesungen über Psychologie* (*Lectures on Psychology*, 1831) arose from a series of private lectures given in the winter of 1829/30 in Dresden. In his major work, *Psyche. Zur Entwicklungsgeschichte der Seele* (*Psyche. On the Developmental History of the Soul*, 1846), he further refined and polished his ideas. In 1866 he published a comparative animal psychology, *Vergleichende Psychologie oder Geschichte der Seele in der Reihenfolge der Thierwelt* (*Comparative Psychology or History of the Soul in its Place in the Sequence of the Animal World*). The first sentence of *Psyche* signals his intent and has a strikingly modern ring: 'The key to the understanding of the conscious life of the soul lies in the realm of the unconscious.'[10] Carus aimed to provide a systematic theory of the unconscious mind and was the first to do so. Later writers, notably Eduard von Hartmann, Ludwig Klages, and Jung, recognised his primacy.[11]

The most important influences on Carus's thinking belonged to the German traditions of *Naturphilosophie*, Idealism, and the late Enlightenment. The broad outline of his system is unmistakably drawn from Schelling's *World-Spirit*, enriched with ideas of organic development from Oken and Leibniz's concept of the monad.[12] For Carus, the unconscious is nature, the 'not yet conscious I' (*noch nicht bewußtes Ich*) of Schelling's *Ideen*.[13] The ultimate substance of the Universe is ideal, Leibnizian monads, whose fundamental attribute is change or 'becoming' (*Werden*), a Leibnizian notion that had been given new life by Oken. Oken also provided Carus with his biologistic angle on the soul. In the *Lectures* Carus quotes Oken's demand that psychologists be first and foremost natural scientists, for the mind is a natural organism: 'mind [is] not something separate from nature, but its purest product and hence its symbol, its language'.[14] Indeed Carus saw his psychology as a continuation of his work in comparative anatomy. His teacher Carl Friedrich Burdach had suggested that the proper starting point for human psychology was comparative animal psychology.[15] This meant Aristotle, who provided Carus with his definition of soul and the idea of classifying souls into different species (*CVP* x). Aspects of his account of consciousness derive from Kant.[16] Arguably his main intellectual creditor was Goethe, as we shall see.

The Universe is a spiritual monadic substance. Whereas in Leibniz's system monads are separate and relate to one another through internal representations, Carus proposes a single organism. The single not only relates to the whole, it gets its being from the whole (*CVP* xii). Thus all individual plants are parts of an ideal whole plant; and by the same token, the whole vegetable world is a single organism (*CVP* 19). This is because the spirit (*Geist*) or idea (*Idee*) is prior to and underlies all physical existence. The empirical proof of this is that in all organisms we can recognise 'the presence of a spiritual (*geistig*) image of its form of existence prior to the existence itself'. Every physical organism has a prior conditioning idea or cause of its existence (*CVP* 23–4).[17] Physical reality stands in the same relation to its *Idee* as a finished work of art does to its original conception in the artist's mind (*CVP* 33–6).

This brings us no closer to understanding the relation of a particular mind to its particular body, which, Carus believes, is a mystery. The closest we can get to it is Aristotle's definition of soul as the entelechy of the body.[18] This entails that we think of mind and body as mutually dependent. Mind is moulded by body and body by mind:

[Mind and body] are . . . to some extent to be considered as the two halves of our earthly existence, but by no means as if one were a merely abstract, intellectual [gedankenhaft] being, and the other a being merely composed mechanically of material elements; rather so that each shows a truly organic life, i.e. it contains all three elements that Aristotle demonstrated were the criteria of all living things, namely the idea, the ethereal material and the form that is expressed by the idea.[19]

Carus distinguishes between three different types of soul, on the basis of their capacities or powers (*CVP* x). The lowest form, found in plants, has no consciousness (*CVP* 45). Animal souls have consciousness of the given world (*Weltbewußtsein*), but not of themselves as subjects of their perceptions. Only humans have self-consciousness. Like Aristotle, Carus thinks that the higher species of soul subsume the lower (*CVP* 118–36).

The unconscious

Carus divides the human mind into four levels, not three, within which there are further developmental stages or subdivisions. The absolute unconscious (*absolut Unbewußtes*) comprises two further stages: a 'general absolute unconscious' (*allgemeines absolut Unbewußtes*), which is the mere organic physical existence possessed by an embryo, and a 'partial absolute unconscious' (*partielles absolut Unbewußtes*) in which the nervous system registers physical processes. Above the two levels of absolute unconscious Carus finds another level of 'relative unconscious' (*relativ Unbewußtes*). This functions as a buffer between consciousness and the absolute unconscious, and is the site of most of our mental activity. Our cognitions are stored here when they are not present to us. The whole mind slips into the relative unconscious when we sleep. Even when we are awake, most of our thinking mind is in the relative unconscious.

The various layers of capacities correspond to different classes of organisms and also to the developmental stages of an individual organism. This is what Carus calls the 'genetic' approach to psychology. He attributes its invention to Goethe and Herder and says that Oken perfected it (*CVP* xi). In the first of his *Lectures* Carus explains his preference for the genetic method. He begins by rejecting what he calls the 'analytical' approach of Faculty Psychology, using arguments similar to those of Schelling and Hegel. The analytical approach leads to 'idolatry' (*Vielgötterei*). Mental capacities are taken for objective things, each distinct from the others and located in its own compartment of the brain, 'like various scholars in their different studies'.[20] Instead of treating statically something that is dynamic, we need to see 'each moment of [the soul's] development'.[21] In support of his argument, Carus quotes from the introduction to Goethe's *Farbenlehre* (*Theory of Colour*):

In fact our attempts to express the essence of a thing are in vain. We are aware of its effects, and a complete history of these effects would I suppose, at best, embrace the essence of the thing. In vain we struggle to portray the character of a person; assemble his actions, his deeds, however, and an image of his character will confront us.[22]

Nature, Carus insists, is in its essence 'eternal becoming' (*ewiges werden*), again quoting Goethe: 'The characteristic feature of nature is thus an *eternal becoming*, and when the poet says:

> The vital process that eternally informs
> All things, embrace you with the bonds that love has wrought;
> To what appears in evanescent forms
> Give substance with the lasting power of thought[23]

then one cannot find more beautiful words to express the essence of natural phenomena and how scientific observation relates to them.'[24]

The nature of change is threefold. All change is from the simple to the complex (*CVP* 14). This kind of change occurs as humans develop their faculties. Secondly, as it becomes more complex, organic life is also individuated. This comports well with the first kind of change, for the more complex an organism is, the more different it is likely to be from other organisms. All human beings begin like all others, but as they develop they acquire characteristics that make them distinct. This process is wholly unconscious and corresponds, Carus says, to the sense of the first stanza of Goethe's poem 'Urworte. Orphisch' ('Primal words: Orphic'):

> Daemon, ΔΑΙΜΩΝ
> When you were granted here your brief admission,
> As sun and planets met that day they charted
> For evermore your growing to fruition
> According to the law by which you started.
> Thus must you be: from self there's no remission;
> Thus long have sibyls, prophets this imparted;
> Nor any time nor any power can shatter
> Imprinted form informing living matter.[25]

The third ingredient of change is temporal duality. Each stage of an organism's development contains within it echoes of its past and seeds of its future. These two aspects Carus calls, with reference to Goethe's unfinished drama *Pandora*, the Epimethean (*epimetheïsch*) and Promethean (*prometheïsch*) principles (*CPS* 24–30).

The function of the unconscious is to maintain and create the organs of life (*CVP* 41–3). The absolute unconscious is present in all organisms. *Geist* embodies itself in material form and exposes itself to the influence of matter. The unconscious is the sum of the effects of its materiality on *Geist* (*CVP* 185–8).[26] For this reason the unconscious is (at first) the same in all members of a species (*CVP* 42–3). In simple organisms it will remain so. In more complex animals the effects of consciousness are reflected back onto the relative unconscious, which is thereby to some extent individuated. The absolute unconscious, however, is completely unindividuated. The unconscious, associated as it is with organic processes, is constantly active. The creation of the unconscious is a process, not a one-off event: the unconscious soul 'is to a certain extent abiding, it is transformative, always destroying and creating anew' – a description reminiscent of Goethe's Storm and Stress period.[27] Most of our mental activity is unconscious (*CPS* 1). This is partly because we never actually forget anything, in the sense that nothing leaves our mind.[28] Everything we experience is stored in the unconscious (*CPS* 101).

In conscious organisms the unconscious develops progressively into world consciousness. Carus conceives of any element of an organic system that is progressive and will play a role in its future development as 'Promethean'. There are some organisms in which 'the manifestation of a radiation of the spiritual life that will in future emerge as consciousness is already preparing its promethean development'.[29] In simple organisms there are four such Promethean precursors of world consciousness (*CPS* 101–8). The first is a nervous system that 'concentrates' (*concentrirt*) the 'stirrings' (*Regungen*) of the non-nervous parts of the body (*CPS* 101–4). The nervous system develops directly as a result of the 'Promethean unconscious dominance of the idea'.[30] The second precursor of consciousness is interaction with an external world through the senses. Third, the mind requires the ability to retain ideas. In a sense this is a retrograde movement, for the mind is clinging to something that belongs to the past. For this reason Carus terms the retaining of impressions 'the Epimethean retention of all of the stirrings of the soul's life'.[31] (In Goethe's *Pandora* Epimetheus describes his main occupation as 'dwelling on what's past, replaying/Swift events in laborious play of thought': 'Vergangnem nach-zusinnen, Raschgeschehenes/Zurückzuführen mühsamen Gedanken-spiels' (10–11). This unconscious capacity corresponds to memory in the conscious mind. The fourth prerequisite of consciousness is the presence of a mass of brain matter sufficient to hold the impressions needed to form ideas (*CPS* 108).

World-consciousness and self-consciousness

World-consciousness always begins as and is underpinned by 'the vague feeling of the condition of one's own [physical] organisation . . . a per-ception or sense that we customarily call the common sense [*Gemein-gefühl*]'.[32] This *Gemeingefühl*, an Aristotelian notion, has two poles of pleasure and pain. It engages with the world through the senses, 'the wakers of the spiritual life'.[33] Carus identifies six senses, the usual five plus a sense of warmth (*CVP* 114). The consciousness of world creates the bulk of our conscious mental life, either directly, when objects of sensation are immediately present to us, or indirectly, when past sensations, having sunk from consciousness into the unconscious, re-emerge. Memory is not a static information storage and retrieval system, but a dynamic process in which waves of information are continuously sinking and rising again into consciousness. Because conscious ideas sink into the unconscious, where they share space with the absolute unconscious, they exercise a continuous submerged influence on consciousness (*CPS* 767).

Consciousness of self is similar to consciousness of world. Just as the latter is only possible for organisms that are aware of the self as part of but also distinct from nature, so too self-consciousness is only possible because we are aware of our relation to other humans. The shift from awareness of nature to awareness of society marks a clean break between animal and human consciousness. No matter how complex animal behaviour becomes, it lacks all social self-awareness. Complex animal behaviour is only the product of consciousness of world or experience. Carus illustrates this with Faust's words on the poodle, 'I see no evil spirit in it, sure enough;/It's just a dog that's trained to do its stuff'.[34] A dog can only have routines of interaction with the world; it cannot develop a sense of how it is distinct from other animals or humans. It is society that constitutes self-consciousness. Consequently, a full and complete human consciousness is only present in humanity as a whole and not in an individual person. This is why societies behave en masse as though they possessed intelligence. Societies are able to see things which their individual components cannot. For instance, society maintains a more or less constant ratio of females to males, whereas if this were left up to an accumulation of the choices of isolated individuals, the ratio of females to males would be entirely arbitrary:

So we arrive at the insight that the true human being is only represented by humanity as a whole, and every individual human is only a particular organ of this higher whole, so that consequently the individual human soul must be seen as one of the infinite ideas that surface and realise themselves in the spirit [Geist] of humanity.[35]

If the existence of self-consciousness depends on society, its content depends on time, as Kant showed (*CPS* 25). Whereas the conscious mind is aware of time, the unconscious mind, which is continuously active, is not, and yet the continuous activity of the unconscious subordinates all individual instants to 'a general time-frame of its existence'.[36] The unconscious divides time into two halves, past and future. It thus possesses its own 'relative eternity' (*relative Ewigkeit*), which is its lifetime. As two parts of a whole, past and future relate to one another organically; the unconscious contains a continuity in which past and future interact (*CPS* 26). In this unconscious relative eternity there is no actual present, however, no isolable moment that can stand on its own. (There is a similarity here with Faust's commitment in the wager never to linger in the present.) The sense of an actual or real present (*eigentliche Gegenwart*) is only possible in consciousness. To a conscious mind the present is immediate and strong, and past and future weaker, presumably because of the power of attention over consciousness. In the unconscious mind there is no present, only an integrated past and future, 'the Promethean and Epimethean [aspects] of the unconsciously creative idea'.[37] Each stage of an organism's development contains elements that belong to its past and its future. For instance, a plant produces a seed which is its own past, the seed from which it grew. In this sense the plant seems to have 'an unconscious memory of . . . past existence' (*eine unbewußte Erinnerung von dem . . . was früher vorhanden war; CPS* 28). Unlike the conscious mind, which has only a weak and patchy knowledge of past and future, the unconscious, with its Promethean and Epimethean principles, gives complete recall, albeit without consciousness. In this sense, the unconscious mind dwarfs consciousness:

Whatever there is in the conscious realm that we call recollection or memory, and even more so what we call prediction, prescience, lags far behind the solidity and security with which this Epimethean and Promethean principle of memory and intimation makes itself felt in the unconscious realm, without any consciousness of the present.[38]

We do not know how unconsciousness emerges into consciousness. All we know is that the unconscious supports and sustains consciousness. In sleep, consciousness sinks into the unconscious to emerge refreshed on waking. Carus compares this aspect of consciousness to Antaeus, who needs contact with earth to maintain his strength (*CVP* 287–8). All conscious activity, immediately it is past, sinks into the unconscious, where it is stored and sustains all our habits (*CPS* 79–80). As the unconscious is also the vegetative principle that sustains our physical existence, it follows that the ideas of consciousness have some influence over our physical existence. Carus believes that this justifies physiognomy and phrenology. This is the basis of his later work *Symbolik der menschlichen Gestalt* (*Symbolism of the Human Form*).

Carus on 'Faust'

Carus's psychological writings promise much, but deliver little in terms of new psychological understanding. They contain many grand ideas, but are disappointingly abstract. Carus's concept of the unconscious says little, chiefly because it is not described in sufficient detail. Moreover, his extreme biologism means that the detail, when it arrives, is often not

psychological. Carus's importance is historical: he kept psychology ethically neutral, emphasised the dynamic nature of mental life, and by sheer
persistence made the idea of a psychology of the unconscious more
plausible. The qualities and flaws of Carus's psychology are equally
present in his writings on Goethe. Of Carus's three books on Goethe,
the *Briefe über Goethes 'Faust' (Letters on Goethe's 'Faust')* are the most
rewarding.[39] Carus read *Faust* from his perspective as a psychologist.
Reading *Faust* as psychology forced Carus to apply his principles to an
individual person, albeit a fictional one, in a way that his psychological
writings did not. However, the interpretation is schematic and leaves
whole aspects of the drama unconsidered.

Carus sees *Faust* as a study in psychological development. To understand *Faust* one must grasp 'the genetic principle of the soul expressed
therein'.[40] Only this can explain the work's aesthetic oddities and extrava-
gances. The most important point to understand is that Faust is not
fully conscious of his goals, as the Lord makes clear in the *Prologue in
Heaven*:

> Though in confusion still he seeks his way,
> Yet I will lead him to the light one day.
> For in the budding sapling the gardener can see
> The promise of the fruit upon the full-grown tree.[41]

Carus sees Faust's soul as progressing, perhaps being drawn, unconsciously and via all manner of illusions and errors, towards 'its highest
divine fulfilment' (*ihre höchste göttliche Befriedigung*). His soul is driven by
an unconscious purpose, and as the gap between his consciousness and his
unconscious varies, he swings between bliss and despair. To represent this,
Goethe has given Faust a blend of positive and negative psychological
characteristics. In some respects Faust is a symbolic figure who represents
humanity in general.[42] His Promethean qualities symbolise the progressive side of the human unconscious. He exemplifies striving and activity.[43]
The negative side of his psyche is his melancholy. Like Albrecht Dürer's
Melencolia i, Goethe's drama captures 'the tormenting desire of the spirit
that wishes to embrace all life's heights and depths'.[44] Carus also sees that
Faust's melancholy and his striving are linked and one follows from the
other. Dissatisfaction with reality is a spur to striving after higher things; a
failure to reach them leads to despair:

Let us then take a fiery soul such as Faust's, that in its very innermost self tends
from absolute striving towards genuine freedom in the purification of all
immoderate desires, but let us at the same time imagine in this soul a violent

attraction towards the press of the world of appearances and let us also imagine it banished to one of those dissonant conditions of life, whose weight can only seem justified to us when we reflect that, without dissonant chords in the part no satisfying progression of higher harmonies would be possible in the whole, and it will become clear to us how painfully, pathologically, and stormily the development of such a soul must weave through myriad binding, releasing, and re-binding processes before it reaches ultimate freedom, how often the arms reaching out through myriad pleasures that mutate into pains must strive upwards, in order finally to attain a higher divinely ordained freedom.[45]

BÜCHNER

As well as being a playwright and a political activist, Büchner was a scientist of some promise and a would-be philosopher. Shortly before his death in 1837 he had taken up a position at the University of Zurich as a lecturer in comparative anatomy and intended also to offer classes on philosophy. He had been taught comparative anatomy, physiology, and natural history by J. B. Wilbrand at Gießen.[46] The trial lecture that Büchner delivered in Zurich in November 1836 presented a *naturphiloso-phisch* account of the nerves of animal skulls. He argued that the ultimate aim of the scientist must be to seek a 'fundamental law informing the entire organic world' (*Grundgesetz für die gesammte Organisation*), echoing the title of Wilbrand's book *Naturphilosophie: Grundgesetz der gesamt-en Organisation* (*Nature Philosophy: The Fundamental Law of All Organisation*).[47] He shared with Goethe, Carus, and the Schellingians the belief that an ideal blueprint or series of related blueprints underlies the whole of nature.

Given these scientific leanings, one might expect Büchner also to have leant in the direction of Idealist philosophy. However, he was deeply sceptical about philosophy in general, Hegel in particular, and indeed about human rationality itself.[48] His philosophy was close in spirit to his fiercely radical politics, and he went so far as to suggest that the rationalism of Descartes and Spinoza gave implicit support to absolutism.[49] The potential for conflict between *Naturphilosophie* and anti-Idealist philosophy was not, as far as one can tell, a matter of concern to Büchner. Had he studied psychology – the nexus of physiology and philosophy – he might have been forced to confront the issue, but there is no evidence in Büchner's writings of a conscious engagement with contemporary psychological theory. In his dramas and the narrative *Lenz*, where a practical, literary engagement with psychology takes place, there is evidence of an unresolved conflict between his *naturphilosophisch* and anti-Rationalist tendencies.

'Woyzeck'

Büchner was writing *Woyzeck* at the same time as working on the trial lecture, and there are several points of contact between the two works.[50] In the first draft of the satirical scene involving holidaying labourers ('Handwerksburschen', H2, 4), one of the drunk apprentices embarks on a parody of teleological theories of life: 'Wherefore is man? Wherefore is man? – But verily I say unto you, how could the farmer, the cooper, the cobbler, the doctor have earned their living if God had not created man? How could the tailor have made his living if God hadn't made men feel ashamed of their nakedness?'[51] Although principally a piece of comical burlesque in the manner of Auerbachs Keller in *Faust i*, the apprentice's *reductio ad absurdum* of teleological philosophy reflects part of Büchner's own attitude to teleological science. Similarly the Doctor, a figure both ridiculous and menacing, holds a Hegelian view of man, in which the fundamental law is the manifestation of reason in mankind. This has led him towards the dubious scientific project of proving that the body is reason's instrument and that the bladder must therefore be subordinated to the will (*BWL* 150). The Doctor is a parody of one of the dogmatic 'philosophers of reason' (*Vernunftphilosophen*) whom Büchner criticised in the trial lecture.

The dramatic psychology of *Woyzeck* is broadly anti-Rationalist, like Büchner's philosophy, and physiological, like his science. The minor characters are rendered in an almost emblematic fashion; they are static rather than dynamic. This lends the play's characterisation an essentialist tenor.[52] Characters appear to represent psychological conditions or drives. These are exposed with a naturalistic attention to the detail of behaviour. In particular, Büchner focuses on quirks of verbal behaviour that represent psychological states. His use of exclamations and incomplete syntax recalls the dramatic language of F. M. Klinger and J. M. R. Lenz, which was very likely his intention, for in his account of the latter's madness in the narrative *Lenz* Büchner has the Storm and Stress playwright formulate an aesthetics that describes, albeit in abstract terms, both Lenz's and his own dramatic practice. This emphasises the physical, unconscious forms of expressions that are half-submerged in ordinary people's behaviour: 'People should try it sometime, they should enter completely into the life of the meanest of men and then reproduce it with every twitch of an eyebrow, every wink and nod, the whole subtle, hardly perceptible play of facial expression.'[53] Lenz explains that this has been his practice as a dramatist. In creating his characters he has emphasised both their ordinariness and their unconscious physiological psychology: 'They are the most everyday people in the world; but the pulse of feeling is the same in almost everyone, the only difference is the thickness of the covering it has to pass through. All you need is the eyes to see and the ears to hear.'[54] Aside from the political point that every sort of person, regardless of class, is worthy of being the subject of art, the thrust seems to be that the essence of a person is in the unconscious expressions of their physiology.

Woyzeck carries out this programme of representing the physiological unconscious, or the emergence of physiological dynamics into consciousness. When Marie responds to the Drum Major's caresses, she is a driven and not a reflective being:

DRUM-MAJOR: Christ almighty, we could breed little drum-majors like bloody rabbits – let's get started, eh? [*he puts his arm around her*]
MARIE [*crossly*]: Get your hands off!
DRUM-MAJOR: Wild animal, that's what you are!
MARIE [*vehemently*]: Just touch me![55]

Marie is not alone in being driven. Woyzeck is driven by anxiety, the Doctor by his ill temper and irritability, the Captain by melancholy. None of them is able fully to control themselves. Woyzeck's urinating in the street is just one (relatively trivial) instance of a general condition of animality. Marie is a 'wild animal'. The Captain reacts emotionally to Woyzeck. The Doctor is prone to fits of anxiety or melancholy, which issue in aggression towards Woyzeck and which he can only control briefly and after a struggle: 'I am calm, quite calm, my pulse is its customary 60, and I am telling you so with the utmost composure. Good God, who's going to bother getting angry with a human, a mere human?'[56]

The power of unconscious drives is matched by the weakness of the intelligence. Humans are dualistic, but asymmetrically so. Our psyche is split between a relatively weak rational part and an extremely powerful, even uncontrollable unconscious part, that is grounded in our physiology. This duality is explored principally through the character of Woyzeck, whose belief in the radical duality of the world acts as a metaphor for the duality of mind. Woyzeck is both incapable of controlling his unconscious side and troublingly aware of his own duality. Indeed, Woyzeck is the one who is most able to express his duality – paradoxically, given the limits on his powers of self-expression that are repeatedly drawn to our attention by his failure to finish his sentences.[57] Woyzeck's *idée fixe* centres on the idea of a conflict between the ordinary, superficial world, and the world's hollow centre: 'Something's moving behind me, under me [*stamps on the ground*] – hollow, do you hear? Everything's hollow down there.'[58] This strange sense of a hidden reality is an insane version of the dualisms that afflicted German philosophy in the eighteenth and early nineteenth centuries. On the surface everything is obvious, too obvious even, for it is fixed and predictable, the very rigidity of the crust 'proving' that there must be a hidden, dynamic core. In an early draft (H2, 2) Woyzeck expresses this belief to Louise (Marie): 'Look around you! It's all stiff, hard, dark, something moving about underneath. Something we can't grasp. It's silent, drives us crazy, but I've got it.'[59]

Woyzeck's belief that the freemasons are at work behind the scenes – a commonly held conspiracy theory – here has a psychological significance. He cannot reconcile the impassive, stable appearance of things with his own desperately strong feelings. His mind is uncontrollably active, and he suffers from constant anxiety. He is aware of powerful urges or compulsions within him that do not square with the way things ordinarily seem to be. He expresses this as a belief that 'something's out there. In the ground'.[60] Yet he is also half aware that the world's mysterious core is actually not out there in the world, but within us. He applies the idea of duality to Marie, as he stares accusingly at her, seeing only the familiar surface, but knowing also that there is a hidden truth: 'No! I don't see nothing, nothing! Oh, you ought to be able to see it, to grab hold of it with your bare hands . . . A sin so big and so fat.'[61] The 'sin' is the unconscious desire that drives her into the arms of the Drum Major, and it is hidden from Woyzeck and, in a sense, from Marie too. Woyzeck is aware of the darkness within, but cannot grasp it. The self is, as he says ominously to her, an abyss: 'Every person's an abyss; it makes you dizzy looking down.'[62] This abyss – from which come the passions that drive us – and not the freemasons, is, along with his miserable circumstances, the real cause of Woyzeck's unhappiness.

CONCLUSION: THE TWIN TRADITIONS OF
GERMAN PSYCHOLOGY

With Schopenhauer, Carus, and Büchner, we reach the threshold of a fully scientific psychology. Psychology developed into an academic discipline in Germany between the second quarter of the eighteenth century and the third quarter of the nineteenth. By the 1870s psychologists were establishing their first research laboratories, where they could pursue empirical research without interference from the Church and social conservatives. Before it achieved autonomy, psychology was mainly practised as philosophy and literature. That is to say, the history of pre-autonomous psychology is, for the most part, a history of the development of psychology in philosophy and literature.

As we have seen, part of the reason for the advanced development of German psychology is the situation in which German philosophy found itself in the seventeenth and early eighteenth centuries. The Semiramist philosophy of the late sixteenth and early seventeenth centuries introduced a new rigour into Aristotelianism. In doing so it created in the tree of philosophical disciplines a branch named *psychologia*, alongside *angelographia* and other doomed enterprises. Following Descartes's attack on Aristotle's doctrine of qualities, German philosophy became anti-Cartesian and anti-dualist. Leibniz was its hero, rescuing the unity of mind and turning mind into an entelechy – an Aristotelian concept. Wolff furnished mind with faculties, the modern equivalents of the powers of the Aristotelian *psychē*. Faculty Psychology was essentially a neo-Aristotelian project.

Psychology had essentially the same function for German philosophers of the eighteenth and early nineteenth centuries. The idea that there existed an unconscious (or unknown or unknowable) part of the mind preserved a wholeness that was felt to be threatened. Leibniz argued that the mind is never inactive and that Descartes was wrong to equate mind with consciousness. He thus avoided the dualism and potential materialism of Descartes and rescued Rationalism from the disrepute it risked falling into in Protestant Europe. This was one of the founding acts of the German Enlightenment, giving to German rationalism its distinctive psychological colouring. Wolff cemented Leibniz's argument and elevated psychology to a position alongside ontology and logic. Kant, though ill-disposed towards Wolff's Rational Psychology, was nonetheless dependent on his theory of mind. One might even say that the *Critique of Pure Reason* has a Leibniz–Wolffian argument at its core. Kant posited an unknowable but necessarily existent mind in order to secure the unity of self and refute Hume's dangerous scepticism. The postulated unknown preserved the wholeness of the known. Schopenhauer made a similar move, though in the opposite direction, for he used the unconscious, or will, to ground a return to Berkeleian idealism. Will is the reality illusion masks. In these various ways, then, the idea of an unconscious mind is of fundamental importance in German thought and is one of the marks that distinguish it. In the British and French intellectual traditions the idea had been available, in the work of Ralph Cudworth for instance, but it was not widely exploited.

Although Wolff did much to popularise philosophy, his psychology was still forbiddingly academic. It had practically no real-world applications, excepting the infant science of aesthetics. The popular profile that psychology achieved in the late eighteenth century was thanks to literature. The breakthrough came in the 1770s. Its main impetus was a reaction against the prevailing rationalist culture, and it drew its ideas chiefly from British empiricism and sensationism. Certain of these – the fashions for melancholy and sympathy – were borrowed in an attempt to define German literary culture against the Francophile culture of the courts. The main change wrought in literary psychology was an overt piece of cultural nationalism. Shakespeare's characterisation became a model because Shakespeare was believed to be the national poet of England and anathema to the Gallic aesthetics that prevailed in Germany. It was not least for these reasons that psychology could serve the overt political aim of portraying the undeserved hurts and unheard protests of men and women of feeling.

Despite moves away from realism in the following decades, the lessons of the 1770s stuck fast. Weimar Classicism espoused an aesthetics based on psychology, presenting itself as a cure for melancholy. It also made melancholy one of its chief subjects, most obviously in *Wallenstein* and *Faust*. The Romantics Kleist and Hoffmann raised questions about the reality of psychological causation, but both still gave psychology a central position, even if it came bundled with the mystical pseudo-science of animal magnetism. Büchner, in a return to the values of the Storm and Stress, joined psychological realism to a bleak social realism. No-one in nineteenth-century Germany would take literary psychological realism further.

It is hard to overlook Goethe's role. His immediate influence was considerable, above all through *The Sorrows of Young Werther*. His longer-term influence on psychology in the nineteenth century, especially through *Faust*, was also deep. For Moritz, *Werther* established the idea of literature as psychopathography. This lay behind Moritz's major projects, the *Magazine for Empirical Psychology* and *Anton Reiser*, which created the genre of the psychological case-history. The second half of his short career was dominated by the attempt to build a new classical aesthetics, in which psychology would play an important role. Moritz's aesthetic ideal was wholeness, which he equated with psychological health. Classical aesthetics was a cure for anxiety and melancholy. Influenced by Moritz, Goethe and Schiller arrived at similar ideas. In a negative example of the classical ideal, Goethe made Faust into an anxious, driven character, the opposite of Goethe's own Epicureanism. Faust's anxiety provided a model for Schopenhauer's conception of anxiety in *The World as Will and Representation* and influenced Carus, the first explicit theorist of the unconscious.

Schopenhauer's biologistic psychology and Moritz's empirical psychology were very different beasts. By 1820, there was not one German tradition of psychology but two: an Idealist tradition, centred on notions of the unconscious derived from Schelling, Kant, and ultimately Leibniz, and an empiricist tradition, which aimed to classify and measure and originated from Wolff's 'Psycheometria'. Tensions between the two tendencies are already evident in Leibniz and Wolff. The break was formally instituted by Kant. In psychological matters, Kant took a quixotic and untenable position. Empirical psychology was not a worthwhile subject, since it could not be mathematised, and so it was doomed to remain anecdotal. In any case, the self was ultimately unknowable. Two interpretations of Kant's psychology emerged in the 1790s and both ran counter to his intentions. The realists interpreted him as having adumbrated a transcendental psychology that they could fill in empirically. His view that all science was reducible to physics could be upheld, and psychology could meet the tests set by it. Herbart, Kant's successor in Königsberg, even proposed a return to Wolff. The Idealists held that Kant had been right to insist on an ultimate unity that bound the phenomena of self together, but wrong to argue that this was unknowable. This issued into the fully Idealist psychology of such writers as Eschenmayer. The heirs of Kant either returned to a psychology that Kant thought he had destroyed or embarked on a psychology that he had held to be impossible.

The fate of Idealist psychology was still more complex. For the early Idealists, Kant had been right: psychology ought not to exist. One of their tactics was to replace psychology with anthropology. The science of man had to have freedom as its premise. The whole design of man – mind and body – clearly aimed at or issued from freedom. This strengthened and gave a new direction to an existing German tradition of philosophical anthropology, which flourished in Idealist circles at first and survived to the middle of the nineteenth century, when it began to be recognised as the philosophical dinosaur it was. Early Romantic writers followed the Idealists in replacing psychology with anthropology. Like

Fichte, Schelling, and Hegel, they could only accept with reservations the realist notions of causation that psychology entailed. Kleist, among others, followed the Idealists in falling for animal magnetism. As an academic subject, animal magnetism was only taken seriously for as long as elements in the Prussian government sponsored it. The Romantics' interest in the empirical and psychiatric traditions of psychology proved to be of more enduring significance. Kleist and Hoffmann continued the line of literary psychopathology that they inherited from Goethe, Schiller, and Moritz. By the 1830s, with Büchner and the beginnings of nineteenth-century literary realism, the influence of Kant and of the Idealists' attack on psychology had ebbed away altogether.

Empirical psychology, the legacy of Wolff, Moritz, Schiller, Goethe, and others, still flourishes. The other legacy of the German tradition of psychology has had difficulty maintaining its position in the world of modern science. The one ingredient of the Idealist ferment that could survive in nineteenth-century academic psychology was the biologism of Schopenhauer and Carus. Freud and Jung resurrected it and made it popular again, with some flourishes of their own. But Freud and Jung are now in their turn largely discredited in academic psychology (although not in the altogether more free-form world of therapy), and whether biologism of this kind will ever make a comeback seems doubtful. It is now more or less academically extinct, and among serious biologists of the mind neo-Darwinian psychology seems to be the only game in town.

Notes

INTRODUCTION

1 For example, Albert M. Reh, *Die Rettung der Menschlichkeit. Lessings Dramen in literaturpsychologischer Sicht*, Bern and Munich: Francke, 1981.
2 Emil Staiger, *Friedrich Schiller*, Zurich: Atlantis, 1967, pp. 142–5.
3 Wolfgang Riedel, *Die Anthropologie des jungen Schiller: Zur Ideengeschichte der medizinischen Schriften und der 'Philosophischen Briefe'*, Würzburg: Königstein & Neumann, 1985; Peter-André Alt, *Schiller. Leben–Werk–Zeit*, 2 vols., Munich: Beck, 2000.
4 Hans-Jürgen Schings, *Melancholie und Aufklärung: Melancholiker und ihre Kritiker in Erfahrungsseelenkunde und Literatur des 18. Jahrhunderts*, Stuttgart: Metzler, 1977. On Jena, see Georg Eckhardt, Matthias John, Temilo van Zantwijk, and Paul Ziche, *Anthropologie und Psychologie um 1800. Ansätze einer Entwicklung zur Wissenschaft*, Cologne, Weimar, and Vienna: Böhlau, 2001.

1 THE 'LONG PAST': PSYCHOLOGY BEFORE 1700

1 Ebbinghaus quoted in, e.g., Edwin G. Boring, *A History of Experimental Psychology*, 2nd edn, Englewood Cliffs, NJ: Prentice Hall, 1950, p. ix; Erwin A. Esper, *A History of Psychology*, Philadelphia and London: Saunders, 1964, p. vi.
2 See, for instance, David B. Claus, *Toward the Soul: An Inquiry into the Meaning of 'Psyche' before Plato*, New Haven and London: Yale University Press, 1981, p. 47; Shirley M. Darcus, 'A person's relation to *phren* in Homer, Hesiod, and the Greek Lyric Poets', *Glotta* 57 (1979), 159–73 (p. 166).
3 On reason in Homer see Joachim Böhme, *Die Seele und das Ich im homerischen Epos. Mit einem Anhang: Vergleich mit den Primitiven*, Leipzig and Berlin: Teubner, 1929, p. 94.
4 Aristotle, *De anima* (*On the Soul*), trans. Hugh Lawson-Tancred, London: Penguin, 1986.
5 D. W. Hamlyn, 'Aristotle's account of *aisthesis* in the *De anima*', *Classical Quarterly* 53 (1959), 6–16.
6 See *Meno*, 80d5–81d4 and *Phaedo*, 64c4–68c3.

7 *Phaedo* 64e4–65d2; see also T. M. Robinson, *Plato's Psychology*, 2nd edn, Toronto: University of Toronto Press, 1995, p. 22 and Gregory Vlastos, 'Anamnesis in the *Meno*', in G. Vlastos (ed.), *Plato's 'Meno' in Focus*, London: Routledge, 1994, pp. 88–111 (pp. 100–5).

8 *Phaedo*, 76c11–13.

9 *Phaedrus*, 250e–253c.

10 Plotinus, *The Enneads*, trans. Stephen MacKenna, London: Faber, 1956, iv.2.1, p. 255 (the soul not an entelechy) and iv.9.1–5, pp. 364–8 (one soul and many bodies).

11 *Ibid.*, v, 3 (49): 3, 35–40 (p. 384).

12 H. J. Blumenthal, *Aristotle and Neoplatonism in Late Antiquity: Interpretations of the 'De anima'*, Ithaca: Cornell University Press, 1996, p. 102.

13 Edward G. Warren, 'Consciousness in Plotinus', *Phronesis* 9 (1964), 83–97 (p. 93).

14 Plotinus, *Enneads*, v, 3 (49): 2, 1–14 (pp. 382–3).

15 Blumenthal, *Aristotle and Neoplatonism*, p. 4.

16 Plotinus, *Enneads*, iv, 4 (28): 8, 16–24 (p. 293).

17 *Ibid*, i, 4: 10, 21–33 (p. 49).

18 Warren, 'Consciousness in Plotinus', pp. 86, 95–6.

19 Marsilio Ficino, *Théologie platonicienne de l'immortalité des âmes*, ed. Raymond Marcel, 3 vols., Paris: Belles-Lettres, 1964–70, vol. ii, p. 139.

20 *Ibid.*, vol. ii, p. 223.

21 *Ibid.*, vol. i, pp. 137–43.

22 Marsilio Ficino, *De vita libri tres*, ed. Martin Plessner, Hildesheim: Olms, 1978, Book 1, Chapters 5–6 [unpaginated: pp. 15–19].

23 Ficino, *Théologie platonicienne*, vol. i, pp. 38–9 and vol. ii, pp. 269–73.

24 *Ibid.*, vol. ii, pp. 291–2.

25 J. A. Passmore, *Ralph Cudworth: An Interpetation* [1951], photo reprint, Bristol: Thoemmes, 1990, pp. 23–4, 30–1.

26 Isabel Rivers, *Reason, Grace, and Sentiment: A Study of the Language of Religion and Ethics in England, 1660–1780*, 2 vols., Cambridge: Cambridge University Press, 1991–2000, vol. i, pp. 25–35.

27 Ernst Cassirer, *The Platonic Renaissance in England*, Nelson: Edinburgh, 1953, p. 8.

28 Ralph Cudworth, *The True Intellectual System of the Universe: Wherein All the Reason and Philosophy of Atheism is Confuted, and Its Impossibility Demonstrated, with a Treatise Concerning Eternal and Immutable Morality*, trans. John Harrison, 3 vols., London: Thomas Tegg, 1845, vol. iii, p. 566.

29 Passmore, *Cudworth*, p. 31.

30 Cudworth, *True Intellectual System*, vol. i, 'Digression on plastic natures', pp. 14–16.

31 *Ibid.*, vol. iii, p. 579.

32 Passmore, *Cudworth*, pp. 24–30.

33 Cudworth, *True Intellectual System*, vol. i, p. 246.

34 *Ibid.*, vol. i, p. 247.

35 Rodolphus Goclenius, ΨΥΧΟΛΟΓΙΑ: *hoc est, De hominis perfectione, animo, et in primis ortu huius, commentationes et disputationes quorundum Theologorum & Philosophorum nostrae aetatis, quos versa pagina ostendit,* Marburg: Egenolph, 1590.

36 Otho Casmannus, *Psychologia anthropologica; sive, animae humanae doctrina (Anthropological Psychology; or, Doctrine of the Human Soul),* Hanau: Anton, 1594.

37 Otho Casmannus, *Secunda pars Anthropologiae: hoc est, Fabrica humani corporis methodice descripta,* Hanau: Anton, 1596 and *Angelographia, seu commentationum disceptationumque* [*sic*] *physicarum prodromus problematicus de angelis seu creatis spiritibus a corpore consortio abiunctis . . . concinnatus,* Frankfurt am Main: Palthen, 1597.

38 '*Psychologia* est doctrina de anima.' Johannes Micraelius, *Lexicon philosophicum terminorum philosophis usitatorum ordine alphabetico sic digestorum, ut inde facile liceat cognosse, praesertim si tam latinus, quam graecus, index praemissus non negligatur, quid in singulis disciplinis quomodo sit distinguendum et definiendum,* Jena: Mamphrasius, 1653, pp. 654–5.

39 Petrus Godartius, *Lexicon philosophicum: item, accuratissima totius philosophiae summa,* 2 vols., 2nd edn, Paris: De la Caille, 1675, vol. 1, pp. 266–304.

40 Stephanus Chauvinus, *Lexicon philosophicum,* 2nd edn, Leeuwarden: Halma, 1713.

41 'Ame . . . Ce qui est le principe de la vie dans les choses vivantes . . . Se dit particulierement en parlant de l'homme, & signifie, Ce qui est en luy, qui le rend capable de penser, de vouloir, & de raisonner.' [Thomas Corneille], *Le dictionnaire des arts et des sciences,* 4 vols., Paris: Coignard, 1694, vol. 1, p. 34; see also vol. 111, p. 29.

42 John Harris, *Lexicon technicum; or, An Universal English Dictionary of the Arts and Sciences: Explaining Not Only the Terms of Art but the Arts Themselves,* London: Daniel Brown *et al.,* 1704, preface [unpaginated, p. i].

43 *Ibid.,* p. vi.

44 Johann Heinrich Zedler, *Großes Universal-Lexicon aller Wissenschaften und Künste, welche bishero durch menschlichen Verstand und Witz erfunden und verbessert worden,* 66 vols., Leipzig and Halle: Zedler, 1732–52, vol. XXIX, p. 1090: 'PSYCHOMETRIA, ist eine zur Zeit noch nicht in Schrifften vorhandene Wissenschafft, welche die mathematische Erkänntniß der Seele ausmachet, und von dem Herrn Christian Wolff in Vorschlag gebracht worden.'

45 '. . . partie de la Philosophie, qui traite de l'ame humaine, qui en définit l'essence, & qui rend raison de ses opérations'. D. Diderot and J. le R. d'Alembert (eds.), *Encyclopédie; ou, Dictionnaire raisonné des arts, des sciences, et des métiers,* 17 vols., Paris: no publ., 1751–65, vol. XIII, p. 543.

46 'Rien est de plus propre que l'étude de la *Psychlogie,* pour remplir des plaisirs les plus vifs, un esprit qui aime les connoisances solides & utiles.' *Ibid.,* vol. XIII, p. 543.

47 *Ibid.,* vol. 1, pp. 327–43.

48 *Ibid.,* vol. 1, pp. 343–53.

49 *Encyclopædia Britannica; or, A Dictionary of Arts and Sciences, compiled upon a new plan. In which the different Sciences and Arts are digested into distinct Treatises and Systems; and the various Technical Terms, &c. are explained as they occur in the order of the Alphabet,* 3 vols., Edinburgh: Bell and Macfarquhar, 1771, vol. III, p. 618–19.

50 *Ibid.*, vol. I, p. 316.

51 *Ibid.*, vol. III, pp. 174–5.

52 William Coward, *Second Thoughts Concerning the Human Soul, demonstrating the Notion of Human Soul, as believ'd to be a spiritual, immortal substance, united to human body, to be a plain heathenish invention* [London]: 1702.

53 Alethius Phylopsyches [*sic*], ΨΥΧΗΛΟΓΙΑ; *or, Serious Thoughts on Second Thoughts . . .*, London: John Nutt, 1702; John Broughton, *Psychologia; or, An Account of the Nature of the Rational Soul*, London: Bennet, 1703.

54 Examples appear in the OED from Cudworth, *True Intellectual System*; [Alexander Gerard], *Marischal College*; Adam Smith, *Wealth of Nations*; and Philip Doddridge, *Course of Lectures on the Principal Subjects in Pneumatology, Ethics, and Divinity.*

2 THE ENLIGHTENMENT: RATIONALISM AND SENSIBILITY

1 Philip Merlan, *Monopsychism, Mysticism, Metaconsciousness: Problems of the Soul in the Neoaristotelian and Neoplatonic Tradition*, The Hague: Martinus Nijhoff, 1963, p. 57.

2 G. W. Leibniz, *Monadology*, paragraphs 2–10, *LPW*, pp. 179–80.

3 *Ibid.*, paragraphs 15–29, *LPW*, pp. 181–3.

4 G. W. Leibniz, *Philosophical Essays*, ed. R. Ariew and D. Garber, Indianapolis: Hackett, 1989, pp. 23–8.

5 G. W. Leibniz, *New Essays on Human Understanding*, trans. P. Remnant and J. Bennett, Cambridge: Cambridge University Press, 1981, p. 54.

6 On the unconscious in Leibniz, see Richard Herbertz, *Die Lehre vom Unbewußten im System des Leibniz*, Abhandlungen zur Philosophie und ihrer Geschichte 20, Halle: Niemeyer, 1905.

7 *KWW* III, p. 117.

8 'Porro quaevis mens, ut recte Plotinus, quemdam in se mundum intelligibilem continet . . . Sed . . . in nobis paucissima distincte noscuntur, caetera confuse velut in chao perceptionum nostrarum latent', quoted in Merlan, *Monopsychism, Mysticism, Metaconsciousness*, p. 61.

9 Leibniz, *Monadology*, paragraph 21, *LPW*, p. 182.

10 *Ibid.*, paragraphs 22–3, p. 182.

11 Leibniz, *New Essays*, pp. 54–5; the quotation is Virgil, *Georgics* IV.393.

12 Georges Gusdorf quoted in Ecole, 'Des rapports de l'expérience et de la raison', p. 617. See also J. G. Sulzer, *Kurzer Begriff aller Wissenschaften und andern Theile der Gelehrsamkeit, worin jeder nach seinem Innhalt, Nuzen, und Vollkommenheit kürzlich beschrieben wird*, 2nd edn, Frankfurt and Leipzig: no publ., 1759, p. 158 (paragraph 206).

13 See also Sulzer, *Kurzer Begriff aller Wissenschaften*, p. 157.
14 Francois H. Lapointe, 'Origin and evolution of the term "psychology"', *American Psychologist* 25 (1970), 640–6 (p. 643).
15 'hub': Charles A. Corr in *WGW* 1.ii.7.
16 Against this, Max Dessoir saw the empirical as only a prelude to the rational psychology (*Geschichte der neueren deutschen Psychologie*, 2nd edn [1909] photo reprint, Amsterdam: Bonset, 1964, p. 8).
17 '. . . dasjenige Ding . . . welches sich seiner und anderer Dinge außer ihm bewußt ist . . . was wir durch die tägliche Erfahrung von [der Seele] wahrnehmen' (*WGW* 1.ii.106).
18 '. . . natura non facit saltum ex obscuritate in distinctionem', quoted in Wolfgang Riedel, 'Erkennen und Empfinden. Anthropologische Achsendrehung und Wende zur Ästhetik bei Johann Georg Sulzer', in Hans-Jürgen Schings (ed.), *Der ganze Mensch. Anthropologie und Literatur im 18. Jahrhundert*, Stuttgart: Metzler, 1994, pp. 410–39 (p. 416).
19 The solution is 157 103 016 871 482 805 817 152 171.
20 Thomas Reid, *Essays of the Intellectual Powers of Man*, ed. A. D. Woozley, London: Macmillan, 1941, p. 3, quoted in Lapointe, 'Origin and evolution of the term "psychology"', p. 643.
21 'Wer weiß, gibt es nicht noch mehr Kräfte, als wir kennen, z. B. den Humour der Britten', quoted in F. A. Carus, *Geschichte der Psychologie*, in *Nachgelassene Werke*, vol. III, Leipzig: Barth & Kummer, 1808, p. 676.
22 Richard J. Blackwell, 'C. Wolff's doctrine of the soul', *Journal of the History of Ideas* 22 (1961), 339–54.
23 *Ibid.*, p. 347.
24 Georg Bernhard Bilfinger, *Dilucidationes philosophicae de Deo, anima humana, mundo, et generalibus rerum affectionibus*, 4th edn, Tübingen: Cotta, 1768.
25 Alexander Gottlieb Baumgarten, *Metaphysica*, 2nd edn, Halle: Hemmerde, 1743.
26 Ursula Franke, *Kunst als Erkenntnis. Die Rolle der Sinnlichkeit in der Ästhetik des Alexander Gottlieb Baumgarten*, Wiesbaden: Franz Steiner, 1972, pp. 39–40.
27 *Ibid.*, p. 47.
28 Baumgarten, *Metaphysica*, p. 140.
29 Franke, *Kunst als Erkenntnis*, p. 37.
30 Georg Friedrich Meier, *Anfangsgründe aller schönen Wissenschaften*, 3 vols., Halle: Hemmerde, 1748.
31 Georg Friedrich Meier, *Beweis, daß keine Materie dencken könne*, Halle: Hemmerde, 1743.
32 Dessoir, *Geschichte der neueren deutschen Psychologie*, p. 27.
33 Georg Friedrich Meier, *Gedancken von Schertzen* [Halle: Hemmerde, 1744], photo reprint, Text und Kontext Sonderreihe 3, Copenhagen: Text und Kontext, 1977.
34 '. . . die Aufmerksamkeit ist . . . die Hand, mit welcher die Seele in ihrem Grunde eine dunkle Vorstellung ergreift, sie in die Höhe hebt und dadurch an das Tageslicht bringt', quoted by Dessoir, *Geschichte der neueren deutschen Psychologie*, pp. 28–9.

35 Meier, *Anfangsgründe aller schönen Wissenschaften*, vol. 11, pp. 5–10.
36 Emil Ermatinger, *Die Weltanschauung des jungen Wieland. Ein Beitrag zur Geschichte der Aufklärung*, Frauenfeld: Huber, 1907, p. 25.
37 '. . . die Natur begeht nirgends einen Sprung', Georg Friedrich Meier, *Versuch einer Erklärung des Nachtwandelns*, Halle: Hemmerde, 1758, pp. 52–7.
38 Johann August Unzer, 'Untersuchung, ob die Träume etwas bedeuten?', in J. A. Unzer, *Sammlung kleiner Schriften. Zur speculativischen Philosophie*, 2 vols., Rinteln and Leipzig: Berth, 1766, pp. 431–9.
39 Ernst Anton Nicolai, *Wirckungen der Einbildungskraft in den menschlichen Cörper aus den Gründen der neuern Weltweisheit hergeleitet*, Halle: Hemmerde, 1744, pp. 32–3.
40 '. . . wenn je ein Zustand unserer Seele im Stande ist, uns die geheimen Gesetze ihrer Thätigkeit zu enträtseln, so ist es der Traum', Pierre Villaume, 'Über die Träume', in: P. Villaume, *Versuche über einige psychologische Fragen*, Leipzig: Crusius, 1789, pp. 1–72 (pp. 15–17: his dream; p. 4: dreams the key to the mind).
41 'Man verfährt hiebey, wie in der Physik mit den körperlichen Dingen, welche man durch Erfahrungen und Versuche kennen lernt. Man könnte also diesen Theil der Psychologie die Experimental[psychologie] nennen', Sulzer, *Kurzer Begriff aller Wissenschaften*, p. 157 (the published text reads 'Experimental-physik', clearly an error).
42 '. . . sind . . . so dunkel und geschehen so plötzlich, daß sie der Aufmerksamkeit sehr leicht entgehen', Sulzer, *Kurzer Begriff aller Wissenschaften*, p. 159.
43 '. . . die dunkeln Gegenden der Seele (wenn man so reden kann) . . . wo sie durch sehr undeutliche und dunkle Begrifffe handelt', *ibid.*, p. 261.
44 '. . . dunkle Vorstellungen sehr merkliche Wirkungen haben können, und daß sich die Seele mit einer beträchtlichen Angelegenheit beschäfftigen kann, ohne eine recht klare Erkenntniß davon zu haben', Johann Georg Sulzer, 'Zergliederung des Begriffs der Vernunft', in J. G. Sulzer, *Vermischte philosophische Schriften*, Leipzig: Weidmann, 1773, pp. 244–81 (p. 261).
45 'Das sind die in dem Innersten der Seele verborgenen Angelegenheiten, die uns zuweilen auf einmal, ohne alle Veranlassung und auf eine unschickliche Art, handeln oder reden, und ohne daß wir daran denken, Dinge sagen lassen, die wir schlechterdings verbergen wollten.' *Ibid.*, p. 261.
46 'in besonderen Beiträgen', *ibid.*, p. 159; cf. Hans Adler, '*Fundus animae* – Der Grund der Seele: Zur Gnoseologie des Dunklen in der Aufklärung', *DVjs* 62 (1988), 197–220 (p. 209).
47 '. . . ein abstraktes Wesen, das mit nichts in der Welt zusammenhängt', Sulzer, *Vermischte philosophische Schriften*, p. 231.
48 '. . . alles, was in keiner Verbindung mit seinem Nachdenken steht, thut er bloß maschinenmässig, und ohne es zu wissen', *ibid.*, p. 231. See Riedel, 'Erkennen und Empfinden', pp. 415–16.
49 Sulzer, *Vermischte philosophische Schriften*, pp. 348–76 (p. 350: single psychic power; p. 351: Thätigkeit; p. 352: continues in sleep; pp. 368–9: contra Descartes; pp. 363–4: immaterial).

50 Alexander Altmann, *Moses Mendelssohn: A Biographical Study*, London: Routledge & Kegan Paul, 1973, p. 45.

51 Moses Mendelssohn, *Briefe über die Empfindungen*, in *Gesammelte Schriften. Jubiläumsausgabe*, 27 vols., Stuttgart: Frommann-Holzboog, 1991, vol. 1, pp. 256–7.

52 *Ibid.*, vol. 1, p. 251.

53 Gotthold Ephraim Lessing, Moses Mendelssohn, and Friedrich Nicolai, *Briefwechsel über das Trauerspiel*, ed. Jochen Schulte-Sasse, Munich: Winkler, 1972, p. 101.

54 Mendelssohn, *Gesammelte Schriften*, vol. 1, p. 384; see also Daniel O. Dahlstrom, 'Introduction', in Moses Mendelssohn, *Philosophical Writings*, ed. D. O. Dahlstrom, Cambridge Texts in the History of Philosophy, Cambridge: Cambridge University Press, 1997, pp. ix–xxx (p. xvii).

55 H. B. Nisbet, 'Lessing's ethics', *Lessing Yearbook* 25 (1993), 1–40, (p. 3).

56 Henry E. Allison, *Lessing and the Enlightenment. His Philosophy of Religion and Its Relation to Eighteenth-Century Thought*, Ann Arbor: University of Michigan Press, 1966, p. 124.

57 *Ibid.*, pp. 125–6.

58 Lessing *et al.*, *Briefwechsel über das Trauerspiel*, p. 55.

59 *Ibid.*, p. 54.

60 *Ibid.*, pp. 55–6.

61 'Der Hauptgedanke ist dieser: es ist wahr, und auch nicht wahr, daß die komische Tragödie . . . die Natur getreu nachahmet; sie ahmet sie nur in einer Hälfte getreu nach und vernachlässiget die andere Hälfte gänzlich; sie ahmet die Natur der Erscheinungen nach, ohne im geringsten auf die Natur unserer Empfindungen und Seelenkräfte dabei zu achten. / In der Natur ist alles mit allem verbunden . . . Aber nach dieser unendlichen Mannigfaltigkeit ist sie nur ein Schauspiel für einen unendlichen Geist. Um endliche Geister an dem Genusse desselben Anteil nehmen zu lassen, mußten diese das Vermögen erhalten, ihr Schranken zu geben, die sie nicht hat; das Vermögen abzusondern und ihre Aufmerksamkeit nach Gutdünken lenken zu können. / Dieses Vermögen üben wir in allen Augenblicken des Lebens; ohne dasselbe würde es für uns gar kein Leben geben; wir würden für allzu verschiedenen Empfindungen nichts empfinden; wir würden ein beständiger Raub des gegenwärtigen Eindruckes sein; wir würden träumen, ohne zu wissen, was wir träumten.'

62 'Von Weinen und Klagen, meinen einzigen Beschäftigungen, ermüdet, sank ich mit halb geschlossenen Augenlidern auf das Bett zurück. Die Natur wollte sich einen Augenblick erholen, neue Tränen zu sammeln. Aber noch schlief ich nicht ganz, als ich mich auf einmal an dem schroffsten Teile des schrecklichsten Felsen sahe. Sie gingen vor mir her, und ich folgte Ihnen mit schwankenden, ängstlichen Schritten, die dann und wann ein Blick stärkte, welchen Sie auf mich zurückwarfen. Schnell hörte ich hinter mir ein freundliches Rufen, welches mir still zu stehen befahl. Es war der Ton meines Vaters – Ich Elende! kann ich denn nichts von ihm vergessen? Ach! wo ihm

sein Gedächtnis ebenso grausame Dienste leistet; wo er auch mich nicht vergessen kann! – Doch er hat mich vergessen. Trost! grausamer Trost für seine Sara! – Hören Sie nur, Mellefont; indem ich mich nach dieser bekannten Stimme umsehen wollte, gleitete mein Fuß; ich wankte und sollte eben in den Abgrund herab stürzen, als ich mich, noch zur rechten Zeit, von einer mir ähnlichen Person zurückgehalten fühlte. Schon wollte ich ihr den feurigsten Dank abstatten, als sie einen Dolch aus dem Busen zog. Ich rettete dich, schrie sie, um dich zu verderben! Sie holte mit der bewaffneten Hand aus – und ach! ich erwachte mit dem Stiche.'

63 '. . . ein weiches und reizloses, obgleich für den sinnlichen Schmerz bisweilen empfindliches Gehirn', Ernst Platner, *Philosophische Aphorismen, nebst einigen Anleitungen zur philosophischen Geschichte*, 2 vols., Leipzig: Schwickert, 1776–82, p. 286.

64 'Welche schmeichelhafte Vorstellung! Ich verliebe mich selbst darein und vergesse es fast, daß in dem Innersten sich noch etwas regt, das ihm keinen Glauben beimessen will. – Was ist es, dieses rebellische Etwas?'

65 MELLEFONT: Nur der Pöbel wird gleich außer sich gebracht, wenn ihn das Glück einmal anlächelt.
NORTON: Vielleicht, weil der Pöbel noch sein Gefühl hat, das bei Vornehmern durch tausend unnatürliche Vorstellungen verderbt und geschwächt wird. Allein in Ihrem Gesichte ist noch etwas anders als Mäßigung zu lesen. Kaltsinn, Unentschlossenheit, Widerwille–'

66 Matthew Bell, *Goethe's Naturalistic Anthropology: Man and Other Plants*, Oxford: Oxford University Press, 1994, pp. 47, 84–5.

67 'Im Schlafe wacht, / Im Wachen schläft ihr Geist, bald weniger / Als Tier, bald mehr als Engel.'

68 'Diesen Morgen lag / Sie lange mit verschloßnem Aug' und war / Wie tot. Schnell fuhr sie auf und rief: 'Horch! horch! / Da kommen die Kamele meines Vaters! / Horch! seine sanfte Stimme selbst!' – Indem / Brach sich ihr Auge wieder, und ihr Haupt, / Dem seines Armes Stütze sich entzog, / Stürzt' auf das Küssen.'

69 Nathan's possessiveness: 'meine Recha' (*LW* 11.210, 83 and 11.214, 227), 'mein Kind' (*LW* 11.213, 178), 'Wenn ich mich wieder je entwohnen müßte, / Dies Kind mein Kind zu nennen!' (*LW* 11.208, 30–1); also *LW* 11.312, 534–8.

70 Monika Fick, '"Verworrene Perzeptionen". Lessings *Emilia Galotti*', *Jahrbuch der Deutschen Schillergesellschaft* 37 (1993), 139–63 (p. 154).

71 Gotthold Ephraim Lessing, *Emilia Galotti*, trans. by Anna Johanna Gode von Aesch, in G. E. Lessing, *'Nathan the Wise', 'Minna von Barnhelm, and Other Plays and Writings'*, ed. Peter Demetz, The German Library 12, New York: Continuum, 1991, p. 77: 'Desto schlimmer – besser; wollt' ich sagen' (*LW* 11.130).

72 Lessing, *Emilia Galotti*, trans. Gode von Aesch, p. 78.

73 Against my view of the Prince, see e.g. Christiane Brown, '"Der widerwärtige Mißbrauch der Macht"; or, "Die Verwandlung der Leidenschaften in tugendhafte Fertigkeiten"', *Lessing Yearbook* 17 (1985), 21–43, and Gisbert Ter-Nedden, *Lessings Trauerspiele. Der Ursprung des modernen Dramas aus dem Geist der Kritik*, Stuttgart: Metzler, 1986, pp. 185–8.

74 Leibniz, *New Essays*, p. 54.

75 Lessing, *Emilia Galotti*, trans. Gode von Aesch, pp. 97–8: 'Aber, es ist wahr; ich bin heut' ungewöhnlich trübe und finster. – Nur sehen Sie, gnädige Frau; – noch einen Schritt vom Ziele, oder noch gar nicht ausgelaufen sein, ist im Grunde eins. – Alles, was ich sehe, alles, was ich höre, alles, was ich träume, prediget mir seit gestern und ehegestern diese Wahrheit. Dieser eine Gedanke kettet sich an jeden andern, den ich haben muß und haben will. – Was ist das? Ich versteh es nicht. – . . . Eines kömmt dann zum andern! – Ich bin ärgerlich; ärgerlich über meine Freunde, über mich selbst – . . . Meine Freunde verlangen schlechterdings, daß ich dem Prinzen von meiner Heirat ein Wort sagen soll, ehe ich sie vollziehe. Sie geben mir zu, ich sei es nicht schuldig: aber die Achtung gegen ihn woll' es nicht anders. – Und ich bin schwach genug gewesen, es ihnen zu versprechen. Eben wollt' ich bei ihm vorfahren' (*LW* 11.156).

76 *Ibid.*, pp. 97–8: 'Das hat gut getan. Mein Blut ist in Wallung gekommen. Ich fühle mich anders und besser' (*LW* 11.160).

77 'Aber daß fremdes Laster uns, wider unsern Willen, zu Mitschuldigen machen kann!' (*LW* 11.150).

78 Lessing, *Emilia Galotti*, trans. Gode von Aesch, p. 134: 'Was Gewalt heißt ist nichts: Verführung ist die wahre Gewalt. – Ich habe Blut, mein Vater; so jugendliches, so warmes Blut, als eine. Auch meine Sinne, sind Sinne. Ich stehe für nichts. Ich bin für nichts gut. Ich kenne das Haus der Grimaldi. Es ist das Haus der Freude. Eine Stunde da, unter den Augen meiner Mutter; – und es erhob sich so mancher Tumult in meiner Seele, den die strengsten Übungen der Religion kaum in Wochen besänftigen konnten' (*LW* 11.203).

79 *Ibid.*, p. 133: 'Als ob wir, wir keinen Willen hätten, mein Vater!' (*LW* 11.202).

80 'Sie wissen, meine Mutter, wie gern ich Ihren bessern Einsichten mich in allem unterwerfe . . . Ich habe keinen Willen gegen den Ihrigen' (*LW* 11.153).

81 Klaus Bäppler, *Der philosophische Wieland. Stufen und Prägungen seines Denkens*, Bern: Francke, 1976, p. 125. See also Charles Elson, *Wieland and Shaftesbury*, New York: Columbia University Press, 1913.

82 '. . . ein immer geschäftiger Trieb, die Tugenden Gottes nachzuahmen', WAA 1.ii.484.

83 Wieland quoted in Ermatinger, *Die Weltanschauung des jungen Wieland*, p. 25.

84 Erich Groß, *C. M. Wielands 'Geschichte des Agathon'. Entstehungsgeschichte*, Berlin: Ebering, 1930, p. 107.

85 Sibylle Gössl, *Materialismus und Nihilismus. Studien zum deutschen Roman der Spätaufklärung*, Würzburg: Königshausen & Neumann, 1987, p. 40: Bonnet, Malebranche, Montesquieu; Groß, *Wielands 'Geschichte des Agathon'*, pp. 66–81: Malebranche, Montesquieu, Bonnet, Helvétius; Rolf Grimminger, 'Roman' in R. Grimminger (ed.), *Hansers Sozialgeschichte der deutschen Literatur vom 16. Jahrhundert bis zur Gegenwart*, vol. III: *Deutsche Aufklärung bis zur Französischen Revolution*, Munich: Hanser, 1980, pp. 635–715 (p. 692): La Mettrie.

86 Grimminger, 'Roman', p. 691.
87 '. . . das Werdende seines Helden . . . alle die Umstände . . . wodurch, und
    wie [der Held] das geworden ist was er ist', Friedrich von Blanckenburg,
    Versuch über den Roman [Leipzig and Liegnitz: Siegert, 1774], photo reprint,
    Stuttgart: Metzler, 1965, p. 150.
88 'Die Absicht des Autors war . . . daß man ganz deutlich möchte begreifen
    können, wie ein solcher Mann – so geboren – so erzogen – mit solchen
    Fähigkeiten und Dispositionen – mit einer solchen besondern Bestimmung
    derselben – nach einer solchen Reihe von Erfahrungen, Entwicklungen und
    Veränderungen – in solchen Glücks-Umständen – an einem solchen Ort und
    in einer solchen Zeit – in einer solchen Gesellschaft – unter einem solchen
    Himmels-Strich – bei solchen Nahrungs-Mitteln (denn auch diese haben
    einen stärkern Einfluß auf Weisheit und Tugend, als sich manche Moralisten
    einbilden) – bei einer solchen Diät – kurz, unter solchen gegebenen
    Bedingungen, wie alle diejenige Umstände sind, in welcher er den Agathon
    bisher gesetzt hat, und noch setzen wird – ein so weiser und tugendhafter
    Mann habe sein können' (WMS 1.830).
89 'Agathon erwiderte den Anblick dieses jungen Sclaven mit einer Aufmerk-
    samkeit, in welcher ein angenehmes Erstaunen nach und nach sich bis zur
    Entzückung erhob. Eben diese Bewegungen enthüllten sich auch in dem
    anmutigen Gesichte des jungen Sclaven; ihre Seelen erkannten einander in
    eben demselben Augenblicke, und schienen durch ihre Blicke schon in
    einander zu fließen, eh ihre Arme sich empfangen, und die von Entzückung
    bebende Lippen – Psyche – Agathon, ausrufen können. Sie schwiegen eine
    lange Zeit; dasjenige, was sie empfanden, war über allen Ausdruck; und
    wozu bedurften sie der Worte? Der Gebrauch der Sprache hört auf, wenn
    sich die Seelen einander unmittelbar mitteilen, sich unmittelbar anschauen
    und berühren, und in einem Augenblick mehr empfinden, als die Zunge der
    Musen selbst in ganzen Jahren auszusprechen vermöchte' (WMS 1.390).
90 'Allein die unmäßigste Schwärmerei hat ihre Grenzen, und weicht endlich
    der Obermacht der Sinnen. Zum Unglück für den Helden unsrer Geschichte
    kamen diese Unsinnigen allmählich aus einer Entzückung zurück, worüber
    sich vermutlich ihre Einbildungskraft gänzlich abgemattet hatte, und bemer-
    kten immer mehr menschliches an demjenigen, den seine ungewöhnliche
    Schönheit in ihren trunknen Augen vergöttert hatte' (WMS 1.387).
91 'Wie ähnlich ist alles dieses einem Traum, wo die schwärmende Phantasie,
    ohne Ordnung, ohne Wahrscheinlichkeit, ohne Zeit oder Ort in Betracht zu
    ziehen, die betäubte Seele von einem Abenteuer zum andern, von der Crone
    zum Bettlers-Mantel, von der Wonne zur Verzweiflung, vom Tartarus ins
    Elysium fortreißt? – Und ist denn das Leben ein Traum, ein bloßer Traum,
    so eitel, so unwesentlich, so unbedeutend als ein Traum?' (WMS 1.400).
92 'Hier hielt Agathon eine Zeitlang inne; sein in Zweifeln verwickelter Geist
    arbeitete sich loszuwinden, bis ein neuer Blick auf die majestätische Natur
    die ihn umgab, eine andre Reihe von Vorstellungen in ihm entwickelte'
    (WMS 1.401).

3 MELANCHOLY TITANS AND SUFFERING WOMEN IN STORM AND
STRESS DRAMA

1 'Natur! Natur! nichts so Natur als Schäkespeares Menschen' (*WA* 1. xxxvii.133).

2 Alan C. Leidner, 'A Titan in extenuating circumstances: Sturm und Drang and the *Kraftmensch*', *Publications of the Modern Language Association* 104 (1989), 178–89 and Jürgen Bolten, 'Melancholie und Selbstbehauptung. Zur Soziogenese des Bruderzwistmotivs im Sturm und Drang', *DVjs* 59 (1985), 265–77.

3 'Gemälde der Empfindung von dritter Hand; nie aber oder selten die unmittelbaren, ersten, ungeschminkten Regungen, wie sie Worte suchen und endlich finden' (*HWS* v.215). Quoted by Thomas Salumets, 'Mündige Dichter und verkrüppelte Helden. F. M. Klingers Trauerspiel *Die Zwillinge*', *Germanic Quarterly* 59 (1986), 401–13 (p. 401).

4 James Engell, *The Creative Imagination: Enlightenment to Romanticism*, Cambridge, MA: Harvard University Press, 1981, pp. 75–6.

5 Gotthold Ephraim Lessing, *Emilia Galotti*, trans. Anna Johanna Gode von Aesch, in G. E. Lessing, *'Nathan the Wise', 'Minna von Barnhelm', and Other Plays and Writings*, ed. Peter Demetz, The German Library 12, New York: Continuum, 1991, p. 134: 'Was Gewalt heißt ist nichts: Verführung ist die wahre Gewalt. – Ich habe Blut, mein Vater; so jugendliches, so warmes Blut, als eine. Auch meine Sinne, sind Sinne. Ich stehe für nichts. Ich bin für nichts gut. Ich kenne das Haus der Grimaldi. Es ist das Haus der Freude. Eine Stunde da, unter den Augen meiner Mutter; – und es erhob sich so mancher Tumult in meiner Seele, den die strengsten Übungen der Religion kaum in Wochen besänftigen konnten' (*LW* 11.203).

6 Albert M. Reh, 'Zu Lessings Charakterzeichnung. Ein Beitrag zur Literaturpsychologie des 18. Jahrhunderts', in Edward P. Harris and Richard E. Schade (eds.), *Lessing in heutiger Sicht. Beiträge zur internationalen Lessing-Konferenz Cincinnati, Ohio 1976*, Bremen: Jacobi, 1977, pp. 169–76.

7 'CLAVIGO. Todt! Marie todt! Die Fackeln dort! ihre traurigen Begleiter! Es ist ein Zauberspiel, ein Nachtgesicht, das mich erschreckt, das mir einen Spiegel vorhält, darin ich das Ende meiner Verräthereien ahnungsweise erkennen soll. – Noch ist es Zeit! Noch! – Ich bebe, mein Herz zerfließt in Schauer! Nein! Nein! du sollst nicht sterben. Ich komme! Ich komme! – Verschwindet, Geister der Nacht, die ihr euch mitängstlichen Schrecknissen mir in den Weg stellt – (*Geht auf sie los.*)' (*WA* 1.xi.119–20).

8 Hans Helmut Hiebel, 'Mißverstehen und Sprachlosigkeit im "bürgerlichen Trauerspiel". Zum historischen Wandel dramatischer Motivationsformen', *Jahrbuch der Deutschen Schiller-Gesellschaft* 27 (1983), 124–53.

9 Gerhard Kaiser, 'Friedrich Maximilian Klingers Schauspiel *Sturm und Drang*', in Manfred Wacker (ed.), *Sturm und Drang*, Wege der Forschung 559, Darmstadt: Wissenschaftliche Buchgesellschaft, 1985, pp. 315–40 (pp. 321–9).

10 Friedrich Maximilian Klinger, *Werke. Historisch-kritische Gesamtausgabe*, ed. Sander L. Gilman *et al.*, Neudruck deutscher Literaturwerke N. F., 21 vols. (in progress), Tübingen: Niemeyer, 1978–, vol. 11, pp. 22–4.

11 Lessing, *Emilia Galotti*, trans. Gode von Aesch, p. 78.

12 Friedrich Beißner, 'Studien zur Sprache des Sturm und Drangs', *Germanisch-Romanische Monatsschrift* 21 (1934), 417–29.

13 E.g. Johann August Unzer, 'Untersuchung, ob die Träume etwas bedeuten?', in J. A. Unzer, *Sammlung kleiner Schriften. Zur speculatirischen Philosophie*, 2 vols., Rinteln and Leipzig: Berth, 1766, pp. 431–9.

14 'Es ist doch immer das Traumreich wie ein falscher Loostopf, wo unzählige Nieten und höchstens kleine Gewinnstchen unter einander gemischt sind. Man wird selbst zum Traum, zur Niete, wenn man sich ernstlich mit diesen Phantomen beschäftigt' (27 December 1788, *WA* IV.ix.68).

15 E.g. Anton Joseph Dorsch, *Beiträge zum Studium der Philosophie. I. Heft. Erste Linien einer Geschichte der Weltweisheit*, Mainz: Alef, 1787, p. 85; Johann Werner Streithorst, *Psychologische Vorlesungen in der litterarischen Gesellschaft zu Halberstadt*, Leipzig: Crusius, 1787, p. 45.

16 Jörg-Ulrich Fechner, 'Leidenschafts- und Charakterdarstellung im Drama (Gerstenberg, Leisewitz, Klinger, Wagner)', in Walter Hinck (ed.), *Sturm und Drang. Ein literaturwissenschaftliches Studienbuch*, Königstein im Taunus: Athenäum, 1978, pp. 175–91 (pp. 177–9).

17 John W. Yolton, *Thinking Matter: Materialism in Eighteenth-Century Britain*, Oxford: Blackwell, 1984.

18 'Man erzählt von Hallern daß, als er einmal eine Treppe herunter und auf den Kopf gefallen war, nachdem er aufgestanden, sich die Nahmen der chinesischen Kaiser nach der Reihe hergesagt, um zu versuchen, ob sein Gedächtniß gelitten habe' (*WA* IV.xv.176).

19 Carl Friedrich Pockels, *Denkwürdigkeiten zur Bereicherung der Erfahrungsseelenlehre und Characterkunde. Ein Lesebuch für Gelehrte und Ungelehrte. Erste Sammlung*, Halle: Renger, 1794, pp. 187–9.

20 'Die Psychologie, was ist sie anders als eine reiche Physik der Seele?': quoted in H. B. Nisbet, *Herder and the Philosophy and History of Science*, Cambridge: MHRA, 1970, p. 252.

21 *Ibid.*, p. 274.

22 '. . . ein Mensch von vollständigen Trieben und Empfindungen' (*HWP* 11.572).

23 Matthew Bell, *Goethe's Naturalistic Anthropology: Man and Other Plants*, Oxford: Oxford University Press, 1994, p. 85.

24 Wolfgang Proß, 'Herder und die Anthropologie der Aufklärung', in Johann Gottfried Herder, *Werke*, ed. W. Proß, 2 vols., Munich: Hanser, 1987–2002, vol. 11, pp. 1190–2.

25 '. . . wie soll ich meinen Hunger nach Empfindungen stillen?' (*SuD* 1.559). See e.g. Samuel Johnson, *Rasselas*, in Johnson, *Samuel Johnson*, ed. D. Greene, Oxford: Oxford University Press, 1984, p. 387.

26 See Bell, *Goethe's Naturalistic Anthropology*, pp. 93–4 and Michael Maurer, *Aufklärung und Anglophilie in Deutschland*, Publications of the German Historical Institute London 19, Göttingen: Vandenhoeck & Ruprecht, 1987.

27 Peter Gay, *The Enlightenment: An Interpretation. Volume 2: The Science of Freedom*, London: Weidenfeld & Nicolson, 1970, p. 167.

28 'Bei jeder Sensation wird [der Säugling], wie aus einem tiefen Traume geweckt, um ihn, wie durch einen gewaltsamen Stoß an eine Idee lebhafter zu erinnern, die ihm seine Lage im Weltall jetzt veranlasset. So entwickeln sich seine Kräfte durch ein Leiden von außen' (*HWS* 11.82).

29 '. . . die ersten Eindrücke in das zarte Wachs unsrer Kindheitsseele gibt uns Farbe und Gestalt des Urteils' (*HWS* iv.38).

30 '. . . benimmt Mut, Genie und Aussicht auf Alles' (*HWS* 1.396–7).

31 Wolfgang Riedel, *Die Anthropologie des jungen Schiller: Zur Ideengeschichte der medizinischen Schriften und der 'Philosophischen Briefe'*, Würzburg: Königstein & Neumann, 1985, p. 20.

32 'Diese Konvulsionen pflanzen sich schnell durch den ganzen Umriß des Nervengebäudes fort, bringen die Kräfte des Lebens in jene Mißstimmung, die seinen Flor zernichtet, und alle Aktionen der Maschine aus dem Gleichgewicht bringen' (*NA* xx.59).

33 'Pietistische Schwärmerei schien den Grund zum ganzen nachfolgenden Übel gelegt zu haben. Sie schärfte sein Gewissen und machte ihn gegen alle Gegenstände von Tugend und Religion äußerst empfindlich, und verwirrte seine Begriffe. Das Studium der Metaphysik machte ihm zuletzt alle Wahrheit verdächtig und riß ihn zum andern Extremo über, so daß er, der die Religion vorhero übertrieben hatte, durch skeptische Grübeleien nicht selten dahin gebracht wurde, an ihren Grundpfeilern zu zweifeln. Diese schwankende Ungewißheit der wichtigsten Wahrheiten ertrug sein vortreffliches Herz nicht. Er strebte nach Überzeugung, aber verirrte auf einen falschen Weg, da er sie suchen wollte, versank in die finstersten Zweifel, verzweifelte an der Glückseligkeit, an der Gottheit, und glaubte sich den unglücklichsten Menschen auf Erden. Alles dies hab ich in häufigen Wortwechseln aus ihm herausgebracht, da er mir von seinem Zustand niemal nichts verschwiegen hat' (*ibid.* xxii.19).

34 J. F. Abel, *Sammlung und Erklärung merkwürdiger Erscheinungen aus dem menschlichen Leben*, 3 vols., Frankfurt and Leipzig: no publ., 1784 (vol. i); Stuttgart: Erhart, 1787–90 (vols. ii and iii), vol. iii, pp. 1–22.

35 Johann Anton Leisewitz, *Julius von Tarent*, ed. W. Keller, Stuttgart: Reclam, 1965, Act ii, Scene v, p. 40.

36 *Ibid.*, Act ii, Scene i, p. 21. See also ii.ii, p. 22: 'Was kann die Liebe nicht – und so viel vermag über das Weib ein Andenken, der Schatten der Liebe, was muß nicht Hoffnung, ihre Seele bei mir tun!'

37 'Ein Diadem erkämpfen ist *gros*. Es wegwerfen ist göttlich. (*Entschlossen.*) Geh unter, Tyrann! Sei frei Genua, und ich (*sanft geschmolzen*) dein *glüklichster* Bürger!' (*NA* iv.64).

38 J. M. R. Lenz, *Philosophische Vorlesungen für empfindsame Seelen. Faksimiledruck der Ausgabe Frankfurt und Leipzig 1780*, ed. Christoph Weiss, St Ingbert: Röhrig, 1994, p. 68.

39 Ilse Graham 'The structure of the personality in Schiller's tragic poetry', in F. Norman (ed.), *Schiller: Bicentenary Lectures*, London: Institute of Germanic Studies, 1960, pp. 104–44 (pp. 106–17).

40 Robert R. Heitner, 'Luise Millerin and the shock motif in Schiller's early dramas', *Germanic Review* 41 (1966), 27–44 (p. 30).

41 Wolf Lepenies, *Melancholie und Gesellschaft*, Frankfurt am Main: Suhrkamp, 1969.

42 'Sie werden lachen, Prinz. – Aber so geht es den Empfindsamen' (*LW* 11.137).

43 'Da sey ihr Gott gnädig! – Wenn ich ein einiges Blatt drinn lesen müßte, so wär ich kapable den Engländer zu machen, und mich an mein Knieband zu hängen' (*SuD* 11.564).

44 'Es hat sich vor meiner Seele wie ein Vorhang weggezogen, und der Schauplatz des unendlichen Lebens verwandelt sich vor mir in den Abgrund des ewig offenen Grabs' (*DjG* IV.139).

45 'Abzusterben für die Welt, die mich so wenig kannte, als ich sie zu kennen wünschte – o welche schwermütige Wollust liegt in dem Gedanken!' (J. M. R. Lenz, *Werke*, ed. K. Lauer, Munich: dtv, 1992, p. 338).

46 *Bitterreiz, ibid.*, p. 452.

47 '. . . diese Klarheit, die mich umgibt, und mir die liebe Dunkelheit, die mich so glücklich machte, auf immer entreißt', *ibid.*, p. 296.

48 *Ibid.*, pp. 24–5.

49 Klinger, *Werke*, 1.III–12.

50 '. . . meine Sinnen [sind] trunken', *ibid.*, 1.118.

51 *Ibid.*, 11.62–4.

52 Johann Wolfgang von Goethe, *Faust. The First Part of the Tragedy, with the Unpublished Scenarios for the Walpurgis Night and the Urfaust*, trans. John R. Williams, Ware: Wordsworth Editions, 1999, p. 215.

53 See Erich Trunz's commentary, *HA* III.522.

54 Lenz, *Werke*, p. 57.

55 '. . . rennt mit dem Kopf gegen die Wand, und sinkt auf den Boden', *ibid.*, p. 301.

56 '. . . wider eine Eiche rennend' (*NA* III.131).

57 Leopold Auenbrugger, *Von der stillen Wuth oder dem Triebe zum Selbstmorde als einer wirklichen Krankheit, mit Original-Beobachtungen und Anmerkungen*, Dessau: Buchhandlung der Gelehrten, 1783, pp. 33–6.

58 Condillac, *Oeuvres philosophiques*, ed. G. LeRoy, 3 vols., Paris: Presses Universitaires de France, 1947–51, vol. 1, p. 122.

59 'Überall schleicht sie mir nach. Schon drei Nächte hintereinander sah ich sie in Totenkleidern; sie winkt mir mit Gebärden, mit Zeichen – ich muß verzweifeln, wenn's noch länger dauert' (*SuD* 11.61).

60 'Ach! Ich kann den Himmel, den schönen weiten Himmel nicht mehr ansehen. Ihr keuschen harmonischen Sterne! Keusch! Lieber Brand, warum sagen die Dichter: die keusche Sterne? – Heiliger Ausdruck! . . . Ihr keuschen Sterne, silberner blasser Mond! leuchtet, leuchtet, ihr leuchtet einem unkeuschen Weibe Angst in die Seele' (*ibid.* 11.27).

61 '. . . die Bilder, die sich treiben und jagen' (*ibid.* 11.59–60).

62 Lenz, *Werke*, p. 11.

63 *Ibid.*, p. 222.

64 'Sie haben Romanen gelesen, wies scheint?', *SuD* 11.546.

65 'Da hatte sie ein Buch gelesen, den Grandison nennen sie's, das hat ihr den Kopf verrückt; sie hatte ein Romanfieber, ein verfluchtes Grandisonenfieber' (*Ibid.* 11.16).

66 *Intrigue and Love*, trans. Charles E. Passage, in Friedrich Schiller, *Plays*, ed. Walter Hinderer, The German Library 15, New York: Continuum, 1983, p. 5: 'Das Mädel setzt sich alles Teufelsgezeug in den Kopf; über all dem Herumschwänzen in der Schlaraffenwelt findet's zuletzt seine Heimat nicht mehr, vergißt, schämt sich, daß sein Vater Miller der Geiger ist' (*NA* v.6–7).

67 'Ich will nichts mehr von ihm wissen, vom ganzen * * nichts. Ein weiblich Aug' sollte nicht hineinschauen. Hätt' mich Gott bewahrt; mit dem Brand wär' ich nie so weit gekommen' (*SuD* 11.22).

68 '. . . daß der Grund davon in seinem Herzen liegt, und daß er auch ohne und Idris das geworden wäre, was er ist', Lenz, *Werke*, p. 346.

69 On music therapy see Werner Friedrich Kümmel, *Musik und Medizin: ihre Wechselbeziehung in Theorie und Praxis von 800 bis 1800*, Freiburg/Breisgau: Alber, 1977.

70 Klinger, *Werke*, 11.18.

71 'Es ist hier nicht von Curen noch von Quacksalbereien die Rede. Wenn wir Phantasie durch Phantasie curiren könnten, so hätten wir ein Meisterstück gemacht' (*WA* 1.xii.54).

72 '. . . wandelt des Nachts in ihren Phantasien' (*ibid.* 1.xii.48).

73 Lenz, *Philosophische Vorlesungen*, p. 51.

74 See e.g. August von Einsiedel, *Ideen*, ed. W. Dobbek, Berlin: Akademie, 1957, p. 92. See also Woodruff D. Smith, 'The social and political origins of German diffusionist ethnology', *Journal of the History of Behavioural Studies* 14 (1978), 103–12.

75 'Weg mit den Vätern!' Lenz, *Werke*, p. 301.

76 Kaiser, 'Klingers Schauspiel *Sturm und Drang*', p. 320.

77 Klinger, *Werke*, 11.52.

78 *Ibid.*, 11.25.

4 EMPIRICAL PSYCHOLOGY AND CLASSICISM: MORITZ, SCHILLER, GOETHE

1 Hans-Jürgen Schings, *Melancholie und Aufklärung: Melancoliker und ihre Kritiker in Erfahrungsseelenkunde und Literatur des 18. Jahrhunderts*, Stuttgart: Metzler, 1977, pp. 256–7.

2 *NA* xxii, 255–6.
3 '. . . wo wir Poeten doch eigentlich zu Hause sind' (*WA* iv.xv.188).
4 Paul Bishop, 'Goethe on the couch: Freud's reception of Goethe', in T. J. Reed, Martin Swales, and Jeremy Adler (eds.), *Goethe at 250: Goethe mit 250; London Symposium/Londoner Symposion*, Publications of the Institute of Germanic Studies 75, Munich: Iudicium, 2000, pp. 177–85 and 'Intellectual affinities between Goethe and Jung, with special reference to *Faust*', *PEGS* 69 (2000), 1–19.
5 Maurice Cranston, *The Solitary Self: Jean-Jacques Rousseau in Exile and Adversity*, London: Allen Lane, 1997, p. xii.
6 Jean Starobinski, *Jean-Jacques Rousseau: Transparency and Obstruction*, Chicago: University of Chicago Press, 1988, p. 192.
7 Jean-Jacques Rousseau, *The Confessions*, trans. J. M. Cohen, Harmondsworth: Penguin, 1953, pp. 169–70: 'Je n'ai pas promis d'offrir au public un grand personage; j'ai promis de me peindre tel que je suis et pour me connoitre dans mon age avancé, il faut m'avoir bien connu dans ma jeunesse. Comme en général les objets font moins d'impression sur moi que leurs souvenirs et que toutes mes idées sont en images, les premiers traits qui se sont gravés dans ma tête y sont demeurés, et ceux qui s'y sont empreints dans la suite se sont plustot combinés avec eux qu'ils ne les ont effacés. Il y a une certaine succession d'affections et d'idées qui modifient celles qui les suivent et qu'il faut connoitre pour en bien juger. Je m'applique à bien développer par tout les prémiéres causes pour faire sentir l'enchainement des effets. Je voudrois pouvoir en quelque façon rendre mon ame transparente aux yeux du lecteur, et pour cela je cherche à la lui montrer sous tous les points de vue, à l'éclairer par tous les jours, à faire en sorte qu'il ne s'y passe pas un mouvement qu'il n'apperçoive, afin qu'il puisse juger par lui-même du principe qui les produit.

'Si je me chargeois du résultat et que je lui disse: tel est mon caractère, il pourroit croire, sinon que je le trompe, au moins que je me trompe. Mais en lui détaillant avec simplicité tout ce qui m'est arrivé, tout ce que j'ai fait, tout ce que j'ai pensé, tout ce que j'ai senti, je ne puis l'induire en erreur à moins que je ne le veuille, encore même en le voulant n'y parviendrois-je pas aisément de cette façon. C'est à lui d'assembler ces élémens et de déterminer l'être qu'ils composent; le résultat doit être son ouvrage, et s'il se trompe alors, toute l'erreur sera de son fait. Or il ne suffit pas pour cette fin que mes recits sont fidelles il faut aussi qu'ile sont exacts. Ce n'est pas à moi de juger de l'importance des faits, je les dois tous dire, et lui laisser le soin de choisir. C'est à quoi je me suis appliqué jusqu'ici de tout mon courage, et je ne me relâcherai pas dans la suite' (*ROC* 1.174–5).
8 Rousseau attacks: Peter France, *Rousseau: 'Confessions'*, Cambridge: Cambridge University Press, 1987, p. 27.
9 *ROC* 1.10; see also *ibid.*, 1.409.
10 *Ibid.*, 1.9.

11 Rousseau, *The Confessions*, p. 25: 'Comme Mlle Lambercier avoit pour nous l'affection d'une mère, elle en avoit aussi l'autorité, et la portois quelquefois jusqu'à nous infliger la punition des enfans, quand nous l'avions méritée. Assez longtems elle s'en tint à la menace, et cette menace d'un châtiment tout nouveau pour moi se sembloit très effrayante; mais après l'execution, je la trouvai moins terrible à l'épreuve que l'attente ne l'avoit été, et ce qu'il y a de plus bisarre est que ce châtiment m'affectiona davantage encore à celle qui me l'avoit imposé' (ROC 1.15).

12 France, *Rousseau*, pp. 40–1.

13 Rousseau, *The Confessions*, p. 23: 'Telles furent les prémiéres affections de mon entrée dans la vie; ainsi commençoit à se former ou se montrer en moi ce coeur à la fois si fier et si tendre, ce caractére efféminé mais pourtant indomptable, qui, flottant toujours entre la foiblesse et le courage, entre la molesse et la vertu, m'a jusq'au bout mis en contradiction avec moi-même, et a fait que l'abstinence et la jouissance, le plaisir et la sagesse, m'ont egalement échappé' (*ROC* 1.12).

14 Mark Boulby, *Karl Philipp Moritz: At the Fringe of Genius*, Toronto and Buffalo: University of Toronto Press, 1979, p. 145; see also pp. 20, 82–3, 93, 94, 100, 114, 241.

15 *Ibid.*, pp. 62–3.

16 Birgit Nübel, *Autobiographische Kommunikationsmedien um 1800. Studien zu Rousseau, Wieland, Herder und Moritz*, Studien zur deutschen Literatur 136, Tübingen: Niemeyer, 1994, p. 213.

17 Gerhard Sauder, *Empfindsamkeit. Bd. 1: Voraussetzungen und Elemente*, Stuttgart: Metzler, 1974, p. 110.

18 Anke Bennholdt-Thomsen and Alfredo Guzzoni, 'Nachwort' in *Gs* x.1–79, p. 46.

19 Nübel, *Kommunikationsmedien*, p. 200. Moritz had probably not read the *Confessions* before writing *Prospect*, but had read about Rousseau's shocking revelations in the *Teutscher Merkur* (*ibid.*, p. 202).

20 Heide Hollmer and Albert Meier, 'Nachwort', in Karl Philipp Moritz, *Werke*, vol. 1: *Dichtungen und Schriften zur Erfahrungsseelenkunde*, Frankfurt am Main: Deutscher Klassiker Verlag, 1999, p. 1300.

21 'Das System der Moral, das wir besitzen, kann immer als ein ohngefährer Grundriß betrachtet werden, damit man doch nicht ganz aufs Ohngefähr hinarbeitet: aber man muß dies System auch so schwankend, wie möglich nehmen; bloß einige Punkte festsetzen, aber noch nicht von einem Punkte zum andern Linien ziehen, sondern nur warten, bis diese Linien gleichsam sich selber ziehen' (*MW* 111.90).

22 Boulby, *Moritz*, pp. 98–9.

23 *Gs* x.iii.1–3.

24 Bennholdt-Thomsen and Guzzoni, 'Nachwort', in *Gs* x.29–31.

25 H. Förstl, M. Angermeyer, and R. Howard, 'Karl Philipp Moritz' *Journal of Empirical Psychology* (1783–1793): an analysis of 124 case reports', *Psychological Medicine* 21 (1991), 299–304 (p. 300).

26 Shaftesbury: Hollmer and Meier in Moritz, *Werke*, vol. 1, pp. 1300–1.
    Tetens: Sauder, *Empfindsamkeit*, p. 119.
27 Hans Joachim Schrimpf, *Karl Philipp Moritz*, Stuttgart: Metzler, 1980,
    p. 168.
28 Hollmer and Meier in Moritz, *Werke*, vol. 1, p. 959. See also Boulby, *Moritz*,
    p. 234; Albert Meier, 'Sprachphilosophie in religionskritischer Absicht.
    Karl Philipp Moritz' *Kinderlogik* in ihrem ideengeschichtlichen Zusammenhang',
    DVjs 67 (1993), 252–66 (p. 255); and Josef Fürnkäs, *Der Ursprung des
    psychologischen Romans. Karl Philipp Moritz' 'Anton Reiser'*, Stuttgart:
    Metzler, 1977, pp. 31, 39–40.
29 Susan Sontag, *Illness as Metaphor*, London: Allen Lane, 1979, p. 50.
30 Karl Philipp Moritz, *Anton Reiser. A Psychological Novel*, trans. by Ritchie
    Robertson, Harmondsworth: Penguin, 1997, p. 8: 'In seiner frühesten Jugend
    hat er nie die Liebkosungen zärtlicher Eltern geschmeckt, nie nach einer
    kleinen Mühe ihr belohnendes Lächeln. Wenn er in das Haus seiner Eltern
    trat, so trat er in ein Haus der Unzufriedenheit, des Zorns, der Tränen und
    der Klagen. Diese ersten Eindrücke sind nie in seinem Leben aus seiner Seele
    verwischt worden und haben sie oft zu einem Sammelplatze schwarzer
    Gedanken gemacht, die er durch keine Philosophie verdrängen konnte' (*MW*
    1.40–1).
31 *Ibid.*, p. 23: 'Vielleicht wäre auch alles im Ehestande besser gegangen, wenn
    Antons Mutter nicht das Unglück gehabt hätte, sich oft für beleidigt und *gern*
    für beleidigt zu halten, auch wo sie es wirklich nicht war, um nur Ursach zu
    haben, sich zu kränken und zu betrüben und ein gewisses Mitleid mit sich
    selber zu empfinden, worin sie eine Art von Vergnügen fand.
    'Leider scheint sie diese Krankheit auf ihren Sohn fortgeerbt zu haben, der
    jetzt noch oft vergeblich damit zu kämpfen hat.
    'Schon als Kind, wenn alle etwas bekamen und ihm sein Anteil hingelegt
    wurde, ohne dabei zu sagen, es sei das seinige, so ließ er ihn lieber liegen, ob
    er gleich wußte, daß er für ihn bestimmt war, um nur die Süßigkeit des
    Unrechtleidens zu empfinden und sagen zu können, alle andre haben etwas
    und ich nichts bekommen! Da er eingebildetes Unrecht schon so stark
    empfand, um so viel stärker mußte er das wirkliche empfinden . . .
    'Oft konnte Anton stundenlang nachdenken und Gründe gegen Gründe
    auf das genaueste abwägen, ob eine Züchtigung von seinem Vater recht oder
    unrecht sei' (*MW* 1.55).
32 *Ibid.*, p. 103: 'Dies Verzeichnis von Reisers Freitischen und den Personen, die
    sie ihm gaben, ist gewiß nicht so unwichtig, wie es manchem vielleicht beim
    ersten Anblick scheinen mag – dergleichen klein scheinende Umstände sind
    es eben, die das Leben ausmachen und auf die Gemütsbeschaffenheit eines
    Menschen den stärksten Einfluß haben' (*MW* 1.137).
33 *Ibid.*, p. 65: 'die Leiden der Einbildungskraft' (*MW* 1.95).
34 *Ibid.*, p. 16: 'inneres Gebet' (*MW* 1.48).
35 *Ibid.*, p. 19: 'die sonderbarste Ideenkombination, die wohl je in einem
    menschlichen Gehirn existiert haben kann' (*MW* 1.51).

36 *Ibid.*, p. 14: 'Auch fing er wirklich zuweilen an, sich mit Nadeln zu pricken und sonst zu peinigen, um dadurch den heiligen Altvätern einigermaßen ähnlich zu werden, da es ihm doch ohnedem an Schmerzen nicht fehlte' (*MW* 1.45).

37 *Ibid.*, p. 23: 'die Süßigkeit des Unrechtleidens' (*MW* 1.55).

38 *Ibid.*, p. 35: '. . . er ward wirklich eine Zeitlang aus einer Art von Mißmut und Verzweiflung, was man einen bösen Buben nennen kann . . . Der Gedanke, daß ihm seine liebsten Wünsche und Hoffnungen fehlgeschlagen und die angetretene Laufbahn des Ruhms auf immer verschlossen war, nagte ihn unaufhörlich, ohne daß er sich dessen immer deutlich bewußt war, und trieb ihn zu allen Ausschweifungen' (*MW* 1.66).

39 *Ibid.*, p. 149 (*MW* 1.185).

40 *Ibid.*, p. 184: 'Nun ging er einmal eines Abends traurig und mißmutig auf der Straße umher – es war schon in der Dämmerung, aber doch nicht so dunkel, daß er nicht von einigen Leuten hätte gesehen werden können, deren Anblick ihm unerträglich war, weil er ihnen ein Gegenstand des Spottes und der Verachtung zu sein glaubte.

'Es war eine naßkalte Luft und regnete und schneiete durcheinander – seine ganze Kleidung war durchnetzt – plötzlich entstand in ihm das Gefühl, *daß er sich selbst nicht entfliehen konnte.*

'Und mit diesem Gedanken war es, also ob ein Berg auf ihm lag – er strebte, sich mit Gewalt darunter emporzuarbeiten, aber es war, als ob die *Last seines Daseins* ihn darniederdrückte.

'Daß er einen Tag wie alle Tage *mit sich aufstehen, mit sich schlafen gehen* – bei jedem Schritte sein verhaßtes Selbst fortschleppen mußte.

'Sein Selbstbewußtsein mit dem Gefühl von *Verächtlichkeit* und *Weggeworfenheit* wurde ihm ebenso lästig wie sein Körper mit dem Gefühl von Nässe und Kälte; und er hätte diesen in dem Augenblick ebenso willig und gerne wie seine durchnetzten Kleider abgelegt – hätte ihm damals ein gewünschter Tod aus irgendeinem Winkel entgegengelächelt' (*MW* 1.223–4).

41 *Ibid.*, p. 27: 'Er [dachte] sich auf einmal ein gänzliches Aufhören von Denken und Empfinden und eine Art von Vernichtung und Ermangelung seiner selbst, die ihn mit Grauen und Entsetzen erfüllte, sooft er wieder lebhaft daran dachte. Seit der Zeit hatte er auch eine starke Furcht vor dem Tode, die ihm manche traurige Stunde machte' (*MW* 1.59).

42 Jutta Osinski, 'Psychologie und Ästhetik bei Karl Philipp Moritz', in Martin Fontius and Anneliese Klingenberg (eds.), *Karl Philipp Moritz und das achtzehnte Jahrhundert. Bestandsaufnahmen–Korrekturen–Neuansätze*, Tübingen: Niemeyer, 1995, pp. 201–14 (pp. 210–13).

43 Samuel Johnson, *Rasselas*, in *Samuel Johnson*, ed. D. Greene, Oxford: Oxford University Press, 1984, p. 387.

44 'Wer mit der meisten Resignation auf den Erfolg arbeitet, der arbeitet sicher am besten' (*MW* 111.292).

45 Matthew Bell, *Goethe's Naturalistic Anthropology: Man and Other Plants*, Oxford: Oxford University Press, 1994, 265–6.

46 'Der Mensch, der andern Glückseligkeit und Zufriedenheit mittheilen will, muß erst selbst völlig glücklich und zufrieden seyn.– Das wird er aber bloß durch Mäßigung seiner Begierden, und eine völlige Resignation' (*MW* III.311).

47 Nübel, *Kommunikationsmedien*, pp. 206–12.

48 *Gs* II.iii.122–4.

49 'Das Laster wird hier mitsamt seinem ganzen innern Räderwerk entfaltet . . . Ich habe versucht, von einem Mißmenschen dieser Art ein treffendes lebendiges Konterfey hinzuwerfen, die vollständige Mechanik seines Lastersystems auseinander zu gliedern . . . Nächst an diesem stehet ein anderer, der vielleicht nicht weniger meiner Leser in Verlegenheit sezen möchte . . . Ein merkwürdiger, wichtiger Mensch, ausgestattet mit aller Kraft, nach der Richtung, die diese bekömmt, nothwendig entweder ein Brutus oder ein Katilina zu werden. Unglükliche Konjunkturen entscheiden für das zweyte und erst am Ende einer ungeheuren Verirrung gelangt er zu dem ersten' (*NA* III.6).

50 Friedrich Schiller, *The Robbers*, in *'The Robbers' and 'Wallenstein'*, trans. F. J. Lamport, Harmondsworth: Penguin, 1979, p. 30: '. . . ist euer Augapfel gewesen bisher' (*NA* III.16).

51 *Ibid.*, p. 29: '. . . der trockne Alltagsmensch, der kalte, hölzerne Franz, und wie die Titelgen alle heissen mögen, die euch der Contrast zwischen ihm und mir mocht eingegeben haben' (*NA* III.14).

52 Friedrich Schiller, *On the Aesthetic Education of Man. In a Series of Letters*, ed. and trans. E. M. Wilkinson and L. A. Willoughby, Oxford: Oxford University Press, 1967, p. xxix.

53 Ilse Graham, 'The structure of the personality in Schiller's tragic poetry', in F. Norman (ed.), *Schiller: Bicentenary Lectures*, London: Institute of Germanic Studies, 1960, pp. 104–44 (p. 106).

54 Wilkinson and Willoughby, introduction to Schiller, *Aesthetic Education*, p. xci.

55 *Phädon; oder, Über die Unsterblichkeit der Seele in drey Gesprächen*, in Moses Mendelssohn, *Gesammelte Schriften. Jubiläumsansgabe*, Stuttgart: Frommann-Holzboog, 1758, III.I, pp. 5–128.

56 Kenneth Dewhurst and Nigel Reeves, *Friedrich Schiller: Medicine, Psychology and Literature*, Oxford: Berg, 1978, pp. 260, 275.

57 Friedrich Schiller, *Intrigue and Love*, trans. Charles E. Passage, New York: Ungar, 1971, p. 53: 'FERDINAND (*hat in der Zerstreuung und Wut eine Violine ergriffen und auf derselben zu spielen versucht – Jetzt zerreißt er die Saiten, zerschmettert das Instrument auf dem Boden und bricht in ein lautes Gelächter aus*)' (*NA* V.57–8).

58 *Ibid.*, p. 53: '. . . die Fugen der Bürgerwelt auseinandertreiben und die allgemeine ewige Ordnung zugrund' stürzen' (*NA* V.57).

59 'Scepticismus und Freidenkerei sind die Fieberparoxysmen des menschlichen Geistes, und müssen durch eben die unnatürliche Erschütterung, die sie in gut organisierte Seelen verursachen, zuletzt die Gesundheit befestigen helfen' (*NA* xx.108).

60 Rose-Marie P. Akselrad, 'Schiller und Karl Philipp Moritz', *Monatshefte* 45 (1953), 131–40.

61 '. . . ein feuriger, groser und empfindender Jüngling': letter to Reinwald, 27 March 1783 (*NA* xxiii.74).

62 'ungewönliche Melancholie' (*ibid.*, vii.2, 183).

63 '*KARLOS kommt langsam und in Gedanken versenkt aus dunkeln Boskagen, seine zerstörte Gestalt verrät den Kampf seiner Seele; einigemal steht er schüchtern still, als wenn er auf etwas horchte . . . man sieht Traurigkeit und Wut in seinen Gebärden abwechseln, er rennt heftig auf und nieder und fällt zuletzt matt auf ein Kanapee*' (*ibid.*, *NA* vi.347).

64 *Don Carlos*, trans. A. Leslie and Jeanne R. Wilson, in Friedrich Schiller, *Plays*, ed. Walter Hinderer, The German Library 15, New York: Continuum, 1983, p. 106:

> KARLOS (*besinnt sich und fährt mit der Hand über die Stirne*):
> Hochwürd'ger Herr – ich habe sehr viel Unglück gehabt
> Mit meinen Müttern. Meine erste Handlung,
> Als ich das Licht der Welt erblickte, war
> Ein Muttermord . . .
> Und meine Neue Mutter – hat sie mir
> Nicht meines Vaters Liebe schon gekostet?
> Mein Vater hat mich kaum geliebt. Mein ganzes
> Verdienst war noch, sein Einziger zu sein.
> Sie gab ihm eine Tochter – O wer weiß,
> Was in der Zeiten Hintergrunde schlummert? (30–40)

65 Anton's lack of parental affection: *MW* i.40–1.

66 Schiller, *Don Carlos*, trans. Leslie and Wilson, pp. iii–12:

> KARLOS   So tief
> Bin ich gefallen – bin so arm geworden,
> Daß ich an unsre frühen Kinderjahre
> Dich mahnen muß – daß ich dich bitten muß,
> Die langvergeßnen Schulden abzutragen,
> Die du noch im Matrosenkleide machtest –
> Als du und ich, zween Knaben wilder Art,
> So brüderlich zusammen aufgewachsen,
> Kein Schmerz mich drückte, als von deinem Geiste
> So sehr verdunkelt mich zu sehn – ich endlich
> Mich kühn entschloß, dich gränzenlos zu lieben,
> Weil mich der Muth verließ, dir gleich zu sein.
> Da fing ich an, mit tausend Zärtlichkeiten

Und warmer Bruderliebe dich zu quälen;
Du, stolzes Herz, gabst sie mir kalt zurück.
Oft stand ich da, und – doch das sahst du nie!
Und heiße, schwere Thränentropfen hingen
In meinem Aug', wenn du, mich überhüpfend,
Vasallenkinder in die Arme drücktest.
Warum nur diese? rief ich trauernd aus:
Bin Ich dir nicht auch herzlich gut? – Du aber,
Du knietest kalt und ernsthaft vor mir nieder:
Das, sagtest du, gebührt dem Königssohn . . .
Ich hatt' es nicht um dich verdient. Verschmähen,
Zerreißen konntest du mein Herz, doch nie
Von dir entfernen. (230–57)

67 *Ibid.*, p. 112: 'und wär' es auch an seinem eig'nen Kinde' (270).

68 *Ibid.*, p. 113: 'daß auf diesem großen Rund der Erde / Kein Elend an das meine gränze' (305–8).

69 *Ibid.*, p. 113: Weltgebräuche,
Die Ordnung der Natur und Roms Gesetze
Verdammen diese Leidenschaft. Mein Anspruch
Stößt fürchterlich auf meines Vaters Rechte.
Ich fühl's, und dennoch lieb ich. Dieser Weg
Führt nur zu Wahnsinn oder Blutgerüste.
Ich liebe ohne Hoffnung – lasterhaft –
Mit Todesangst und mit Gefahr des Lebens –
Das seh ich ja, und dennoch lieb ich. (310–18)

70 *Ibid.*, p. 114:

MARQUIS: Ach! Und ihr Vater, Prinz –

KARLOS: Unglücklicher! Warum an den mich mahnen!
Sprich mir von allen Schrecken des Gewissens;
Von meinem Vater sprich mir nicht . . .

MARQUIS: Sie hassen Ihren Vater!

KARLOS: Nein! Ach nein!
Ich hasse meinen Vater nicht – doch Schauer
Und Missetäters Bangigkeit ergreifen
Bei den zwo fürchterlichen Sylben mich.
Kann ich dafür, wenn eine knechtische
Erziehung schon in meinem jungen Herzen
Der Liebe zarten Keim zertrat? – Sechs Jahre
Hatt' ich gelebt, als mir zum erstenmal der
Fürchterliche, der, wie sie mir sagten,
Mein Vater war, vor Augen kam. Es war

An einem Morgen, wo er steh'nden Fußes
Vier Bluturtheile unterschrieb. Nach diesem
Sah ich ihn nur, wenn mir für ein Vergehn
Bestrafung angekündigt ward – O Gott!
Hier fühl' ich, daß ich bitter werde – (338–58)

71 *Ibid.*, p. 115:

Wie Furien des Abgrunds folgen mir
Die schauerlichsten Träume. Zweifelnd ringt
Mein guter Geist mit gräßlichen Entwürfen;
Durch labyrinthische Sophismen kriecht
Mein unglücksel'ger Scharfsinn, bis er endlich
Vor eines Abgrunds gähem Rande stutzt – (386–91)

72 J. F. Abel, *Sammlung und Erklärung merkwürdiger Erscheinungen aus dem menschlichen Leben*, 3 vols., Frankfurt and Leipzig: no publ., 1784 (vol. I); Stuttgart: Erhart, 1787–90 (vols. II and III).

73 '. . . die Beschaffenheit und Stellung der Dinge, welche einen solchen Menschen umgaben, bis der gesammelte Zunder in seinem Inwendigen Feuer fing' (*NA* XVI.9).

74 '. . . die *unveränderliche* Struktur der menschlichen Seele . . . die *veränderlichen* Bedingungen, welche sie von außen bestimmten' (*ibid.*, XVI.9).

75 '. . . [den Leser] überrascht es nun nicht mehr, in dem nämlichen Beete, wo sonst überall heilsame Kräuter blühen, auch den giftigen Schierling gedeihen zu sehen', (*ibid.*, XVI.9).

76 'Die Natur hatte seinen Körper verabsäumt. Eine kleine unscheinbare Figur, krauses Haar von einer unangenehmen Schwärze, eine plattgedrückte Nase und eine geschwollene Oberlippe, welche noch überdies durch den Schlag eines Pferdes aus ihrer Richtung gewichen war, gab seinem Anblick eine Widrigkeit, welche alle Weiber von ihm zurückscheuchte und dem Witz seiner Kameraden eine reichliche Nahrung darbot' (*ibid.*, XVI.10).

77 Wolfgang Riedel, *Die Anthropologie des jungen Schiller: Zur Ideengeschichte der medizinischen Schriften und der 'Philosophischen Briefe'*, Würzburg: Königstein & Neumann, 1985, pp. 242–4.

78 *Ibid.*, p. 242. The conceptual framework for Grammont's case – and hence also the Prince in *Der Geisterseher* – probably came from Abel, who published the case of a pendular religious melancholic in his *Sammlung und Erklärung merkwürdiger Erscheinungen aus dem menschlichen Leben*, pp. 1–22.

79 'Eine bigotte, knechtische Erziehung . . . hatte seinem zarten Gehirne Schreckbilder eingedrückt, von denen er sich während seines ganzen Lebens nie ganz losmachen konnte. Religiöse Melancholie war eine Erbkrankheit in seiner Familie; die Erziehung, welche man ihm und seinen Brüdern geben ließ, war dieser Disposition angemessen, die Menschen, denen man ihn anvertraute, aus diesem Gesichtspunkt gewählt, also entweder Schwärmer

oder Heuchler . . . Diese schwarze nächtliche Gestalt hatte die ganze Jugendzeit unsers Prinzen . . . Alle seine Vorstellungen von Religion hatten etwas fürchterliches an sich, und eben das Grauenvolle und Derbe war es, was sich seiner lebhaften Einbildungskraft zuerst bemächtigte und sich auch am längsten darin erhielt. Sein Gott war ein Schreckbild, ein strafendes Wesen; seine Gottesverehrung knechtisches Zittern oder blinde, alle Kraft und Kühnheit erstickende Ergebung. Allen seinen kindischen und jugendlichen Neigungen, denen ein derber Körper und eine blühende Gesundheit um so kraftvollere Explosionen gab, stand die Religion im Wege; mit allem, woran sein jugendliches Herz sich hängte, lag sie im Streite; er lernte sie nie als eine Wohltat, nur als eine Geißel seiner Leidenschaften kennen. So entbrannte allmählich ein stiller Groll gegen sie in seinem Herzen, welcher mit einem respektvollen Glauben und blinder Furcht in seinem Kopf und Herzen die bizarreste Mischung machte – einen Widerwillen gegen einen Herrn, vor dem er in gleichem Grade Abscheu und Ehrfurcht fühlte' (*NA* xvi.103).

80 Karl Philipp Moritz, 'Versuch einer Vereinigung aller Schönen Künste und Wissenschaften unter dem Begriff des in sich Vollendeten', *Berlinische Monatsschrift* 5.3 (March, 1785), 225–36.

81 'Übrigens haben seine philosophischen Untersuchungen sehr glücklich auf sein Gemüth gewirkt, und ihn aus einer schrecklichen Seelenlage gerissen, wie er selbst gesteht. Sein Geist hat durch anstrengendes Denken über seine Hypochondrie gesiegt', 3–6 January 1789 (*ibid.*, xxv.177–8).

82 '. . . Nachahmung ist ein niedrer Grad von Vollkommenheit' (*ibid.*, NA xxv.155).

83 'Bei der Vereinzelung und getrennten Wirksamkeit unsrer Geisteskräfte, die der erweiterte Kreis des Wissens und die Absonderung der Berufsgeschäfte notwendig macht, ist es die Dichtkunst beinahe allein, welche die getrennten Kräfte der Seele wieder in Vereinigung bringt, welche Kopf und Herz, Scharfsinn und Witz, Vernunft und Einbildungskraft in harmonischem Bunde beschäftigt, welche gleichsam den *ganzen Menschen* in uns wieder herstellt' (*ibid.*, xxii.245).

84 'Am meisten vermißt man die Idealisierkunst bei Hn. B., wenn er Empfindung schildert . . . Sie sind nämlich nicht bloß Gemälde dieser eigentümlichen (und sehr undichterischen) Seelenlage, sondern sie sind offenbar auch *Geburten* derselben. Die Empfindlichkeit, der Unwille, die Schwermut des Dichters sind nicht bloß der *Gegenstand*, den er besingt, sie sind leider auch oft der *Apoll*, der ihn begeistert . . . ein Dichter nehme sich ja in Acht, mitten im Schmerz den Schmerz zu besingen . . . Aus der sanften und fernenden Erinnerung mag er dichten . . . aber ja niemals unter der gegenwärtigen Herrschaft des Affekts, den er uns schön versinnlichen soll . . . Das Idealschöne wird schlechterdings nur durch eine Freiheit des Geistes,

durch eine Selbsttätigkeit möglich, welche die Übermacht der Leidenschaft aufhebt' (*ibid.*, XXII.255–6).

85 'Nur die heitre, die ruhige Seele gebiert das Vollkommene. Kampf mit äußern Lage und Hypochondrie, welche überhaupt jede Geisteskraft lähmen, dürfen am allerwenigsten das Gemüt des Dichters belasten, der sich von der Gegenwart loswickeln und frei und kühn in die Welt der Ideale emporschweben soll. Wenn es auch noch so sehr in seinem Busen stürmt, so müsse Sonnenklarheit seine Stirne umfließen' (*ibid.*, XXII.258).

86 Dieter Borchmeyer, *Macht und Melancholie. Schillers 'Wallenstein'*, Frankfurt am Main: Athenäum, 1988.

87 Schiller, *Wallenstein*, in *'The Robbers' and 'Wallenstein'*, trans. Lamport, p. 254:

> Du redst, wie dus verstehst. Wie oft und vielmals
> Erklärt ich dirs! – *Dir* stieg der Jupiter
> Hinab bei der Geburt, der helle Gott;
> Du kannst in *die* Geheimnisse nicht schauen.
> Nur in der Erde magst du finster wühlen,
> Blind, wie der Unterirdische, der mit dem bleichen
> Bleifarbnen Schein ins Leben dir geleuchtet.
> Das Irdische, Gemeine magst du sehn,
> Das Nächste mit dem Nächsten klug verknüpfen;
> Darin vertrau ich dir und glaube dir.
> Doch was geheimnisvoll bedeutend webt
> Und bildet in den Tiefen der Natur, –
> Die Geisterleiter, die aus dieser Welt des Staubes
> Bis in die Sternenwelt, mit tausend Sprossen,
> Hinauf sich baut, an der die himmlischen
> Gewalten wirkend auf und nieder wandeln, –
> Die Kreise in den Kreisen, die sich eng
> Und enger ziehn um die zentralische Sonne –
> *Die* sieht das Auge nur, das entsiegelte,
> Der hellgebornen, heitern Joviskinder. (*Die Piccolomini*, 966–85)

88 *Ibid.*, p. 420:

> GORDON: Wohl dreißig Jahre sinds. Da strebte schon
> Der kühne Mut im zwanzigjährgen Jüngling.
> Ernst über seine Jahre war sein Sinn,
> Auf große Dinge männlich nur gerichtet,
> Durch unsre Mitte ging er stillen Geists,
> Sich selber die Gesellschaft, nicht die Lust,
> Die kindische, der Knaben zog ihn an,
> Doch oft ergriffs ihn plötzlich wundersam,
> Und der geheimnisvollen Brust entfuhr,
> Sinnvoll und leuchtend, ein Gedankenstrahl,

> Daß wir uns staunend ansahn, nicht recht wissend,
> Ob Wahnsinn, ob ein Gott aus ihm gesprochen.
>
> (*Wallensteins Tod*, 2548–59)

89 *Ibid.*, p. 420:

> BUTTLER: Dort wars, wo er zwei Stock hoch niederstürzte,
> Als er im Fensterbogen eingeschlummert,
> Und unbeschädigt stand er wieder auf.
> Von diesem Tag an, sagt man, ließen sich
> Anwandlungen des Wahnsinns bei ihm spüren.
>
> GORDON: Tiefsinniger wurd er, das ist wahr, er wurde
> Katholisch. Wunderbar hatt ihn das Wunder
> Der Rettung umgekehrt. Er hielt sich nun
> Für ein begünstigt und befreites Wesen,
> Und keck wie einer, der nicht straucheln kann,
> Lief er auf schwankem Seil des Lebens hin. (2560–70)

90 *Ibid.*, p. 374:

> Dir wird ein ruhigeres Los! – Auch wir,
> Ich und dein Vater, sahen schöne Tage,
> Der ersten Jahre denk ich noch mit Lust.
> Da war er noch der fröhlich Strebende,
> Sein Ehrgeiz war ein mild erwärmend Feuer,
> Noch nicht die Flamme, die verzehrend rast.
> Der Kaiser liebte ihn, vertraute ihm,
> Und was er anfing, das mußt ihm geraten.
> Doch seit dem Unglückstag zu Regenspurg,
> Der ihn von seiner Höh herunter stürzte,
> Ist ein unsteter, ungeselliger Geist
> Argwöhnisch, finster, über ihn gekommen.
> Ihn floh die Ruhe, und dem alten Glück,
> Der eignen Kraft nicht fröhlich mehr vertrauend
> Wand er sein Herz den dunkeln Künsten zu,
> Die keinen, der sie pflegte, noch beglückt. (1394–1409)

91 'Wallenstein fiel, nicht weil er Rebell war, sondern er rebellirte, weil er fiel' (*NA* XVIII.329).

92 See *Wallenstein's Camp*, 591–5 and *The Piccolomini*, II, vii.

93 Lesley Sharpe, '*Der Verbrecher aus verlorener Ehre*: an early exercise in Schillerian psychology', *German Life and Letters* 33 (1980), 102–10.

94 Schiller, *Wallenstein*, trans. Lamport, p. 168: '[Die Kunst] sieht den Menschen in des Lebens Drang / Und wälzt die größre Hälfte seiner Schuld / Den unglückseligen Gestirnen zu' (Prolog, 108–10).

95 'der Puritaner dumpfe Predigtstuben' (415).

96 *Mary Stuart*, in Friedrich Schiller, *Mary Stuart; Joan of Arc*, trans. Robert David MacDonald, Birmingham: Oberon, 1987, pp. 26–7: 'Des Himmels wundervolle Rettungshand / Glaubt' ich in dieser Fügung zu erkennen, / Ein lauter Ruf des Schicksals war sie mir, / Das *meinen* Arm gewählt, Euch zu befreien' (539–42).

97 'gleicher Strenge furchtbare Gerechtigkeit' (35–6).

98 'Greueltaten ohne Namen, / Schwarze Verbrechen verbirgt dies Haus' (967–8).

99
                den Anblick selbst
Des lieben Angesichts, den heißerflehten,
Versagt' ich mir, den strengen Vater scheuend,
Der, von des Argwohns ruheloser Pein
Und finster grübelndem Verdacht genagt,
Auf allen Schritten mir die Späher pflanzte. (1362–7)

100
                Der liebte
Von jeher, sich verborgen in sich selbst
Zu spinnen und den Ratschluß zu bewahren
Im unzugangbar fest verschlossenen Gemüt. (1451–4)

101
        Der Streit ist abgeschlossen zwischen mir
Und dem geliebten Bruder! Den erklär ich
Für meinen Todfeind und Beleidiger
Und werd ihn hassen wie der Hölle Pforten,
Der den erloschnen Funken unsres Streits
Aufbläst zu neuen Flammen. (575–80)

102 'Nicht Männerliebe darf dein Herz berühren', 411 (*NA* ix.181); 'Eine reine Jungfrau / Vollbringt jedwedes Herrliche auf Erden, / Wenn sie der irdschen Liebe widersteht', 1087–9 (*NA* ix.207); see also Ilse Graham, *Schiller's Drama: Talent and Integrity*, London: Methuen, 1974, pp. 178–83.

103 Jasper Griffin, *Homer on Life and Death*, Oxford: Oxford University Press, 1980, pp. 54–5.

104 *Joan of Arc*, in Schiller, *Mary Stuart; Joan of Arc*, p. 173:

    Nicht mein Geschlecht beschwöre! Nenne mich nicht Weib.
    Gleichwie die körperlosen Geister, die nicht frein
    Auf irdsche Weise, schließ ich mich an kein Geschlecht
    Der Menschen an, und dieser Panzer deckt kein Herz. (608–11)

105 *Ibid.*, p. 175:

      In Mitleid schmilzt die Seele, und die Hand erbebt,
      Als bräche sie in eines Tempels heilgen Bau,
      Den blühenden Leib des Gegners zu verletzen;
      Schon vor des Eisens blanker Schneide schaudert mir,

> Doch wenn es not tut, alsbald ist die Kraft mir da,
> Und nimmer irrend in der zitternden Hand regiert
> Das Schwert sich selbst, als wär es ein lebendger Geist. (680–6)

106 On the theme of vision, see Frank M. Fowler, 'Sight and insight in Schiller's *Die Jungfrau von Orleans*', *Modern Language Review* 68 (1973), 367–79; David B. Richards, 'Mesmerism in *Die Jungfrau von Orleans*', *Publications of the Modern Language Association* 91 (1976), 856–70.

107 'JOHANNA *erhebt das Schwert mit einer raschen Bewegung gegen ihn, läßt es aber, wie sie ihn ins Gesicht faßt, schnell wieder sinken*' (2479).

108 Schiller, *On the Aesthetic Education of Man*, p. 119: 'der von Gesetzen einseitig beherrschte oder geistig angespannte Mensch wird aufgelöst und in Freiheit gesetzt'.

109 'Der Zwang von Begriffen': Ulrich Tschierske, *Vernunftkritik und Subjektivität. Studien zur Anthropologie Friedrich Schillers*, Tübingen: Niemeyer, 1988, pp. 17–34.

110 Schiller, *On the Aesthetic Education of Man*, p. 89: 'der nachtheilige Einfluß einer überwiegenden Rationalität . . . diese gewaltthätige Usurpation der Denkkraft' (*NA* xx.350).

111 'Die sogenannten *untern* Seelenkräfte sind wie schlafende Löwen, die man oft beßer thut nicht zu wecken, weil man sie nicht sogleich zum Schweigen bringen kann', 10 June 1792 (*ibid.*, xxvii.144).

112 '. . . entehrende Verwandtschaft mit dem Stoff' (*ibid.*, xx.412).

113 'Manchmal gedenke ich Rousseaus und seines hypochondrischen Jammers, und doch wird mir begreiflich, wie eine so schöne Organisation verschoben werden konnte. Fühlt ich nicht solchen Anteil an den natürlichen Dingen und säh ich nicht, daß in der scheinbaren Verwirrung hundert Beobachtungen sich vergleichen und ordnen lassen, wie der Feldmesser mit einer durchgezogenen Linie viele einzelne Messungen probiert, ich hielte mich oft selbst für toll', Naples, 17 March 1787 (*WA* 1.xxxi.58).

114 '. . . [die] völlige Entäußerung von aller Prätension . . . [die] Treue das Auge licht sein zu lassen' (*ibid.*, iv.viii.50).

115 'Ich muß erst mein Auge bilden, mich zu sehen gewöhnen' (*ibid.*, iii.i.206).

116 '. . . eine ganz andre Elasticität des Geistes' (*ibid.*, iii.i.176).

117 '. . . glücklicher Humor . . . ohne daß ich im mindsten aufgespannt bin hab ich den schönsten Genuß und gute Betrachtung' (*ibid.*, iii.i.19–20).

118 'Wenn ich auch gleich für meine Person an der Lehre des Lucrez mehr oder weniger hänge und alle meine Prätensionen in den Kreis des Lebens einschließe; so erfreut und erquickt es mich doch immer sehr, wenn ich sehe daß die allmütterliche Natur für zärtliche Seelen auch zartere Laute und Anklänge in den Undulationen ihrer Harmonien leise tönen läßt und dem endlichen Menschen auf so manche Weise ein Mitgefühl des Ewigen und Unendlichen gönnt', 2 February 1789 (*ibid.*, iv.ix.78).

119 Letter to C. G. Heyne, 24 July 1788 (*ibid.*, iv.ix.vii–viii); see also *ibid.*, 1. xlviii.214.

120 Bell, *Goethe's Naturalistic Anthropology*, p. 75.
121 Johann Wolfgang von Goethe, *The Sorrows of Young Werther*, trans. Michael Hulse, Harmondsworth: Penguin, 1989, p. 107: 'Das klare Wetter konnte wenig auf sein trübes Gemüt wirken, ein dumpfer Druck lag auf seiner Seele, die traurigen Bilder hatten sich bei ihm festgesetzt, und sein Gemüt kannte keine Bewegung als von einem schmerzlichen Gedanken zum andern' (*WA* 1.xix.214).
122 'Je vollkommner das Empfindungsvermögen für eine gewisse Gattung des Schönen ist, um desto mehr ist es in Gefahr, sich zu täuschen, sich selbst für Bildungskraft zu nehmen und auf die Weise durch tausend mißlungene Versuche seinen Frieden mit sich selbst zu stören' (*MW* 11.565).
123 On feelings of loss, see e.g. Aaron T. Beck, *Cognitive Therapy and the Emotional Disorders*, Harmondsworth: Penguin, 1989, pp. 57–60.
124 'Diese herrliche Gegenwart regt mein Innerstes auf, fordert mich zur Tätigkeit auf, und was kann ich tun, was tue ich! Da setz' ich mich hin und schreibe und beschreibe' (*WA* 1.xix.197).
125 'Endlich schien ein leidenschaftlicher Traum sie zu beunruhigen, sie seufzte tief, veränderte heftig die Stellung, stammelte den Namen eines Geliebten und schien ihre Arme gegen ihn auszustrecken. "Komm!" rief sie endlich mit vernehmlicher Stimme, "komm, mein Freund, in meine Arme, oder ich schlafe wirklich ein"' (*ibid.* 1.xix.219).
126 Goethe, *The Sorrows of Young Werther*, p. 66: 'ein ewig verschlingendes, ewig wiederkäuendes Ungeheuer' (*WA* 1.xix.76).
127 *Ibid.*, p. 65: 'das, was des Menschen Glückseligkeit macht . . . die Quelle seines Elendes [geworden ist]' (*WA* 1.xix.73).
128 Johann Wolfgang von Goethe, *Faust The First Part of the Tragedy, with the Unpublished Scenarios for the Walpurgis Night and the Urfaust*, trans. John R. Williams, Ware: Wordsworth Editions, 1999, 24–32:

> Drum hab ich mich der Magie ergeben,
> Ob mir durch Geistes Krafft und Mund
> Nicht manch Geheimniss werde kund.
> Dass ich nicht mehr mit saurem Schweis
> Rede von dem was ich nicht weis.
> Dass ich erkenne was die Welt
> Im innersten zusammenhält,
> Schau alle Würckungskrafft und Saamen
> Und thu nicht mehr in Worten kramen.

129 Goethe, *Faust*, trans. Williams, 410–13:

> Und fragst du noch warum dein Herz
> Sich inn' in deinem Busen klemmt?
> Warum ein unerklärter Schmerz
> Dir alle Lebensregung hemmt?

130 On dichotomous thinking and other cognitive distortions, see Beck, *Cognitive Therapy*, pp. 89–95.

131 Matthew Bell, 'Sorge, Epicurean Psychology, and the Classical *Faust*', *Oxford German Studies* 28 (1999), 82–130.

132 David Konstan, *Some Aspects of Epicurean Psychology*, Philosophia antiqua 25, Leiden: Brill, 1973.

133 E.g. Lucretius, *De rerum natura*, 11.19 and 45–6.

134 *Ibid.*, 111.31–93.

135 E.g. dust and worms (403), smoke, musty odours, skeletons, bones (416–17), confinement (642).

136 'Ein Donnerwort hat mich hinweggerafft' (622), Faust sees himself cast back 'ins ungewisse Menschenlos' (629), he is a worm squashed beneath a traveller's foot (652–5). Cf. the fear of transience in his desire to enjoy 'ew'ges Licht' (1074–88).

137 *Faust*, trans. Williams, 640–51.

138 Albrecht Schöne, in Johann Wolfgang Goethe, *Sämtliche Werke, Briefe, Tagebücher und Gespräche*, ed. Friedmar Apel *et al.*, 40 vols., section 1, vol. VII: *Faust*, 2 vols., ed. Albrecht Schöne (Bibliothek deutscher Klassiker, 114), 4th rev. edn, Frankfurt am Main: Deutscher Klassiker Verlag, 1999, vol. VII/2, pp. 223–4.

139 Han Arens, 'Haus und Hof . . . Weib und Kind' in, *Kommentar zu Goethes 'Faust i'*, Heidelberg: Winter, 1982, p. 111.

140 Lucretius, *Von der Natur der Dinge*, trans. K. L. von Knebel, Leipzig: Göschen, 1821, 111. 37–40.

141 Lucretius, *On the Nature of the Universe*, trans. R. E. Latham, rev. John Godwin, Harmondsworth: Penguin, 1994, pp. 67–8.

142 Goethe, *Faust*, trans. Williams, 712–17:

> Hier ist es Zeit, durch Taten zu beweisen,
> Daß Manneswürde nicht der Gotteshöhe weicht,
> Vor jener dunkeln Höhle nicht zu beben,
> In der sich Phantasie zu eigner Qual verdammt,
> Nach jenem Durchgang hinzustreben,
> Um dessen engen Mund die ganze Hölle flammt.

143 Goethe, *Faust*, trans. Williams, 1024–9:

> Hier saß ich oft gedankenvoll allein
> Und quälte mich mit Beten und mit Fasten.
> An Hoffnung reich, im Glauben fest,
> Mit Thränen, Seufzen, Händeringen
> Dacht' ich das Ende jener Pest
> Vom Herrn des Himmels zu erzwingen.

144 David Luke, 'Notes', in Johann Wolfgang von Goethe, *Faust. Part One*, trans. D. Luke, Oxford: Oxford University Press, 1987, p. 152.

145 Goethe, *Faust*, trans. Williams, 1562–5:

> Auch muß ich, wenn die Nacht sich niedersenkt,
> Mich ängstlich auf das Lager strecken;
> Auch da wird keine Rast geschenkt,
> Mich werden wilde Träume schrecken.

146 Lucretius, *On the Nature of the Universe*, pp. 68–9.
147 Goethe, *Faust*, trans. Williams, 1699–1702:

> Werd ich zum Augenblicke sagen:
> Verweile doch! du bist so schön!
> Dann magst du mich in Fesseln schlagen,
> Dann will ich gern zugrunde gehn!

148 Rousseau, *Reveries of the Solitary Walker*, trans. Peter France, Harmonds-worth: Penguin, 1979, p. 88: 'Tout est dans un flux continuel sur la terre: rien n'y garde une forme constante et arrêtée, et nos affections qui s'attachent aux choses extérieures passent et changent necessairement comme elles. Toujours en avant et en arriére de nous, elles rappellent le passé qui n'est plus ou previennent l'avenir qui souvent ne doit point être: il n'y a rien là de solide à quoi le coeur se puisse attacher. Aussi n'a-t-on guére ici-bas du plaisir qui passe; pour le bonheur qui dure je doute qu'il y soit connu. A peine est-il dans nos plus vives jouissances un instant où le coeur puisse véritablement nous dire: *Je voudroit que cet instant durât toujours*; et comment peut-on appeler bonheur un état fugitif qui nous laisse encor le coeur inquiet et vide, qui nous fait regreter quelque chose avant, ou desirer encor quelque chose après?' (*ROC* I.1046).
149 Hans Arens, *Kommentar zu Goethes 'Faust II',* Heidelberg: Winter, 1989, p. 918.
150 Lucretius, *De rerum natura* II. 48.
151 Lucretius, *On the Nature of the Universe*, pp. 93–4.
152 Goethe, *Faust*, trans. Williams, 302–3: 'Ihn treibt die Gärung in die Ferne, / Er ist sich seiner Tollheit halb bewußt.'

5 IDEALISM'S CAMPAIGN AGAINST PSYCHOLOGY

1 '... die größten Tendenzen des Zeitalters', Friedrich Schlegel, *Schriften zur Literatur*, ed. W. Rasch, Munich: Hanser, 1970, p. 45.
2 '. . . nicht zur Erweiterung, sondern zur Läuterung unserer Vernunft' (*KWW* III.63, B25/A11).
3 '... bisher zu sehr in ihrem Werte verkannt, oder wenigstens [schlummerte sie] zu wenig beachtet im Schatten der Philosophie', A. C. A. Eschenmayer, *Psychologie*, ed. P. Krumme, Frankfurt am Main, Berlin, and Vienna: Ullstein, 1982, p. iii.

4 'Seit der großen Revolution, die durch Kant veranlaßt wurde, ist [die Psychologie] aus der spekulativen Philosophie ausgestoßen', Henrik Steffens, 'Über die wissenschaftliche Behandlung der Philosophie', in Wilhelm Bietak (ed.), *Romantische Wissenschaft*, Deutsche Literatur, Reihe Romantik 13, Leipzig: Reclam, 1940, pp. 281–94 (p. 281).

5 W. H. Walsh, 'Self-knowledge', in Ralph C. S. Walker (ed.), *Kant on Pure Reason*, Oxford Readings in Philosophy, Oxford: Oxford University Press, 1982, pp. 150–75 (p. 153).

6 'In der Psychologie erforschen wir uns selbst nach unseren Vorstellungen des inneren Sinnes' (*KWW* x.417).

7 See also the 'Kollegnachschrift' quoted in Vladimir Satura, *Kants Erkenntnispsychologie in den Nachschriften seiner Vorlesungen über empirische Psychologie, Kant-Studien*, Ergänzungshefte 101, Bonn: Bouvier, 1971, p. 29.

8 'Die Psychologie ist für menschliche Einsichten nichts mehr und kann auch nichts mehr werden, als Anthropologie, d.i. als Kenntnis des Menschen, nur auf die Bedingung eingeschränkt, so fern er sich als Gegenstand des inneren Sinnes kennt' (*KWW* v.648). See also *KWW* iv.707, A848/B876.

9 '. . . [sie gehört] nicht in die Transzendentalphilosophie, sondern in die Psychologie' (*ibid.*, iii.149, B152).

10 *Grundlegung zur Metaphysik der Sitten*, preface, *KWW* vi.13–15, Bvii–xiii, and *Kritik der praktischen Vernunft*, preface, *KWW* vi.113–14, A15–17.

11 '. . . [eine] subtile u[nd] in meinen Augen auf ewig vergebliche Untersuchung' (*KAA* x.145).

12 'Wer den Naturursachen nachgrübelt, worauf z. B. das Erinnerungsvermögen beruhen möge, kann über die im Gehirn zurückgelassenen Spuren von Eindrücken, welche die erlittenen Empfindungen hinterlassen, hin und her (nach dem Cartesius) vernünfteln; muß aber dabei gestehen: daß er in diesem Spiel seiner Vorstellungen bloßer Zuschauer sei, und die Natur machen lassen muß, indem er die Gehirnnerven und Fasern nicht kennt, noch sich auf der Handhabung derselben zu seiner Absicht versteht: mithin alles theoretische Verünfteln hierüber reine Verlust ist' (*KWW* x.399).

13 Herman-Jean de Vleeschauwer, *The Development of Kantian Thought. The History of a Doctrine*, London: Nelson, 1962, pp. 39–41.

14 '. . . eine reine Moralphilosophie zu bearbeiten, die von allem, was nur empirisch sein mag und zur Anthropologie gehört, gesäubert wäre', *Grundlegung zur Metaphysik der Sitten*, preface (*KWW* vi.13, BAviii–ix).

15 P. F. Strawson, *The Bounds of Sense: An Essay on Kant's 'Critique of Pure Reason'*, London and New York: Routledge, 1989, pp. 16–18, 33–5, 171–2, 241–3.

16 Immanuel Kant, *Critique of Pure Reason*, trans. Paul Guyer and Allen W. Wood, The Cambridge Edition of the Works of Immanuel Kant, Cambridge: Cambridge University Press, 1998, p. 341: 'Also beziehen sich alle Begriffe und mit ihnen alle Grundsätze, so sehr sie auch a priori möglich sein mögen, dennoch auf empirische Anschauungen, d.i. auf Data zur möglichen Erfahrung. Ohne dieses haben sie gar keine objektive Gültigkeit, sondern sind ein bloßes Spiel' (*KWW* iii.270, B298).

17 *Ibid.*, p. 372: 'Leibniz intellektuierte die Erscheinungen, so wie Locke die Verstandesbegriffe . . . insgesamt sensifiziert' (*KWW* III.293, B327/A271).

18 *Ibid.*, p. 193–4: 'Gedanken ohne Inhalt sind leer, Anschauungen ohne Begriffe sind blind' (*KWW* III.98, A51/B75).

19 Ralph C. S. Walker, *Kant*, The Arguments of the Philosophers, London: Routledge, 1978, pp. 76–7.

20 ' . . . die Handlung, verschiedene Vorstellungen zu einander hinzuzutun, und ihre Mannigfaltigkeit in einer Erkenntnis zu begreifen' (*KWW* III.116, B103/A77).

21 De Vleeschauwer, *Development of Kantian Thought*, p. 83.

22 Gary Hatfield, *The Natural and the Normative: Theories of Spatial Perception from Kant to Helmholtz*, Cambridge, MA: MIT Press, 1990, p. 101.

23 Patricia Kitcher, *Kant's Transcendental Psychology*, New York and Oxford: Oxford University Press, 1990, pp. 13–14.

24 *Ibid.*, p. 9.

25 Alfred Hegler, *Die Psychologie in Kants Ethik*, Freiburg: Mohr, 1891, p. 6.

26 De Vleeschauwer, *Development of Kantian Thought*, p. 69.

27 Johann Nicolas Tetens, *Philosophische Versuche über die menschliche Natur und ihre Entwicklung*, 2 vols., Leipzig: Weidmann, 1777, vol. 1, p. 118.

28 Kant, *Critique of Pure Reason*, p. 239: 'Daß die Einbildungskraft ein notwendiges Ingrediens der Wahrnehmung selbst sei, daran hat wohl noch kein Psychologe gedacht' (*KWW* III.176, A121).

29 *Ibid.*, p. 273: 'Dieser Schematismus unseres Verstandes . . . ist eine verborgene Kunst in den Tiefen der menschlichen Seele, deren wahre Handgriffe wir der Natur schwerlich jemals abraten, und sie unverdeckt vor Augen legen werden' (*KWW* III.190, B180–1/A141).

30 P. F. Strawson, 'Imagination and Perception', in Ralph C. S. Walker (ed.), *Kant on Pure Reason*, Oxford Readings in Philosophy, Oxford: Oxford University Press, 1982, pp. 82–99 (p. 84).

31 Satura, *Kants Erkenntnispsychologie*, pp. 153–4.

32 Jürgen Bona Meyer, *Kant's Psychologie*, Berlin: Hertz, 1870, pp. 51–64.

33 Walsh, 'Self-Knowledge', p. 156.

34 ' . . . eine Aufsuchung der Ursache einer gegebenen Wirkung, und in so fern [hat es] etwas einer Hypothese Ähnliches an sich' (*KWW* III.16, Axviii).

35 Thomas Love Peacock, *Nightmare Abbey; Crotchet Castle*, Harmondsworth: Penguin, 1969, pp. 44, 67, 83.

36 'Ich muß gestehen, daß dieser Anstand mich bey dem Studio der Kantischen Philosophie nicht wenig aufgehalten hat, so daß ich verschiedene Jahre hintereinander die Kritik der reinen Vernunft immer wieder von vorne anfangen mußte, weil ich unaufhörlich darüber irre wurde, daß ich ohne jene Voraussetzung [i.e. causation] in das System nicht hineinkommen, und mit jener Voraussetzung darinn nicht bleiben konnte', Friedrich Heinrich Jacobi, *Werke*, 6 vol., photo reprint, Darmstadt: Wissenschaftliche Buchgesellschaft, 1976, vol. II, p. 304.

37 Johann Gottlieb Fichte, Letter to F. A. Weißhuhn, August/September 1790 (*FGA* iii.i.168).

38 'Das absolute Subjekt, das Ich, wird nicht durch empirische Anschauung gegeben, sondern durch intellectuelle gesetzt; und das absolute Object, das Nicht-Ich, ist das ihm entgegengesetzte' (*ibid.*, 1.ii.48).

39 'Überhaupt welches ist denn der Inhalt der Wissenschaftslehre in zwei Worten? Dieser: die Vernunft ist absolut selbständig; sie ist nur für sich; aber für sie ist auch nur sie. Alles sonach, was sie ist, muß in ihr selbst begründet seyn, und nur aus ihr selbst, nicht aber aus Etwas außer ihr erklärt werden, zu welchem, außer ihr, sie nicht gelangen könnte, ohne sich selbst aufzugeben. Kurz: die Wissenschaftslehre ist transscendentaler Idealismus', (*ibid.*, 1.iv.227).

40 '. . . dasjenige, dem Leiden zugeschrieben wird, und insofern nicht *Thätigkeit*, heißt das bewirkte (der *Effect*, mithin von einer andern abhängende und keine Ur-Realität)' (*ibid.*, 1.ii.294).

41 'Jenes ursprüngliche *Setzen* nun, und *Gegensetzen*, und *Theilen* ist NB. kein *Denken*, kein *Anschauen*, kein *Empfinden*, kein *Begehren*, kein *Fühlen* u.s.f., sondern es ist die *gesammte Thätigkeit* des menschlichen Geistes, die keinen Namen hat, die im Bewußtseyn nie vorkommt, die *unbegreiflich* ist; weil sie das durch alle besondern (u[nd] lediglich insofern ein Bewußtseyn bildende) Akte des Gemüths *bestimmbare*, keineswegs aber ein *bestimmtes* ist', 2 July 1795 (*ibid.*, iii.ii.344).

42 '. . . das Ich sezt ursprünglich schlechthin sein eignes Seyn' (*Ibid.*, 1.ii.261).

43 'Dieser Wechsel des Ich in und mit sich selbst, da es sich endlich und unendlich zugleich setzt – ein Wechsel, der gleichsam in einem Widerstreite mit sich selbst besteht, und dadurch sich selbst reproducirt, indem das Ich unvereinbares vereinigen will, jezt das unendliche in die Form des endlichen aufzunehmen versucht, jetzt, zurückgetrieben, es wieder außer derselben sezt, und in dem nemlichen Momente abermals es in die Form der Endlichkeit aufzunehmen versucht – ist das Vermögen der *Einbildungskraft*' (*ibid.*, 1. ii.359).

44 'Merke auf dich selbst: kehre deinen Blick von allem, was dich umgiebt, ab, und in dein Inneres – ist die erste Forderung, welche die Philosophie an ihren Lehrling thut' (*ibid.*, 1.iv.186).

45 Joachim Widmann, *Johann Gottlieb Fichte. Einführung in seine Philosophie*, Sammlung Göschen, Berlin: de Gruyter, 1982, p. 12.

46 Ernst Platner, *Anthropologie für Ärzte und Weltweise*, Leipzig: Dyck, 1772.

47 'Jedes Thier *ist*, was er ist; der Mensch allein ist ursprünglich gar nichts. Was er seyn soll, muß er werden und – da er doch ein Wesen für sich seyn soll – durch sich selbst werden. Die Natur hat alle ihre Werke vollendet, nur vom Menschen zog sie die Hand ab und übergab ihn gerade dadurch sich selbst. Bildsamkeit, als solche, ist der Charakter der Menschheit' (*FGA* 1.iii.379).

48 E.g. *NS* iv.48, 109–10.

49 'Sich nach den Dingen, oder die Dinge nach sich *richten* – ist eins' (*ibid.*, 11.589).

50 ' . . . die transscendente Natur ist zugleich immanent – so auch die immanente Person ist transcendent zugleich – und auch umgekehrt' (*ibid.*, 11.57).

51 ' . . . ein encyclopaedischer systematischer Index oder Plan unsers Geistes' (*ibid.*, 11.583).

52 John Neubauer, *Bifocal Vision: Novalis' Philosophy of Nature and Disease*, Chapel Hill, NC: University of North Carolina Press, 1971, pp. 49, 104. On Brownianism, see *NS* 111.383, 388, 407–8.

53 'Thus one must, as an educated person, be able to be, as *body and soul*, irritable and sensitive at *will*.' ('So muß man, als gebildeter M[ensch] überhaupt *Körper und Seele* – reizbar und Sensibel nach *Belieben* seyn können. Der vollkommenste Mensch hat alle Constitutionen samt ihren Veränderungen in seiner Gewalt'; *NS* 111.350.)

54 'In the same way as we can set our organ of thinking in motion at will . . . so too we must *learn* to move, restrict, unite, separate the internal organs of our body . . . Then each person will become his own doctor – and be able to acquire a complete, reliable, and exact sense of his own body – then humans will at last be truly independent of nature, and perhaps even be in a position to restore lost limbs, kill themselves by a pure act of will, and thereby at last attain true insights into body – soul – the world, life – death and the spirit world . . . Fichte taught – and discovered the active use of the organ of thinking. Indeed Fichte was the first to discover the active use of the organs at all. Intellectual intuition is nothing other than this.' ('Auf dieselbe Art, wie wir unser Denkorgan in beliebige Bewegung setzen . . . auf eben dieselbe Art müssen wir auch die innern Organe unsers Körpers bewegen, hemmen, vereinigen, vereinzeln, *lernen* . . . Dann wird jeder sein eigner Arzt sein – und sich ein vollständiges, sichres und genaues Gefühl seines Körpers erwerben können – dann wird der Mensch erst wahrhaftig unabhängig von der Natur, vielleicht im Stande sogar seyn verlorne Glieder zu restauriren, sich blos durch seinen Willen zu tödten, und dadurch erst wahre Aufschlüsse über Körper–Seele–Welt, Leben–Tod und Geisterwelt zu erlangen . . . Fichte hat den thätigen Gebrauch des Denkorgans gelehrt – und entdeckt. Hat Fichte etwa die Gesetze des thätigen Gebrauchs der Organe überhaupt entdeckt. Intellectuale Anschauung ist nichts anders'; *ibid.*, 11.583).

55 John Neubauer, *Novalis*, Twayne's World Authors 556, Boston: Twayne, 1980, p. 144.

56 ' . . . a free recreation of the bound imagination' (' . . . eine freie Erholung der gebundenen Phantasie'; *NS* 1.199).

57 ' . . . how the world came into being through wondrous sympathy' (' . . . wie durch wundervolle Sympathie die Welt entstanden'; *ibid.*, 1.220); ' . . . the almighty sympathy of nature' ('die allmächtige Sympathie der Natur'; 1.225).

58 'ERREG[UNGS]THEOR[IE]. Aller Reitz soll nur temporell, nur *Erziehungsmittel*, nur Veranlassung zur Selbstthätigkeit seyn. BILD[UNGS] LEHRE D[ER] NATUR. Die Natur soll moralisch werden. Wir sind ihre *Erzieher* – ihre moralischen *Tangenten* – ihre moralischen Reitze' (*ibid.*, 111.252).

59 'Hier ist nun schlechterdings nie Psychologie' (*FGA*, 11.v.333).
60 'Kontrast der Form und des Stoffs . . . philosophische Groteske': Friedrich Schlegel, *Schriften zur Literatur*, ed. W. Rasch, Munich: Hanser, 1970, p. 32.
61 'Die sogenannte Psychologie gehört auch zu den Larven, die die Stellen im Heiligthum eingenommen haben, wo ächte Götterbilder stehn sollten' (*NS* III.435).
62 ' . . . die Psychologie . . . hat . . . die notwendige Tendenz . . . alles Hohe und Ungemeine herabzuwürdigen . . . Die großen Thaten und Charaktere der vergangenen Zeit in dem herrlichen Leben der alten Welt erscheinen, unter das psychologische Messer genommen, als das natürliche Resultat einiger ganz begreiflicher Motive. Die Ideen der Philosophie erklären sich aus mehreren sehr groben psychologischen Täuschungen' (*SWS* III.271).
63 *Ibid.*, III.284.
64 ' . . . so daß der Geist zu einem bloßen Aggregat von selbständigen Kräften wird' (*HGW*, x.12; see also 1.355, v.46–7).
65 ' . . . befindet sich noch immer in einem höchst schlechten Zustande' (*ibid.*, x.238–9; see also VII.48–9).
66 See e.g. *FGA* 11.iv.71.
67 'Die Phänomenologie des Geistes soll an die Stelle der psychologischen Erklärungen . . . treten' (*HGW* III.593).
68 C. C. E. Schmid, 'Kann Psychologie als eine eigene selbständige Wissenschaft noch ferner geduldet werden?' *Anthropologisches Journal* 3 (1803), 93–127 (p. 94).
69 Gottfried Keller, *Der grüne Heinrich*, ed. C. Heselhaus, Munich: Hanser, 1958, vol. IV, pp. 568–86.
70 Johann Friedrich Herbart, *Sämtliche Werke*, ed. Karl Kehrbach and Otto Flügel, 19 vols., Aalen: Scientia, 1989, vol. IV, p. 297.
71 'Kant bediente sich der Seelenvermögen . . . und es ist nicht leicht, seine Kritiken von dieser Form zu entkleiden', Herbart, *Werke*, vol. IV, p. 307.
72 *Ibid.*, vol. IV, p. 304.
73 *Ibid.*, vol. II, vol. 2, pp. 210–15.
74 *Ibid.*, vol. IV, pp. 369–86.
75 David E. Leary, 'The philosophical development of the conception of psychology in Germany, 1780–1850', *Journal of the History of the Behavioral Sciences* 14 (1978), 113–21 (p. 119).
76 A. C. A. Eschenmeyer, *Psychologie*, ed. P. Krumme, Frankfurt am Main, Berlin, and Vienna:Ullstein, 1982.

6   ROMANTICISM AND ANIMAL MAGNETISM

1 Reinhard Mocek, *Johann Christian Reil (1759–1813). Das Problem des Übergangs von der Spätaufklärung zur Romantik in Biologie und Medizin in Deutschland*, Frankfurt am Main: Lang, 1995, p. 143. Contrast Theodore Ziolkowski, *German Romanticism and Its Institutions*, Princeton, NJ: Princeton University Press, 1990, pp. 181–7.

2 Reinhard Mocek, 'J. C. Reil', in Walther Killy and Rudolf Vierhaus (eds.), *Deutsche biographische Enzyklopädie*, 13 vols., Munich: Saur, 1998, vol., p. 208.
3 E.g. *RR* 27.
4 Franz Loquai, *Künstler und Melancholie in der Romantik*, Frankfurt am Main: Lang, 1984, pp. 34–5.
5 'Am Anfang führen meistens Mittel, die Furcht machen, am schnellsten zum Ziel. Selbst solche Kranke, die durch Güte gezogen werden müssen, fodern in dieser Periode eine ernsthafte Behandlung, um ihnen Achtung für ihre Vorgesetzte einzuflössen. Sie ähneln den Kindern, die es versuchen ihren Willen durchzusetzen, aber bald einlenken, wenn ihrem Vorsatze ein schmerzhaftes Hinderniss in den Wege gestellt wird' (*RR* 224).
6 'Zarte und furchtsame Subjekte können durch ein rauhes Anfahren, durch Drohungen oder durch den bloßen Anblick einer schauderhaften Scene zum Gehorsam gebracht werden' (*ibid.*, 227).
7 Mocek, *Johann Christian Reil*, p. 143.
8 Reinhard Mocek, 'Johann Christian Reil', in Walther Killy and Rudolf Vierhaus (eds.), *Deutsche biographische Enzyklopädie*, vol. VIII, Munich: K. G. Saur, 1998, p. 209.
9 Johann Christian Reil and Johann Christoph Hoffbauer (eds.), *Beyträge zur Beförderung einer Curmethode auf psychischem Wege*, 2 vols., Vienna: Doll, 1808, I.24–39; II.1–44, 107–53.
10 '. . . die man zu dem Gebiet des sogenannten Wunderglaubens gezählt hat', Gotthilf Heinrich von Schubert, *Ansichten von der Nachtseite der Natur-wissenschaft*, Dresden: Arnold, 1808, p. 2.
11 'Endlich werden wir in mannigfaltigen Erscheinungen, das Eingreifen des künftigen, höheren Daseyns, in das jetzige minder vollkommene anerkennen, und wie der tief in uns schlummernde Keim eines neuen Lebens, in gewißen Momenten, wo die Kräfte des jetzigen ruhen, deutlich hervorbricht', Schubert, *Ansichten*, p. 22.
12 '. . . ein beständiges Streben . . . der innigen Vereinigung mit der Gesamtmasse des Planeten' (*ibid.*, p. 177).
13 Peter Krebs, *Die Anthropologie des Gotthilf Heinrich von Schubert*, Cologne: Orthen, 1940, pp. 31–2.
14 *Ibid.*, p. 350.
15 *Ibid.*, p. 336.
16 *Ibid.*, p. 337–40.
17 *Ibid.*, p. 344.
18 Gotthilf Heinrich von Schubert, *Die Symbolik des Traumes* [1814], photo reprint, Heidelberg: Schneider, 1968, p. i.
19 *Ibid.*, p. 99–101.
20 *Ibid.*, p. 3.
21 'Wir drücken in jener Sprache durch einige wenige hieroglyphische, seltsam aneinander gefügte Bilder . . . in Momenten mehr aus, als wir mit Worten in ganzen Stunden auseinander zu setzen vermöchten' (*ibid.*, p. 1).
22 '. . . die Sprache der Poesie und der Offenbarung' (*ibid.*, p. 13).

23 *Ibid.*, p. 56.
24 ' . . . eine allgemeine verbreitete stätige, aüsserst feine Flüssigkeit, welche ihrer Natur nach die Fähigkeit hat alle Arten von Bewegung anzunehmen, dieselbe mitzutheilen, und fortzupflanzen', Franz Anton Mesmer, *Abhandlung über die Entdeckung des thierischen Magnetismus* [Karlsruhe edn of 1781], Tübingen: Edition Diskord, 1985, p. 47.
25 *Ibid.*, pp. 11–12.
26 ' . . . ein allgemeines Heil- und Verwahrungs-Mittel gegen alle Krankheiten' (*ibid.*, p. 4).
27 On Mesmer's early years, see Ernst Benz, *Franz Anton Mesmer und die philosophischen Grundlagen des animalischen Magnetismus*, Wiesbaden: Steiner, 1977; Anneliese Ego, *'Animalischer Magnetismus' oder 'Aufklärung'. Eine mentalitätsgeschichtliche Studie zum Konflikt um ein Heilkonzept im 18. Jahrhundert*, Epistemata 68, Würzburg: Königshausen und Neumann, 1991; Maria M. Tatar, *Spellbound. Studies on Mesmerism and Literature*, Princeton, NJ: Princeton University Press, 1978.
28 Robert Darnton, *Mesmerism and the End of the Enlightenment in France*, Cambridge, MA: Harvard University Press, 1968, pp. 92–105. On the fashion for sensibility, see A. J. de Montegre, *Du magnétisme animal et de ses partisans, ou recueil de piéces importantes sur cet objet*, Paris: Colas, 1812, p. 4.
29 Mesmer, *Abhandlung*, p. 199.
30 'Dieser Zustand stellt den Menschen so dar, wie er von Natur aus ist, ohne durch den Gebrauch der Sinne oder durch einen fremden Einfluß anders geartet zu seyn', Franz Anton Mesmer, *Mesmerismus. Oder System der Wechselwirkungen, Theorie und Anwendung des thierischen Magnetismus als die allgemeine Heilkunde zur Erhaltung des Menschen*, ed. Karl Christian Wolfart, Berlin: Nicolai, 1814, p. 23.
31 J. P. F. Deleuze, *Practical Instruction in Animal Magnetism*, trans. T. C. Hartshorn, Providence, RI: Cranston, 1837, p. 58.
32 Mesmer, *Mesmerismus*, pp. 243–59.
33 On the German reception of animal magnetism 1775–1800, see Ego, *'Animalischer Magnetismus' oder 'Aufklärung'*.
34 Eberhard Gmelin, *Über thierischen Magnetismus. In einem Brief an Herrn Geheimen Rath Hoffmann in Mainz*, 2 vols., Tübingen: Heerbrandt, 1787, vol. 11, pp. 10–11
35 *Ibid.*, vol. 2, pp. 164, 177. On Gmelin's and Böckmann's observations, see also Johann Lorenz Böckmann (ed.), *Archiv für Magnetismus und Somnambulismus*, 8 vols., Strasbourg: Akademische Buchhandlung, 1787–8, vol. 1, p. 13.
36 Gmelin, *Über thierischen Magnetismus*, vol. 11, p. 157.
37 Böckmann (ed.), *Archiv*, vol. 1, p. 32.
38 *Ibid.*, vol. 11, p. 81.
39 Eberhard Gmelin, *Materialien für die Anthropologie*, 2 vols., Tübingen: Cotta, 1791; Heilbronn and Rothenburg/Tauber: Claß, 1793, vol. 1, pp. 3–45.

40 'In unserer Seele liegt ein gewisses dunkles Gefühl . . . genommen aus der Kenntniß unsers Körpers, unserer Seele und der Dinge außer uns . . .' (*ibid.*, vol. 1, p. 207).

41 Gmelin, *Über thierischen Magnetismus*, vol. 11, pp. 204–6.

42 Arnold Wienholt, *Beytrag zu den Erfahrungen über den thierischen Magnetismus*, Hamburg: Hoffmann, 1787; *Einleitung in sein Werk über die Heilkraft des thierischen Magnetismus*, Lemgo: Meyer, 1800; *Heilkraft des thierischen Magnetismus nach eigenen Beobachtungen*, Lemgo: Meyer, 1802.

43 Ego, *'Animalischer Magnetismus' oder 'Aufklärung'*, p. 172.

44 Carl Alexander Ferdinand Kluge, *Versuch einer Darstellung des animalischen Magnetismus als Heilmittel*, Berlin: Realschulbuchhandlung, 1811.

45 '. . . alles individuelle Daseyn ist nur ein einseitiger Reflex des Ganzen', Christoph Wilhelm Hufeland, *Über Sympathie*, Weimar: Landes-Industrie-Comptoir, 1811, p. 1.

46 *Ibid.*, p. 43.

47 '. . . allgemeines Gesetz der Sympathie . . . unter zwei in einem sympathetischen Verhältniß stehenden Subjecten, die Lebensform des einen durch die Wirkungssphäre des andern bestimmt wird, und der in diesem Verhältniß als der active oder positive zu betrachtender Organismus sich dem andern gleichsam assimilirt und auf ihn seine eigene gesunde oder kranke Lebensform überträgt' (*ibid.*, pp. 220–1).

48 'Unserm Vaterlande ist es . . . ausschließlich vorbehalten, diese den französischen Aerzten unbegreiflich und daher unglaublich gebliebenen Entdeckungen und Lehren zu bestätigen, und für die Nachwelt ausser fernern Zweifel zu setzen. In Berlin, der Pflegerin alles Guten, wird sich zuerst diese hohe Bestimmung erfüllen', Karl Christian Wolfart, 'Über die Erweckung von Mesmers Lehre, und die Anwendung des sogenannten thierischen Magnetismus', *Miszellen für die neueste Weltkunde* 83 (14 October 1812), 329–31 (pp. 329–30).

49 'Aus der Erkenntniß des innersten Triebwerkes des Weltalls, von allem was da ist, was war und noch seyn wird, kann allein die wahre Idee des sogenannten thierischen Magnetismus herkommen, und diese Erkenntniß liegt wiederum in der ganzen Lehre, die nichts anders ist, als die *wahre Naturphilosophie*, oder die *Physik der Natur* sowohl in geistiger als körperlicher Richtung, was eben darin zur Einheit sich verbunden findet' (*ibid.*, p. 329).

50 '. . . ein blinder Empirismus' (*ibid.*, p. 329).

51 '. . . der Nachlaß der Irritabilität, d.h. des thätigen Wechselverhältnisses zwischen Muskel und Nerven' (*ibid.*, p. 329).

52 *Ibid.*, pp. 329–31.

53 Georg Kieser, *System des Tellurismus oder thierischen Magnetismus. Ein Handbuch für Naturforscher und Aerzte*, 2 vols., Leipzig: Herbig, 1822.

54 *Ibid.*, vol. 1, p. 67.

55 *Ibid.*, vol. 1, pp. 92–3.

56 *Ibid.*, vol. 11, p. 15.

57 *Ibid.*, vol. 1, p. 198.

58 *Ibid.*, vol. 1, p. 234.

59 *Ibid.*, vol. 1, pp. 248–62.

60 On Christ's date of birth see *ibid.*, vol. 1, p. 95; on focusing magnetism see *ibid.*, vol. 1, pp. 448–78.

61 '. . . ein Blick in ihre [i.e. der Seele] geheime Werkstätte', A. C. A. Eschenmayer, *Versuch die scheinbare Magie des thierischen Magnetismus aus physischen und psychologischen Gründen zu erklären*, Vienna: Haas, 1816, p. 26.

62 *Ibid.*, p. 58.

63 '. . . eine geistige Zeugung durch geistige Begattung' (*ibid.*, p. 124).

64 'Die geistige Zeugung und Begattung, wie wir sie im thierischen Magnetismus sehen, [ist] ein von dem Naturelement der Generations-Organe aufwärtsgehender Proceß, in welchem die Seele am Ende sich über ihr Zeitleben erhebt' (*ibid.*, pp. 125–6).

65 On language: 'Even the sole thing we possess, Language, is not fit to portray the soul, and what it [i.e. Langauge] gives us are only scattered fragments' ('Selbst das einzige, das wir besitzen, die Sprache taugt nicht dazu, sie kann die Seele nicht malen, und was sie uns gibt sind nur zerrissene Bruchstücke'), letter to Ulrike von Kleist, 5 February 1801 (*KWS* 11.626). See also 'Über die allmähliche Verfertigung der Gedanken beim Reden' ('On the gradual production of thoughts whilst speaking': *KWS* 11.319–24).

66 Tatar, *Spellbound*, Chapter 3.

67 Heinrich von Kleist, *Penthesilea*, in *Five Plays*, trans. Martin Greenberg, New Haven and London: Yale University Press, 1988, p. 234: 'Mein ewiger Gedanke, wenn ich wachte, / Mein ewger Traum warst du!' (2187–8).

68 *Ibid.*, 864–6, 610–12.

69 *Ibid.*, 986, 1054.

70 *Ibid.*, 34–8, 116–21.

71 Tatar, *Spellbound*, pp. 48–81.

72 Kleist, *Penthesilea*, trans. Martin Greenberg, p. 179.

73 '. . . as often as, after annual calculations . . .' ('so oft nach jährlichen Berechnungen . . .'), 2026.

74 'Die Geschichte eines wohlüberlegten Mordes, den eine, übrigens vernünftig scheinende Schwangere an ihrem Mann beging, zu dessen Fleisch sie einen unwiderstehlichen Appetit bekommen, steht bey Reil S. 394. Die Unglückselige salzte noch das Fleisch des Ermordeten ein, um recht lange daran zu haben. Auch solche Beobachtungen erinnern an den Schweden-borgischen Satz, daß in jener Welt wollüstige Liebe sich in Lust sich gegenseitig zu morden verwandle, und an die schon längst anerkannte Verwandschaft der Wollust (Fleischeslust) und Mordlust', Schubert, *Symbolik*, 122–3. See Ralph Tymms, 'Alternation of personality in the dramas of Heinrich von Kleist and Zacharias Werner', *Modern Language Review* 37 (1942), 64–73.

75 Kleist, *Penthesilea*, trans. Martin Greenberg, p. 268: 'Sie sank weil sie zu stolz und kräftig blühte! / Die abgestorbne Eiche steht im Sturm, / Doch die gesunde stürzt er schmetternd nieder, / Weil er in ihre Krone greifen kann' (3040–3).

76 'Wenn der Sturm kleine Flammen auslöscht, große aber noch größer macht, inwiefern ist er mit dem Unglück zu vergleichen?', 11–12 January, 1801, (*KWS* 11.613).

77 Kleist, *Penthesilea*, trans. Martin Greenberg, p. 218: 'Das Unglück sagt man läutert die Gemüter, / Ich, du geliebte, ich empfand es nicht; / Erbittert hat es, Göttern mich und Menschen / In unbegriffner Leidenschaft empört' (1686–9).

78 'Selbstmord in Worten': Elisabeth Madlener, *Die Kunst des Erwürgens nach Regeln. Von Staats- und Kriegskünsten, preußischer Geschichte und Heinrich von Kleist*, Pfaffenweiler: Centaurus, 1994, p. 156.

79 *Ibid.*, p. 268: '. . . jetzt steig ich in meinen Busen nieder, / Gleich einem Schacht, und grabe, kalt wie Erz, / Mir ein vernichtendes Gefühl hervor. / Dies Erz, dies läutr' ich in der Glut des Jammers / Hart mir zu Stahl' (3028–29).

80 'Je frischer und kräftiger der äußere Mensch vegetirt, desto ohnmächtiger wird der innere, der sich dann in die Bilderwelt der dunkeln Gefühle und des Traumes zurückzieht, je kräftiger dagegen der innere Mensch auflebt, desto mehr muß der äußere absterben. Eine nur gar zu alte Erfahrung! Was jener am liebsten will, ist diesem nichts nütze, was dieser verlangt, ist jenem ein Gift. Beyde Naturen dieses seltsamen Zweygespannes fodern laut ihr Recht, das keine der andern aufopfern will; die eine zieht dahin, die andere dorthin, und in der unselig seligen Mitte schwebt der Mensch, gerissen nach zwey Seiten, öfters von dem widerspänstigen Gespann zerrissen; unvermeidlich, immer die eine begünstigt mit der andern im tödlichen Kriege', Schubert, *Symbolik*, 69–70. See Tymms, 'Alternation of personality', p. 71.

81 Jürgen Barkhoff, *Magnetische Fiktionen. Literarisierungen des Mesmerismus in der Romantik*, Stuttgart: Metzler, 1995, pp. 244–5.

82 *Ibid.*, pp. 240–1.

83 Böckmann, *Archiv*, vol. 11, p. 81.

84 Barkhoff, *Magnetische Fiktionen*, p. 246.

85 Friedrich Röbbeling, *Kleists 'Käthchen von Heilbronn'* [Halle: Niemeyer, 1913], photo reprint, Tübingen: Niemeyer, 1973, p. 84.

86 *Ibid.*, pp. 81–6.

87 *Ibid.*, p. 83.

88 'So werden sich unsre Seelen auch in dem dritten Gegenstande zusammentreffen' (*KWS* 11. 517).

89 'Flucht ins Positive': Jochen Schmidt, *Heinrich von Kleist. Studien zu seiner poetischen Verfahrensweise*, Tübingen: Niemeyer, 1974, p. 245. On the play's irony: Gerd Ueding, 'Zweideutige Bilderwelt: *Das Käthchen von Heilbronn*', in Walter Hinderer (ed.), *Kleists Dramen. Neue Interpretationen*, Stuttgart:

Reclam, 1981, pp. 172–87; Anthony Stephens, *Heinrich von Kleist: The Dramas and Stories*, Oxford and Providence, RI: Berg, 1994, pp. 127–56.

90 Barkhoff, *Magnetische Fiktionen*, p. 247.

91 *The Prince of Homburg*, in Heinrich von Kleist, *Selected Writings*, ed. and trans. David Constantine, London: Dent, 1997, p. 138: '. . . wie weit ers treibt' (64).

92 *Ibid.*, p. 204: 'Die Schule dieser Tage durchgegangen, / Wollt ihrs zum vierten Male mit ihm wagen?' (1822–3).

93 See Spiridion Wukadinovic, *Kleist-Studien*, Stuttgart and Berlin: Cotta, 1904, pp. 173–92.

94 Kleist, *The Prince of Homburg*, trans. Constantine, pp. 174–5: 'Sieh, diese Augen, Tante, die dich anschaun, / Will man mit Nacht umschatten, diesen Busen / Mit mörderischen Kugeln mir durchbohren. / Bestellt sind auf dem Markte schon die Fenster, / Die auf das öde Schauspiel niedergehn, / Und der die Zukunft, auf des Lebens Gipfel, / Heut wie ein Feenreich, noch überschaut, / Liegt in zwei engen Brettern duftend morgen, / Und ein Gestein sagt dir von ihm: er war!' (984–92).

95 *Ibid.*, p. 141: '. . . von Gold und Silber strahlend'.

96 For Homburg's visions see 355–65, 777–81, 899–907, 981–92, 1030–6, 1039–52.

97 John M. Ellis, '*Prinz Friedrich von Homburg*. A Critical Study, Berkeley: University of California Press, 1970, pp. 7–9.

98 E. T. A. Hoffmann, *Briefwechsel*, ed. Friedrich Schnapp, 3 vols., Munich: Winkler, 1967–9, vol. 1, p. 166.

99 *Ibid.*, vol. 1, p. 335.

100 *Ibid.*, vol. 1, pp. 403–9.

101 *Ibid.*, vol. 1, p. 461.

102 '. . . die Wunder eines höheren Reichs verkünden' (*HSB* 54).

103 'die Erkenntnis der Duplizität . . . , von der eigentlich allein unser irdisches Sein bedingt ist' (*ibid.*, 54).

104 'Es gibt eine innere Welt, und die geistige Kraft, sie in voller Klarheit, in dem vollendetsten Glanze des regesten Lebens zu schauen, aber es ist unser irdisches Erbteil, daß eben die Außenwelt, in der wir eingeschachtet, als der Hebel wirkt, der jene Kraft in Bewegung setzt. Die inneren Erscheinungen gehen auf in dem Kreise, den die äußeren um uns bilden und den der Geist nur zu überfliegen vermag in dunklen geheimnisvollen Ahnungen, die sich nie zum deutlichen Bilde gestalten' (*ibid.*, 54).

105 'Jeder prüfe wohl, ob er auch wirklich das geschaut, was er zu verkünden unternommen, ehe er es wagt laut damit zu werden' (*ibid.*, 55).

106 Helmut Pfotenhauer, 'Exoterische und esoterische Poetik in E. T. A. Hoffmanns Erzählungen', *Jahrbuch der Jean-Paul-Gesellschaft* 17 (1982) 129–44.

107 '. . . alle mögliche Bücher über den Wahnsinn' (*HSB* 20).

108 Uwe Japp, 'Das serapiontische Prinzip', in Heinz Ludwig Arnold (ed.), *E. T. A. Hoffmann. Text + Kritik Sonderband*, Munich: Text + Kritik, 1992, pp. 63–75.

109 'Überdem dünkt mich, daß die merkwürdige Historie vom redenden Türken gerade von Haus aus fragmentarisch angelegt ist. Ich meine, die Fantasie des Lesers oder Hörers soll nur ein paar etwas heftig Rucke erhalten und dann sich selbst beliebig fortschwingen' (*HSB* 354).

110 'Nichts ist mir mehr zuwider als wenn in einer Erzählung, in einem Roman, der Boden, auf dem sich die fantastische Welt bewegt hat, zuletzt mit dem historischen Besen so rein gekehrt wird, daß auch kein Körnchen, kein Stäubchen bleibt, wenn man so ganz abgefunden nach Hause geht, daß man gar keine Sehnsucht empfindet noch einmal hinter die Gardinen zu kucken' (*ibid.*, 355).

111 'Hier ist es nun das Fantastische . . . das keck in das Alltagsleben hineinfährt, und alles zu oberst und unterst dreht' (*ibid.*, 90).

112 John Reddick, 'E. T. A. Hoffmann', in Alex Natan (ed.), *German Men of Letters. Volume v: Twelve Literary Essays*, London: Oswald Wolff, 1969, pp. 77–105.

113 '. . . ein gewisser ironisierender Ton . . . der den trägen Geist stachelt oder ihn vielmehr ganz unvermerkt mit gutmütiger Miene wie ein böser Schalk hineinverlockt in das fremde Gebiet' (*HSB* 254).

114 '. . . [der] versteckter Poet, dessen Äußerungen mit den Ansichten und den Neigungen des gewöhnlichen sinnlichen Lebens in einem beständigen ironischen Widerspruch stehen', Schubert, *Symbolik*, p. 56.

115 Compare *RR* 312–13.

116 Schubert, *Ansichten*, p. 350.

117 '. . . daß der Liebe höchste Seligkeit, die Erfüllung des Geheimnisses im Tode aufgeht', E. T. A. Hoffmann, *Die Elixiere des Teufels; Lebens-Ansichten des Katers Murr*, ed. Walter Müller-Seidel and Wolfgang Kron, Munich: Winkler, 1961, p. 153; cf. Schubert, *Ansichten*, p. 76.

118 Hoffmann, *Die Elixiere des Teufels*, p. 437; cf. *RR* 398–9.

119 '. . . und andere . . . die über Schlaf und Traum geschrieben und die ich nicht gelesen' (*HFN* 525).

120 Georg Reuchlein, *Bürgerliche Gesellschaft, Psychiatrie und Literatur: zur Entwicklung der Wahnsinnsthematik in der deutschen Literatur des späten 18. und frühen 19. Jahrhunderts*, Munich: Fink, 1986, pp. 358–61, and Auhuber, 'E. T. A. Hoffmanns produktive Rezeption der zeitgenössischen Medizin und Psychologie', *Mitteilungen der E. T. A. Hoffmann-Gesellschaft* 32 (1986), 89–99 (pp. 91–2).

121 '. . . das gänzliche Aufgeben des eignen Ichs, diese trostlose Abhängigkeit von einem fremden geistigen Prinzip . . . Grausen und Entsetzen' (*HSB* 273).

122 Tatar, *Spellbound*, pp. 130–40.

123 E. T. A. Hoffmann, *Tales*, ed. Victor Lange, The German Library 26, New York: Continuum, 1982, p. 17: 'innerlich erbeben'.

124 Auhuber, 'E. T. A. Hoffmanns produktive Rezeption der zeitgenössischen Medizin und Psychologie', p. 90; Maria M. Tatar, 'Mesmerism, Madness, and Death in E. T. A. Hoffmann's *Der goldne Topf*', *Studies in Romanticism* 14 (1975) 365–89.

125 Tatar, 'Mesmerism, madness, and death', p. 375.

126 *Ibid.*, pp. 375-6(cf. *RR* 192).

127 *Ibid.*, pp. 379-80(cf. *RR* 211–12).

128 Hoffmann, *Tales*, pp. 24–5: 'Schon war er in der Nähe des Koselschen Gartens, da setzte sich der Wind in den weiten Überrock und trieb die Schöße auseinander, daß sie wie ein Paar große Flügel in den Lüften flatterten, und es dem Studenten Anselmus, der verwunderungsvoll dem Archivarius nachsah, vorkam, als breite ein großer Vogel die Fittiche aus zum raschen Flug.– Wie der Student nun so in die Dämmerung hineinstarrte, da erhob sich mit krächzendem Geschrei ein weißgrauer Vogel hoch in die Lüfte, und er merkte nun wohl, daß das weiße Geflatter, was er noch immer für den davonschreitenden Archivarius gehalten, schon eben der Geier gewesen sein müsse, unerachtet er nicht begreifen konnte, wo denn der Archivarius mit einemmal hingeschwunden' (*HFN* 150).

129 Hartmut Steinecke, *Unterhaltsamkeit und Artistik. Neue Schreibarten in der deutschen Literatur von Hoffmann bis Heine*, Berlin: Erich Schmidt, 1998, p. 39.

130 Hoffmann, *Tales*, p. 52: '. . . die unglückliche Zeit, wenn die Sprache der Natur dem entarteten Geschlecht der Menschen nicht mehr verständlich [ist]' (*HFN* 177).

131 Hoffmann, *Tales*, p. 50: '. . . als sei er von der holden, lieblichen Gestalt so ganz und gar umschlungen und umwunden, daß er sich nur mit ihr regen und bewegen könne, und als sei es nur der Schlag ihres Pulses, der durch seine Fibern und Nerven zittere' (*HFN* 176).

132 Hoffmann, *Tales*, p. 54: 'doch . . . mußte er zuweilen unwillkürlich an Veronica denken, ja manchmal schien es ihm, als träte sie zu ihm hin und gestehe errötend, wie herzlich sie ihn liebe und wie sie danach trachte, ihn den Phantomen, von denen er nur geneckt und verhöhnt werde, zu entreißen. Zuweilen war es, als risse eine fremde plötzlich auf ihn einbrechende Macht ihn unwiderstehlich hin zur vergessenen Veronica, und er müsse ihr folgen, wohin sie nur wolle, als sei er festgekettet an das Mädchen' (*HFN* 181).

133 Hoffmann, *Tales*, p. 57: 'Da war es dem Anselmus als beginne ein Kampf in seinem Innern – Gedanken – Bilder – blitzten hervor und vergingen wieder – der Archivarius Lindhorst – Serpentina – die grüne Schlange – endlich wurde es ruhiger, und alles Verworrene fügte und gestaltete sich zum deutlichen Bewußtsein . . . Er wunderte sich selbst über seine Träumereien und schrieb sie lediglich seinem durch die Liebe zu Veronica exaltierten Seelenzustande sowie der Arbeit bei dem Archivarius Lindhorst zu, in dessen Zimmern es noch überdem so sonderbar betäubend dufte' (*HFN* 182).

134 Steinecke, *Unterhaltsamkeit*, p. 39.

135 The theory that he commits suicide seems to me to lack textual support; see James M. McGlathery, 'The suicide motif in E. T. A. Hoffmann's *Der goldne Topf*', *Monatshefte* 58 (1966) 115–23. On Anselmus's similarity to the narrator, see Steinecke, *Unterhaltsamkeit*, p. 40.

136 Kenneth Negus, *E. T. A. Hoffmann's Other World. The Romantic Author and his New Mythology*, Philadelphia: University of Pennsylvania Press, 1965, p. 92. My reading follows John M. Ellis, 'Clara, Nathanael and the narrator: interpreting Hoffmann's *Der Sandmann*', *Germanic Quarterly* 54 (1981), 1–18. Sigmund Freud, *The Standard Edition of the Complete Works of Sigmund Freud*, ed. James Strachey, 24 vols., London: Hogarth Press/ Institute of Psychoanalysis, 1957, vol. XVII, pp. 231–2.

137 Stefan Ringel writes of an 'alternating erosion and restoration of a closed image of a finite reality' ('Abfolge von Irritation und Wiederherstellung des geschlossenen Bildes einer endlichen Wirklichkeit'), *Realität und Einbildungskraft im Werk E. T. A. Hoffmanns*, Cologne: Georg Büchner, 1997, p. 201.

138 Hoffmann, *Tales*, p. 286: 'Gibt es eine dunkle Macht, die so recht feindlich und verräterisch einen Faden in unser Inneres legt, woran sie uns dann festpackt und fortzieht auf einem gefahrvollen, verderblichen Wege, den wir sonst nicht betreten haben würden –gibt es eine solche Macht, so muß sie in uns sich wie wir selbst gestalten, ja unser Selbst werden; denn nur *so* glauben wir an sie und träumen ihr den Platz ein, dessen sie bedarf, um jenes geheime Werk zu vollbringen' (*HFN* 16–17).

139 Hoffmann, *Tales*, p. 286: '. . . alles Entsetzliche und Schreckliche . . . nur in Deinem Innern vorging' (*HFN* 15).

140 *Ibid.*, p. 293: '. . . der Tod, der mit Klaras Augen ihn freundlich anschaut' (*HFN* 24).

141 *Ibid.*, p. 294: 'Du lebloses, verdammtes Automat!' (*HFN* 25).

142 Ellis, 'Clara, Nathanael and the narrator', pp. 10–11.

143 Hoffmann, *Tales*, p. 283: '. . . ein dunkles Verhängnis wirklich einen trüben Wolkenschleier über mein Leben gehängt hat, den ich vielleicht nur sterbend zerreiße' (*HFN* 13).

144 Silvio Vietta, 'Romantikparodie und Realitätsbegriff im Erzählwerk E. T. A. Hoffmanns', *Zeitschrift für deutsche Philologie* 100 (1981), 575–91(pp. 581–2).

7   AFTER ROMANTICISM: THE PHYSIOLOGICAL UNCONSCIOUS

1 Lancelot Law Whyte, *The Unconscious before Freud*, London: Friedmann, 1978, p. 71.

2 Schopenhauer cited: Sigmund Freud, *The Standard Edition of the Complete Works of Sigmund Freud*, ed. James Strachey, London: Hogarth Press / Institute of Psychoanalysis, 1957, vol. IV, pp. 36, 66, 90, 263; his influence denied: vol. XIV, p. 15.

3 Christopher Janaway, *Self and World in Schopenhauer's Philosophy*, Oxford: Oxford University Press, 1989, p. 70–1.

4 '*Thing in itself* means what is present independently of our perception, hence what actually exists. For Democritus this means organised matter; it was still essentially that for Locke; for Kant it was = X, for me *will*.' ('*Ding an sich* bedeutet das unabhängig von unserer Wahrnehmung Vorhandene, also das eigentlich Seiende. Dies war dem Demokritos die geformte Materie; dasselbe war es im Grunde noch Locke, Kanten war es = X, mir Wille'; *SWL* v.109).

5 Mathew Bell, *Goethe's Naturalistic Anthropology: Man and Other Plants*, Oxford: Oxford University Press, 1994, pp. 184–8, 211–28.

6 Arthur Schopenhauer, *The World as Will and Representation*, trans. E. F. J. Payne, 2 vols., New York: Dover, 1969, vol. 1, p. 330: 'Die Genitalien sind viel mehr als irgendein anderes äußeres Glied des Leibes bloß dem Willen und gar nicht der Erkenntnis unterworfen . . . die Genitalien [sind] der eigentliche *Brennpunkt* des Willens und folglich der entgegengesetzte Pol des Gehirns, des Repräsentanten der Erkenntnis, d.i. der anderen Seite der Welt, der Welt als Vorstellung. Jene sind das lebenerhaltende, der Zeit endloses Leben zusichernde Prinzip . . . Die Erkenntnis dagegen gibt die Möglichkeit der Aufhebung des Wollens, der Erlösung durch Freiheit, der Überwindung und Vernichtung der Welt' (*SWL* 1.452; see also *SWL* v.200–1).

7 *Ibid.*, vol. 1, p. 309: 'Alles Streben entspringt aus Mangel, aus Unzufriedenheit mit seinem Zustande, ist also Leiden, solange es nicht befriedigt ist; keine Befriedigung ist aber dauernd, vielmehr ist sie stets nur der Anfangspunkt eines neuen Strebens. Das Streben sehen wir überall vielfach gehemmt, überall kämpfend; solange also immer als Leiden: kein letztes Ziel des Strebens, also kein Maß und Ziel des Leidens' (*SWL* 1.425).

8 *Ibid.*, vol. 1, p. 315: 'Die unaufhörlichen Bemühungen, das Leiden zu verbannen, leisten nichts weiter, als daß es seine Gestalt verändert. Diese ist ursprünglich Mangel, Not, Sorge um die Erhaltung des Lebens. Ist es, was sehr schwer hält, geglückt, den Schmerz in dieser Gestalt zu verdrängen, so stellt er sogleich sich in tausend andern ein, abwechselnd nach Alter und Umständen – als Geschlechtstrieb, leidenschaftliche Liebe, Eifersucht, Neid, Haß, Angst, Ehrgeiz, Geldgeiz, Krankheit usw. usw. Kann er endlich in keiner andern Gestalt Eingang finden, so kommt er im traurigen, grauen Gewand des Überdrusses und der Langenweile, gegen welche denn mancherlei versucht wird. Gelingt es endlich, diese zu verscheuchen, so wird es schwerlich geschehn, ohne dabei den Schmerz in einer der vorigen Gestalten wieder einzulassen und so den Tanz von vorne zu beginnen; denn zwischen Schmerz und Langerweile wird jedes Menschenleben hin und her geworfen' (*SWL* 1.432).

9 For examples of Carus's paintings, see Marianne Prause, *Carl Gustav Carus. Leben und Werk*, Berlin: Deutscher Verlag für Kunstwissenschaft, 1968.

10 'Der Schlüssel zur Erkenntnis vom bewußten Seelenleben liegt in der Region des Unbewußtseins' (p. 1).

11 Eduard von Hartmann, *Philosophie des Unbewußten. Speculative Resultate nach inductiv-naturwissenschaftlicher Methode*, 3 vols., 12th edn, Leipzig: Kröner, 1923 [1860], vol. 1, pp. viii, 32–3. On Klages, see e.g. Ludwig Klages, *Zur Ausdruckslehre und Characterkunde*, Heidelberg: Kampmann, 1926, p. 310. For Jung on Carus, see the entries for Carus in the index of C. G. Jung, *The Collected Works of C. G. Jung*, ed. H. Read *et al.*, 20 vols. London and New York: Routledge & Kegan Paul, 1953–79, vol. xx.

12 Reinhard Abeln, *Unbewußtes und Unterbewußtes bei C. G. Carus und Aristoteles*, Meisenheim am Glan: Anton Hain, 1970, p. 7; Werner Felber and Otto Bach, 'Carl Gustav Carus und das Unbewußte. Ein philosophisch-psychologisches Entwicklungskonzept im 19. Jahrhundert', in Günter Heidel (ed.), *Carl Gustav Carus: Opera et efficacitas. Beiträge des wissenschaftlichen Symposiums zu Werk und Vermächtnis von Carl Gustav Carus am 22. September 1989*, Dresden: Carus-Akademie, 1990, pp. 117–26 (p. 121).

13 Felber and Bach, 'Carl Gustav Carus und das Unbewußte', p. 120.

14 '. . . der Geist [ist] nichts von der Natur Verschiedenes, nur ihre reinste Ausgeburt und daher ihr Symbol, ihre Sprache' (*CVP* 39–40).

15 Christoph Bernoulli, *Die Psychologie von Carl Gustav Carus und deren geistesgeschichtliche Bedeutung*, Jena: Diederichs, 1925, p. 8.

16 Abeln, *Unbewußtes und Unterbewußtes*, p. 7.

17 '. . . das Vorhandensein eines geistigen Bildes ihrer Daseinsform vor dem Dasein selbst', 'bestimmende Idee', die bedingende Ur-Sache ihres Daseins' (*CVP* 24).

18 *CPS* 4; see also Carl Gustav Carus, *Physis. Zur Geschichte des leiblichen Lebens*, Stuttgart: Scheitlin, 1851, p. 18.

19 '. . . sie sind als gewissermaßen zwei Hälften unseres irdischen Daseyns bildend zu betrachten, aber keinesweges so, daß die eine ein blos abstraktes, blos gedankenhaftes, die andere ein blos aus materiellen Elementen maschinenartig zusammengehaltenes Wesen darstellte, sondern so, daß *jedes* ein wahrhaft *organisches* Leben zeigt, d. h. daß es alle drei Elemente enthält, welche Aristoteles schon als die Criterien eines jeden Lebendigen darstellt, nämlich die Idee, das ätherische Material und die Form, welche letztere durch die Idee ausgedrückt wird', Carus, *Physis*, p. 482.

20 '. . . wie verschiedene Gelehrte in verschiedenen Studirzimmern' (*CVP* 22).

21 '. . . alle Momente ihrer [i.e. der Seele] Entwickelung' (*CVP* 24).

22 'Denn eigentlich unternehmen wir umsonst, das Wesen eines Dinges auszudrücken. Wirkungen werden wir gewahr, und eine vollständige Geschichte dieser Wirkungen umfaßte wohl allenfalls das Wesen jenes Dinges. Vergebens bemühen wir uns, den Charakter eines Menschen zu schildern; man stelle dagegen seine Handlungen, seine Thaten zusammen, und ein Bild des Charakters wird uns entgegentreten' (*CVP* 23, quoting *WA* 11.1.ix).

23 Johann Wolfgang Goethe, *Faust. The First Part of the Tragedy, with the Unpublished Scenarios for the Walpurgis Night and the Urfaust*, trans. John R. Williams, Ware: Wordsworth Editions, 1999, lines 346–9, pp. 12–13.

24 Das Charakteristische der Natur ist also ein *ewiges Werden*, und wenn der Dichter sagt:

> Das Werdende, das ewig wirkt und lebt,
> Umfaß euch mit der Liebe holden Schranken,
> Und was in schwankender Erscheinung schwebt,
> Befestiget mit daurenden Gedanken.

So kann man nicht schöner das Wesen der Naturerscheinung, und wie sich die wissenschaftliche Betrachtung zu demselben verhalte, ausdrücken. (*CVP* 11).

25 Johann Wolfgang Von Goethe, *Selected Poems*, trans. John Whaley, London: Dent, 1998, p. 123:

> Daemon ΔΑΙΜΩΝ
> Wie an dem Tag, der dich der Welt verliehen,
> Die Sonne stand zum Gruße der Planeten,
> Bist alsobald und fort und fort gediehen
> Nach dem Gesetz, wonach du angetreten.
> So mußt du sein, dir kannst du nicht entfliehen,
> So sagten schon Sibyllen, so Propheten;
> Und keine Zeit und keine Macht zerstückelt
> Geprägte Form, die lebend sich entwickelt. (*CPS* 75)

26 Abeln, *Unbewußtes und Unterbewußtes*, pp. 15–16.

27 '. . . sie [*sc.* die unbewußte Seele] ist in gewissem Maße andauernd, sie ist umgestaltend, immer zerstörend und neu bildend' (*CPS* 24).

28 Abeln, *Unbewußtes und Unterbewußtes*, p. 34.

29 '. . . die Erscheinung einer künftig als Bewußtsein sich offenbarenden Strahlung des Seelenlebens prometheïsch sich vorbereitet' (*CPS* 37).

30 '. . . prometheïsches Unbewußtes Walten der Idee' (*CPS* 104).

31 '. . . das epimetheïsche Festgehaltensein aller Anregungen des Seelenlebens' (*CPS* 104–5).

32 '. . . das unbestimmte Gefühl des Zustandes der eignen Organisation . . . , eine Wahrnehmung oder ein Sinn, welche wir mit dem Namen des Gemeingefühls zu nennen pflegen' (*CPS* 111).

33 '. . . die Wecker des Seelenlebens' (*CVP* 48).

34 Goethe, *Faust*, lines 1172–3, pp. 36–7. 'Ich finde nicht die Spur / Von einem Geist, und alles ist Dressur' (*CVP* 48).

35 'So kommen wir zu dem Erkenntniß, daß nur die Menschheit der wahre Mensch sei, und jeder einzelne Mensch nur ein besonderes Organ dieses höhern Ganzen, daß folglich die einzelne menschliche Seele angesehen werden müsse als eine der unendlichen im Geiste der Menschheit aufsteigenden und sich verwirklichenden Ideen' (*CVP* 85).

36 '. . . eine allgemeine Zeit seines Daseins' (*CPS* 25).

37 ' . . . [das] Prometheïsche und Epimetheïsche der unbewußt schaffenden Idee' (*CPS* 27).

38 'Alles, was wir im bewußten Leben Gedächtniß, Erinnerung nennen, und noch weit mehr alles, was wir in dieser Region Voraussehen, Vorauswissen nennen, [bleibt] doch gar weit zurück hinter der Festigkeit und Sicherheit, mit welcher in der Region des unbewußten Lebens dieses epimetheïsche und prometheïsche Princip, dieses Erinnerungs- und Vorahnungsvermögen, noch ohne alles Bewußtsein einer Gegenwart, geltend macht.' (*CPS* 28).

39 Carl Gustav Carus, *Briefe über Goethes 'Faust'*, Hamburg: Kurt Saucke, 1837 (first published Leipzig: Gerhard Fleischer, 1835); *Göthe. Zu dessen näherem Verständniß*, Leipzig: August Weichardt, 1843; *Goethe, dessen Bedeutung für unsere und die kommende Zeit*, Vienna: Wilhelm Braumüller, 1863.

40 ' . . . das darin ausgesprochene genetische Princip der Seele', Carus, *Briefe über Goethes 'Faust'*, p. 352.

41 *Faust*, trans. Williams, 308–11: 'Wenn er mir jetzt auch nur verworren dient, / So werd ich ihn bald in die Klarheit führen. / Weiß doch der Gärtner, wenn das Bäumchen grünt, / Daß Blüt und Frucht die künft'gen Jahre zieren', Carus, *Briefe über Goethes 'Faust'*, pp. 48–50.

42 Carus, *Briefe über Goethes 'Faust'*, p. 35.

43 *Ibid.*, p. 49.

44 ' . . . die qualvolle Sehnsucht des alle Höhen und Tiefen erfassen wollenden Geistes' (*ibid.*, p. 48).

45 'Nehmen wir nun eine Feuer-Seele, gleich der des Faust, ihrer innersten Eigenthümlichkeit nach von unbedingtem Streben gegen ächtes Freisein in Läuterung von allem Ungemäßen gerichtet, denken wir aber in dieser Seele zugleich eine heftige Anziehung gegen das Drängen der Erscheinungswelt und überdieß sie in eines jener dissonirenden Verhältnisse des Lebens verwiesen, dessen Druck uns nur gerechtfertigt wird, wenn wir daran gedenken, daß ohne dissonirende Akkorde im Einzelnen keine befriedigende Fortschreitung höherer Harmonie im ganzen möglich wäre, und es wird uns begreiflich, wie schmerzlich, krankhaft und stürmisch die Entwicklung einer solchen Seele durch tausendfältig bindende, lösende und wieder bindende Vorgänge zu endlicher Freiheit sich hindurch winden müsse, wie endlich suchend die Arme oft durch tausendfältige, zu Leiden sich wandelnde Freuden aufstreben müsse, um zu höherer gottsinniger Freiheit zu gelangen', Carus, *Briefe über Goethes 'Faust'*, pp. 48–50.

46 John Reddick, *Georg Büchner: The Shattered Whole*, Oxford: Oxford University Press, 1994, p. 39.

47 Georg Büchner, *On Cranial Nerves* [*Über Schädelnerven*], in: *Complete Plays, 'Lenz' and Other Writings*, trans. John Reddick, Harmondsworth: Penguin, 1993, p. 184.

48 Letter to Gutzkow, November 1835: 'My brain is being addled by the study of philosophy; I am getting to know the paltriness of the human mind from yet another side. But so be it! If we could only imagine that the holes in our trousers were palace windows, We could live like kings; as it is, we're

miserably cold', Büchner, *Complete Plays, 'Lenz' and Other Writings*, p. 203; 'Ich werde ganz dumm in dem Studium der Philosophie; ich lerne die Armseligkeit des menschlichen Geistes wieder von einer neuen Seite kennen. Meinetwegen! Wenn man sich nur einbilden könnte, die Löcher in unsern Hosen seien Palastfenster, so könnte man schon wie ein König leben, so aber friert man erbärmlich', Georg Büchner, *Sämtliche Werke*, ed., H. Poschmann, 2 vols., Frankfurt am Main: Deutscher Klassiker Verlag, 1992–9, vol. II, p. 420. A schoolmate reported his 'sometimes arrogant disdain for the conjuring tricks of Hegelian dialectics and definitions' ('manchmal übermüthiger Hohn über Taschenspielerkünste hegelscher Dialektik und Begriffsformulationen'), Büchner, *Sämtliche Werke*, vol. II, p. 934. See also the letter to his family of February 1834: 'Intellect is in any case only a very minor aspect of our inner being' Büchner, *Complete Plays, 'Lenz', and Other Writings*, p.92 'der *Verstand* . . . ist nur eine sehr geringe Seite unseres geistigen Wesens' (*BWL* 253).

49 Büchner, *Sämtliche Werke*, vol. II, p. 955. On the connection between philosophy and politics, see Reddick, *Büchner*, pp. 36–7.

50 Reddick, *Büchner*, p. 336.

51 Büchner, *Woyzeck*, in *Complete Plays, 'Lenz' and Other Writings*, p. 129: 'Warum hat Gott die Mensche geschaffe? Das hat auch sei Nutz. Was würde der Landmann, der Schuhmacher, der Schneider anfange, wenn er für die Mensche kei Schuh, kei Hose machte? Warum hat Gott den Mensche das Gefühl der Schamhaftigkeit eingeflößt? Damit der Schneider lebe kann' (*BWL* 138).

52 Reddick, *Büchner*, pp. 10, 337–8.

53 Büchner, *Lenz*, in *Complete Plays, 'Lenz' and Other Writings*, p. 149: 'Man versuche es einmal und senke sich in das Leben des Geringsten und gebe es wieder, in den Zuckungen, den Andeutungen, dem ganz feinen, kaum bemerkten Mienenspiel' (*BWL* 76).

54 *Ibid.*, p. 149: 'Es sind die prosaischsten Menschen unter der Sonne; aber die Gefühlsader ist in fast allen Menschen gleich, nur ist die Hülle mehr oder weniger dicht, durch die sie brechen muß. Man muß nur Aug und Ohren dafür haben' (*BWL* 76).

55 Büchner, *Woyzeck*, in *Complete plays, 'Lenz' and Other Writings*, pp. 120–1:

> TAMBOUR-MAJOR: Sapperment, wir wollen eine Zucht von
> Tambour-Majors anlegen. He? *Er umfaßt sie*
> MARIE: *verstimmt*. Laß mich!
> TAMBOUR-MAJOR: Wild Tier!
> MARIE: *heftig*. Rühr mich an! (H4, 6; *BWL* 150).

56 Büchner, *Woyzeck*, in *Complete Plays, 'Lenz' and Other Writings* p. 121: 'Ich bin ruhig, ganz ruhig, mein Puls hat seine gewöhnlichen 60, und ich sag's Ihm mit der größten Kaltblütigkeit. Behüte wer wird sich über einen Menschen ärgern! ein Menschen!' (H4, 8; *BWL* 151).

57 Reddick, *Büchner*, p. 328.

58 Büchner, *Woyzeck*, in *Complete Plays, 'Lenz' and Other Writings*, p. 113: 'Es geht hinter mir, unter mir (*stampft auf den Boden*) hohl, hörst du? Alles hohle da unten' (H4, 1; *BWL* 145).

59 'Sieh um dich! Alles starr, fest, finster, was regt sich dahinter. Etwas, was wir nicht fasse. Geht still, was uns von Sinnen bringt, aber ich hab's aus' (H2, 2; *BWL* 136).

60 'Draußen liegt was. Im Boden' (H1, 13; *BWL* 131).

61 Büchner, *Woyzeck*, in *Complete Plays, 'Lenz' and Other Writings*, p. 125: 'Hm! Ich seh nichts, ich seh nichts. O, man müßt's sehen. man müßt's greifen könne mit Fäusten . . . Eine Sünde so dick und so breit . . . ' (H4, 7; *BWL* 150).

62 'Jeder Mensch ist ein Abgrund, es schwindelt einem, wenn man hinabsieht' (H2, 8; *BWL* 143).

Bibliography

PRIMARY SOURCES (*up to c. 1850*)

Abel, J. F., *Sammlung und Erklärung merkwürdiger Erscheinungen aus dem menschlichen Leben*, 3 vols., Frankfurt and Leipzig: no publ., 1784 (vol. I); Stuttgart: Erhart, 1787–90 (vols. II and III).

Alt, Peter-André, *Schiller. Leben-Werk-Zeit*, 2 vols., Munich: Beck, 2000.

Aristotle, *De anima (On the Soul)*, trans. Hugh Lawson-Tancred, London: Penguin, 1986.

Auenbrugger, Leopold, *Von der stillen Wuth oder dem Triebe zum Selbstmorde als einer wirklichen Krankheit, mit Original-Beobachtungen und Anmerkungen*, Dessau: Buchhandlung der Gelehrten, 1783.

Baumgarten, Alexander Gottlieb, *Metaphysica*, 2nd edn, Halle: Hemmerde, 1743.

Bilfinger, Georg Bernhard, *Dilucidationes philosophicae de Deo, anima humana, mundo, et generalibus rerum affectionibus*, 4th edn, Tübingen: Cotta, 1768.

Blanckenburg, Friedrich von, *Versuch über den Roman* [Leipzig and Liegnitz: Siegert, 1774]. Photo reprint, Stuttgart: Metzler, 1965.

Böckmann, Johann Lorenz (ed.), *Archiv für Magnetismus und Somnambulismus*, 8 vols., Strasbourg: Akademische Buchhandlung, 1787–8.

Broughton, John, *Psychologia; or, An Account of the Nature of the Rational Soul*, London: Bennet, 1703.

Büchner, Georg, *Complete Plays, 'Lenz' and Other Writings*, trans. John Reddick, Harmondsworth: Penguin, 1993.

Sämtliche Werke, ed. H. Poschmann, 2 vols., Frankfurt am Main: Deutscher Klassiker Verlag, 1992–9.

Carus, Carl Gustav, *Briefe über Goethes 'Faust'*, Hamburg: Kurt Saucke, 1837 (first published Leipzig: Gerhard Fleischer, 1835).

Göthe. Zu dessen näherem Verständniß, Leipzig: August Weichardt, 1843.

Physis. Zur Geschichte des leiblichen Lebens, Stuttgart: Scheitlin, 1851.

Goethe, dessen Bedeutung für unsere und die kommende Zeit, Vienna: Wilhelm Braumüller, 1863.

Casmannus, Otho, *Secunda pars Anthropologiae: hoc est, Fabrica humani corporis methodice descripta*, Hanau: Anton, 1596.

Angelographia, seu commentationum disceptationumque [*sic*] *physicarum prodromus problematicus de angelis seu creatis spiritibus a corpore consortio abiunctis ... concinnatus*, Frankfurt am Main: Palthen, 1597.

Chauvinus, Stephanus, *Lexicon philosophicum*, 2nd edn, Leeuwarden: Halma, 1713.

Condillac, *Oeuvres philosophiques*, ed. G. LeRoy, 3 vols., Paris: Presses Universitaires de France, 1947–51.

Corneille, Thomas, *Le dictionnaire des arts et des sciences*, 4 vols., Paris: Coignard, 1694.

Coward, William, *Second Thoughts Concerning the Human Soul, demonstrating the Notion of Human Soul, as believ'd to be a spiritual, immortal substance, united to human body, to be a plain heathenish invention* [London]: 1702.

Cudworth, Ralph, *The True Intellectual System of the Universe: Wherein All the Reason and Philosophy of Atheism is Confuted, and Its Impossibility Demonstrated, with a Treatise Concerning Eternal and Immutable Morality*, trans. John Harrison, 3 vols., London: Thomas Tegg, 1845.

Deleuze, J. P. F., *Practical Instruction in Animal Magnetism*, trans. T. C. Hartshorn, Providence, RI: Cranston, 1837.

Diderot, D. and J. le R. d'Alembert (eds.), *Encyclopédie; ou, Dictionnaire raisonné des arts, des sciences, et des métiers*, 17 vols., Paris: no publ., 1751–65.

Dorsch, Anton Joseph, *Beiträge zum Studium der Philosophie. I. Heft. Erste Linien einer Geschichte der Weltweisheit*, Mainz: Alef, 1787.

Einsiedel, August von, *Ideen*, ed. W. Dobbek, Berlin: Akademie, 1957.

Encyclopædia Britannica; or, A Dictionary of Arts and Sciences, compiled upon a new plan. In which the different Sciences and Arts are digested into distinct Treatises and Systems; and the various Technical Terms, &c. are explained as they occur in the order of the Alphabet, 3 vols., Edinburgh: Bell and Macfarquhar, 1771.

Eschenmayer, A. C. A., *Versuch die scheinbare Magie des thierischen Magnetismus aus physischen und psychologischen Gründen zu erklären*, Vienna: Haas, 1816.

Psychologie, ed. P. Krumme, Frankfurt am Main, Berlin, and Vienna: Ullstein, 1982.

Ficino, Marsilio, *Théologie platonicienne de l'immortalité des âmes*, ed. Raymond Marcel, 3 vols., Paris: Belles-Lettres, 1964–70.

De vita libri tres, ed. Martin Plessner, Hildesheim: Olms, 1978.

Commentarium in Phedrum, in Michael J. B. Allen, *Marsilio Ficino and the Phaedran Charioteer*, Berkeley and Los Angeles: University of California Press, 1981, pp. 65–129.

Gmelin, Eberhard, *Über thierischen Magnetismus. In einem Brief an Herrn Geheimen Rath Hoffmann in Mainz*, 2 vols., Tübingen: Heerbrandt, 1787.

Materialien für die Anthropologie, 2 vols., Tübingen: Cotta, 1791; Heilbronn and Rothenburg/Tauber: Claß, 1793.

Goclenius, Rodolphus, ΨΥΧΟΛΟΓΙΑ: *hoc est, De hominis perfectione, animo, et in primis ortu huius, commentationes et disputationes quorundum Theologorum & Philosophorum nostrae aetatis, quos versa pagina ostendit*, Marburg: Egenolph, 1590.

Lexicon philosophicum, quo tanquam clave philosophiae fores aperiuntur, Frankfurt am Main: Becker, 1613.

Lexicon philosophicum graecum, opus sane omnibus philosophiae alumnis valde necessarium cum perspicientia philosophysici sermonis plurimum etiam ad cognitionem rerum utile, Marburg: Hutwelcker, 1615.

Godartius, Petrus, *Lexicon philosophicum: item, accuratissima totius philosophiae summa*, 2 vols., 2nd edn, Paris: De la Caille, 1675.

Goethe, Johann Wolfgang von, *The Sorrows of Young Werther*, trans. Michael Hulse, Harmondsworth: Penguin, 1989.

Selected Poems, trans. John Whaley, London: Dent, 1998.

Faust. The First Part of the Tragedy, with the Unpublished Scenarios for the Walpurgis Night and the Urfaust, trans. John R. Williams, Ware: Wordsworth Editions, 1999.

Harris, John, *Lexicon technicum; or, An Universal English Dictionary of the Arts and Sciences: Explaining Not Only the Terms of Art but the Arts Themselves*, London: Daniel Brown *et al.*, 1704.

Helvétius, Claude-Adrien, *Oeuvres complètes*, 3 vols., Paris: Lepetit, 1818.

Herbart, Johann Friedrich, *Sämtliche Werke*, ed. Karl Kehrbach and Otto Flügel, 19 vols., Aalen: Scientia, 1989.

Hoffmann, E. T. A., *Die Elixiere des Teufels; Lebens-Ansichten des Katers Murr*, ed. Walter Müller-Seidel and Wolfgang Kron, Munich: Winkler, 1961.

Briefwechsel, ed. Friedrich Schnapp, 3 vols., Munich: Winkler, 1967–9.

Tales, ed. Victor Lange, The German Library 26, New York: Continuum, 1982.

Hufeland, Christoph Wilhelm, *Über Sympathie*, Weimar: Landes-Industrie-Comptoir, 1811.

Jacobi, Friedrich Heinrich, *Werke*, 6 vols. [Leipzig: Fleischer, 1812–25], photo reprint, Darmstadt: Wissenschaftliche Buchgesellschaft, 1976.

Jakob, Ludwig Heinrich, *Grundriß der Erfahrungsseelenlehre*, Halle: Hemmerde und Schwetschke, 1791.

Johnson, Samuel, *Samuel Johnson*, ed. D. Greene, Oxford: Oxford University Press, 1984.

Kant, Immanuel, *Critique of Pure Reason*, trans. Paul Guyer and Allen W. Wood, The Cambridge Edition of the Works of Immanuel Kant, Cambridge: Cambridge University Press, 1998.

Ketter, Gottfried, *Der grüne Heinrich*, ed. C. Heselhaus, Munich: Hanser, 1958.

Kieser, Georg, *System des Tellurismus oder thierischen Magnetismus. Ein Handbuch für Naturforscher und Aerzte*, 2 vols., Leipzig: Herbig, 1822.

Kleist, Heinrich von, *Five Plays*, trans. Martin Greenberg, New Haven and London: Yale University Press, 1988.

Selected Writings, ed. and trans. David Constantine, London: Dent, 1997.

Klinger, Friedrich Maximilian, *Werke. Historisch-kritische Gesamtausgabe*, ed. Sander L. Gilman *et al.*, Neudruck deutscher Literaturwerke N. F., 21 vols. (in progress), Tübingen: Niemeyer, 1978–.

Kluge, Carl Alexander Ferdinand, *Versuch einer Darstellung des animalischen Magnetismus als Heilmittel*, Berlin: Realschulbuchhandlung, 1811.

Leibniz, G. W., *New Essays on Human Understanding*, trans. P. Remnant and J. Bennett, Cambridge: Cambridge University Press, 1981.

Philosophical Essays, ed. R. Ariew and D. Garber, Indianapolis: Hackett, 1989.

Leisewitz, Johann Anton, *Julius von Tarent*, ed. W. Keller, Stuttgart: Reclam, 1965.

Lenz, J. M. R., *Werke*, ed. K. Lauer, Munich: dtv, 1992.

Philosophische Vorlesungen für empfindsame Seelen. Faksimiledruck der Ausgabe Frankfurt und Leipzig 1780, ed. Christoph Weiss, St Ingbert: Röhrig, 1994.

Lessing, Gotthold Ephraim, *Emilia Galotti*, trans. Anna Johanna Gode von Aesch, in G. E. Lessing, *'Nathan the Wise', 'Minna von Barnhelm', and Other Plays and Writings*, ed. Peter Demetz, The German Library 12, New York: Continuum, 1991.

Lessing, Gotthold Ephraim, Moses Mendelssohn and Friedrich Nicolai, *Briefwechsel über das Trauerspiel*, ed. Jochen Schulte-Sasse, Munich: Winkler, 1972.

Lucretius, *Von der Natur der Dinge*, trans. K. L. von Knebel, Leipzig: Göschen, 1821.

On the Nature of the Universe, trans. R. E. Latham, rev. John Godwin, Harmondsworth: Penguin, 1994.

Meier, Georg Friedrich, *Beweis, daß keine Materie dencken könne*, Halle: Hemmerde, 1743.

Gedancken von Schertzen [Halle: Hemmerde, 1744], photo reprint, Text und Kontext Sonderreihe 3, Copenhagen: Text und Kontext, 1977.

Anfangsgründe aller schönen Wissenschaften, 3 vols., Halle: Hemmerde, 1748.

Versuch einer Erklärung des Nachtwandelns, Halle: Hemmerde, 1758.

Mendelssohn, Moses, *Gesammelte Schriften. Jubiläumsausgabe*, 27 vols., Stuttgart: Frommann-Holzboog, 1991.

Mesmer, Franz Anton, *Mesmerismus. Oder System der Wechselwirkungen, Theorie und Anwendung des thierischen Magnetismus als die allgemeine Heilkunde zur Erhaltung des Menschen*, ed. Karl Christian Wolfart, Berlin: Nicolai, 1814.

Abhandlung über die Entdeckung des thierischen Magnetismus [Karlsruhe edn of 1781], Tübingen: Edition Diskord, 1985.

Micraelius, Johannes, *Lexicon philosophicum terminorum philosophis usitatorum ordine alphabetico sic digestorum, ut inde facile liceat cognosse, praesertim si tam latinus, quam graecus, index praemissus non negligatur, quid in singulis disciplinis quomodo sit distinguendum et definiendum*, Jena: Mamphrasius, 1653.

Montegre, A. J. de, *Du magnétisme animal et de ses partisans, ou recueil de pièces importantes sur cet objet*, Paris: Colas, 1812.

Moritz, Karl Philipp, *Anton Reiser. A Psychological Novel*, trans. Ritchie Robertson, Harmondsworth: Penguin, 1997.

'Versuch einer Vereinigung aller schönen Künste und Wissenschaften unter dem Begriff des in sich Vollendeten' *Berlinische Monatsschrift* 5.3 (March, 1785), 225–36.

Nicolai, Ernst Anton, *Wirckungen der Einbildungskraft in den menschlichen Cörper aus den Gründen der neuern Weltweisheit hergeleitet*, Halle: Hemmerde, 1744.

Peacock, Thomas Love *Nightmare Abbey; Crotchet Castle*, Harmondsworth: Penguin, 1969.

Phylopsyches, Alethius [*sic*], *ΨΥΧΗΛΟΓΙΑ or, Serious Thoughts on Second Thoughts ...*, London: John Nutt, 1702.

Platner, Ernst, *Anthropologie für Ärzte und Weltweise*, Leipzig: Dyck, 1772.
   Philosophische Aphorismen, nebst einigen Anleitungen zur philosophischen Geschichte, 2 vols., Leipzig: Schwickert, 1776–82.

Plotinus, *The Enneads*, trans. Stephen MacKenna, London: Faber, 1956.

Pockels, Carl Friedrich, *Denkwürdigkeiten zur Bereicherung der Erfahrungs-seelenlehre und Characterkunde. Ein Lesebuch für Gelehrte und Ungelehrte. Erste Sammlung*, Halle: Renger, 1794.

Reid, Thomas, *Essays of the Intellectual Powers of Man*, ed. A. D. Woozley, London: Macmillan, 1941.

Reil, Johann Christian and Johann Christoph Hoffbauer (eds.), *Beyträge zur Beförderung einer Curmethode auf psychischem Wege*, 2 vols., Vienna: Doll, 1808.

Rousseau, Jean-Jacques, *The Confessions*, trans. J. M. Cohen, Harmondsworth: Penguin, 1953.
   Reveries of the Solitary Walker, trans. Peter France, Harmondsworth: Penguin, 1979.

Schiller, Friedrich, *On the Aesthetic Education of Man. In a Series of Letters*, ed. and trans. E. M. Wilkinson and L. A. Willoughby, Oxford: Oxford University Press, 1967.
   Intrigue and Love, trans. Charles E. Passage, New York: Ungar, 1971.
   'The Robbers' and 'Wallenstein', trans. F. J. Lamport, Harmondsworth: Penguin, 1979.
   Plays, ed. Walter Hinderer, The German Library 15, New York: Continuum, 1983.
   Mary Stuart; Joan of Arc, trans. Robert David MacDonald, Birmingham, UK: Oberon, 1987.

Schlegel, Friedrich, *Schriften zur Literatur*, ed. W. Rasch, Munich: Hanser, 1970.

Schmid, C. C. E., 'Kann Psychologie als eine eigene selbständige Wissenschaft noch ferner geduldet werden?' *Anthropologisches Journal* 3 (1803), 93–127.

Schopenhauer, Arthur, *The World as Will and Representation*, trans. E. F. J. Payne, 2 vols., New York: Dover, 1969.

Schubert, Gotthilf Heinrich von, *Ansichten von der Nachtseite der Natur-wissenschaft*, Dresden: Arnold, 1808.
   Die Symbolik des Traumes [1814], photo reprint, Heidelberg: Schneider, 1968.

Steffens, Henrik, 'Über die wissenschaftliche Behandlung der Philosophie', in Wilhelm Bietak (ed.), *Romantische Wissenschaft*, Deutsche Literatur, Reihe Romantik 13, Leipzig: Reclam, 1940, pp. 281–94.

Streithorst, Johann Werner, *Psychologische Vorlesungen in der litterarischen Gesellschaft zu Halberstadt*, Leipzig: Crusius, 1787.

Sulzer, Johann Georg, *Kurzer Begriff aller Wissenschaften und andern Theile der Gelehrsamkeit, worin jeder nach seinem Innhalt, Nuzen, und Vollkommenheit kürzlich beschrieben wird*, 2nd edn, Frankfurt am Main and Leipzig: no publ., 1759.

Vermischte philosophische Schriften, Leipzig: Weidmann, 1773.

Tetens, Johann Nicolas, *Philosophische Versuche über die menschliche Natur und ihre Entwicklung*, 2 vols., Leipzig: Weidmann, 1777.

Unzer, Johann August, 'Untersuchung, ob die Träume etwas bedeuten?', in J. A. Unzer, *Sammlung kleiner Schriften. Zur speculativischen Philosophie*, 2 vols., Rinteln and Leipzig: Berth, 1766, pp. 431–9.

Villaume, Pierre, *Versuche über einige psychologische Fragen*, Leipzig: Crusius, 1789.

Wienholt, Arnold, *Beytrag zu den Erfahrungen über den thierischen Magnetismus*, Hamburg: Hoffmann, 1787.

Einleitung in sein Werk über die Heilkraft des thierischen Magnetismus, Lemgo: Meyer, 1800.

Heilkraft des thierischen Magnetismus nach eigenen Beobachtungen, Lemgo: Meyer, 1802.

Wolfart, Karl Christian, 'Über die Erweckung von Mesmers Lehre, und die Anwendung des sogenannten thierischen Magnetismus', *Miszellen für die neueste Weltkunde* 83 (14 October 1812), 329–31.

Zedler, Johann Heinrich, *Großes Universal-Lexicon aller Wissenschaften und Künste, welche bishero durch menschlichen Verstand und Witz erfunden und verbessert worden*, 66 vols., Leipzig and Halle: Zedler, 1732–52.

SECONDARY LITERATURE

Abeln, Reinhard, *Unbewußtes und Unterbewußtes bei C. G. Carus und Aristoteles*, Meisenheim am Glan: Anton Hain, 1970.

Adler, Hans, '*Fundus animae* – Der Grund der Seele: Zur Gnoseologie des Dunklen in der Aufklärung', *DVjs* 62 (1988), 197–220.

Akselrad, Rose-Marie P., 'Schiller und Karl Philipp Moritz', *Monatshefte* 45 (1953), 131–40.

Allen, Séan, *The Plays of Heinrich von Kleist*, Cambridge: Cambridge University Press, 1996.

Allison, Henry E., *Lessing and the Enlightenment. His Philosophy of Religion and Its Relation to Eighteenth-Century Thought*, Ann Arbor: University of Michigan Press, 1966.

Altmann, Alexander, *Moses Mendelssohn: A Biographical Study*, London: Routledge & Kegan Paul, 1973.

Arens, Hans, *Kommentar zu Goethes 'Faust I'*, Heidelberg: Winter, 1982.
  Kommentar zu Goethes 'Faust II', Heidelberg: Winter, 1989.
Auhuber, Friedhelm, 'E. T. A. Hoffmanns produktive Rezeption der zeitgenössischen Medizin und Psychologie', *Mitteilungen der E. T. A. Hoffmann-Gesellschaft* 32 (1986), 89–99.
Bäppler, Klaus, *Der philosophische Wieland. Stufen und Prägungen seines Denkens*, Bern: Francke, 1976.
Barkhoff, Jürgen, *Magnetische Fiktionen. Literarisierungen des Mesmerismus in der Romantik*, Stuttgart: Metzler, 1995.
Beck, Aaron T., *Cognitive Therapy and the Emotional Disorders*, Harmondsworth: Penguin, 1989.
Beißner, Friedrich, 'Studien zur Sprache des Sturm und Drangs', *Germanisch-Romanische Monatsschrift* 21 (1934), 417–29.
Bell, Matthew, *Goethe's Naturalistic Anthropology: Man and Other Plants*, Oxford: Oxford University Press, 1994.
  'Sorge, Epicurean psychology, and the classical *Faust*', *Oxford German Studies* 28 (1999), 82–130.
Bennholdt-Thomsen, Anke and Alfredo Guzzoni, 'Nachwort' in *Gs* X.1–79.
Benz, Ernst, *Franz Anton Mesmer und die philosophischen Grundlagen des animalischen Magnetismus*, Wiesbaden: Steiner, 1977.
Bernoulli, Christoph, *Die Psychologie von Carl Gustav Carus und deren geistesgeschichtliche Bedeutung*, Jena: Diederichs, 1925.
Bishop, Paul, 'Goethe on the couch: Freud's reception of Goethe', in T. J. Reed, Martin Swales and Jeremy Adler (eds.), *Goethe at 250: Goethe mit 250; London Symposium/Londoner Symposion*, Publications of the Institute of Germanic Studies 75, Munich: Iudicium, 2000, pp. 177–85.
  'Intellectual affinities between Goethe and Jung, with special reference to *Faust*', *PEGS* 69 (2000), 1–19.
Blackwell, Richard J., 'C. Wolff's doctrine of the soul', *Journal of the History of Ideas* 22 (1961), 339–54.
Blumenthal, H. J., *Aristotle and Neoplatonism in Late Antiquity: Interpretations of the 'De anima'*, Ithaca: Cornell University Press, 1996.
Böhme, Joachim, *Die Seele und das Ich im homerischen Epos. Mit einem Anhang: Vergleich mit den Primitiven*, Leipzig and Berlin: Teubner, 1929.
Bolten, Jürgen, 'Melancholie und Selbstbehauptung. Zur Soziogenese des Bruderzwistmotivs im Sturm und Drang', *DVjs* 59 (1985), 265–77.
Borchmeyer, Dieter, *Macht und Melancholie. Schillers 'Wallenstein'*, Frankfurt am Main: Athenäum, 1988.
Boring, Edwin G., *A History of Experimental Psychology*, 2nd edn, Englewood Cliffs, NJ: Prentice Hall, 1950.
Boulby, Mark, *Karl Philipp Moritz: At the Fringe of Genius*, Toronto and Buffalo: University of Toronto Press, 1979.
Brown, Christiane, '"Der widerwärtige Mißbrauch der Macht"; or, "Die Verwandlung der Leidenschaften in tugendhafte Fertigkeiten"', *Lessing Yearbook* 17 (1985), 21–43.

Carus, Friedrich August, *Geschichte der Psychologie*, in *Nachgelassene Werke*, vol. III, Leipzig: Barth & Kummer, 1808.

Cassirer, Ernst, *The Platonic Renaissance in England*, Nelson: Edinburgh, 1953.

Claus, David B., *Toward the Soul: An Inquiry into the Meaning of 'Psyche' before Plato*, New Haven and London: Yale University Press, 1981.

Cranston, Maurice, *The Solitary Self: Jean-Jacques Rousseau in Exile and Adversity*, London: Allen Lane, 1997.

Dahlstrom, Daniel O., 'Introduction', in Moses Mendelssohn, *Philosophical Writings*, ed. D. O. Dahlstrom, Cambridge Texts in the History of Philosophy, Cambridge: Cambridge University Press, 1997, pp. ix–xxx.

Damrau, Peter, 'The reception of English puritan literature in Germany', unpubl. Ph.D. dissertation, London, 2003.

Danziger, Kurt, *Constructing the Subject: Historical Origins of Psychological Research*, Cambridge: Cambridge University Press, 1990.

Darcus, Shirley M., 'A person's relation to *phren* in Homer, Hesiod, and the Greek Lyric Poets', *Glotta* 57 (1979), 159–73.

Darnton, Robert, *Mesmerism and the End of the Enlightenment in France*, Cambridge, MA: Harvard University Press, 1968.

Dessoir, Max, *Geschichte der neueren deutschen Psychologie*, 2nd edn. [1909], photo reprint, Amsterdam: Bonset, 1964.

Dewhurst, Kenneth and Nigel Reeves, *Friedrich Schiller: Medicine, Psychology and Literature*, Oxford: Berg, 1978.

Eckhardt, Georg, Matthias John, Temilo van Zantwijk, and Paul Ziche, *Anthropologie und Psychologie um 1800. Ansätze einer Entwicklung zur Wissenschaft*, Cologne, Weimar, Vienna and Böhlau, 2001.

Ecole, Jean, 'Des rapports de l'expérience et de la raison ou l'analyse de l'âme dans la *Psychologia empirica* de Christian Wolff', *Giornale di metafisica* 21 (1966), 589–617.

Ego, Anneliese, *'Animalischer Magnetismus' oder 'Aufklärung'. Eine mentalitätsgeschichtliche Studie zum Konflikt um ein Heilkonzept im 18. Jahrhundert*, Epistemata 68, Würzburg: Königshausen und Neumann, 1991.

Ellis, John M., *'Prinz Friedrich von Homburg'. A Critical Study*, Berkeley: University of California Press, 1970.

'Clara, Nathanael and the narrator: interpreting Hoffmann's *Der Sandmann*', *Germanic Quarterly* 54 (1981), 1–18.

Elson, Charles, *Wieland and Shaftesbury*, New York: Columbia University Press, 1913.

Engell, James, *The Creative Imagination: Enlightenment to Romanticism*, Cambridge, MA: Harvard University Press, 1981.

Epstein, Seymour, 'The self-concept revisited; or, a theory of a theory', *American Psychologist* 28 (1973), 404–16.

Ermatinger, Emil, *Die Weltanschauung des jungen Wieland. Ein Beitrag zur Geschichte der Aufklärung*, Frauenfeld: Huber, 1907.

Esper, Erwin A., *A History of Psychology*, Philadelphia and London: Saunders, 1964.

Fechner, Jörg-Ulrich, 'Leidenschafts- und Charakterdarstellung im Drama (Gerstenberg, Leisewitz, Klinger, Wagner)', in Walter Hinck (ed.), *Sturm und Drang. Ein literaturwissenschaftliches Studienbuch*, Königstein in Taunus: Athenäum, 1978, pp. 175–91.

Felber, Werner and Otto Bach, 'Carl Gustav Carus und das Unbewußte. Ein philosophisch-psychologisches Entwicklungskonzept im 19. Jahrhundert', in Günter Heidel (ed.), *Carl Gustav Carus: Opera et efficacitas. Beiträge des wissenschaftlichen Symposiums zu Werk und Vermächtnis von Carl Gustav Carus am 22. September 1989*, Dresden: Carus-Akademie, 1990, pp. 117–26.

Fick, Monika, '"Verworrene Perzeptionen". Lessings Emilia Galotti', *Jahrbuch der deutschen Schillergesellschaft* 37 (1993), 139–63.

Förstl, H., M. Angermeyer, and R. Howard, 'Karl Philipp Moritz' *Journal of Empirical Psychology* (1783–1793): an analysis of 124 case reports', *Psychological Medicine* 21 (1991), 299–304.

Fowler, Frank M., 'Sight and insight in Schiller's *Die Jungfrau von Orleans*', *Modern Language Review* 68 (1973), 367–79.

France, Peter, *Rousseau: 'Confessions'*, Cambridge: Cambridge University Press, 1987.

Franke, Ursula, *Kunst als Erkenntnis. Die Rolle der Sinnlichkeit in der Ästhetik des Alexander Gottlieb Baumgarten*, Wiesbaden: Franz Steiner, 1972.

Freud, Sigmund, *The Standard Edition of the Complete Works of Sigmund Freud*, ed. James Strachey, 24 vols., London: Hogarth Press/Institute of Psychoanalysis, 1957.

Fürnkäs, Josef, *Der Ursprung des psychologischen Romans. Karl Philipp Moritz' 'Anton Reiser'*, Stuttgart: Metzler, 1977.

Gay, Peter, *The Enlightenment: An Interpretation. Volume 1: The Rise of Modern Paganism*, London: Weidenfeld & Nicolson, 1967.

The Enlightenment: An Interpretation. Volume 2: The Science of Freedom, London: Weidenfeld & Nicolson, 1970.

Gössl, Sibylle, *Materialismus und Nihilismus. Studien zum deutschen Roman der Spätaufklärung*, Würzburg: Königshausen & Neumann, 1987.

Graham, Ilse, 'The structure of the personality in Schiller's tragic poetry', in F. Norman (ed.), *Schiller: Bicentenary Lectures*, London: Institute of Germanic Studies, 1960, pp. 104–44.

Schiller's Drama: Talent and Integrity, London: Methuen, 1974.

Griffin, Jasper, *Homer on Life and Death*, Oxford: Oxford University Press, 1980.

Grimminger, Rolf, 'Roman' in R. Grimminger (ed.), *Hansers Sozialgeschichte der deutschen Literatur vom 16. Jahrhundert bis zur Gegenwart*, vol. III: *Deutsche Aufklärung bis zur Französischen Revolution*, Munich: Hanser, 1980, pp. 635–715.

Groß, Erich, *C. M. Wielands 'Geschichte des Agathon'. Entstehungsgeschichte*, Berlin: Ebering, 1930.

Hacking, Ian, *The Social Construction of What?*, Cambridge, MA and London: Harvard University Press, 1999.

Hamlyn, D. W., 'Aristotle's account of *aisthesis* in the *De anima*', *Classical Quarterly* 53 (1959), 6–16.

Hartmann, Eduard von, *Philosophie des Unbewußten. Speculative Resultate nach inductiv-naturwissenschaftlicher Methode*, 3 vols., 12th edn, Leipzig: Kröner, 1923 [1860].

Hatfield, Gary, *The Natural and the Normative: Theories of Spatial Perception from Kant to Helmholtz*, Cambridge, MA: MIT Press, 1990.

Hegler, Alfred, *Die Psychologie in Kants Ethik*, Freiburg: Mohr, 1891.

Heitner, Robert R., 'Luise Millerin and the shock motif in Schiller's early dramas', *Germanic Review* 41 (1966), 27–44.

Henry, John, 'A Cambridge Platonist's materialism: Henry More and the concept of soul', *Journal of the Warburg and Courtauld Institutes* 49 (1986), 172–95.

Herbertz, Richard, *Die Lehre vom Unbewußten im System des Leibniz*, Abhandlungen zur Philosophie und ihrer Geschichte 20, Halle: Niemeyer, 1905.

Heyd, Michael, *'Be Sober and Reasonable'. The Critique of Enthusiasm in the Seventeenth and Early Eighteenth Centuries*, Leiden: E. J. Brill, 1995.

Hiebel, Hans Helmut, 'Mißverstehen und Sprachlosigkeit im "bürgerlichen Trauerspiel". Zum historischen Wandel dramatischer Motivationsformen', *Jahrbuch der Deutschen Schiller-Gesellschaft* 27 (1983), 124–53.

Hollmer, Heide and Albert Meier, ' Nachwort', in Karl Philipp Moritz, *Werke*, vol. 1: *Dichtungen und Schriften zur Erfahrungsseelenkunde*, Frankfurt am Main: Deutscher Klassiker Verlag, 1999.

Janaway, Christopher, *Self and World in Schopenhauer's Philosophy*, Oxford: Oxford University Press, 1989.

Japp, Uwe, 'Das serapiontische Prinzip', in Heinz Ludwig Arnold (ed.), *E. T. A. Hoffmann. Text + Kritik Sonderband*, Munich: Text + Kritik, 1992.

Jost, Walter, *Von Ludwig Tieck zu E. T. A. Hoffmann. Studien zur Entwicklungsgeschichte des romantischen Subjektivismus*, Frankfurt am Main: Diesterweg, 1921.

Jung, C. G., *The Collected Works of C. G. Jung*, ed. H. Read *et al.*, 20 vols., London and New York: Routledge & Kegan Paul, 1953–79.

Kaiser, Gerhard, 'Friedrich Maximilian Klingers Schauspiel *Sturm und Drang*', in Manfred Wacker (ed.), *Sturm und Drang*, Wege der Forschung 559, Darmstadt: Wissenschaftliche Buchgesellschaft, 1985, pp. 315–40.

Karoli, Christa, *Ideal und Krise enthusiastischen Künstlertums in der deutschen Romantik*, Bonn: Bouvier, 1968.

Kiernan, Colm, *Enlightenment and Science in Eighteenth-Century France*, Banbury: Voltaire Foundation, 1973.

Kitcher, Patricia, *Kant's Transcendental Psychology*, New York and Oxford: Oxford University Press, 1990.

Kondylis, Panajotis, *Die Aufklärung im Rahmen des neuzeitlichen Rationalismus*, Stuttgart: Klett-Cotta, 1986.

Konstan, David, *Some Aspects of Epicurean Psychology*, Philosophia antiqua 25, Leiden: Brill, 1973.

Krebs, Peter, *Die Anthropologie des Gotthilf Heinrich von Schubert*, Cologne: Orthen, 1940.

Kristeller, Paul Oskar, *The Philosophy of Marsilio Ficino*, Columbia Studies in Philosophy 6, New York: Columbia University Press, 1943.

Kuhn, Thomas S., *The Structure of Scientific Revolutions*, Chicago and London: University of Chicago Press, 1962.

Kümmel, Werner Friedrich, *Musik und Medizin: ihre Wechselbeziehung in Theorie und Praxis von 800 bis 1800*, Freiburg/Breisgau: Alber, 1977.

Langen, August, *Der Wortschatz des deutschen Pietismus*, Tübingen: Niemeyer, 1968.

Lapointe, Francois H., 'Origin and evolution of the term "psychology"', *American Psychologist* 25 (1970), 640–6.

Leary, David E., 'The philosophical development of the conception of psychology in Germany, 1780–1850', *Journal of the History of the Behavioral Sciences* 14 (1978), 113–21.

Leidner, Alan C., 'A Titan in extenuating circumstances: Sturm und Drang and the *Kraftmensch*', *Publications of the Modern Language Association* 104 (1989), 178–89.

Lepenies, Wolf, *Melancholie und Gesellschaft*, Frankfurt am Main: Suhrkamp, 1969.

Livingston, Donald W., *Philosophical Melancholy and Delirium. Hume's Pathology of Philosophy*, Chicago: University of Chicago Press, 1998.

Loquai, Franz, *Künstler und Melancholie in der Romantik*, Frankfurt am Main: Lang, 1984.

Luke, David, 'Notes', in Johann Wolfgang von Goethe, *Faust. Part One*, trans. D. Luke, Oxford: Oxford University Press, 1987.

McGlathery, James M., 'The suicide motif in E. T. A. Hoffmann's *Der goldne Topf*', *Monatshefte* 58 (1966), 115–23.

McKenzie, E. C., *British Devotional Literature and the Rise of German Pietism*, St Andrews: University of St Andrews Press, 1984.

Madlener, Elisabeth, *Die Kunst des Erwürgens nach Regeln. Von Staats- und Kriegskünsten, preußischer Geschichte und Heinrich von Kleist*, Pfaffenweiler: Centaurus, 1994.

Manuel, Frank E., *The Changing of the Gods*, Hanover, NH: University of New England Press, 1983.

Mattenklott, Gert, *Melancholie in der Dramatik des Sturm und Drang*, Königstein: Athenäum, 1985.

Maurer, Michael, *Aufklärung und Anglophilie in Deutschland*, Publications of the German Historical Institute London 19, Göttingen: Vandenhoeck & Ruprecht, 1987.

Meier, Albert, 'Sprachphilosophie in religionskritischer Absicht. Karl Philipp Moritz' Kinderlogik in ihrem ideengeschichtlichen Zusammenhang', *DVjs* 67 (1993), 252–66.

Merlan, Philip, *Monopsychism, Mysticism, Metaconsciousness: Problems of the Soul in the Neoaristotelian and Neoplatonic Tradition*, The Hague: Martinus Nijhoff, 1963.

Meyer, Jürgen Bona, *Kant's Psychologie*, Berlin: Hertz, 1870.

Mintz, Samuel I., *The Hunting of Leviathan: Seventeenth-Century Reactions to the Materialism and Moral Philosophy of Thomas Hobbes*, Cambridge: Cambridge University Press, 1962.

Mocek, Reinhard, *Johann Christian Reil (1759–1813). Das Problem des Übergangs von der Spätaufklärung zur Romantik in Biologie und Medizin in Deutschland*, Frankfurt am Main: Lang, 1995.

'Johann Christian Reil', in Walther Killy and Rudolf Vierhaus (eds.), *Deutsche biographische Enzyklopädie*, 13 vols., vol. VIII, Munich: K. G. Saur, 1998, p. 209.

Negus, Kenneth, *E. T. A. Hoffmann's Other World. The Romantic Author and his New Mythology*, Philadelphia: University of Pennsylvania Press, 1965.

Neubauer, John, *Bifocal Vision: Novalis' Philosophy of Nature and Disease*, Chapel Hill, NC: University of North Carolina Press, 1971.

Novalis, Twayne's World Authors 556, Boston: Twayne, 1980.

Nisbet, H. B., *Herder and the Philosophy and History of Science*, Cambridge: MHRA, 1970.

'Lessing's ethics', *Lessing Yearbook* 25 (1993), 1–40.

Norris, Christopher, *Against Relativism. Philosophy of Science, Deconstruction, and Critical Theory*, Oxford: Blackwell, 1997.

Nübel, Birgit, *Autobiographische Kommunikationsmedien um 1800. Studien zu Rousseau, Wieland, Herder und Moritz*, Studien zur deutschen Literatur 136, Tübingen: Niemeyer, 1994.

O'Daly, Gerald, *Augustine's Philosophy of Mind*, London: Duckworth, 1987.

Osinski, Jutta, 'Psychologie und Ästhetik bei Karl Philipp Moritz', in Martin Fontius and Anneliese Klingenberg (eds.), *Karl Philipp Moritz und das achtzehnte Jahrhundert. Bestandsaufnahmen–Korrekturen–Neuansätze*, Tübingen: Niemeyer, 1995.

Passmore, J. A., 'The malleability of man in eighteenth-century thought', in Earl R. Wasserman (ed.), *Aspects of the Eighteenth Century*, Baltimore: Johns Hopkins University Press, 1965, pp. 21–46.

Ralph Cudworth: An Interpetation [1951], photo reprint, Bristol: Thoemmes, 1990.

Pfotenhauer, Helmut, 'Exoterische und esoterische Poetik in E. T. A. Hoffmanns Erzählungen', *Jahrbuch der Jean-Paul-Gesellschaft* 17 (1982), 129–44.

Pocock, J. G. A., *Barbarism and Religion. Volume One: The Enlightenments of Edward Gibbon, 1737–1764*, Cambridge: Cambridge University Press, 1999.

Porter, Roy and Mikuláš Teich (eds.), *The Enlightenment in National Context*, Cambridge: Cambridge University Press, 1981.

Prause, Marianne, *Carl Gustav Carus. Leben und Werk*, Berlin: Deutscher Verlag für Kunstwissenschaft, 1968.

Price, Lawrence Marsden, *English Literature in Germany*, University of California Publications in Modern Philology 37, Berkeley and Los Angeles: University of California Press, 1953.

Proß, Wolfgang, 'Herder und die Anthropologie der Aufklärung', in Johann Gottfried Herder, *Werke*, ed. W. Proß, 2 vols., Munich: Hanser, 1987.

Reddick, John, 'E. T. A. Hoffmann', in Alex Natan (ed.), *German Men of Letters. Volume* V: *Twelve Literary Essays*, London: Oswald Wolff, 1969.

  Georg Büchner: The Shattered Whole, Oxford: Oxford University Press, 1994.

Reh, Albert M., 'Zu Lessings Charakterzeichnung. Ein Beitrag zur Literaturpsychologie des 18. Jahrhunderts', in Edward P. Harris and Richard E. Schade (eds.), *Lessing in heutiger Sicht. Beiträge zur internationalen Lessing-Konferenz Cincinnati, Ohio 1976*, Bremen: Jacobi, 1977.

  Die Rettung der Menschlichkeit. Lessings Dramen in literaturpsychologischer Sicht, Bern and Munich: Francke, 1981.

Reuchlein, Georg, *Bürgerliche Gesellschaft, Psychiatrie und Literatur: zur Entwicklung der Wahnsinnsthematik in der deutschen Literatur des späten 18. und frühen 19. Jahrhunderts*, Munich: Fink, 1986.

Richards, David B., 'Mesmerism in *Die Jungfrau von Orleans*', *Publications of the Modern Language Association* 91 (1976), 856–70.

Riedel, Wolfgang, *Die Anthropologie des jungen Schiller: Zur Ideengeschichte der medizinischen Schriften und der 'Philosophischen Briefe'*, Würzburg: Königstein & Neumann, 1985.

  'Erkennen und Empfinden. Anthropologische Achsendrehung und Wende zur Ästhetik bei Johann Georg Sulzer', in Hans-Jürgen Schings (ed.), *Der ganze Mensch. Anthropologie und Literatur im 18. Jahrhundert*, Stuttgart: Metzler, 1994, pp. 410–39.

Ringel, Stefan, *Realität und Einbildungskraft im Werk E. T. A. Hoffmanns*, Cologne: Böhlau, 1997.

Rivers, Isabel, *Reason, Grace, and Sentiment: A Study of the Language of Religion and Ethics in England, 1660–1780*, 2 vols., Cambridge: Cambridge University Press, 1991–2000.

Röbbeling, Friedrich, *Kleists 'Käthchen von Heilbronn'* [Halle: Niemeyer, 1913], photo reprint, Tübingen: Niemeyer, 1973.

Robinson, T. M., *Plato's Psychology*, 2nd edn, Toronto: University of Toronto Press, 1995.

Salumets, Thomas, 'Mündige Dichter und verkrüppelte Helden. F. M. Klingers Trauerspiel *Die Zwillinge*', *Germanic Quarterly* 59 (1986), 401–13.

Satura, Vladimir, *Kants Erkenntnispsychologie in den Nachschriften seiner Vorlesungen über empirische Psychologie*, Kant-Studien, Ergänzungshefte 101, Bonn: Bouvier, 1971.

Sauder, Gerhard, *Empfindsamkeit. Bd. 1: Voraussetzungen und Elemente*, Stuttgart: Metzler, 1974.

Schings, Hans-Jürgen, *Melancholie und Aufklärung: Melancholiker und ihre Kritiker in Erfahrungsseelenkunde und Literatur des 18. Jahrhunderts*, Stuttgart: Metzler, 1977.

Schmidt, Jochen, *Heinrich von Kleist. Studien zu seiner poetischen Verfahrensweise*, Tübingen: Niemeyer, 1974.

Die Geschichte des Genie-Gedankens in der deutschen Literatur, Philosophie und Politik, 1750–1945. Bd. I: Von der Aufklärung bis zum Idealismus, Darmstadt: Wissenschaftliche Buchgesellschaft, 1985.

Schrimpf, Hans Joachim, *Karl Philipp Moritz*, Stuttgart: Metzler, 1980.

Sharpe, Lesley, '*Der Verbrecher aus verlorener Ehre*: an early exercise in Schillerian psychology', *German Life and Letters* 33 (1980), 102–10.

Smith, Woodruff D., 'The social and political origins of German diffusionist ethnology', *Journal of the History of Behavioural Studies* 14 (1978), 103–12.

Sontag, Susan, *Illness as Metaphor*, London: Allen Lane, 1979.

Staiger, Emil, *Friedrich Schiller*, Zurich: Atlantis, 1967.

Starobinski, Jean, *Jean-Jacques Rousseau: Transparency and Obstruction*, Chicago: University of Chicago Press, 1988.

Steinecke, Hartmut, *Unterhaltsamkeit und Artistik. Neue Schreibarten in der deutschen Literatur von Hoffmann bis Heine*, Berlin: Erich Schmidt, 1998.

Stephens, Anthony, *Heinrich von Kleist: The Dramas and Stories*, Oxford and Providence, RI: Berg, 1994.

Strawson, P. F., 'Imagination and perception', in Ralph C. S. Walker (ed.), *Kant on Pure Reason*, Oxford Readings in Philosophy, Oxford: Oxford University Press, 1982, pp. 82–99.

The Bounds of Sense: An Essay on Kant's 'Critique of Pure Reason', London and New York: Routledge, 1989.

Tatar, Maria M., 'Mesmerism, madness, and death in E. T. A. Hoffmann's *Der goldne Topf*', *Studies in Romanticism* 14 (1975), 365–89.

Spellbound. Studies on Mesmerism and Literature, Princeton, NJ: Princeton University Press, 1978.

Ter-Nedden, Gisbert, *Lessings Trauerspiele. Der Ursprung des modernen Dramas aus dem Geist der Kritik*, Stuttgart: Metzler, 1986.

Tschierske, Ulrich, *Vernunftkritik und Subjektivität. Studien zur Anthropologie Friedrich Schillers*, Tübingen: Niemeyer, 1988.

Tymms, Ralph, 'Alternation of personality in the dramas of Heinrich von Kleist and Zacharias Werner', *Modern Language Review* 37 (1942), 64–73.

Ueding, Gerd, 'Zweideutige Bilderwelt: *Das Käthchen von Heilbronn*', in Walter Hinderer (ed.), *Kleists Dramen. Neue Interpretationen*, Stuttgart: Reclam, 1981.

Vietta, Silvio, 'Romantikparodie und Realitätsbegriff im Erzählwerk E. T. A. Hoffmanns', *Zeitschrift für deutsche Philologie* 100 (1981), 575–91.

Vlastos, Gregory, '*Anamnesis* in the *Meno*', in G. Vlastos (ed.), *Plato's 'Meno' in Focus*, London: Routledge, 1994, pp. 88–111.

Vleeschauwer, Herman-Jean de, *The Development of Kantian Thought. The History of a Doctrine*, London: Nelson, 1962.

Walker, Ralph C. S., *Kant*, The Arguments of the Philosophers, London: Routledge, 1978.

Walsh, W. H., 'Self-knowledge', in Ralph C. S. Walker (ed.), *Kant on Pure Reason*, Oxford Readings in Philosophy, Oxford: Oxford University Press, 1982, pp. 150–75.

Warren, Edward G., 'Consciousness in Plotinus', *Phronesis* 9 (1964), 83–97.

Whyte, Lancelot Law, *The Unconscious before Freud*, London: Friedmann, 1978.

Widmann, Joachim, *Johann Gottlieb Fichte. Einführung in seine Philosophie*, Sammlung Göschen, Berlin: de Gruyter, 1982.

Wukadinovic, Spiridion, *Kleist-Studien*, Stuttgart and Berlin: Cotta, 1904.

Yolton, John W., *Thinking Matter: Materialism in Eighteenth-Century Britain*, Oxford: Blackwell, 1984.

Zammito, John H., *Kant, Herder, and the Birth of Anthropology*, Chicago and London: University of Chicago Press, 2002.

Ziolkowski, Theodore, *German Romanticism and Its Institutions*, Princeton, NJ: Princeton University Press, 1990.

Index of names and places

Subject index